Los Angeles Police Department Meltdown

The Fall of the Professional-Reform Model of Policing

Advances in Police Theory and Practice Series

Series Editor: Dilip K. Das

Financial Crimes: A Global Threat
Maximillian Edelbacher, Peter Kratcoski, and Michael Theil

Police Integrity Management in Australia:
Global Lessons for Combating Police Misconduct
Louise Porter and Tim Prenzler

The Crime Numbers Game: Management by Manipulation
John A. Eterno and Eli B. Silverman

The International Trafficking of Human Organs: A Multidisciplinary Perspective
Leonard Territo and Rande Matteson

Police Reform in China
Kam C. Wong

Mission-Based Policing
John P. Crank, Dawn M. Irlbeck, Rebecca K. Murray, Mark Sundermeier

The New Khaki: The Evolving Nature of Policing in India
Arvind Verma

Cold Cases: An Evaluation Model with Follow-up Strategies for Investigators
James M. Adcock and Sarah L. Stein

Policing Organized Crime: Intelligence Strategy Implementation
Petter Gottschalk

Security in Post-Conflict Africa: The Role of Nonstate Policing
Bruce Baker

Community Policing and Peacekeeping
Peter Grabosky

Community Policing: International Patterns and Comparative Perspectives
Dominique Wisler and Ihekwoaba D. Onwudiwe

Police Corruption: Preventing Misconduct and Maintaining Integrity
Tim Prenzler

Los Angeles Police Department Meltdown

The Fall of the Professional-Reform Model of Policing

James Lasley

CRC Press
Taylor & Francis Group
Boca Raton London New York

CRC Press is an imprint of the
Taylor & Francis Group, an **informa** business

CRC Press
Taylor & Francis Group
6000 Broken Sound Parkway NW, Suite 300
Boca Raton, FL 33487-2742

First issued in paperback 2019

ISBN-13: 978-1-4398-9917-5 (hbk)
ISBN-13: 978-0-367-86699-0 (pbk)

Library of Congress Cataloging-in-Publication Data

Lasley, James R.
Los Angeles Police Department meltdown : the fall of the professional-reform model of policing / James Lasley.
p. cm. -- (Advances in police theory and practice series ; 14)
Includes bibliographical references and index.
ISBN 978-1-4398-9917-5
1. Los Angeles (Calif.). Police Dept. 2. Police administration--California--Los Angeles. 3. Police--California--Los Angeles. 4. Police corruption--California--Los Angeles. I. Title.

HV8148.L55L37 2012
363.209764'94--dc23 2012006796

Visit the Taylor & Francis Web site at
http://www.taylorandfrancis.com

and the CRC Press Web site at
http://www.crcpress.com

To all the LAPD street officers whose voices were never heard.

Contents

Series Preface

While the literature on police and allied subjects is growing exponentially, its impact upon day-to-day policing remains small. The two worlds of research and practice of policing remain disconnected even though cooperation between the two is growing. A major reason is that the two groups speak in different languages. The research work is published in hard-to-access journals and presented in a manner that is difficult to comprehend for a layperson. On the other hand, the police practitioners tend not to mix with researchers and remain secretive about their work. Consequently, there is little dialogue between the two and almost no attempt to learn from one another. Dialogue across the globe, among researchers and practitioners situated in different continents, is, of course, even more limited.

I attempted to address this problem by starting the IPES, www.ipes.info, where a common platform has brought the two together. IPES is now in its 15th year. The annual meetings that constitute most major annual events of the organization have been hosted in all parts of the world. Several publications have come out of these deliberations, and a new collaborative community of scholars and police officers has been created whose membership runs into several hundreds.

Another attempt was to begin a new journal, aptly called *Police Practice and Research: An International Journal* (PPR), which has opened the gate to practitioners to share their work and experiences. The journal has attempted to focus upon issues that help bring the two onto a single platform. PPR completed its 10th year in 2009. It is certainly evidence of growing collaboration between police research and practice that PPR, which began with four issues a year, expanded into five issues in its fourth year, and now it is issued six times a year.

Clearly, these attempts, despite their success, remain limited. Conferences and journal publications do help create a body of knowledge and an association of police activists, but cannot address substantial issues in depth. The limitations of time and space preclude larger discussions and more authoritative expositions that can provide stronger and broader linkages between the two worlds.

It is this realization of the increasing dialogue between police research and practice that has encouraged many of us—my close colleagues and I, connected closely with IPES and PPR across the world—to conceive and implement a new attempt in this direction. *Advances in Police Theory and*

Practice is a series that seeks to attract writers from all parts of the world. Further, the attempt is to find practitioner contributors. The objective is to make the series a serious contribution to our knowledge of the police as well as to improve police practices. The focus is not only on work that describes the best and successful police practices, but also one that challenges current paradigms and breaks new ground to prepare a police for the 21st century. The series seeks comparative analysis that highlights achievements in distant parts of the world, as well as one that encourages an in-depth examination of specific problems confronting a particular police force.

Continuing the book series mission is the present work: *Los Angeles Police Department Meltdown: The Fall of the Professional-Reform Model of Policing.* This book relies on qualitative research methods to explore what is perhaps the most significant event to impact the practice of American policing during the last half century. The event specifically investigated is the organizational meltdown of the LAPD following both national and international criticism of the department's aggressive police tactics after mass media exposure of the Rodney King incident. The causes and dynamics of the meltdown are examined through firsthand written statements of officers that capture an unprecedented candid account of why and how one of the world's most respected policing agencies ultimately failed as a model for modern police administration. Specifically, the book provides insights on how police administrators can avoid experiencing an organizational meltdown similar to that occurring at the LAPD. Most importantly, it truly bridges the gap between research and practice by providing a scientific organizational analysis from which both students of police management and practicing police administrators can create their own policies and solutions for solving significant problems facing police organizations in a changing world.

It is hoped that through this series it will be possible to accelerate the process of building knowledge about policing and help bridge the gap between the two worlds—the world of police research and that of police practice. This is an invitation to police scholars and practitioners across the world to come and join in this venture.

Dilip K. Das, PhD
Founding President, International Police Executive Symposium (IPES), www.ipes.info
Founding editor in chief, Police Practice and Research: An International Journal *(PPR), www.tandf.co.uk/journals*

International Police Executive Symposium

Police Practice & Research
An International Journal

Preface

Anyone who has ever been involved in the world of policing knows that it is extremely rare, if not ever the case, when the "blue code of silence" is broken—that is, when a police officer is willing to tell outsiders the real truth about his or her job. However, there are those times and places in history when a critical event "rocks" a policing agency so hard that it causes the code to break by itself. This is what happened at the Los Angeles Police Department sometime during 1991, shortly after media exposure of the Rodney King incident went viral on news broadcasts throughout the nation. Fortunately, the testimonials of hundreds of LAPD officers who broke their professional silence during this unprecedented time in modern policing are captured in written form and presented in this book. But what caused these officers to become so outraged that they were begging for anyone outside of the department to listen to their story about what it was like to be an LAPD police officer during the post-King era? The discovery of this cause is also presented in this book.

The book's title, *Los Angeles Police Department Meltdown: The Fall of the Professional-Reform Model of Policing*, was selected because it reflects the likely explanation for why the blue code of silence at LAPD was broken. Both the title and the explanation it reflects were not my inspiration, but that of the LAPD chief of police himself: the late Chief Daryl F. Gates. Over 20 years ago, shortly after the King incident had occurred, Chief Gates contacted me and asked if I would conduct a personnel study of the department and its officers. I was interested and met with him. During this meeting he was quite candid. He told me that the LAPD was having an "organizational meltdown" and he wanted me to find out what was causing it and if it could be fixed. In addition, he said that the outcome would probably help him decide if he would resign as chief or continue to struggle in the job in order to save what he called "the LAPD's policing method." What he was referring to was the professional-reform model of policing started at the department some 40 years earlier by Chief William H. Parker.

The professional-reform model is LAPD's contribution to modern policing. Most people know how it works because of television shows like *Dragnet* and *Adam-12*, which were based on the model's policing tactics. It is called professional because police officers were taught to make decisions based on fact rather than emotion. It was called reform because it replaced

LAPD's use of the political model of policing, which had led to the corruption of officers by exposure to political influences. Eventually, Parker's transformation of the department from the political to professional model caused the LAPD to achieve national recognition as American's premier policing agency. The department's motto "to protect and to serve" can be seen on police cars throughout the world.

Needless to say, I accepted Chief Gates' challenge to research the underlying causes of LAPD's meltdown and its detrimental effects on the professional-reform model of policing. Unlike any other prior (or perhaps future) researcher of the LAPD, I was allowed to enter the inner sanctum of the department to record the broken blue code of silence. Equally rare were Chief Gates' words regarding the restrictions/freedoms granted to me as a researcher in the department: He said, "Consider the LAPD as your research laboratory.... I believe you have your head screwed on right." On a personal level, I was honored to be the researcher selected to study Parker's legacy at the LAPD during its final days. Now, this book forever records a time and place in policing history that has come and gone but will not be forgotten.

Acknowledgments

First and foremost, my most extreme gratitude must be given to the late Chief Daryl F. Gates for his selecting me as the researcher to study the final days of the professional-reform model of policing within the LAPD. Equally important to the outcome of this study were the support, encouragement, and kind words given to me by LAPD Assistant Chief Robert Vernon (Ret.) during many discussions on the sixth floor of Parker Center. In many ways, he is responsible for my entry into the world of policing research and to my ongoing interest in the LAPD. My sincere thanks also go out to LAPD Deputy Chief Art Lopez (Ret.) for supporting my research efforts within the department at the time of this study. Other persons contributing directly or indirectly to the study's outcome include Prof. George T. Felkenes, Prof. W. Garrett Capune, Dep. Nikos Guskos (Los Angeles Sheriff's Department), Prof. James Farris (USAF Office of Special Investigations, Ret.), Prof. James Larson (San Diego PD, Ret.), Prof. James Guffey (Oakland PD, Ret.), and members of the Inland Blue Line. Gratitude must also be extended to LeRoy A. Scheller Jr. (USMC, Ret.) for his technical support and inspirational ideas. And a special thanks is in order to Lt. Michael Hooper (LAPD, Ret.) of the California Commission on Peace Officer Standards and Training POST for his invaluable academic insights regarding the LAPD's Davis era. Finally, the John Randolph Haynes and Dora Haynes Foundation of Los Angeles, California, must be thanked for its interest in and generous financial support for the completion of this study, much of which was done by the author while serving as a Haynes Foundation Faculty Fellow.

Finally, Taylor & Francis Senior Editor Carolyn Spence and the Taylor & Francis editorial and production staff must be afforded extreme gratitude and thanks for their professional support of this project.

About the Author

James Lasley is professor of criminal justice at California State University, Fullerton. He has worked in the field of law enforcement and research, most extensively with the Los Angeles Police Department, which includes the design, implementation, and analysis of LAPD's Operation Cul De Sac (a short documentary detailing this work is also accessible on YouTube at http://www.youtube.com/results?search_query=operation+cul+de+sac). His prior academic appointments include Washington State University, Arizona State University, the University of Southern California, and National University. He has also served as a consultant to the California Commission on Peace Officer Standards and Training (POST) to establish standards and methods for police officer driver training.

Parker's Thin Blue Line
The Professional-Reform Model (PRM) of Policing: Historical Overview

1

PRM was established and created as the "new" general model of police operations for the LAPD in 1950 by Chief William H. Parker. It served to replace LAPD's reliance on the political model of policing, which was also America's first and oldest police organizational paradigm (see "The Pre-Parker Era" below).[1] Parker devised PRM primarily as a means to overcome corrupt police practices, such as officer involvement in gambling, prostitution, and other organized crime rackets that had plagued the LAPD prior to his becoming chief. Furthermore, he directly blamed the political model for causing LAPD officer corruption because it failed to insulate police officers from undue influences of politicians and community members. Parker believed that the only way to keep his police force "clean" from untoward influences was to build a professional and emotional wall between the LAPD, its officers, and the outside world.

The new LAPD officers, under PRM, were trained or retrained to have a tough, unemotional, yet objective demeanor to the public. In effect, this new outlook toward the police officers' role in the community would create both personal and emotional distance from politicians and the community—which Parker felt was an essential ingredient for creating police officers and a policing organization that was capable of repelling corruption. The "new LAPD officers" were taught to view themselves as a professional crime-fighting army whose mission was to wage war against crime and criminals who were now viewed as "the enemy." Their method of operation would be to gather the facts surrounding criminal activities from community members without becoming emotionally involved in the plight of crime victims. Emotion, according to PRM, served to cloud an officer's judgment when attempting to act in an objective manner when enforcing the law. New LAPD operational rules and policies were created by Parker as well. In effect, he transformed the department's existing management style into that of a paramilitary organization where the chief of police had power and authority over his police like a general commanding his troops.

Parker's PRM policing methods quickly caught the attention of countless other U.S. police agencies that were quick to copy LAPD by replacing the old political model with their own version of PRM.[2] By the early 1960s nearly all police considered LAPD to be the world's premier policing agency, and it was generally acknowledged that Parker's PRM was the most effective means for operating a police organization. After Parker died in 1966, LAPD continued to be the standard bearer for PRM, most notably under the leadership and tenure of two individuals to serve as the department's chief of police. The first, Chief Edward Davis, who was Parker's successor from 1969 to 1978, and Chief Daryl Gates, who followed Davis as chief of LAPD from 1978 to 1992. It was during the final year of Gates' term as chief that PRM was ultimately abandoned as the official organizational model of policing at the LAPD. As the foregoing discussion suggests, the history of PRM can be best explained in terms of four distinct eras: the pre-Parker era (prior to 1950), the Parker era (1950–1966), the Davis era (1969–1978), and the Gates era (1978–1992). The following sections examine each of these eras and provide a brief history of PRM within the LAPD organization.

The Pre-Parker Era

The Political Model and LAPD Corruption

As previously mentioned, prior to the creation of the PRM in 1950, policing in Los Angeles and other major cities throughout America operated under what was referred to as the political model. This organizational method was also termed the "corruption model" due to the fact that politicians were afforded exclusive powers to control the every move of police agencies within their jurisdiction. For example, in Los Angeles as well as other major cities, including New York and Chicago, the mayor-elect appointed the chief of police, who then appointed every rank-and-file police officer. Conceivably, each time a new mayor was elected, so too could a new police chief be appointed, resulting in a firing and rehiring of the city's entire police force.[3]

Because all police effectively served at the will of the mayor, an elected official, police officers were able to retain their jobs only if they remained in good favor with the public and political entities. During this era of policing, police fostered close personal contacts and relationships with citizens they served in an effort to maintain the political status quo. This "closeness" with the public was viewed by many experts as the cause of massive widespread internal corruption of police organizations and a warped mob-like style of law enforcement in the streets.

Police corruption began to gain momentum in Los Angeles sometime during the mid-1920s, ironically around the time Chief William Parker began his career with the LAPD in 1927. Events and allegations involving corrupt LAPD officers reached their peak during the 1930s under the political administration of Mayor Frank L. Shaw, who was elected in 1933.

Shaw and his brother "Joe" (appointed to the position of private secretary to the LA mayor),[4] according to numerous investigative sources at the time, were instrumental in creating ties between the LAPD, Los Angeles City Hall, and LA-based organized crime figures. Prostitution, gambling, and murder-for-hire rings were among the many illegal activities flourishing in the city, and tolerated by the LAPD, under Shaw's corrupt political regime. Shaw was ousted from office by public recall in 1938.[5]

Parker Inherits a Tarnished Badge

During the 1940s, the allure of Hollywood coupled with growing social tensions within LA's residential melting pot created further problems within the organizational environment of the LAPD. In the aftermath of the *Zoot Suit Riots*, occurring over a one-week period in East Los Angeles during the summer of 1943, the department's image was again tarnished by national criticism over how LAPD officers handled the incident. Critics contended that officers failed to take action against angry mobs of U.S. servicemen targeting and assaulting male Latino youths known as *Pachucos*, who wore a distinctive style of dress called a zoot suit. Further allegations of police racism were supported by the fact that the vast majority of those arrested by LAPD during the riots were Latinos and not soldiers.[6]

The department's future reputation was also affected by numerous high-profile cases. Perhaps the most notable among these was dubbed by the media the *Black Dahlia Murder*. In July 1947, the dead body of would-be Hollywood actress Elizabeth Short was discovered in an empty lot within a Los Angeles suburb. Short, whose favorite movie was *The Blue Dahlia* and favorite color was black (ergo, the nickname "Black Dahlia"), was the victim of a macabre murder—with her body being severed in two with a surgically precise incision below the torso, the corners of her mouth slashed to resemble a smile, and ligature marks on her arms and legs from being restrained during likely torture sessions. This case dealt yet another crushing blow to the public image of the LAPD, but this time to its much revered detective squad who "always got their man." Despite their best efforts, LA super sleuths were unable to obtain a solid suspect lead. The Black Dahlia's killer was never found.

The Parker Era

Parker's Police Professionalism

On August 9, 1950, William H. Parker was sworn in as LAPD chief of police, and soon thereafter Parker's sweeping organizational changes in the department's policies and operational study marked the beginnings of PRM in Los Angeles. Parker's idea of reform was based on the operational philosophy that police corruption was a product of cops that got too physically, emotionally, and politically close to the community. He believed that distance between police and the public was the key to stemming the tide of corruption that plagued LAPD in the past. During Parker's first year in office, he put his theory into action by implementing numerous organizational changes that were instrumental in introducing PRM to the LAPD and to the world as the first professional model of policing.

To create physical distance, the pre-Parker style of foot beat patrol, which fostered face-to-face interaction with community members, was replaced with patrol beats in police cruisers, which minimized the potential for the public's casual interpersonal contact with officers. Next, officers were retrained in a community relations style that emphasized a hard-nosed, stoic demeanor in order to create an emotional barrier between themselves and the personalities of ordinary citizens. According to Parker's plan, such measures would enable police not only to distance themselves psychologically from the public, but also to objectively gather "just the facts" about crime-related matters. Finally, Parker insulated himself from political and other outside influences by breaking ties with governmental entities and affording himself civil service job protection so that he no longer had to serve at the will of the mayor, city council, or external citizen review boards. Thus, within a very short time, Blue took on a life of its own with the LAPD.[7]

LAPD's "Clean Cop" Image

Parker strived to create a refined public image of the LAPD police officer that embodied honesty, integrity, objectivity, and toughness. This was in direct opposition to the public's perception of the department's officers of the past, who had a reputation for hard drinking, dishonesty, and an unkempt physical appearance. The new cohort of police recruits was drawn from pools of applicants who had served in the military, many of whom were ex-Marines. It was assumed that this type of individual would more than meet all of the department's desired police officer qualifications—including organizational loyalty, respect for authority, and physical ability. Most of LAPD's new academy graduates, when they hit the streets of LA, were Caucasian males who were younger, taller, stronger, better trained, higher paid, and in general "more physically imposing" than their LAPD police officer predecessors.[8] As one former recruit from this era recalled, "We carried ourselves in a certain way and had a certain look that was a sort of body language that meant … we are the law."

Under PRM, the department also hired women officers. In fact, historically speaking, LAPD is credited with hiring the world's first female "municipal cop," Alice Stebbins Wells, in 1910. However, only a handful of women officers were hired during the Parker era and LAPD policies kept a clear division between the duties of men and women on the force. Women police officers carried a badge that read "Police Woman," while the men's badge read "Police Man." The police woman's appearance was clearly feminine. She wore a small nurse-style hat, blouse with a bowtie, a waist-high uniform jacket, skirt, nylons, and pump-style shoes and carried her service revolver as well as handcuffs in a purse with a shoulder strap. In general, women police officers did not patrol, and their enforcement duties were restricted to female and juvenile offenders. Department policy prohibited them from arresting men or teenage boys.

Quasi-Military Style of Management

Central to the administrative goal of PRM was to restructure LAPD into a quasi-military organization. The Office of Chief of Police was the strategic apex of all departmental decision making, similar to a general's function in the military. All of LAPD's policies and operational mandates originated with the chief and were administered in a top-down style to high-ranking deputy chiefs to commanders to captains to lieutenants to sergeants to officers and detectives on the streets. The superior-subordinate style of communication was strictly adhered to, and the flow of information from the bottom of the organization to the top was not tolerated. Chief Parker assumed that the department could not operate as an effective crime-fighting machine without a management style that demanded complete and utter subordination of the officers.[9]

Perhaps the most vital organizational change implemented during the Parker era was the creation of an organizational philosophy that the LAPD knew what was best for its officers and for the creation of a safe environment within the city of Los Angeles. Parker strongly believed that citizen recommendations for internal change within the department were to be taken under advisement but by no means used to supplant the wisdom of the chief and his command staff. Even sensitive issues such as police officer misconduct were handled by the Office of Chief of Police and LAPD internal review boards. Like doctors, lawyers, and other persons in the professions, professionalized LAPD officers should be and were able to police themselves without interference from politicians and the public who did not adequately understand the police function. Thus, LAPD was transformed into an organizational fortress that was impenetrable by outside influences, yet functioned "to protect and to serve" in a manner it deemed best fit for the public good.

The Thin Blue Line

Whether or not you were a friend or foe of LAPD depended on which side of Chief Parker's "thin blue line" you were on. This imaginary boundary stretched somewhere across the city of Los Angeles (and perhaps the nation) and was defined on Parker's weekly television show *The Thin Blue Line*, which aired in 1952. According to Parker, on one side of the line was law and order, and on the other was civil and social anarchy. LAPD was, in many ways, the line itself: a professionalized police force that was like a dam holding back a potential killer flood of depraved humanity and crime. Parker's weekly mantra was one of gloom and doom for Angelinos if the LAPD should falter. If any force, be it political or otherwise, should weaken the thin blue line, Armageddon would surely result in the Los Angeles community.

A clear majority of LA citizenry was on Parker's side of the line. Supporters of Parker's new LAPD were mainly Caucasian working- or middle-class persons who were taught by Parker to believe in and to support the department's efforts in maintaining the thin blue line. As a result, whether or not they truly agreed with Parker, most Angelinos and the media never questioned LAPD officers' methods of and motivations for enforcing the law. Regardless of how the police got things done, most persons believed that supporting their officers was necessary to provide safety as well as to preserve the culture on their side of the line. On the other side of the line were those in LA who challenged the department's authority or operational style—either head on by breaking the law or philosophically by calling the LAPD's integrity and benevolence into question. A good deal of LA's ethnic minority community at the time—consisting primarily of Latinos, African Americans, and Asians—was either pushed, pulled, or self-selected to be on the wrong side of the thin blue line. Also included on the wrong side of the line were persons who had political disagreements with policing tactics used under the department's application of PRM. Today's critics of PRM contend that during the Parker era, culture, crime, and political ideology were all lumped together in the same place, which most Angelinos and the LAPD perceived to be the opposing side of the line.[10]

Intelligence Gathering

It's true that when the color red is mixed with blue the result is purple; however, for LAPD officers serving during the Parker era, such a color combination was an utter impossibility. As for Chief Parker himself, the color red symbolized one of the largest threats to social order in the city of Los Angeles: communism. In fact, long before Parker took the reins of LAPD, the department operated a series of "secret" squads to combat potential threats by communist organizations and their operatives—as well as any other organization posing a social, economic, or political threat to status quo Los Angeles culture. Most famous among the police counterintelligence units was the LAPD Red Squad, which was operated by Parker's predecessor, Chief James E. Davis. Amid allegations of scandal and corruption, the Red Squad was disbanded just prior to Parker's arrival at the LAPD.

However, after a short time in office, Chief Parker resurrected the Red Squad; however, this time under a new name: the G-2 Squad. The basic function of G-2 was to gather intelligence on the actions of persons and groups ranging from labor unions, which could threaten LA business operations, to Hollywood's Screen Actors Guild, where left-wing communist actors could be hiding during the Cold War. For the most part, Parker and his G-2 Unit functioned as a clandestine intelligence gathering unit. G-2 information files, only accessible to Parker and his elite staff, contained enough "dirt" to sully the reputation of any group or person that dared to cross the department's legal or political path. To Parker, intelligence was power that could be used to solidify allies of the LAPD as well as to squash those who were considered enemies of the department.[11]

The Bloody Christmas

One of LAPD's most significant early challenges was to deal with a situation involving allegations of police brutality against Latino suspects being held in the department's central jail facility on Christmas morning of 1951. According to media accounts and court testimony chronicling the event, LAPD officers attending a Christmas Eve celebration at the jail facility severely brutalized a group of five Latino suspects who were being detained as crime suspects. It was also revealed that the officers involved in the attack had been drinking and were intoxicated at the time of the altercation. Despite suffering very serious wounds, none of the injured suspects as killed.

In defense of his officers, Chief Parker investigated the allegations of officer brutality from inside LAPD with his newly established Internal Affairs Division. As a result of recent changes to the city charter under Parker's advisement, citizens were no longer able to review matters of police misconduct. Although Parker used the incident to denounce police brutality in general, his investigation failed to produce significant wrongdoing on the part of the accused officers. The LA grand jury found otherwise, indicting each of the LAPD officers named in the brutality complaint. However, LAPD escaped the controversy relatively unscathed due to Chief Parker's ability to deflect the seriousness of "Bloody Christmas" by reminding the public that any effort to undermine the authority of the department would likely result in the Los Angeles community losing the war on crime. Members of the Latino community, on the other hand, claimed that the event was proof that the LAPD could successfully run roughshod over anyone or group that attempted to question the department's policing practices. Perhaps this was also the first time and place the efficacy of PRM as a policing operational style had been called into question.[12]

LAPD and the Media

LAPD became a Hollywood icon, primarily because of actor Jack Webb's fascination with the department and law enforcement in general. Largely as the result of teaming up with Chief Parker, Webb created several hit television shows that portrayed LAPD and its professional model of policing in a highly positive, if not surreal, light. The most famous of these TV dramas was *Dragnet*, named for a large-scale coordinated effort by police to apprehend criminals. In the series, which first aired during the 1950s, Webb played Sergeant Joe Friday, the quintessential professional LAPD officer who as a plainclothes detective approached each case in the characteristic Parker professional policing style. Web also produced the TV show *Adam-12*, which portrayed the role of patrol officers in a similar fashion.

Webb was perhaps the LAPD's and Parker's best ally, and perhaps an unsuspecting public relations guru for police officers operating under PRM. It was the popularity of Webb's innovative near-reality coverage of true LAPD cases and the far-reaching effects of the television media that propelled LAPD into worldwide stardom not only with civilians, but also within police organizational culture. The overall effects of this media blitz were twofold. First, Webb's flawless image of LAPD officers helped to stir up strong public support for the department and to cause citizens to rally around the agency in times of trouble. Second, police agencies from the United States to Singapore strived to emulate everything about the LAPD, from its organizational style to the "to protect and to serve" motto displayed on the side of a black-and-white patrol unit. To this day, one can still find timeless symbols of homage to Jack Webb for his positive media portrayals of the LAPD: Awards are given to officers bearing his character Friday's classic #714 badge number, police banquets are held in his honor, and even the LAPD police academy auditorium at Elysian Park bears his name.[13]

The Watts Riots

During the early 1960s, tensions mounted between LAPD and the African-American community of South Central Los Angeles, known then as Watts. Allegations of LAPD officer mistreatment of African-American citizens abounded both in the press and on the streets. Amid scathing criticisms from the Watts community and religious leads, Chief Parker held tight to the department's operational manifesto that "criminals could be recognized by their appearance and demeanor." This, in turn, paved the way for accusations that the LAPD employed a unique brand of racial profiling that enabled officers to target, arrest, and perhaps kill African Americans with legal impunity.

The LAPD's reputation received a major bruising in Watts during 1962 in the fallout of an event involving the shooting of Nation of Islam (NOI)

Secretary Ronald Stokes and six other NOI members by LAPD officers. After being stopped in his vehicle by LAPD officers, Stokes returned to his mosque—where he was again approached by police. Officers shot and killed Stokes after having a brief struggle with him. Hearing the shots fired, several armed NOI members responded to the scene, prompting a gun battle between them and the LAPD. The incident raised antipolice sentiments to an unprecedented high among African-American Angelinos, whose disdain for the LAPD was further fueled by a highly charged speech by civil rights leader Malcolm X calling for revenge in Watts against Chief Parker and his officers. Political reverberations from the incident reached Washington, D.C., prompting the U.S. Commission on Civil Rights to investigate LAPD's treatment of Black Muslims.[14]

The PRM policing style survived a near knockout punch in 1965, and perhaps received permanent wounds, when Watts "went off" into a six-day riot (known as the Watts Riots), which is still considered one of the nation's worst inner-city racial upheavals. The powder keg of tension was initially sparked when an angry crowd of Watts residents protested what they perceived to be the unjust arrest of an African-American motorist and his family by the California Highway Patrol. The incident soon erupted into a firestorm of mob violence, with tens of thousands of participants fighting and looting in the streets of Watts. Being greatly outnumbered, Chief Parker called for the assistance of the National Guard and the declaration of martial law in the city of Los Angeles. When the riots finally ended, and the final score was tallied, the statistics indicated that LAPD officers' battle wounds were not nearly as bad as those of their opponents. Of the 1,032 injured in the riots, 90 were police officers; of the 35 persons killed, 2 were police officers—but not from the LAPD. Following the riots, Chief Parker placed a gag order on his troops: They were not to talk to anyone about what went on in Watts. Parker's official statements about the riots included observations such as "The rioters were the criminal element in Watts…. We [the LAPD] are on top and they are on the bottom…. The rioters acted like monkeys in a zoo." In a recent interview, an LAPD officer who was a first responder to the Watts riots stated the following about Parker's handling of the incident: "The way we handled things under the control of Chief Parker got things under control in about 24 hours after the whole thing started. We were given orders to shoot looters on sight and we did … our use of force was effective, but it was misrepresented as brutality in the media."

The final official word on the riots came from the McCone Commission in 1965, which published a report citing numerous factors, including poor schools, unemployment, decreasing house values, and the like, as potential causes of the social unrest in Watts. Much to the dismay of many civic and governmental leaders who reviewed the report's findings, neither the LAPD nor its alleged police mistreatment of African-American citizens in Watts was directly addressed. Again, it appeared as though the LAPD's war on crime in Los Angeles had emerged victorious over the war on poverty that raged in Watts.

Parker Passes

On the night of July 16, 1966, Chief William Parker passed away of a massive heart attack at the age of 64 after receiving a standing ovation for a speech he had given to a group of 1,500 Marines. Parker's body was later transported in a motorcade consisting of some 300 full-dress motorcycle officers to Los Angeles City Hall, where his body lay in state within the building's rotunda, where all admirers were permitted to pay him their final respects. His funeral was the largest in LAPD history. Los Angeles police headquarters, known to police as the "Glass House," was named Parker Center in his honor. A life-size bronze bust of Parker also adorns the entrance of LAPD police headquarters. Parker's passing raised many questions in the minds of both his friends and foes regarding LAPD's future destiny. While it was true that Parker had many protégés within the department that supported his PRM operational methods, would one of them be appointed to the position of chief? And if so, would they or could they fill Parker's shoes and maintain the thin blue line in Los Angeles?

The Davis Era

Choosing Parker's Successor

LAPD went through three new chiefs (Thad Brown, appointed interim chief following Parker's death; Thomas Reddin, appointed chief in 1967; and Roger Murdock, appointed interim chief following Reddin's retirement) in the two years immediately following Parker's passing in 1966 until finding the "right fit" in 1969: Edward Davis. Chief Davis had a tough public persona and was known for making outrageous comments to the media. Most of all, as a loyal follower of Parker, he carried on the tradition of PRM at LAPD.[15] However, given the turbulent social environment in Los Angeles and the nation during the late 1960s, Davis saw fit to adapt Parker's professional policing model to the times. In doing so, he created the Basic Car Plan. This was LAPD's first attempt at reaching out to the community, especially in riot-torn Watts. The plan involved stabilizing the patrol area of LAPD officers so they "could get to know" the citizens and place they protected and served. "Team policing," as the method was also called, entailed a series of community-oriented measures to build bonds between the LA public and

LAPD officers, such as social get-togethers at citizens' homes to discuss neighborhood crime and police-community relations problems.

However, when it came to the war on crime, Davis saw eye to eye with Parker regarding the application of PRM and its policing methods utilized by officers on the street. Allegations of street level justice meted out by police under the guise of crime control still abounded. Political demonstrations were quelled by baton-wielding cops who still espoused Parker's "spare the baton and spoil the crook" philosophy. The "choke hold" was introduced as a use of force option for LAPD officers in lieu of using a baton, kick, or other form of blunt force technique. The method left no scars, but functioned to block blood to the suspect's brain by pressure to the carotid artery on the side of the neck, causing unconsciousness within less than 10 seconds—and perhaps death, if applied incorrectly or to the wrong suspect. In retrospect, an officer who worked for LAPD under the Davis administration stated the following about the advent of the choke hold: "We used the choke hold all the time instead of shooting a suspect…. I believe a lot more suspects were taken into custody alive because we were able to use the choke hold back in those days."

The "New Age" Crime Wave

The middle years of PRM during the late 1960 to early 1970s were highlighted by a wave of new crime and criminals that brought the world's attention to Los Angeles and the LAPD. During this period the department confronted a new style of political nemesis: one with a gun, and perhaps a twisted political agenda or a warped criminal mind, or both. First, there was the assassination of Senator Robert Kennedy while giving his acceptance speech at the downtown Ambassador Hotel after winning the California Democratic primary election in 1968. Political conspiracy theories swirled around the event due to assassin Sirhan Sirhan's Middle Eastern background. Then there was the Black Panther Shootout in 1969, when LAPD's newly former SWAT unit engaged in a five-hour gun battle with Panther members at their Los Angeles headquarters—where all suspects surrendered alive. And next was the strange, warped, politically motivated crime saga of the Symbionese Liberation Army (SLA).[16] After gaining national notoriety by kidnapping newspaper heiress Patricia Hearst, and then having her join their ranks as a bank robber, the SLA became the target of the LAPD. In 1974, six members of the group were killed in their Los Angeles hideout after a lengthy gun battle with LAPD officers when the dwelling in which they were holed up erupted into flames, perhaps as the result of heat from police tear gas canisters or an explosion of the group's own Molotov cocktails.

Crazed criminals with uncertain agendas also tested LAPD's psychological crime-fighting prowess during the 1960s and 1970s. After Susan Atkins, famed member of the Manson family, scrawled the words "Death To Pigs" with her bloody hands after murdering pregnant actress Sharon Tate and her unborn child, it was clear that LAPD was now dealing with the likes of a *criminal noir* that its officers had never before encountered. The arrest of "Helter Skelter" crazed Charles Manson, Atkins, and other members of "Charlie's family" was not the end of the road for the LAPD's encounter with the criminally disturbed mind. Next came along the challenge of unlocking the twisted mind of a serial killer responsible for dumping the nude bodies of young females on remote LA hillsides, all of whom were the apparent victims of rape, torture, and strangulation. The case, referred to by the media as the "Hillside Strangler," was eventually solved by the LAPD's arrest of two cousins, Kenneth Bianchi and Angelo Buono, who worked in tandem to seduce and kill at least 10 women by the time they were brought into custody in 1979.[17]

Perhaps even more deranged was the plight of the "Alphabet Bomber" during the mid-1970s. In this case, LAPD officers locked horns with the tormented mind of a man who informed television news sources that he would set bombs to kill persons in locations spelling out the name of a group to which he belonged—Aliens of American. The first bomb, representing the letter A, was placed at Los Angeles International Airport, where it exploded killing 3 and wounding 36. The Alphabet Bomber was responsible for several other bombings and attempted incendiary attacks throughout the Los Angeles area, and continued to taunt LAPD detectives by providing communiqués to them prior to each of his crimes. His penchant for communicating with LAPD ultimately led to his arrest when, while under surveillance, he was seen by police in his car preparing one of his infamous precrime tape-recorded messages.

The Gates Era

In 1978, following the retirement of Chief Davis, Daryl Gates was appointed the 49th LAPD chief of police. During the later years of Parker's administration, Daryl Gates served as one of the chief's elite assistants and, in many respects, was an on-the-job trainee of how to run the department under PRM. As Parker's aid, Gates was instrumental in developing the nation's first SWAT unit (Special Weapons and Tactics Team) in response to the growing threat of urban terror attacks in the Los Angeles area. He is also credited with the creation of other innovative programs, such as DARE (Drug Abuse Resistance Education) and Neighborhood Watch. Although many considered Gates a clone of Parker, history would prove otherwise. To say that Gates was a strong advocate of PRM would be an understatement. He whole-heartedly embraced the model as the central operating method of the LAPD during his tenure as chief. In fact, Gates went to great lengths to preserve the basic

BOX 1.1: TIMELINE OF ADMINISTRATIVE AND OPERATIONAL CHANGES OCCURRING AT LAPD DURING THE DAVIS ERA[18]

1967: Creation of the student worker program. Enabled student workers to enter the police academy as recruit officers before attaining age 21.

1967: Special Investigations Section (SIS) formed. Provided for intense investigation and surveillance of the highly skilled criminal.

1967: Commercial Auto Theft Section (BAD CATS) formed. Concentrated on the professional car thief rather than the joyrider.

1967: Creation of the Office of Planning and Control. Purpose of the office was the study of change needed in ensuing years in order to proactively initiate procedures and adjustments in deployment to address emergent trends.

1967: Automated Field Interview (AFI) system created. Automated officers' records of field interviews.

1969: Advent of Basic Car Plan. Divided Los Angeles into mini-neighborhoods and turned them over to individual teams of nine radio car officers. Officers were told, "This piece of territory now belongs to you. You'll have to earn the help and friendship of the people who live here. Meet with them at every opportunity. Never stop communicating."

1969: Implementation of the Police Role in Government program in 30 junior and senior high schools. Program received the George Washington Honor Medal Award from the Freedoms Foundation at Valley Forge. The program involved a full semester of elective study and provides insight into scores of topics concerned with police policies and the law and how they relate to young people.

1969: Creation of Neighborhood Watch. Born of the Basic Car Plan. Block meetings of citizens were carried out as often as required by their day-to-day crime situations. National recognition came when the federal government funded a similar program for sponsorship by the National Sheriffs' Association.

1969: ASTRO (Air Support to Regular Operations) implemented. Amplified the LAPD's powers of observation, deterrence, and response vis-a-vis the use of helicopter units.

1969: AWWS (Automated Want and Warrant System) fully operational. Provided instantaneously determination of whether an individual is wanted on a criminal charge.

1971: Chief Davis chaired the Task Force on Police, National Advisory Commission on Criminal Justice Standards and

Training. Documented methods for preventing and reducing crime for all size agencies. In addition, this documentation "may well be called the 'Bible' of law enforcement since nothing equal to its scope has ever been available."

1971: Career Police Plan. Provided for incremental increases in salary, based on a combination of higher education and job experience, for patrol officer ranks. Was a "giant forward stride toward enhancing the professional quality of police service." Created four pay grade positions: police officer I through police officer III+1.

1972: Team policing piloted. Consolidated patrol, traffic, and crime investigation into a single unit (team). Each team functions as a mini-department for a specific neighborhood. However, unlike a small town agency the teams have immediate access to the total resources of the LAPD.

1973: Criminalistics laboratory. Without equal among local agencies, thanks to federal grants enabling acquisition of highly sophisticated equipment. Only one of three agencies in the nation to possess the sound spectrographic analyzer—voiceprint equipment.

1973: Multimedia Instruction for Law Enforcement (MILE). Enabled recruits to learn at their own pace via multimedia instructional packages within individual study carrels equipped with videocassette players, eliminating the frustrating competition inherent in lockstep training methods. Allowed concentration on academic areas that individuals respectively find most difficult.

1973: Civilianization. Increased civilian employment relieved large numbers of sworn personnel for reassignment to line positions (jail and station security assignments as well as command positions in support operations—property division and supply division).

1973: Decentralization of Office of Operations. Created four geographic bureaus to increase responsiveness to local or area crime problems.

1973: Unisex. Classification of "police woman" eliminated. All sworn personnel undergo same training and designated "police officers."

1973: Child abuse detail formed within juvenile division. Recorded another first in law enforcement by implementing, in collaboration with medical authorities, a new approach to combating the battered child syndrome.

1973: Initiated development of computer-aided ECCCS (Emergency Command Control Communications System), subsidized via a $2 million federal grant.

1974, May 17: Symbionese Liberation Army (SLA) shootout. Demonstrated the ability of SWAT to gain an objective without endangering the safety of uninvolved citizens. 3,772 rounds of SLA ammunition was fired, but no casualties were sustained by citizens or officers.

1974: Body armor. Acquired for all field personnel.

1976: DEFT (Development and Evaluation of a Firearms Training Facility). Only firearms training simulator of its kind in the world. Optimal training program designed to develop the ability of officers to handle complex, conflict-laden situations in which the use of firearms may be required. Important training tool to help ensure strict adherence to use of force policy.

aspects of PRM at LAPD, such as (1) maintaining a small police-to-citizen ratio to enable quicker, more flexible police responses to crime; (2) insulating the department from political and community influences; (3) maintaining the tough, hard-nosed officer image; and (4) gathering intelligence on persons or organizations that may pose an outside threat to the LAPD.

When Daryl Gates took over the helm of LAPD, he would be the final chief to represent PRM and the professional police officer to both citizens and law enforcement. Gates would serve as the department's leader for a total of 14 years, a length of service that was only surpassed by Chief Parker's 16-year tenure in the same position. Gates fondly referred to LAPD as the "Big Blue Machine," or just "Big Blue" for short. He was noted for his strong support of the average patrol officer on the street, which he believed to be "the backbone of the department." As one officer reflected about Gates: "He was an extremely fair chief when there was an officer discipline issue and with him you always knew as an officer on the street that he 'had your back' against everyone that was out there attacking the way we did things."

The War on Crime Continues

Under Gate's leadership, LAPD's crime control muscle reverted back to the Parker "hook and book" style of policing, and once again turned away from the community. The scourge of serial killing still made its chilling presence in Los Angeles during the 1980s when Doug Clarke and Carol Bundy (the "Sunset Slayers") were leaving decapitated bodies throughout the city. Gates' detective squad handily solved this case and others like it to once again prove to the community that criminals could not escape the long arm of the law when enforced by LAPD. However, the department and Gates himself also came under extreme media fire in the highly publicized Eulia Love case, which perhaps marked the beginnings of growing discontent with aggressive policing taking place in minority communities. Love, an African-American female, was shot and killed by LAPD officers outside her home when she threw a knife at them after having a heated argument over an unpaid utility bill. Gates supported the officers' decision to use deadly force under departmental policies, drawing further complaints that LAPD's method of enforcement advocated the use of strong-arm tactics against persons of color. This negative sentiment was further fueled by media accounts painting Gates as a racist and claiming that he referred to Latinos as "lazy" and African Americans as "not normal people."[19]

However, the most serious crime control challenge to be encountered by Gates and PRM was the growing threat of LA street gangs. The LAPD had dealt with gang crime in the past, but nothing like that of the open drug-fueled and territorial warfare of African-American and Latino gang members. Chief Gates met the problem head on with the creation of CRASH (Community Resources Against Street Hoodlums). CRASH units specialized in targeting, arresting, and ultimately suppressing street gangs throughout Los Angeles inner-city neighborhoods. Considered most dangerous, and targeted by LAPD most often, were African Americans belonging to rival Crips and Bloods (or Piru) gangs. During the late 1980s, the introduction of gang distribution networks of crack cocaine in South Central LA and fights over their control caused an urban battlefield where more blood was spilled on the streets than in any other time in LAPD's history. But this war on crime was much different from that of the Parker era. The department's roughly 7,000 officers were outnumbered by the more than 20,000 confirmed gang members in LA; its firepower, consisting of 9-mm handguns and 12-gauge shotguns, was no match for the fully automatic AK-47 and Uzi assault weapons used by street gangs.

In order to flex muscles in a show of force against gangs, LAPD implemented several highly controversial field tactics. First, all persons in suspected "gang neighborhoods" were automatically "proned out" (made to lie face down on the ground with hand and feet spread) for even minor traffic violations. The greatest show of force, however, was the "gang sweep" carried out under the name "Operation Hammer." The Hammer, which was carried out typically on weekend nights, involved some 100 or more LAPD officers descending in unison on inner-city ghettos making mass arrests of hundreds of suspected gang members. Many believe that these aggressive tactics marked the beginning of LAPD's "us versus them" mentality that spread from the criminal element to the ordinary citizen—which drove a permanent wedge between LAPD and the public, causing the latter to believe that they were no longer being protected and served by the department.

Changing Times

LAPD walked the walk and talked the talk of toughness during the final years of PRM in the late 1980s. However, unlike the old days of the war on crime, the self-centered management style and aggressive policing style of PRM now appeared to be feared rather than revered by community members and politicians alike. In particular, the media and politicians who once supported LAPD gradually began to distance themselves from the department, as the professional police officer became perceived as more of bully rather than savior in the public's point of view. No longer was the elite SIS (Special Investigative Section) unit of detectives, who shadowed LA's most dangerous felons until catching them during the act of a serious crime and often gunning them down, seen as an effective means of preserving Parker's idea of the thin blue line. Rather, it was viewed as a hallmark of overly aggressive policing—as was the use of a Sherman tank as a battering ram—that had run amok in the city of Los Angeles.[20]

And no longer was the department's "get tough on crime" talk well received by the public. Chief Gates, who was the mouthpiece for LAPD's *neo-Parker* police professionalism, no longer sang to the choir as did Parker—instead, he was viewed as speaking from a bully pulpit. His comments about LAPD's war on crime, made in a similar vein to Parker's, were less likely to fly over the sea of public criticism. When Gates made his famous statement comparing the crime of marijuana smoking to treason, the public recoiled, and it became clear that the life span of the PRM professional cop might soon be over.

New Officer Diversity

Events occurring during the 1980s also forced LAPD to reevaluate the effectiveness of PRM. The old cast used to mold an image of an imposing, chiseled male LAPD officer was about to be recast. As the result of a civil lawsuit filed against LAPD, *Fanchon Blake v. City of Los Angeles*, the "look" of rank and file of LAPD patrol officers was changed radically. The suit, which was filed by then female LAPD sergeant Fanchon Blake, alleged that LAPD's past hiring and promotional practices discriminated against women and minorities. Proponents for the plaintiff presented evidence that very few women relative to men were promoted above the rank of sergeant and that the department's height requirement systematically excluded large numbers of women and minority recruits from being hired. Needless to say, Sergeant Blake prevailed in the case, resulting in the imposition of a consent decree against the department requiring the proactive hiring of women and minority applicants.

Adding to the above turmoil from within the patrol ranks of LAPD was the controversy surrounding the resignation of an openly gay officer named Mitchell Grobeson. He alleged that his resignation was due to antigay discriminatory actions taken against him by his fellow LAPD officers. Antigay epithets were written on his police car and on his locker inside the police station; backups failed to arrive when summoned to crime scenes he was working; and even worse, the department failed to do anything about it. These and other related actions prompted Grobeson to take legal action against LAPD for a host of issues relating to an untoward workplace, including discrimination and harassment. Eventually, proponents of Parker's original professional police officer image would have to accept the fact that many officers would eventually "come out" in the LAPD uniform.[21]

The King Incident and Gates' 10-Point Plan

On the night of March 19, 1991, it can be argued that the stage was set for the demise of PRM as a viable policing model for the LAPD or any other police agency. That night, African-American Rodney King received "power stroke" blows from the PR24 batons of four LAPD patrol officers who had stopped him after traveling high speeds on LA freeways. The event was videotaped and shown on news channels across the world. Officers involved claimed that King was under the influence of drugs and noncompliant to their demands, therefore justifying the use of force under LAPD policy guidelines. King, on the other hand, claimed that the officers who beat him were not merely a few bad apples, but instead they exemplified only four of an entire barrel of bad apples within the LAPD.

It quickly became clear that LAPD and PRM were suffering from mortal wounds dealt by the March 1991 Rodney King incident. It seemed as though the walls that were build decades ago by Chief Parker to shield the LAPD from outside threats were caving in on Chief Gates and his last bastion of professional policing. After the King incident, the department was now under investigation by the FBI, the Los Angeles District Attorney, the Los Angeles Police Commission, the LA Mayor's Office, and numerous civil rights organizations. In an attempt to counter the sudden wave of organizational scrutiny, and perhaps deflect some of the mounting negative accusations levied against the department, Chief Gates assembled a 10-point plan to make right any possible wrongs inside LAPD that may have led to the King incident. Some of the sweeping changes suggested by Gates included:

- Performing a comprehensive examination of use of force policies and training
- Executing an internal review of all potential police brutality complaints against officers by citizens
- Using the department's psychological staff to profile officers who may have overly aggressive tendencies
- Closely monitoring communications between officers for foul, racist, or other inappropriate language
- Developing a toll-free hotline for citizens to directly call LAPD internal affairs officers to lodge complaints against officers for inappropriate behavior
- Looking for nonlethal substitutes for the police baton, pistol, and other potentially lethal weapons in the LAPD use of force arsenal

In sum, all of the above reforms were direct threats to PRM and the preservation of professional policing within the LAPD organization. Possibly, the 10-point plan was merely a means to deflect outsiders from criticizing the LAPD's operational style in the wake of the King incident. Conversely, if Gates' intentions outlined in the plan were genuine, it may be safe to say that Chief William Parker was rolling over in his grave the day this last-ditch effort to save PRM from extinction was released to the LAPD and the public. With the issuance of the above reforms, it was clear that Chief Gates was forced for the first time in his leadership of the LAPD to soften Parker's thin blue line.[22]

The Christopher Commission

When it became clear that Gates' efforts to reform the LAPD would not suffice to relieve public criticism of the department in the wake of the King beating, outside experts were called in for consultation by order of the LA mayor, Tom Bradley. Bradley, a former LAPD officer himself, had a rather contemptuous relationship with Chief Gates, and with the professional model of policing. Bradley proposed his own plan to restore the LAPD back to health, but his plan would require radical surgery of the department's policies and operational practices—performed by many outside political practitioners. Eventually, both the Gates and Bradley plans for organizational change within the LAPD were merged under one main plan that was to be executed by an independent neutral commission headed by ex-U.S. Secretary of State Warren Christopher. Christopher had prior experience in such matters, having been instrumental in the review of the LAPD practices following the Watts riots.[23]

The Christopher Commission was assembled from countless experts representing the legal, judicial, academic, political, and law enforcement arenas. It officially convened for the first time on April 1, 1991, with the express goal to investigate the LAPD from the inside out by obtaining any and all available information on factors that may have contributed to the King incident. After gathering documents, reviewing cases, interviewing officers, and otherwise looking in every inner recess of the LAPD, the commission produced a 228-page report outlining what it felt to be numerous systemic flaws with the department and recommendations on how to fix them. Excessive use of force and racial insensitivity were LAPD's main character flaws highlighted in the report's findings. Moreover, the department was criticized for either failing to react, covering up, or rewarding such behaviors known to have been carried out against citizens by its officers.

The changes suggested by Christopher and his associates, in the eyes of Parker's professional police force, focused primarily on removing the shroud of secrecy that insulated the internal organizational sphere of the LAPD from external oversight and installing political mechanisms capable of performing external reviews of departmental operations. In addition, the report identified the age-old "us versus them" mantra of professional policing as a growing tumor that was killing the department's ability to foster emotional sensitivity toward citizens. Removing this aspect of the department could only be done by reinstilling the "C word" (i.e., "community") within the LAPD officer vocabulary. The Christopher Commission recommended that it was time for the LAPD to shake off Sergeant Joe Friday's Dragnet persona and his "just the facts, ma'am" dialogue so that police officers could once again move closer to the community. Perhaps the most scathing recommendation of the report was for the removal of Daryl Gates from the Office of Chief and the appointment of new leadership of the LAPD. This request was seconded by the city's mayor, Tom Bradley, who also called for the immediate resignation of Chief Gates following the report's release on July 10, 1991. The Los Angeles Police Commission also echoed Bradley's demand for the ouster of Chief Gates. However, it would be almost 1 year from this time that Gates would eventually step down as chief of LAPD on his own accord.[24]

The Los Angeles Riots

The evening of April 29, 1992, after the acquittal of four LAPD officers who had been on criminal trial for the beating of Rodney King, several events

BOX 1.2: KEY INVESTIGATIVE FINDINGS OF THE CHRISTOPHER COMMISSION[25]

Los Angeles and Its Police Force

1. Between 1960 and 1989, the rate of violent crime in Los Angeles was twice the national average.
2. Policing in Los Angeles is compounded by its vast geographic area and diversity of its population.
3. Of the six largest U.S. police departments, LAPD has the fewest officers per resident and per square mile.

Excessive Force

1. Significant numbers of officers repetitively misused force and ignore department guidelines regarding use of force. This group had received inadequate supervisory and management attention.
2. Forty-four officers were identified as having six or more allegations of excessive force for the period 1986 through 1990. Officers' performance evaluations generally did not give an accurate picture of the officers' disciplinary history.
3. Review of mobile digital terminals' messages revealed a disturbing incidence of improper messages, including scores in which officers talked about beating suspects and eagerness to be involved in violent confrontations with suspects.
4. Lack of monitoring or controlling of officers' MDT messages by supervisors.
5. Review of instances of 83 civil lawsuits between 1986 and 1990 revealed deficient investigations, and discipline was frequently light or nonexistent.

Racism and Bias

1. Bias within LAPD was not confined to officers' treatment of the public, but was also reflected in conduct directed to fellow officers who are members of racial or ethnic groups.
2. Bias also takes the form of gender and sexual orientation discrimination.
3. Female officers were subjected to a double standard and subtle harassment.
4. Too few minority officers were in managerial positions.
5. Female officers utilized a style of policing that minimizes use of excessive force.

Community Policing

1. LAPD organizational culture emphasized crime control over crime prevention, and this isolated the police from the communities they serve.
2. Officers were evaluated by statistical measures (e.g., number of arrests and calls handled) and were rewarded for being "hard-nosed." This creates a "siege" mentality that alienates the officer from the community.
3. Too many officers viewed citizens with resentment and hostility.
4. LAPD should implement community policing on a citywide basis, and this will require a fundamental change in values.

Recruitment

1. Background investigation offers the best hope for screening out violence-prone applicants.
2. Officers should be retested periodically to determine both psychological and physical problems.
3. Supervisors must understand their role to include training and counseling officers to cope with the problems policing can often entail.

Training

1. In academy training, increase emphasis on verbal skills rather than physical force to control potentially volatile situations.
2. In academy training, increase hours dedicated to cultural awareness.
3. Increase requirements for becoming a field training officer (FTO). "The most influential training received by a probationer comes from the example set by his or her FTO."

Promotion, Assignment, and Other Personnel Issues

1. The incidence of "not sustained" personnel complaints should be considered in the review process for promotion and coveted assignments.
2. Increase incentives for patrol assignments.
3. Officers should be rotated periodically to preclude their remaining in one geographic location for an inordinate period of time.
4. Complaint histories should be considered in assignment of problem officers who may be using force improperly.

Personnel Complaints and Officer Discipline

1. Overhaul the disciplinary system, from intake through adjudication.
2. Create the position of inspector general within the police commission with the responsibility to oversee the disciplinary process.
3. Address the greatest barrier to effective investigation: the code of silence.

Structural Issues

1. Police commission staff should be placed under the control of an independent civilian chief of staff, rather than the existing situation with a sworn staff officer.
2. The chief of police should serve a five-year term, renewable at the discretion of the police commission for one additional five-year term.
3. Selection, tenure, discipline, and removal of the chief of police should be exempted from existing civil service provisions.
4. The chief of police should be appointed by the mayor, with advice from the police commission.

occurred that marked the certain end of PRM as an operating model at LAPD—and as a viable policing model in general. First, one of the largest urban riots in the nation's history was touched off just hours after the King case verdict was announced, commonly referred to as the Great Los Angeles Riots of 1992. From the flashpoint of the riots in South Central Los Angeles, lawlessness in the streets of Los Angeles and surrounding cities quickly spread out of control and could not be controlled by the LAPD. Persons were attacked, fires were set, and buildings were looted and ransacked by thousands of rioters (many of which were believed to be criminals seeking opportunities to steal during the confusion of the riots). More than 50 persons were killed and over 1,000 injuries were reported over the 6 days that the violence persisted. The LAPD, which seemed helpless to control LA's riot-torn streets, was assisted by the military and various outside police agencies in order to regain control of the city. Rodney King himself was even enlisted to help calm the rioters when he appeared on television uttering his famous words, "Can't we all just get along!"[26]

Following the riots, critics of the LAPD stepped up pressure for Chief Gates' removal and called for sweeping reforms of the Gates administration, which had kept PRM alive as the preeminent policing model of Los Angeles. Furthermore, Chief Gates and his officers were considered by most outside observers of the LA Riots as the core problem for the eruption of what many experts believe to be the worst racially motivated riot in history. Postriot political fallout prompted further external review of LAPD policies, procedures, and operations by the Webster Commission. The Webster Commission convened during May 1992 (and completed its report during October 1992) in the wake of the Los Angeles Riots, which occurred after the acquittal of the officers on trial for beating Rodney King. The charge to the Webster Commission was to ascertain the nature of the LAPD's response to the civil disorder, as well as its level of preparation. The findings included the following:

- By early 1992 the problems of the inner city—gangs, crack cocaine, poverty, and racial and ethnic tension—made Los Angeles a tinderbox.
- There was a lack of emergency preparedness—and training—in the period before the verdicts for the accused officers were announced.
- The response to the riots was disorganized in that city government and police leaders did not appear to work well together.
- Several senior police commanders, including the chief of police, apparently found it difficult under the pressure of the event to make decisions and provide effective direction.
- The police department has grown aloof and removed from the city and its people—it must now become involved in a working partnership with the citizens.
- Chief Gates promoted the professional model of policing, in which aggressive crime fighting, rather than crime prevention, is the principal objective.
- Chief Gates moved the department away from contact with the community by placing more and more of his officers outside regular patrol functions and into highly trained, technically sophisticated specialized units that had little day-to-day contact with the community.
- The LAPD must change from the professional model to a more community-oriented approach if it is to regain the confidence of the people.
- Reduce the emphasis on specialized units and reemphasize the importance of patrol duties as the cornerstone for a new area-based problem-solving approach.
- The chief of police should actively participate in a program of developing citywide plans and training programs for emergency preparedness that also reasonably anticipates contingencies.[27]

Ironically, before the above Webster Commission report findings regarding the LAPD were made public, Chief Gates stepped down as chief of LAPD on June 28, 1992. On this day, it can be argued with relative certainty, the professional-reform model of policing faced extinction in the Los Angeles community much in the same way dinosaurs eventually became extinct in a changing habitat. In a matter of months after Gates' removal, most of the reforms recommended by the Webster and Christopher Commissions were implemented within the LAPD. Most important among these was the replacement of PRM as LAPD's operational style with a new model of policing based on reducing interpersonal barriers between citizens and police to form crime-solving partnerships that would, in effect, replace the thin blue line. This style of policing, however, was a condition of the pre-Parker era that was believed to breed corruption and led to initial creation of PRM at LAPD—and begs one critical question about the future of policing without PRM: How can a policing agency have an effective war on crime and battle officer corruption and at the same time rub elbows with the community?

References

1. Orlando Wilson and William H. Parker. *Parker on Police*. Springfield, IL: Charles Thomas, 1957.
2. Art R. Sjoquist. *History of the Los Angeles Police Department*. Los Angeles: Los Angeles Police Revolver and Athletic Club, 1984.
3. Martin Schiesl. Behind the Badge: The Police and Social Discontent in Los Angeles Since 1950. In Martin Schiesl and Norman Klein (eds.), *20th Century Los Angeles: Power, Promotion and Social Conflict*. Claremont, CA: Regina, 1990.
4. Ibid.
5. Sarah Alisa Kramer. *William H. Parker and the Thin Blue Line: Politics, Public Relations and Policing in Postwar Los Angeles* [PhD dissertation]. Washington, DC: American University, 2007.
6. Ibid.
7. James Gazell. William H. Parker, Police Professionalization and the Public: An Assessment. *Journal of Police Science and Administration*, 4(1), 1976.
8. Ibid.
9. Ibid.
10. Joe Domanik, *To Protect and to Serve. LAPD's Century of War in a City of Dreams*. New York: Pocket Books, 1994.
11. Ibid.
12. Edward J. Escobar. Bloody Christmas and the Irony of Police Professionalism: The Los Angeles Police Department, Mexican American, and Police Reform in the 1950s. *Pacific Historical Review*, 72, 2003.
13. Jack Webb. *The Badge: The Inside Story of One of America's Great Police Departments*. New York: Prentice-Hall, 1958.
14. Ibid.
15. Mike Davis. *City of Quartz: Excavating the Future in Los Angeles*. London: Verso, 1990.
16. Ibid.
17. Ibid.

18. Michael Hooper. California Commission on Peace Officer Standards and Training. Personal correspondence, May 15, 2011.
19. Daryl F. Gates. *Chief: My Life in the LAPD*. New York: Bantam, 1992.
20. Ibid.
21. George T. Felkenes and Peter Unsinger. *Diversity, Affirmative Action and Law Enforcement*. Springfield, IL: Charles C Thomas, 1992.
22. Daryl F. Gates. Personal correspondence, June 30, 1991.
23. Christopher Commission. *Report of the Independent Commission of the Los Angeles Police Department*. Los Angeles, CA: LAPD, 1991.
24. Ibid.
25. Ibid.
26. Lou Cannon. *Official Negligence: How Rodney King and the Riots Changed Los Angeles and the LAPD*. New York: Times Books, 1997.
27. William Webster and Hubert Williams. *The City in Crisis: Los Angeles*. Los Angeles, CA: City of Los Angeles, 1991.

The Study
A Qualitative Analysis of LAPD's Organizational Dying Declarations

2

Criminal Intent and Organizational Death

Those who study the life and death of organizations claim that, in many respects, an organization is like a person. It has a life cycle involving birth, life, and death. During its living years, an organization grows and thrives as well as develops a unique identity and culture. The death of an organization is commonly brought about by old age, a terminal illness, or perhaps by an unfortunate accident. On more rare occasions, however, organizations may become the victims of homicide. The homicide may be justifiable, or in self-defense, if those who are responsible for the death felt that their life was in imminent danger by the organization's actions at the time of the killing. Alternatively, the organization's killer may have been acting "in the heat of passion," having lost control over finding the organization in an untoward or provocative situation. Last, and most disturbing, are situations involving the malicious, intentional killing of an organization in cold blood. In these cases, the killer may have acted alone or with others in the execution of a plan—for revenge or profit or both—to cut short the life of a vibrant, thriving organization.

Whether or not an organization was the victim of homicide is a question that, for most organizational deaths, remains unanswered. New organizations, with new leadership, emerge quickly to replace the operations and memories of those that have died. Occasionally, however, there is some evidence occurring at the time of death that can be used by investigators to determine if the organization's demise was the product of foul play. Most powerful and convincing among the potential clues left at the death scene is the dying declaration. Simply defined, a dying declaration is "the last dying words from someone who is aware of their impending death, that relate in some way to the cause or circumstances surrounding death."[1] They are considered to be credible and trustworthy evidence because it is assumed that individuals who know they are about to die, and have knowledge regarding a homicide, will speak the truth before death in an effort for justice to be done among the living.

This qualitative study contains, and is based upon, the collection of dying declarations obtained from within the LAPD during a time that is herein defined as an organizational meltdown. Simply defined, this term refers to a sudden and complete failure of an organization. Applied to the LAPD, this term refers to a specific point in time when the department and its officers were no longer able to function in the manner in which they had been functioning in the past. The organizational culture and PRM policing model that they had relied upon for the last 40 years was also no longer functional. In effect, when Parker's policing model suddenly died of heretofore unknown causes, LAPD officers lost their sense of professional identity, purpose, and mission both within the organization and in the outside community.

In this chapter, the research study process is explained. In particular, methods used to examine the nature and extent of what has come to be known as the LAPD organizational meltdown are presented. Central to the findings produced in this investigation is the qualitative analysis of hundreds of written interviews obtained from officers during the department's meltdown period. The interviews or organizational dying declarations, as they are referred to in the sections that follow, are presented in the officers' own handwriting to further illustrate the emotions underlying their written attitudes and observations. Through a systematic analysis of these data it is the main research goal of this study to determine the root cause or causes of the LAPD meltdown and to provide policy recommendations for avoiding similar future occurrences within other policing or other organizational environments.

Determining Whether or Not to Pull the Plug

Days after the Christopher Commission report was released on July 10, 1991, Chief Gates contacted the author, who had performed independent evaluations of the department in the past, requesting that he perform a "special study" to determine "just how bad" the LAPD's reputation was in the LA community and if it could, at all, be fixed. This author responded to Gates' plea for help and volunteered to do a full statistical workup of the department's perception within the community, and to provide recommendations to the chief regarding how his and the department's reputation could be restored in the community as well as among his troops. Chief Gates accepted the offer through a correspondence sent to the author dated July 22, 1991 (Figure 2.1) and further clarified his intentions to cooperate with an

LOS ANGELES POLICE DEPARTMENT

DARYL F. GATES
Chief of Police

TOM BRADLEY
Mayor

P. O. Box 30158
Los Angeles, Calif. 90030
Telephone:
(213) 485-3202
Ref #: 9.4

July 22, 1991

Dr. James Lasley, Associate Professor
Department of Criminal Justice
California State University, Fullerton
800 North State College Boulevard
Fullerton, California 92634

Dear Dr. Lasley:

The Los Angeles Police Department welcomes your offer to design a survey instrument and conduct four quarterly public opinion surveys in the 18 Police Department Areas of the City of Los Angeles. I understand that the purpose of these surveys will be to learn public opinions and priorities on police service in the various neighborhoods of Los Angeles. From these surveys, I hope to learn what real or perceived problems may exist in Police Department relationships with the public.

I understand that you will conduct these surveys at no cost to the City of Los Angeles and without a contract or any binding agreement between you and the City of Los Angeles or any of its agents. I understand completely that you must conduct the surveys independent of Police Department or City influence in order to produce a research product that is valid and credible.

The Police Department will cooperate fully in your research. Please let me know if I can assist in your efforts to obtain funding, including writing letters in support of your efforts. The help that you request from us and that which we provide must not influence the outcome of your research. Please help me insure that this restriction is not violated.

I anticipate that you and your staff will want to meet with various Department representatives and obtain maps and other data held by the Department. I have directed Captain Dan Watson, Commanding Officer, Planning and Research Division, to give special attention to any needs you or your staff may have. He can be reached at (213) 485-2636.

AN EQUAL EMPLOYMENT OPPORTUNITY – AFFIRMATIVE ACTION EMPLOYER

(a)

Dr. James Lasley
Page Two
9.4

The Police Department has cooperated with California State University, Fullerton, in past criminal justice research, and we have been very pleased with your work. I look forward to reading your research report as soon as it is made available to the public.

Very truly yours,

DARYL F. GATES
Chief of Police

(b)

Figure 2.1 Original letter from Chief Daryl F. Gates authorizing the independent study of factors relating to LAPD's organizational meltdown.

LOS ANGELES POLICE DEPARTMENT

DARYL F. GATES
Chief of Police

TOM BRADLEY
Mayor

P. O. Box 30158
Los Angeles, Calif. 90030
Telephone:
(213) 485-3202
Ref #: 9.4

August 2, 1991

Dr. James Lasley, Associate Professor
Department of Criminal Justice
California State University, Fullerton
800 North State College Boulevard
Fullerton, California 92634

Dear Dr. Lasley:

Attached are the formal statements of the mission, motto, objectives, and standard of conduct of the Los Angeles Police Department. The defining elements in each of these statements have been underscored or, in the case of the standard of conduct, listed separately. I would welcome learning from your surveys how people in the various neighborhoods of Los Angeles feel about Police Department performance on these elements.

I have also enclosed a copy of the complete Manual of the Los Angeles Police Department and Human Relations in the Police Service, from which the above statements are taken. These publications are comprehensive documentation of what we believe our job to be and how we believe we should be doing it. You may find them useful in your efforts to learn how we succeed or fail in meeting the expectations of the people we serve.

In general, three kinds of information would be useful in guiding future Department operations:

1. Current public opinion on the quality of service in each of the 18 Police Department Areas;

2. How that opinion was formed (direct experience, friends, relatives, radio, television, newspaper, etc.); and

3. Current public expectations and priorities on various types of police service.

AN EQUAL EMPLOYMENT OPPORTUNITY – AFFIRMATIVE ACTION EMPLOYER

(a)

Dr. James Lasley
Page two
9.4

As I said in my July 22 letter, you have my full support in your research. At the same time, please insure that Police Department involvement does not influence the outcome of that research. The work you are doing is vital to the future of policing in Los Angeles. I sincerely appreciate your volunteering to perform this critical public service.

Very truly yours,

DARYL F. GATES
Chief of Police

Enclosures

(b)

Figure 2.2 Follow-up letter from Chief Daryl F. Gates outlining LAPD's identifying the Department's research priorities for discovering factors relating to the meltdown.

independent research examination of the LAPD in a second letter dated August 2, 1991 (Figure 2.2).

Around this time, mounting media, community, and political pressures were being placed on Gates and his entire department over the King beating. Having already been asked by the LA mayor to resign, and suffering an 80% disapproval rating in a *Los Angeles Times* newspaper poll, Gates held strong to his civil service job protection and hoped that the author's study might help provide a "Hail Mary" strategy to restoring the community's confidence in him and in the department. Finding a successful strategy for preserving the status quo LAPD also meant that Parker's professional-reform model of policing would live on. But when definite signs of plummeting officer morale of a catastrophic proportion began to surface from patrol officers to air support units, it soon became apparent to the chief that LAPD was suffering from organizational bleeding not only externally, but internally as well.

In the past, LAPD officers had always remained loyal to the Department and to the war on crime—despite shots taken at the organization from politicians, civil rights groups, and community members. Ostensibly, this was no longer the case. Thus, in order to stop the internal organizational bleeding and to stabilize the departmental patient, Gates requested of the author that the focus of the departmental analysis be shifted immediately to ills within the organization itself rather than on the outside community perception of the chief and LAPD in general. Gates stated that he feared "the LAPD was melting down" and "chaos" within the department and within the streets of Los Angeles could become an unfortunate consequence of this organizational meltdown.

According to Gates' plans, the objectives of this "special internal study" were twofold. First, the study was to be carried out in such a way as to tap into his officers' inner-most feelings about what they felt was the main reason the department was "dying" and about to undergo a total meltdown; and the study's second objective was to determine if the officers could recommend any possible antidote that might provide a cure in order to save the department? Ultimately, the results of this study would be the determining factor regarding (1) whether or not to pull the plug on the professional-reform model of policing and (2) to help Chief Gates in deciding whether or not to call it quits as the LAPD's last leader to support the model.

The Thin Blue "Flat" Line

Work on the special internal study of the LAPD's organizational wounds began during the first week of August 1991. The author was given complete autonomy to perform the study, and there were no restrictions placed on the investigation process. However, there was an express directive from Gates that the analysis should focus on ways to restore the health of the organization based on the recommendations of LAPD patrol officers, whom as a group he considered "the backbone" of the department. First, he wanted to know if and how he could restore their confidence in him and in the department; second, if there was enough time, he wanted to know if the LAPD's reputation could be restored in the community.

During the first week of December 1991, the information contained in this study was gathered by the author from 320 officers representing various ranks, from patrol to upper administration, selected for inclusion in this study. The officer sample was not gathered randomly, but rather purposively. The sample represents both males and females, ethnic minorities (Latinos, African-Americans), and officers whose date of hire was during the Parker, Davis, and Gates eras—thus, encompassing the entire life span of the LAPD professional policing model. These officers provided in writing a brief statement of their opinion regarding the primary reason(s) why the LAPD and its policing methods (i.e., the professional model) were facing rejection not only by LA citizens, but also by themselves or by the public. Getting wind of the study, the police officers' union, the Police Protective League, tried to secure a court injunction against the investigation for fear that it would turn up something that could be used against officers in future collective bargaining agreements.

The union-initiated delay and other problems caused by departmental politics resulted in the author's inability to perform a full examination of the study data until the end of April 1992. Prior to then, the actual written documents obtained from the officers and presented in this study remained in a cardboard box that was tapped shut and secured in a storage area located on the sixth floor of Parker Center. The only identifying information on the box was the author's business card, which was affixed to its lid. Unfortunately, prior to the time the author was able to recover the contents of the box the LA Riots erupted on April 29, 1992. Two months later Chief Gates would step down from his post and the LAPD would be infiltrated by numerous outside examiners who were investigating Gates' and the department's role in both the King incident and the LA Riots. This also meant that the information contained in the box at Parker Center, and its contents comprised of the officers' written interview data, took on new significance: They were now dying declarations of the LAPD organization that were perhaps the only true recorded record of how and why the departmental meltdown occurred. In addition, the results of the internal study could reveal how the meltdown may have contributed to the professional-reform model's demise at the hand of the LAPD administration.

Admissibility of the Evidence

Little did the author know at the time of his involvement with this special study that the information being gathered would, in fact, be the last documentation ever obtained from the LAPD while it operated under the professional model of policing. Fortunately, various voices from within the department were forever recorded as organizational dying declarations of the professional model of policing. These voices, which collectively reflect final breaths taken by a living police organization, were obtained from LAPD officers who witnessed firsthand the meltdown, collapse, and ultimate death of police professionalism as it was once known. Within these officer accounts lies the truth regarding how the policing model died, and perhaps whether or not the situation should indeed be investigated as an accidental death or one of a homicidal nature "at the hands of another." However, in order for a dying declaration to be afforded credibility, the law of evidence outlines several requirements that must be met by those documenting and providing the declaration. Each of these is discussed below within the context of the situation at hand:

1. *The form of dying declaration or the manner in which it was obtained is immaterial—it can be written or oral, verified or unverified.* The dying declarations were gathered in a variety of ways. The majority, approximately 80%, were obtained during the roll call period immediately before the beginning of the officers' patrol shift during the first and second weeks in December 1991. The remaining 20% of declarations were procured directly from officers either during or after their patrol shift. When asked whether they were willing to be a witness in the investigation of their agency's downfall, in a rare abandonment of the blue code of silence, the officers welcomed the opportunity for their voices on the impending death of the LAPD to be finally heard. Each dying declaration was provided in the officer's own handwriting for authenticity purposes. Information on the officer's gender, race, and date of hire was also gathered by the author. At the time the declarations were gathered, the officers were informed that it was likely their statements would be read by the chief of police, the media, and otherwise made public. The general response to this advisement was "I don't give a ****"—thus, ostensibly, the thin blue line that had created a "what happens inside LAPD stays inside LAPD" culture was now ostensibly broken. Thus, the officers represented in this study were voluntary and informed participants as required under the ethical guidelines of conducting qualitative research.
2. *The declaration must be made with the belief of immediate death—even if there are hopes of recovery.* According to the ancient legal principle

upon which the dying declaration is founded, "the mind, impressed with the awful idea of approaching dissolution, acts under a sanction equally powerful with that which it is presumed to feel by solemn appeal to God upon an oath."[1] Thus, the primary question to be answered here with regard to the professional policing era's demise is this: Are the LAPD officers' dying declarations merely the reflections of overexaggerated feelings resulting from an emotional reaction to the turbulent times following the King incident, or are they accurate witness accounts from "insiders" who were finally willing to tell their story during the first time in history time that the LAPD was "caught with its pants down"? Based on the psychological theory of dying declarations, each individual testimony should be considered good evidence if it can be assumed that at the time it was written the witnessing officer believed LAPD was on the brink of death. This is true regardless of whether or not the officer believed the department would ever make a recovery. Under these circumstances, the officer statements may be considered equivalent to those that would be taken under legal oath. In a research sense, we then can conclude that they possess a certain degree of validity or truthfulness regarding the experiential nature of the LAPD organizational meltdown.

3. *Death can be delayed days or even weeks and the declaration is still valid.* The exact time the meltdown began and the professional era of policing died is unknown and can only be estimated through conjecture. For purposes of this study it is assumed that LAPD organizational culture began melting down sometime after the Rodney King incident occurred on March 3, 1991. Likewise, it is also assumed that the professional era ended at or shortly after 3:15 p.m. on Wednesday, April 29, 1992, following the public announcement of the jury verdict fully acquitting three of the four LAPD officers charged with criminally assaulting Rodney King. There were certain signs of the meltdown by later in the evening that same day, evidenced by a crowd of several hundred protesters gathered outside of LAPD's Parker Center headquarters throwing rocks, smashing windows, and attempting to catch the building ablaze. The declarations from LAPD patrol officers presented here were gathered approximately four months prior to this point in time. However, according to legal custom, this gap in time does not necessarily taint the evidence presented in the dying declarations. According to the logic handed down in past court rulings:

> The rule as to the admissibility of dying declarations does not require that they should have been made while the sufferer is

> literally breathing his last breath. It is enough that they were made when he understands that his injuries are fatal and he believes that death is near at hand.

Thus, the validity of LAPD officers' dying declarations should not be minimized or discounted by the fact alone that they were obtained at a time that was months in advance of the professional era's actual death. Again, it is the degree to which the officers believed in the ultimate demise of the professional-reform model at the LAPD that is key in determining the potential accuracy of their written eyewitness accounts. Thus, traditional time-bound threats to the validity and reliability of observational data due to memory fading on the part of participants are not likely to distort the accuracy of the officer observations presented in this study[2] (Figure 2.3).

Chief Gates' 10 Point Plan

MARCH 27, 1991

PRESS RELEASE

THE AFTERMATH OF THE RODNEY KING INCIDENT HAS BEEN AN EXCEEDINGLY DIFFICULT AND TRYING TIME. FEELINGS OF BETRAYAL AND SHOCK HAVE BEEN EXPERIENCED BY BOTH COMMUNITY MEMBERS AND DEPARTMENT PERSONNEL. THERE IS NO DOUBT FROM ANY QUARTER THAT A NUMBER OF THOSE OFFICERS INVOLVED IN THE KING INCIDENT MUST BE, AND WILL BE, BROUGHT BEFORE THE BARS OF THE CRIMINAL AND ADMINISTRATIVE JUSTICE. THERE IS UNANIMOUS CONSENSUS THAT THERE MUST BE A THOROUGH AND DILIGENT SEARCH FOR ANY UNDERLYING REASONS WHY THOSE OFFICERS ENGAGED IN SUCH LAWLESSNESS. WE MUST LOOK FOR ANY AND ALL CONDITIONS THAT MAY HAVE CONTRIBUTED TO THE DEVELOPMENT OF ATTITUDES AND PATTERNS OF BEHAVIOR THAT COULD HAVE LED TO THIS KIND OF GROSS MISCONDUCT. WE MUST DETERMINE WHY SUCH INDICATORS, IF THEY DID EXIST, WERE NOT DETECTED.

FLAWS THAT ARE FOUND IN ANY PART OF THE PROCESS THAT TRANSFORMS A CITIZEN INTO A POLICE OFFICER MUST BE CORRECTED. IMPROVED METHODS FOR INSTILLING IN OUR RECRUITS A REVERENCE FOR THE LAW AND A MORE COMPASSIONATE UNDERSTANDING AND APPRECIATION FOR THE CULTURAL DIVERSITY OF THE RESIDENTS WE SERVE MUST BE DEVELOPED.

Figure 2.3 Press release issued by Chief Gates outlining a "10 Point Plan" to investigate causes relating to the King Incident within LAPD. The present study was included as one of the points, and was the only point under Gates' plan that was actually carried out.

Missing in Action

Approximately one week after the riots had subsided, the author contacted officials at Parker Center in order to check on the status of the special internal study and to hopefully secure the original dying declarations secured from the officers. However, after several phone calls to several individuals, he was informed that the box could not be located. This prompted the author to gain permission from LAPD to examine the storage area where the information was last placed in hopes that the box had been overlooked or perhaps moved to another place in the building. Upon inspection, the corner of the room where the box was last seen appeared exactly the same as it was before the riots—with the exception of the missing box. A search of other likely locations within Parker Center turned up nothing. The author was informed that the box had perhaps been sent back to the university where the author was employed. However, workers at the university mailroom reported that they had not received the box. After months of calling, searching, and waiting, it appeared that the odds of recovering the original dying declarations were slim to none.

In May 2006, when the author approached his university office at sometime before noon to start his teaching schedule for the day, he noticed a yellowed cardboard box in the hallway outside of the office door. On its lid was his business card, which was an older version and now somewhat yellowed. After examining the box's exterior to make sure it was not some sort of student prank, or worse an explosive device, the author realized this was the "missing box" containing the dying declarations gathered by him from LAPD officers over 20 years ago. Miraculously, the box contained no water damage and appeared to be relatively intact. The tape that had secured the contents had come loose in some places, but was not torn or removed. From all visible indications, the box had never been opened.

Upon opening the box, the author found all of the original written dying declarations in especially good condition. How the box got home to its rightful owner is yet to be determined. One theory is that a conscientious person who came across the box without knowledge of its contents was merely doing a good deed by returning it. The other theory, which is more conspiracy based, is that an LAPD "insider" with knowledge of the special internal study intentionally removed the box from the Parker Center so that the officers' statements would never be read. Perhaps a guilty mind or sense of conscience prompted the preservation and delayed return of the original dying declarations. Regardless of the motives behind the box's return, now the officers' voices can be heard, and the original statements can be used as proof to verify the authenticity of their comments regarding the LAPD meltdown and fall of the professional model of policing.

Research Methodology: Preparing for an Organizational Autopsy

This study, like most based on qualitative research principles, is decidedly exploratory in nature. Unlike traditional quantitative studies that begin with a theory upon which specific hypotheses are constructed and then tested (i.e., deductive logic), the present research approach follows inductive logic. That is, specific observations are first examined for thematic content, and then hypotheses are constructed that lead to the construction of an overall theory used to explain the research problem. In the case of the present study, there are many possible ways that the officers' declarations could be grouped in order to provide some sort of collective meaning and interpretation. Consideration was given to grouping them by the available officer demographics: ethnicity, date of hire, or gender. To do so would presume that any one of these factors would provide the most important reason for the LAPD's organizational meltdown and the professional policing model's failure.

However, the decision was made to group the statements on the basis of common themes because therein (it is here assumed) lies the best clues to discovering the best explanation for how and why the meltdown occurred within the LAPD organization. In doing so, an analysis of these themes can then be used to perform an organizational autopsy of the LAPD's internal policing culture to discover specific causes of the meltdown and the professional model's fall from grace. Furthermore, analogous to a pathologist inspecting a corpse during a postmortem medical examination, the contents of the dying declarations can be utilized to determine the model's probable organizational manner of death. That is, did the professional model die as the result of an accident, a suicide, natural causes, or a homicide? And if the latter conclusion is reached, should the killing of the model be considered a case of organizational murder at the hands of another (e.g., disloyal LAPD officers, politicians, the media, Rodney King)?

Officer Sample

The study sample was selected by examining each of the officers' written interview statements for usable content. Specifically, the officers' comments were inspected for specific, logical, and legible observations identifying one or more causal factors likely leading to LAPD's organizational meltdown. Surprisingly, the vast majority of the officer statements contained specific identifiable causes and were included in the immediate analysis. Excluded from the sample were 82 of 320 (or approximately 25%) officer comments initially gathered for study. These were not included due to space limitations,

Table 2.1 Demographic Composition of Final Study Sample (N = 238)

	N	%	% LAPD (1991)
	Gender		
Male	215	90.3	88.1
Female	23	9.7	11.9
	Race		
Caucasian	182	76.5	63.9
Hispanic	38	16.0	20.1
African American	18	4.8	13.1
	Age		
Less than 30 years	59	24.8	NA
21–40 years	117	49.2	NA
41 years or more	62	26.0	NA
	Experience		
6 years or less	59	24.8	NA
7–20 years	121	50.1	NA
21 years or more	58	25.1	NA
	Chief When Hired		
Parker	26	10.9	NA
Reddin	14	5.9	NA
Davis	88	40.0	NA
Gates	110	43.2	NA

Note: % LAPD denotes percent of given officer demographics for the total department during 1991, the year the study was executed. NA denotes information not available for study comparisons.

redundant content, or illegible/illogical responses (these and all other original officer comments can be viewed in the downloadable database that accompanies this book). The final study sample consisted of 238 officer comments. Limited demographic information was provided by each of these officers and is presented in Table 2.1. As the table shows, percentage breakdowns associated with officer gender revealed that females in the study sample, compared to the percentage of females in the general LAPD officer population in 1991[3] (the year this study was conducted), were slightly underrepresented by approximately 2%. The same comparisons for officer race revealed that Caucasian officers were overrepresented in the sample by approximately 13%. The number of minority officers included in the sample was approximately 12% less than that shown for the LAPD officer population. Most underrepresented in the study were African American officers, whose presence was nearly three times greater in the LAPD population than in the study sample.

Theme Development

The primary methodological foundation of this study is based on the creation and analysis of substantive themes relating to the probable cause(s) of the LAPD organizational meltdown, which were interpreted from the officers' written comments. The method of theme development followed a specific to general process. First, each officer comment was examined for one or more identifiable causes of the meltdown. Admittedly, this was somewhat of a subjective process, but for the most part, the specific causes were readily identifiable. The following is a list of themes generated from this initial analytical step:

- Citizen alienation of LAPD and its officers
- Officer cynicism toward their job and the LAPD
- Department doesn't care about street officers
- LAPD administrators "sold out" to politicians and the community
- Affirmative action policies ruined the department
- Officers support the department—no matter what happens
- Citizens and politicians are "bashing" the LAPD
- The LAPD has bad training
- The LAPD has bad management and administrators
- Officers support Chief Gates
- Officers don't support Chief Gates
- The Rodney King incident ruined the department
- The Christopher Commission ruined the department
- Mayor Bradley and special interest groups ruined the department
- Aggressive policing should be maintained over community-based policing
- Aggressive policing should not be maintained over community-based policing
- More citizen contact is needed
- Better promotion and hiring practices for street officers

Next, the method of analytical parsimony was used to generate a smaller set of more manageable general theme categories. Basically this involved regrouping each of the above specific themes based on their overall commonalties regarding the cause(s) of the LAPD organizational meltdown. This process did not prove difficult because there appeared to be a clear consensus among officers regarding the main general causes of the meltdown.

In all, there were four main theme (or cause) categories identified, which were factors relating to either: (1) the Rodney King incident; (2) outside interference and attacks against the department by politicians, special interest groups, and others at the community level; (3) unfair hiring and promotional practices imposed by the department as the result of court-mandated affirmative action policies; and (4) mismanagement and other activities by the LAPD administration judged to be inappropriate by street level officers.

Presentation of Findings

The study findings are based on an analysis of the above four main theme categories. The following five chapters contain results from qualitative analyses of the officer comments, and present the narrative of each comment and, in some cases, actual written statements. The actual statement is provided because much can be learned from an examination of the "body language" contained in the officer's writing. It is often the case that the emotion of the officer's comment is clearly visible in how the writing is composed and presented. (Bear in mind that these comments were to be viewed by Chief Gates and other top LAPD administrators, as well as by the researcher.) The chapter that immediately follows is a qualitative analysis of officer comments performed in order to determine if indeed an organizational meltdown of the LAPD did occur and, if so, the extent of the damage it caused to the professional model of policing. Respectively, Chapters 4 to 7 contain qualitative analyses of the likely impact of the King incident, politicians and others groups, affirmative action policies, and LAPD administrators on the LAPD meltdown. Specifically these analyses were performed to determine which, if any, of these potential causes of the meltdown were detrimental to the professional model of policing. Chapter 8 contains the only quantitative analysis performed in the study. Here, officer comments are converted to quantitative data and empirical analyses are performed in order to test various hypothetical conclusions drawn from earlier qualitative results. Overall conclusions and policy implications for the study findings are discussed in Chapter 9.

Study Limitations and Database

Space does not permit the inclusion of all written materials gathered from the officer sample. Statements that have been excluded were done so because either they were relatively similar in content to those that were included or they did not provide information that was relevant to the issue at hand. To preserve authenticity, each officer interview is presented in its natural state, that is, as it was originally written in the officer's own handwriting.

This was done to illustrate the emotion that is expressed by the officers in their own unique writing styles. All efforts were made to present each officer statement in its entirety; however, some may have been reduced in length, but none was edited for substantive content. All statements contain a transcription of the officer's handwriting for ease of reading as well as brief biographical information about the officer who was interviewed. All officer interviews contained in this study, in addition to those that have not been included, are made available by the researcher for additional inspection and analysis in the study's supplemental downloadable external database.

References

1. Bryan A. Garner (Ed.), Black's Law Dictionary (9th ed.), St. Paul, MN: West Publishing, 2009.
2. N.K. Denzin and Y.S. Lincoln. *Handbook of Qualitative Research* (2nd ed.). Thousand Oaks, CA: Sage Publications, 2000.
3. George T. Felkenes and Peter Unsinger. *Diversity, Affirmative Action and Law Enforcement*. Springfield, IL: Charles C Thomas, 1992.

3 Assessing the Meltdown

Was There a Meltdown?

This first research question that must be answered by an examination of the study data before proceeding further is: Was there indeed a meltdown that took place within the LAPD organization? Although there is ample evidence generated by the media[1] and other second-hand sources outside of the organization suggesting that a meltdown must have occurred following the Rodney King incident, evidence of a deep and widespread internal breakdown of the LAPD's organizational functioning during this time period has never been presented. Some skeptics may argue that a true meltdown of any great magnitude did not actually occur, but was rather a mere presumption based on the fact that any organization enduring such an extreme amount of public negativity as that directed at the LAPD would or should be in utter operational chaos. After all, the professional policing model at LAPD has had a history of surviving past attacks from the department's outside "enemies."[2]

However, in the present case, the data suggest that LAPD did in fact suffer an extremely intense and systemic meltdown—one of a magnitude perhaps never before experienced by the organization or its administrators and officers. Of the entire sample of officer responses, only four interviews (two representing lieutenants and the Parker era) expressed a theme that the department was operating "as usual" despite erroneous outside perceptions that the organization was rendered dysfunctional following public, political, and media fallout from the Rodney King incident.

Theme 1: Temporary Damage—"Things Will Go Back to Normal"

#1

> It's been a rough year but, we will bounce back. We all need to work together. Service is #1 that's why we are all here—I think that is the general feeling among uniformed ofc's (90%)....
>
> (Police Officer, Male, Hispanic, 24 years old, 2 years PO, 2 years LAPD, Chief when hired: Gates) (Figure 3.1)

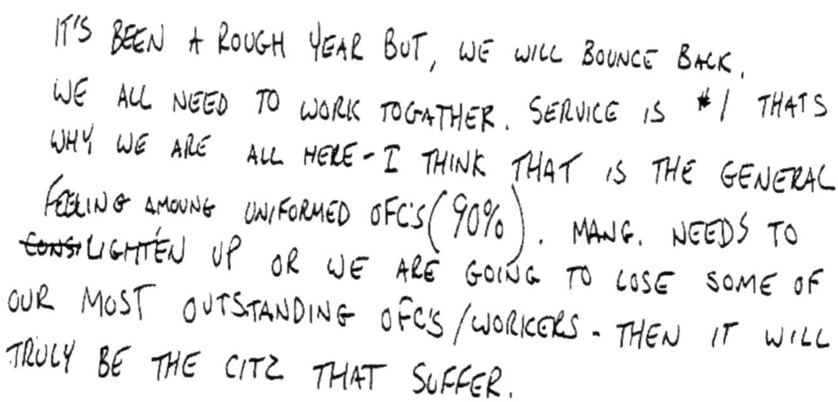
IT'S BEEN A ROUGH YEAR BUT, WE WILL BOUNCE BACK.
WE ALL NEED TO WORK TOGATHER. SERVICE IS #1 THATS
WHY WE ARE ALL HERE - I THINK THAT IS THE GENERAL
FEELING AMOUNG UNIFORMED OFC'S (90%). MANG. NEEDS TO
~~CONST~~ LIGHTEN UP OR WE ARE GOING TO LOSE SOME OF
OUR MOST OUTSTANDING OFC'S / WORKERS - THEN IT WILL
TRULY BE THE CITZ THAT SUFFER.

Figure 3.1 Statement Transcription: It's been a rough year but, we will bounce back. We all need to work together. Service is #1 that's why we are all here—I think that is the general feeling among uniformed officers (90%). Management needs to lighten up or we are going to lose some of our most outstanding officers/workers—then it will truly be the citizens that suffer (see Officer Informant statement #1).

#2

We should be careful not to over react to criticism from the uninformed or those who are historically anti-LAPD. We should continue to have faith in the Depts. goals and procedures. That is not to say that we can't improve. But to say that if there is not clear evidence that change is needed [then] let's not!

(Lieutenant, Male, Caucasian, 54 years old, 31 years PO, 29 years LAPD, Chief when hired: Parker) (Figure 3.2)

#3

In the final analysis this is a great job that pays well when you take an honest look at the Department (The Christopher Commission did not) we do an outstanding job for the community. We can always improve, however all organizations can. Given the number of people we have and the size of the job of policing Los Angeles, we are superstars. We must look beyond our detractors both inside the organization and outside and continue down the road we know is correct. I am confident the community supports us and is in concert with most of our actions. I see the support everyday in the way the community treats my officers and how they appreciate their efforts. As I have watched the political environment since the Rodney King case I am convinced that our detractors have no concept or interest in what is best for the people that live and work in Los Angeles. This means we have a responsibility to hang in and do the right thing and ensure that the community gets what it wants and deserves in the way of police service.

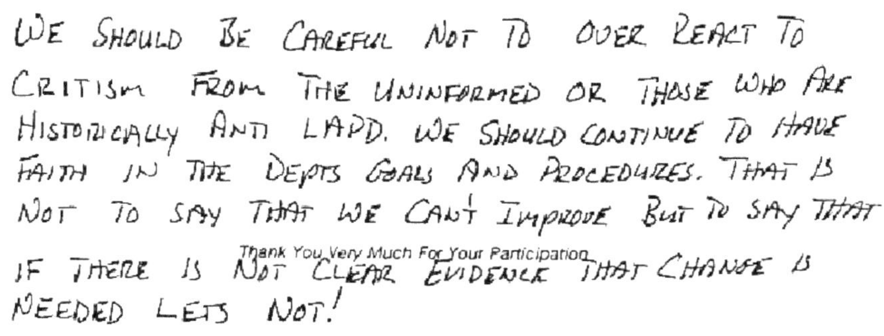
WE SHOULD BE CAREFUL NOT TO OVER REACT TO CRITISM FROM THE UNINFORMED OR THOSE WHO ARE HISTORICALLY ANTI LAPD. WE SHOULD CONTINUE TO HAVE FAITH IN THE DEPTS GOALS AND PROCEDURES. THAT IS NOT TO SAY THAT WE CAN'T IMPROVE BUT TO SAY THAT IF THERE IS NOT CLEAR EVIDENCE THAT CHANGE IS NEEDED LETS NOT!

Thank You Very Much For Your Participation

Figure 3.2 Statement Transcription: We should be careful not to over react to criticism from the uninformed or those who are historically anti-LAPD. We should continue to have faith in the Department's goals and procedures. That is not to say that we can't improve. But to say that if there is not clear evidence that change is needed let's not! (see Officer Informant statement #2).

(Lieutenant, Male, Caucasian, 50 years old, 27 years PO, 27 years LAPD, Chief when hired: Parker)

#4

… I am proud to be a Los Angeles Police Officer. I will be a sergeant soon. I have been offered work outside law enforcement and I have resisted the temptations. I know I cannot change the world alone but dadgumit if I'm not going to change a part of it—alone or with help. We have the potential to be number one but I don't think it means much to be "self proclaimed number one." If we work hard our status will return; overall, we don't deserve the number ranking today….

(Police Officer, Male, Hispanic, 27 years old, 9 years PO, 4 years LAPD, Chief when hired: Gates)

The near unanimity of opinion among officers was that LAPD had indeed suffered an organizational meltdown. Furthermore, an examination of the entire sample suggested that this observation was not restricted to just one particular officer demographic, but was shared by officers regardless of rank, gender, ethnicity, age, length of service on the LAPD, or the chief under which they were originally hired as a police officer. Below are just few of the many themes/statements that support this conclusion.

Theme 2: Permanent Damage—"The Department Is Melting Down"

#5

This ship is dead in the water….

(Police Officer, Male, Caucasian, 45 years old, 22 years PO, 22 years LAPD, Chief when hired: Davis) (Figure 3.3)

Figure 3.3 Statement Transcription: This ship is dead in the water…(see Officer Informant statement #5).

#6

There is no unity in this organization. There is a double standard and duplicity throughout the department. Management has no realistic idea how to effectively manage the organization. Each commander and deputy chief has their own agenda with no concern for the department. There is too much micro management at the bureau level. Captains and above do not have a clue what proper and effective discipline is. Some people are disciplined when they should not be and some are not disciplined when they should be. Some discipline is unfairly based on sex and race. Ideas from senior supervisors are not sought. There is a very low feeling about the department at this time. I have never seen it this bad in my 28 years.

(Sergeant, Male, Caucasian, 50 years old, 28 years PO, 28 years LAPD, Chief when hired: Parker)

#7

Why don't you people get out of your Ivory Offices and back on the street so you can see the Deep "Shit" this Department is really in.

(Police Officer, Male, Caucasian, 43 years old, 16 years PO, 16 years LAPD, Chief when hired: Davis) (Figure 3.4)

#8

This department is so caught up with how the public views it and the media until it has forgotten about the police officers. We risk our lives every night for the citizens of LA and never receive a thanks. This department does not stand behind it's ofcrs. This causes a lot of stress on us because we know that the department is not going to stand behind us. LAPD officers moral is very low.

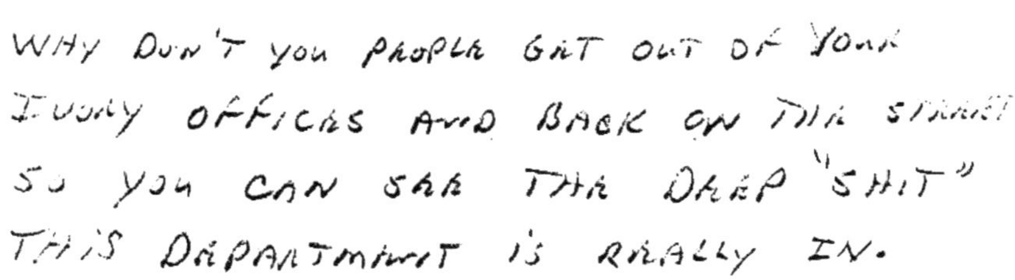

Figure 3.4 Statement Transcription: Why don't you people get out of your Ivory Offices and back on the street so you can see the Deep "Shit" this Department is really in (see Officer Informant statement #7).

I AM UNHAPPY WITH THE FUNCTION OF THE ENTIRE DEPT. BUT, I AM THANKFUL TO HAVE A JOB.

Figure 3.5 Statement Transcription: I am unhappy with the function of the entire dept. But, I am thankful to have a job (see Officer Informant statement #9).

(Police Officer, Female, African American, 23 years old, 1 year PO, 1 year LAPD, Chief when hired: Gates)

#9

I am unhappy with the function of the entire dept. But, I am thankful to have a job.

(Police Officer, Male, African American, 25 years old, 3 years PO, 3 years LAPD, Chief when hired: Gates) (Figure 3.5)

#10

At this time I am looking for work with a different police dept. I strongly feel this dept is becoming an unfavorable place to work. The good people of LA will suffer in the end from all the radical changes this dept. is going through.

(Police Officer, Male, Hispanic, 27 years old, 4 years PO, 4 years LAPD, Chief when hired: Gates)

How Extensive Was the Meltdown?

Meltdowns within organizations can be either far-reaching or restricted to various subunits within an organization. In the latter case, a small group of officers may express discontent and make it seem to the outside world that all officers share in their negative views toward their work environment. On the other hand, in the former instance, the effects of a meltdown are felt at all levels of the organization and disrupt its normal operational capabilities. The following comments, which were expressed in the comments of nearly all officers, suggest that the effects of the meltdown had an endemic effect that spread throughout the entire LAPD organization and perhaps was instrumental in killing the professional policing model:

#11

Personally, I feel the problems plaguing the LAPD are so serious and so abundant that there is no hope for restoring this organization to what it once was. Frankly, I can no longer care. It used to be fun to come to work. I couldn't wait for the next day. I never wanted to go home. No longer! I can't wait for my 20. I'm out of here. What's really unfortunate about this is that at one time I cared; I'm very good at what I do. I squarely place the blame on the shoulder of the depts. top

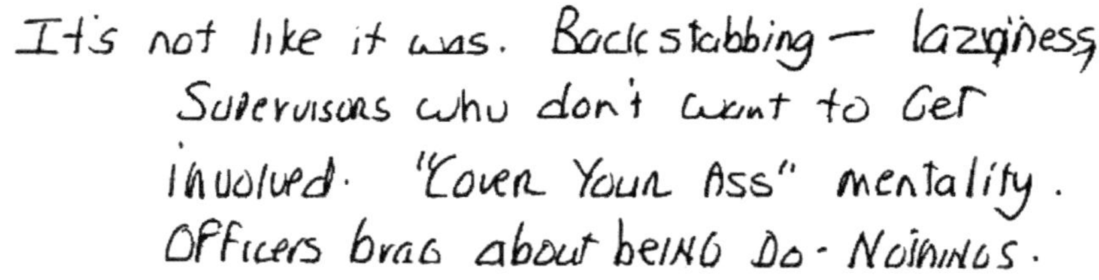

It's not like it was. Backstabbing— lazginess
Supervisors who don't want to Get
involved. "Cover Your Ass" mentality.
Officers brag about being Do-Nothings.

Figure 3.6 Statement Transcription: It's not like it was, Backstabbing—laziness, supervisors who don't want to get involved "Cover You Ass" mentality. Officers brag about being Do-Nothings (see Officer Informant statement #12).

administrators. You have no idea what we have to put up with. If you do you should be fired for inaction.

(Detective, Male, Caucasian, 41 years old, 18 years PO, 18 years LAPD, Chief when hired: Davis)

#12

It's not like it was, Backstabbing—laziness, supervisors who don't want to get involved "Cover You Ass" mentality. Officers brag about being Do-Nothings.

(Police Officer, Male, Caucasian, 44 years old, 22 years PO, 22 years LAPD, Chief when hired: Davis) (Figure 3.6)

#13

There's not enough time to list everything & it will take 15–20 years to turn it around if they start now. We have already promoted too many Bozo's that have a lot of years left with the LAPD. Good Luck. Glad I'm leaving, maybe I can get my blood pressure down when I have to constantly think about how fucked up we are.

(Sergeant, Male, Caucasian, 50 years old, 28 years PO, 28 years LAPD, Chief when hired: Parker) (Figure 3.7)

#14

Two decades ago I joined this department because it was a proud, professional and autonomous organization. In the intervening years it has been besieged by mettling outsiders for self-serving political interests. Today the department is tarnished and impotent. No wonder morale is low and esprit de corps absence. Still, despite all this discouragement, I am proud of what I do and I am proud to be a member of this department. Unfortunately, I am skeptical that this or any other survey will make a difference.

(Detective, Male, Caucasian, 44 years old, 19 years PO, 19 years LAPD, Chief when hired: Davis)

#15

We have lost control. Its evident in that the majority of the ofcrs are dissatisfied with work. I believe that command staff has lost sight of

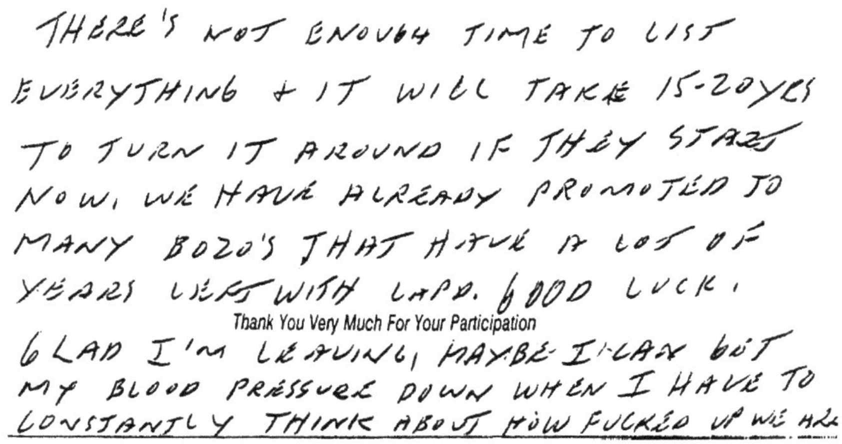
THERE'S NOT ENOUGH TIME TO LIST
EVERYTHING + IT WILL TAKE 15-20YRS
TO TURN IT AROUND IF THEY START
NOW, WE HAVE ALREADY PROMOTED TO
MANY BOZO'S THAT HAVE A LOT OF
YEARS LEFT WITH LAPD. GOOD LUCK.
Thank You Very Much For Your Participation
GLAD I'M LEAVING, MAYBE I CAN GET
MY BLOOD PRESSURE DOWN WHEN I HAVE TO
CONSTANTLY THINK ABOUT HOW FUCKED UP WE ARE

Figure 3.7 Statement Transcription: There's not enough time to list everything & it will take 15–20 years to turn it around if they start now. We have already promoted too many Bozo's that have a lot of years left with the LAPD. Good Luck. Glad I'm leaving, maybe I can get my blood pressure down when I have to constantly think about how fucked up we are (see Officer Informant statement #13).

the goals of the ultimate goal of any police dept.—to jail the bad guy and have a positive effect and outcome on crime. Ofcrs are scared to work, to get involved & will be in this state until our community realizes that we cannot effectively work until they back off and stop yelling police brutality every time an arrest is made. Community based policing is good if directed at the good people of our community. Vermin still need to be put in jail. I did not come here for the $—I earned 10+K more/year elsewhere. We also need better police ofcr selection. If we cant lure the intelligent & mature individual to come on board, or keep choosing our ofcrs from a pool of designed minorities who cannot even coherently read, write or think, where are we expected to be in 10 years. I'll be surprised if our outcome is not dismal.

(Police Officer, Male, Hispanic, 39 years old, 3 years PO, 3 years LAPD, Chief when hired: Gates)

Was the Meltdown Rapid or Slow?

A meltdown like that occurring at LAPD may often appear as though it was the product on a single devastating critical event that serves to quickly destabilize and then rapidly destroy all normal organizational functioning. On the other hand, the critical event presumed to be the immediate cause of the department's destruction may in fact be a symptom of long-standing organizational problems that just simply reached a breaking point. An outsider's view of LAPD during the time of the meltdown would suggest the most likely single and rapidly acting cause of the meltdown would have been the public's reaction (including political and media attacks on the department) to the Rodney King incident. Surprisingly, there were only a handful of officer interviews in support of this perspective—from which the following statement was taken:

#16

If these questions [about organizational effectiveness] were asked before Rodney King you would have had a totally different outlook. The press has screwed us big time.

(Police Officer, Female, Hispanic, 29 years old, 8 years PO, 8 years LAPD, Chief when hired: Gates) (Figure 3.8)

#17

One thing that is evident to me over the 19½ years of service on this police dept.—that the Brass governs by "management by crisis"; in other words, the leaders of this dept. are "Reactionaries"—not visionaries. I truly believe that any and all changes now taking place, including this survey, is only the result of Rodney King. It's too bad; all the changes on this dept. have come as a result of an outside pressure and not because of leadership and innovation.

(Detective, Male, Caucasian, 41 years old, 20 years PO, 20 years LAPD, Chief when hired: Davis)

#18

How secure are the people of this city in their homes, neighborhoods, places of business? Have these liberal commissions go into the neighborhoods and ask. The answer may surprise them, but not those of us who deal with the victim & others affected by crime & drugs. The entire elected establishment & media went to extremes to slam this dept. for the "King" incident. Pick any weekend of the year and count the gang drive-by shootings alone. Count the dead bodies. Ask the surviving relatives if they want a kinder & gentler dept. or do they want us to do our job of maintaining law and order. I have seen an unbelievable deterioration in our ability to control the streets of this city. It's getting worse. We need more officers, many more to fight crime.

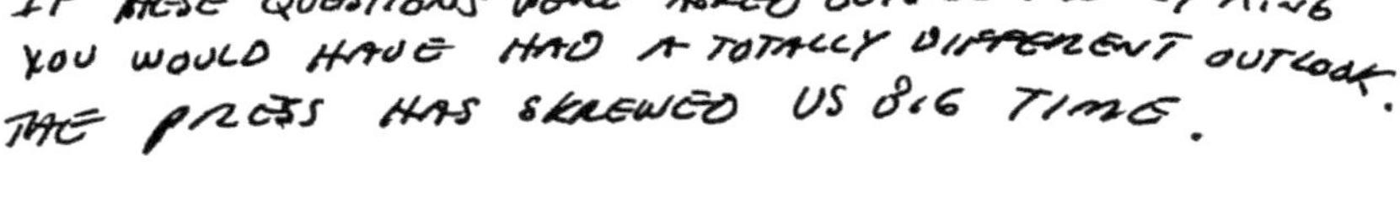

Figure 3.8 Statement Transcription: If these questions were asked before Rodney King you would have had a totally different outlook. The press has screwed us big time (see Officer Informant statement #16).

(Detective, Male, Caucasian, 47 years old, 26 years PO, 26 years LAPD, Chief when hired: Parker)

Although some officers believed the department meltdown had a rapid onset fueled by both internal and external reactions to the King incident, a sizable number of other officers did not. They proposed an alternative hypothesis in support of a much more slowly developing organizational meltdown. In particular, they proposed that the King incident was merely “the straw that broke the LAPD’s back” after years of gradual failure and decay of the professional policing model both inside and outside of the department. Below are interviews that reflect various subthemes upon which this conclusion is drawn.

Subtheme 1: Persistent Problems Were Ignored

#19

Just more lip service. The same problems exist now as 25 years ago. Nothing has been done. The complaints have been ignored.

(Sergeant, Male, Caucasian, 47 years old, 25 years PO, 25 years LAPD, Chief when hired: Parker) (Figure 3.9)

#20

In my 22 years of service, I have seen LAPD service going down the tubes. I feel sorry for the good people in this city. They deserve more. I grew up in New York and saw the decay of that city. I feel LA is going the same way. Politics and police don’t mix.

(Detective, Male, Caucasian, 44 years old, 22 years PO, 22 years LAPD, Chief when hired: Davis) (Figure 3.10)

#21

Narcotics Div. of LAPD is totally corrupt & ineffective! The people of LA are getting ripped off by the calls for service which are horrible! We need more uniform cops and the department is so top heavy I am surprised it hasn’t collapsed! The morale of troops in the field is in the basement which is reflective onto the citizens! A new Chief is not the answer it is a major overhaul of the specialized units which

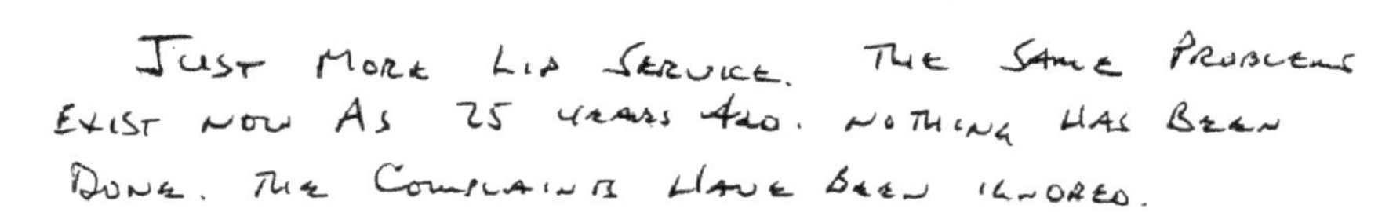
JUST MORE LIP SERVICE. THE SAME PROBLEMS EXIST NOW AS 25 YEARS AGO. NOTHING HAS BEEN DONE. THE COMPLAINTS HAVE BEEN IGNORED.

Figure 3.9 Statement Transcription: Just more lip service. The same problems exist now as 25 years ago. Nothing has been done. The complaints have been ignored (see Officer Informant statement #19).

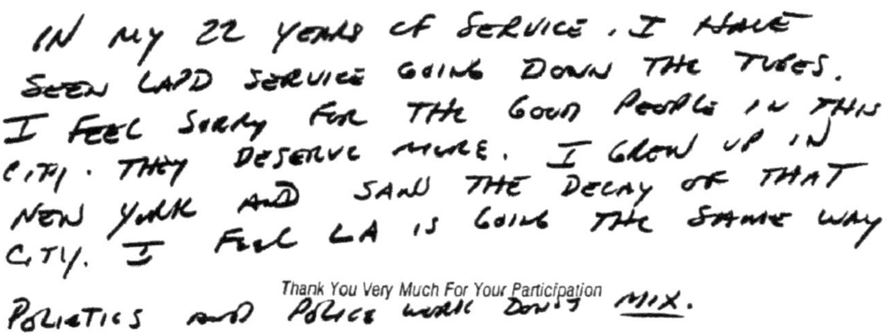
IN MY 22 YEARS OF SERVICE, I HAVE
SEEN LAPD SERVICE GOING DOWN THE TUBES.
I FEEL SORRY FOR THE GOOD PEOPLE IN THIS
CITY. THEY DESERVE MORE. I GREW UP IN
NEW YORK AND SAW THE DECAY OF THAT
CITY. I FEEL LA IS GOING THE SAME WAY.
Thank You Very Much For Your Participation
POLITICS AND POLICE WORK DON'T MIX.

Figure 3.10 Statement Transcription: In my 22 years of service, I have seen LAPD service going down the tubes. I feel sorry for the good people in this city. They deserve more. I grew up in New York and saw the decay of that city. I feel LA is going the same way. Politics and police don't <u>mix</u> (see Officer Informant statement #20).

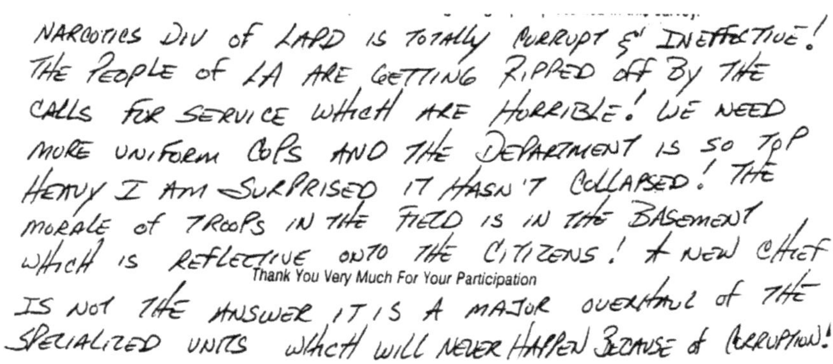
NARCOTICS DIV OF LAPD IS TOTALLY CORRUPT & INEFFECTIVE!
THE PEOPLE OF LA ARE GETTING RIPPED OFF BY THE
CALLS FOR SERVICE WHICH ARE HORRIBLE! WE NEED
MORE UNIFORM COPS AND THE DEPARTMENT IS SO TOP
HEAVY I AM SURPRISED IT HASN'T COLLAPSED! THE
MORALE OF TROOPS IN THE FIELD IS IN THE BASEMENT
WHICH IS REFLECTIVE ONTO THE CITIZENS! A NEW CHIEF
Thank You Very Much For Your Participation
IS NOT THE ANSWER IT IS A MAJOR OVERHAUL OF THE
SPECIALIZED UNITS WHICH WILL NEVER HAPPEN BECAUSE OF CORRUPTION!

Figure 3.11 Statement Transcription: Narcotics Division of LAPD is totally corrupt & ineffective! The people of LA are getting ripped off by the calls for service which are horrible! We need more uniform cops and the department is so top heavy I am surprised it hadn't collapsed! The morale of troops in the field is in the basement which is reflective onto the citizens! A new Chief is not the answer it is a major overhaul of the specialized units which will never happen because of corruption! Ad [Administration for] vice, Ad [Administration for] Narc [Narcotics Division] totally good ol' boys corrupt (see Officer Informant statement #21).

will never happen because of corruption! Ad vice, Ad Narc Totally good ol' boys corrupt.

(Police Officer, Male, Caucasian, 35 years old, 8 years PO, 8 years LAPD, Chief when hired: Gates) (Figure 3.11)

Subtheme 2: Discontent Over Hiring Practices

#22

I believe the hiring practices of this City do not allow us to get the best type of person for this job and the way the scoring of the tests is a way to get certain groups of people promoted not on merit but on their minority status in life. I used to be proud of this job. I don't know what I am now!! No wonder our patrol cops just want to do the basics....

(Police Officer, Male, Caucasian, 45 years old, 18 years PO, 18 years LAPD, Chief when hired: Davis)

#23

I know for a fact that a # of my fellow white-male ofcrs have grown to resent the depts affirmative action efforts. I find this very disturbing. My feelings about this dept have deteriorated greatly over the past several years. Upper-level mgt cares only about themselves and almost nothing about those who are out there putting their lives & reputations on the line for this dept daily. My greatest fear is that once Gates retires our next Chief will seek to appease every ctz group etc. & he to will show little concern & respect for "The Little Guy" He too will over react as has been done for years.

(Police Officer, Male, African American, 33 years old, 9 years PO, 7 years LAPD, Chief when hired: Gates)

#24

Morale is bad enough. So why does this department treat its white male officers as evil? Be fair and equal to everyone except white males. Let's strive to treat everyone for any position fairly. The most qualified get the job rather than we don't have a minority so get one. The leadership of this department should stop kissing everyone's ass so everyone will like us. That's not our job. We put bad guys in jail to protect & serve the public, that's our job. So let's stop making excuses to everyone, and do our job.

(Sergeant, Male, Caucasian, 43 years old, 20 years PO, 20 years LAPD, Chief when hired: Davis)

Subtheme 3: Poor or Inadequate Training

#25

I have 2½ years as a uniform sergeant but I am currently a detective. I waited over a year to attend Sergeant's school after I was promoted. Poor police service which I rec. while living in Foothill Div (as a police officer) was a major consideration in moving my family out of the City of Los Angeles to Ventura County.

(Detective, Male, Caucasian, 37 years old, 12 years PO, 12 years LAPD, Chief when hired: Gates)

#26

There is a piss poor training at the academy. What's this stuff about everybody makes it....

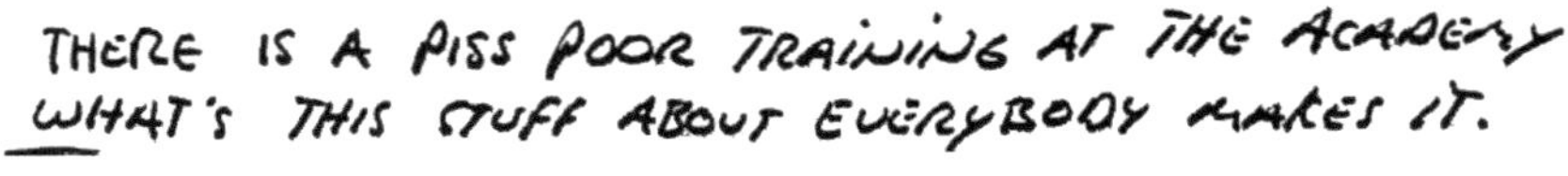
THERE IS A PISS POOR TRAINING AT THE ACADEMY
WHAT'S THIS STUFF ABOUT EVERYBODY MAKES IT.

Figure 3.12 Statement Transcription: There is a piss poor training at the academy. What's this stuff about everybody makes it. The City Attorney's office has let this City down (see Officer Informant statement #26).

(Police Officer, Male, Hispanic, 34 years old, 11 years PO, 11 years LAPD, Chief when hired: Gates) (Figure 3.12)

#27

In regard to academy training, I feel my entire 6mts in academy was mostly useless. Shooting, tactics and radio communications was most important. The field is completely different then the academy. Community relations is important however officer safety overrides everything else.

(Police Officer, Female, African American, 23 years old, 1 year PO, 1 year LAPD, Chief when hired: Gates)

#28

Training at the academy is a waste of time & manpower. Academy training is set up to last 3 days, when it could be done in one.

(Police Officer, Male, Caucasian, 49 years old, 25 years PO, 25 years LAPD, Chief when hired: Parker)

#29

Allow any ofcr who want to go to extra training the opportunity. I have signed up for many training schools including drivers, gang, narco and have not gone to any because of only 5–6 a division can go. Fine, but don't overlook that 50 ofcrs signed up. Not because they see it as a day off (some do) but because they desperately want to be trained. Give them the knowledge they are hungry for!!

(Police Officer, Male, Caucasian, 30 years old, 7 years PO, 7 years LAPD, Chief when hired: Gates)

#30

If the Dept. would spend more time in training officers in self defense, they would raise the confidence level of ofcrs and, reduce the percentage of out of policy shootings....

(Police Officer, Male, African American, 30 years old, 4 years PO, 4 years LAPD, Chief when hired: Gates)

#31

Should be more self-defense training for ofcrs after 1 year.

(Police Officer, Male, African American, 53 years old, 22 years PO, 22 years LAPD, Chief when hired: Davis)

Subtheme 4: Ineffective or Unresponsive Administration and Management

#32

Captains/staff/command ofcrs need to put on a blue suit and get out in the field. They're the ones who need "in service" training and get their heads out of the clouds. They appear to be brain washed spineless worms attempting to make a name for themselves, no matter what the cost.

(Police Officer, Male, Caucasian, 33 years old, 7 years PO, 7 years LAPD, Chief when hired: Gates)

#33

This is by no means the dept. I joined nearly 20 years ago. We've bent over backwards for some and ignored many. The double standard that exists between brass and sgts, dets and ofcrs is a pity. It's just now being exposed now more than ever before. The people in the mainstream of the dept will go nowhere unless connected to the brass or a particular group. We need to promote the police profession and those dedicated people who carry on despite obstacles from the police executives, politicians, and the misguided public. Despite my feeling I will always be faithful to the public I serve and my chosen profession—law enforcement.

(Detective, Male, Caucasian, 42 years old, 20 years PO, 20 years LAPD, Chief when hired: Davis)

#34

This dept. has always treated ofcrs as children. Sometimes when I come to work, I feel like a 10 year old kid. After the Foothill Incident the mis-trust of ofcrs by upper brass had increased. I'm a 25 year vet & I resent being mis-trusted by anyone.

(Detective, Male, Caucasian, 48 years old, 25 years PO, 25 years LAPD, Chief when hired: Parker) (Figure 3.13)

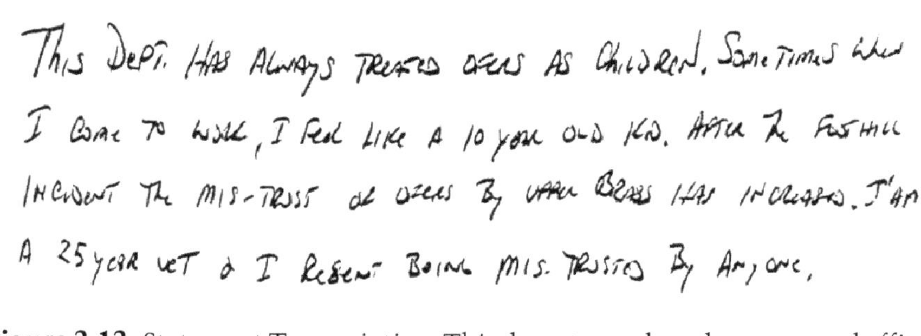

Figure 3.13 Statement Transcription: This department has always treated officers as children. Sometimes when I come to work, I feel like a 10 year old kid. After the Foothill Incident the mistrust of officers by upper brass had increased. I'm a 25 year veteran & I resent being mistrusted by anyone (see Officer Informant #34).

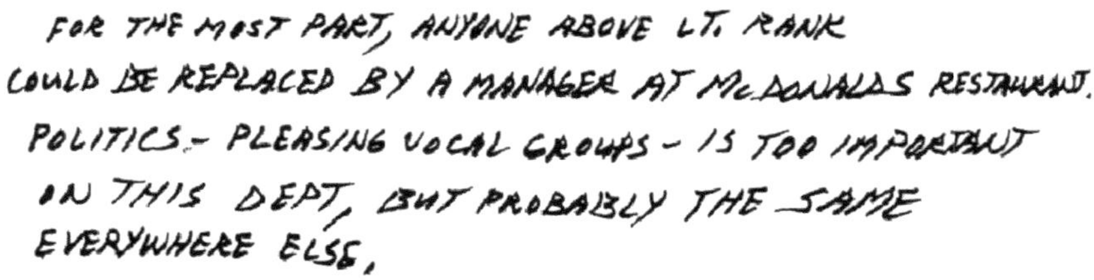
FOR THE MOST PART, ANYONE ABOVE LT. RANK
COULD BE REPLACED BY A MANAGER AT McDONALDS RESTAURANT.
POLITICS - PLEASING VOCAL GROUPS - IS TOO IMPORTANT
ON THIS DEPT, BUT PROBABLY THE SAME
EVERYWHERE ELSE.

Figure 3.14 Statement Transcription: For the most part, anyone above Lieutenant rank could be replaced by a manager at McDonald's restaurant. Politics—pleasing vocal groups—is too important on this dept, but probably the same everywhere else (see Officer Informant statement #36).

#35

The staff from capt & above are nothing but back stabbing, self serving thiefs. This deps need to get rid of more than ½ of these do nothing people. They think they are Gods & don't know what the streets are like and don't care. They care nothing about the citizens of LA & don't care. All they want is their own power & making themselves jobs where no one knows what they are doing from capt. up. Why do you need two capts of the Divisions. You will have answers which say nothing. (Officer information not available)

#36

For the most part, anyone above Lt. rank could be replaced by a manager at McDonald's restaurant....

(Police Officer, Male, Caucasian, 44 years old, 22 years PO, 22 years LAPD, Chief when hired: Davis) (Figure 3.14)

#37

You forgot Air Support! We're not surprised. We can tell by the way everyone is concerned how we feel about what kind of helicopter we fly. Our management does not speak for the line pilots + (observers), especially our deceased ones. We could even save you money!

(Police Officer, Male, Caucasian, 39 years old, 16 years PO, 16 years LAPD, Chief when hired: Davis) (Figure 3.15)

Subtheme 5: Inadequate Equipment and Poor Working Conditions

#38

I work a small specialized unit. We can't get enough cars, radios and other equipment to properly do our jobs. We use our own pagers, mobile phones, and whatever else we can borrow just to make it thru the day....

(Detective, Male, N/A, 40 years old, 15 years PO, 15 years LAPD, Chief when hired: Davis)

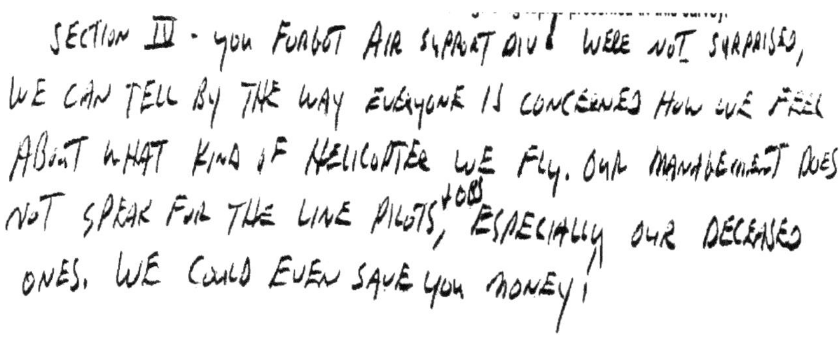
SECTION IV - YOU FORGOT AIR SUPPORT DIV! WERE NOT SURPRISED, WE CAN TELL BY THE WAY EVERYONE IS CONCERNED HOW WE FEEL ABOUT WHAT KIND OF HELICOPTER WE FLY. OUR MANAGEMENT DOES NOT SPEAK FOR THE LINE PILOTS +OBS, ESPECIALLY OUR DECEASED ONES. WE COULD EVEN SAVE YOU MONEY!

Figure 3.15 Statement Transcription: Section IV (referring to the a section of the study questionnaire asking for the specific LAPD Division where the Officer Informant is assigned to work)—You forgot Air Support! We're not surprised. We can tell by the way everyone is concerned how we feel about what kind of helicopter we fly. Our management does not speak for the line pilots + (observers), especially our deceased ones. We could even save you money! (see Officer Informant statement #37).

#39

Working conditions are tragic for Detectives throughout the City. We are 50 years behind the times in working conditions, work space, computers, etc....

(Detective, Male, Caucasian, 43 years old, 20 years PO, 20 years LAPD, Chief when hired: Davis)

#40

... Our police facilities are terrible. They are dirty, uncomfortable and loaded with safety and health hazards. There is never enough equipment (cars, rovers, computers or even reports) to do the job and station security does not exist....

(Police Officer, Male, Caucasian, 28 years old, 7 years PO, 7 years LAPD, Chief when hired: Gates)

#41

1. Re-instate the choke hold
2. New MDT'S Rovers; comm. System
3. Cages in veh's; spotlights on veh's (dual) Upright shotgun racks; put one-piece plastic (hard) seats in rear of veh's.
4. Adopt a semi-auto hi-capacity shotgun (modern) or a dual operation (i.e., super 90 M1 or M3) w/a tac light forearm.
5. Adopt a cloth badge for outerwear (foul/inclement weather)
6. Revamp all combat/hand-to-hand (dangerously inefficient)
7. Allow use of Glock; Sig-Saur etc 9mm

(Police Officer, Male, Caucasian, 25 years old, 2 years PO, 2 years LAPD, Chief when hired: Gates)

#42

LAPD does an outstanding job with the resources we have available. One of our main problems is lack of personnel and adequate equipment. We have a 25,000 person problem and are trying to solve it with 8,000 people. In 20 years we have only marginally increased the department size in the light of an enormous increase in crime and complexity of service. We are inundated with requests for service and are simply overloaded. Patrol division personnel are detectives are burning out. In addition, upper managements lack of direction is contributing to low morale. We need 1. More people 2. Better equipment 3. Better facilities 4. Better upper management leadership. I could write 20 pages easily on this topic—out of room.

(Sergeant, Male, Caucasian, 44 years old, 23 years PO, 23 years LAPD, Chief when hired: Reddin)

What Caused the Meltdown?

Taken together, the above officer statements suggest clearly that LAPD did endure an organizational meltdown, which perhaps produced significant changes in the department's internal and external operations. Also suggested in the previous analysis is that there are many potential factors that may have served as causes of the meltdown. These include declining officer morale, poor training, ineffective management, negative community reactions to the Rodney King incident, as well as many other organizational and extra-organizational variables. In the chapters that follow, further research investigations are undertaken to gain a deeper understanding of these and other specific causes that perhaps precipitated the meltdown. Research questions to be answered include:

- Was there just one main cause of the meltdown or were there multiple causes?
- Which cause(s) of the meltdown produced the greatest impact on the LAPD organization?
- Did the meltdown begin inside or outside of the LAPD organization?
- How did the meltdown impact the delivery of police services to citizens?
- What was the LAPD's administrative reaction to the meltdown?
- Could the organizational effects of the meltdown have been minimized or avoided?

Did the Meltdown Kill the Professional Model?

The primary substantive question to be answered by findings from this study is: What was the relationship between the meltdown and the fall of the professional model of policing within the LAPD? There are several possible theoretical scenarios. First, the meltdown may have provided such a strong organizational "knockout punch" to the professional model that it was immediately and permanently abandoned by the LAPD. In this case, the meltdown played a direct causal role in the death of the professional model. Alternatively, the meltdown could have had an indirect effect in producing the professional model's demise. It is possible that the meltdown was merely a catalyst for igniting various other preexisting organizational factors that were the real (or direct) cause for abandoning the professional model. Last, the meltdown may have not caused any harm to the professional model. Theoretically speaking, the relationship between the meltdown and the fall may be totally spurious; that is, both events happened at the same time, creating the appearance that they caused one another—but in reality, were causally unrelated.

Although causal inferences drawn from data such as those (i.e., qualitative in nature) included in this study are highly speculative at best, the formulation of theoretical insights into the professional model's fall are nonetheless possible. To this end, officer statements are initially presented and analyzed for thematic content; next, the themes are used to created hypotheses about probable relationships between the meltdown (as the cause) and the fall of the professional model (the effect); finally, theory will be developed in an attempt to explain why the meltdown occurred and how the professional model failed. In the final analysis, the latter theoretical explanation will be used to answer a very important substantive question: What was the manner of death of the professional model? Just as in the real world, an autopsy may reveal a definitive cause of death (e.g., a heart attack). This one cause, however, can be explained in terms of various situational facts that explain the manner of its occurrence. For example, the heart attack may have been caused *naturally* by old age or *accidentally* by physical overexertion. Likewise, the heart attack could have resulted from a *suicide* involving an intentional overdose of drugs. Lastly, the heart attack could have resulted from an intentional poisoning by another person desiring to commit *murder*. Each of these manners of death can be equally applied within the context of an organizational autopsy of the LAPD. Thus, through a detailed examination of the study data, an attempt will be made to discover whether the professional model died as the result of an unintentional organizational affliction such as advanced age or an administrative accident. On the other hand, if the organizational autopsy performed here suggests that the professional model's death was intentional—either by a self-inflicted wound or at the malicious hands of another—the ultimate aim of this study will be to determine the underlying organizational motivation for the commission of this act resulting in the model's untimely passing.

References

1. Ronald N. Jacobs. *Race, Media, and the Crisis of Civil Society: From Watts to Rodney King*. Cambridge: Cambridge University Press, 2000.
2. Glynn B. Martin. LAPD Chief Parker: A Product of His Time. *Los Angeles Times* OP ED. Retrieved from http://www.latimes.com/news/opinion/la-oew-martin28-2009jan28,0,5287776.story

The Rodney King Incident

4

There is little doubt that the Rodney King incident served, in some way, to help trigger the LAPD meltdown. However, the question remains: Was the King incident the primary cause of the organizational chaos and disorder within the department that is believed to have precipitated the fall of the professional model of policing? As previously mentioned in Chapter 3, officer statements suggested that the meltdown was definitely "put into motion" following both internal and external reactions to the King affair, but it remains to be discovered if these reactions gained enough traction to bring forth the professional model's demise.

Prior to actually examining the content of all officer statements included in this study, one might assume that the King incident was first and foremost on most officers' minds when it came to explaining the major causes of the organization's meltdown. Surprisingly, however, among the 238 statements collected from the study sample interviews there were relatively few officers (approximately 10%) that directly made mention of the King incident—either explicitly or implicitly. In fact, as the following statement suggests, there may have been a prevailing attitude in the department (at least at the patrol level) that the whole Rodney King affair was "a bad joke" that was not to be taken as seriously as other, deeper problems that were causing the LAPD organization to melt down:

#43

> I'm sick and tired of hearing about "poor Rodney King!"
>
> (Police Officer, Male, Hispanic, 30 years old, 5 years PO, 5 years LAPD, Chief when hired: Gates) (Figure 4.1)

Possible Explanations

The Justified Use of Force Explanation

Immediately following the King incident's news-breaking coverage, seen locally in Los Angeles and quickly spreading as the top story around the world, the LAPD formulated a firm line of defense to explain the actions of the Foothill Division officers at the scene. The department's defense strategy was an attempt to convince the public that the officers' use of force against King

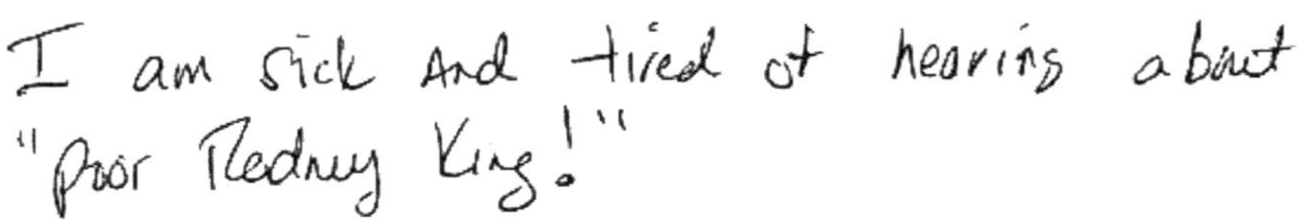
I am sick And tired of hearing about "Poor Rodney King!"

Figure 4.1 Statement Transcription: I'm sick and tired of hearing about "poor Rodney King!" (see Officer Informant statement #43).

was not malicious, but rather a professional response to the seemingly dangerous situation that confronted them. Moreover, the department asserted that the use of force seen on television was justified under departmental use of force policies that were based under laws outlined in the California Penal Code, which outlines rules for the level of force that may be used by all peace officers in the state in specific situations.[1]

According to state and departmental policies at the time, LAPD officers were permitted to use whatever force was reasonable and necessary to maintain control over the suspect or to prevent the suspect's escape from custody. In applying their force, the officers were required to abide by what is known as the ladder of escalation and de-escalation. The ladder begins with verbal commands for compliance (i.e., "get down on your knees and remain still") and, if not followed by a suspect, can escalate to the next level, allowing the officer to apply a firm grip to the suspect. If the grip is ineffective, then physical "pain" compliance holds (such as wristlocks) may be used to gain control over the suspect.[2]

If the above compliance steps of the ladder are deemed by the officer to be ineffective or inappropriate given the seriousness of the circumstances, the situation escalates to what is termed the intermediate level of force. At this level several force options are available for use by officers, including chemical agents, batons, kicks, tasers, saps, leg sweeps, and swarm techniques. Finally, if the latter methods are not capable of gaining control over the suspect, an officer may decide to use deadly force (shooting or choke hold, according to LAPD policy). Most critical to this process is the decision to escalate or de-escalate the level of force based on the changing situation of how much control the officer has over the suspect. For example, an officer may have gained control over a suspect temporarily after spraying him or her with a chemical agent, only to have the suspect overcome the effects of the chemical and become increasingly noncompliant. That being the case, the officer must again apply the appropriate level of force given this new situation. The escalation and de-escalation process may repeat itself over a prolonged time period—involving various levels of force—until the suspect has been permanently controlled by the officer.

In their defense of the officers involved in the King incident, LAPD use of force experts advanced the argument that the use of baton blows and kicks to gain the compliance of King at the scene was justifiable as an intermediate-level force. In addition, the department argued that the situation at the scene was made to intentionally "look bad" by the news media, which aired a shortened version of the original videotaped crime scene. The original videotape, according to the following statement obtained from an LAPD informant, was intentionally altered by the media to omit sights and sounds that vindicated the officers' justifiable use of force against King:

> … When the officers first arrived at the scene, King, who was a really large guy, jumped out of his car flailing his arms all over the place and running over in the direction of the officers screaming, "I'm not fucking going back to prison…. You're not going to send me back to fucking prison!" At that point, the officers had to assume they were dealing with an experienced felon who could be dangerous. But this part at the very beginning of the tape was cut out by the news media because they said the tape was too long. And then you can clearly see in the tape that King would keep getting up after he was hit by the officers' batons. A normal suspect stays still and complies … not like King. Officers are justified to keep using their batons until he quits trying to get up and possibly attack the officers. The tape just didn't show this side of the situation.[3]

To bolster the defense of the officers' actions during the King incident, the LAPD further argued that King was thought to be under the influence of the drug PCP at the time the use of force took place—as the latter LAPD informant further points out:

> … King was tased with enough volts to knock out a horse, but he just kept on coming. Any logical officer seeing the taser have no effect like that on a suspect would believe, and rightfully so, that that suspect is on some sort of drugs or out of their mind…. At that time, PCP was a real popular drug and it causes people to have a lot of strength and feel no pain. Anyway, the guy was strong, mad, feeling no pain from the taser gun that had given him all of its juice, so what else could the officers do but to use their batons? King was lucky they didn't use deadly force the way he was acting…. At the time all of this happened, there is no doubt in my mind that the officers were acting professionally and according to our [the department's] use of force policy and the use of force laws for the state. It all just looked bad on TV after all was said and done.

Another LAPD informant added additional support to the notion that officers responding to the King incident were not reacting maliciously but professionally, because of the inherently good-natured sergeant [Stacey Koon] who was directing their actions at the scene:

> I worked with the Sergeant Koon at the LAPD lockup and I knew him well. He was a very good-natured guy and cared about how people were treated. Much more than a lot of other officers I've worked with. I remember one night a tranny came into the jail where we were working who was all drunk or drugged up. They guy fell flat on his face, passed out on the floor in front of everybody who were there on duty. Everybody just ignored the guy. Sergeant Koon was the only guy who ran over and gave the tranny mouth-to-mouth to try to save his life. Nobody else was willing to do that…. God knows what kind of diseases you would get. But, Sergeant Koon had a good heart and stepped up to the plate. A guy like that doesn't let his officer just beat up a suspect so he can get some sort of cheap thrill out of it. And if you think everybody around here goes around wanting to beat suspects that's a bunch of bullshit![4]

The "Few Bad Apples" Explanation

Those who supported the department during the King affair, yet believed that the use of force against King was unjustified and not within policy or legal guidelines, formulated a second defense: The few bad apples explanation. In other words, the King incident was really an isolated incident caused by officers who represented a few bad apples in a barrel of good officers (representing the majority of the department) who would have reacted to the situation in a much more professional, less violent manner. In fact, insiders within the LAPD organization who were in agreement with this idea had formulated a theory to explain that the officers who were the few bad apples at the King crime scene may have not even been bad themselves, but rather the victims of bad timing. The following statement obtained from an LAPD officer informant explains this perspective on the King incident:

> … Well, it goes like this. There seems to be this strange thing that happens sometimes when we have a roll call training on a certain tactic to use in the field. After the training, and after roll call is over, and after we roll into the field, there seems to be an excessive amount of officers who get involved with whatever it was the training was about. Like, the other day, we had a roll call training about hot pursuits … sure enough, that night we had a couple of them. We usually don't have any on a regular shift…. Ok, so here's the idea about King…. As I heard it, the night the whole King thing went down, there was a roll call training about baton use and how to do power stroke with it. You know, the kind of back-and-forth hard hitting that was used on King. I even heard that Powell, the officer who did all the hitting, was being made fun of at that roll call by all the guys in the room. They kept yelling out, calling him "Limp Wrist, Limp Wrist, Limp Wrist," making fun of him for a time when they saw him practicing his power stroke outside on the lot. I think that night both Powell and King happened to be in the wrong place and the wrong time.

> The roll call effect might have taken over and Powell might have been showing everybody that he wasn't a "Limp Wrist" like everybody said at roll call.[5]

If the King incident was indeed an isolated incident caused by a handful of out-of-control rogue officers this would give credence to the idea the meltdown was possibly a knee-jerk reaction by the department as well as the community to a perceived problem of an overaggressive policing culture at LAPD that simply did not exist in reality. This would mean, quite simply, that getting rid of the professional model of policing based on the assumption that the King incident represented how all LAPD officers would react in a similar situation was tantamount to "throwing the baby out with the bathwater."

The "Tip of the Iceberg" Explanation

Whereas the two explanations listed above suggest the professional model of policing as implemented by the LAPD played no role in the Rodney King incident, a third theory, the tip of the iceberg perspective, assumes that the King affair was a true personification of the model and the policing culture it created within the LAPD organization. Proponents of this explanation, which were largely comprised of Los Angeles politicians, special interest groups, and selected members of the community, believed that the aggressive style of policing displayed at the King scene was systemic within the LAPD organization and encouraged within the department's culture of violence. As one informant representing a prominent Los Angeles-based special interest group stated:

> ... The beating of Rodney King recorded on that videotape was nothing more than the LAPD caught with its pants down. There were many, many more incidents just like that one and probably worse beatings were given to citizens—especially Black ones. That's the way the LAPD is run. Beat 'em first, especially if they're Black, then ask questions later. We're damn lucky that beating was caught on video to bring some sunshine in on LAPD to heal the infections of violent thinking that has festered within the department for generations. Could you imagine what the city would be like today, and the treatment of the minority groups, if the King beating wasn't caught on video?[6]

Thus, proponents of the above explanation would argue that the professional model of policing had developed an officer mind-set that had permeated the thinking of most officers within the LAPD organization. In such a policing culture not only would the majority of the department support the officers' actions taken in the King incident, but attempts to preserve the professional model within the LAPD organization would also be executed by top-ranking LAPD administrators (such as the justified use of force defense described above). The traditional Parker approach to handling such a situation would be to defend the department and its officers against outside political and community attacks at all costs. In addition, the decision whether or not the officers at the King scene acted appropriately, according to Parker's leadership style, would be an issue to be handled by the department's Internal Affairs Division—not by outsiders conducting a "trial by media" of the officers involved in the King incident.

Officer Statements and Themes

As stated above, there were a paucity of comments received from officers that could be used to bear light on the King incident and its likely impact on the LAPD meltdown or reasons underlying the professional model's abandonment within the department. All available statements regarding the King affair could be grouped into the following themes listed below.

Theme 1: Media Distortion and Political Manipulation of the King Incident

The majority of officer comments concerning the King incident, which are included in the section that follows, contain themes that imply the King affair was intentionally used by LAPD detractors to "bash" the department and its officers. Specifically, these officers felt that the news media, politicians, and others who were—for various reasons—at odds with the LAPD used the Rodney King incident to further their own personal agendas by creating a distorted, negative image of the department. This image, according to many of the officers, painted an inaccurate public picture of the LAPD as a violent, racist, and perhaps corrupt policing organization. Furthermore, these officers believed the department was undeserving of such criticism levied against them by outsiders and that they had done nothing wrong to deserve the harsh criticism of their policing practices following the King incident. In addition, the following set of statements suggest that poor officer morale, increased street crime, impaired community relations, and political corruption were some of the possible negative side effects of the media's negative treatment of the officers and department in the wake of the King affair.

#44

> How secure are the people of this city in their homes, neighborhoods, places of business? Have these liberal commissions go into the neighborhoods and ask. The answer may surprise them, but not those of us who deal with the victim & others affected by crime & drugs. The entire elected establishment & media went to extremes to

slam this dept. for the “King” incident. Pick any weekend of the year and count the gang drive-by shootings alone. Count the dead bodies. Ask the surviving relatives if they want a kinder & gentler dept. or do they want us to do our job of maintaining law and order. I have seen an unbelievable deterioration in our ability to control the streets of this city. It’s getting worse. We need more officers, many more to fight crime.

(Detective, Male, Caucasian, 47 years old, 26 years PO, 26 years LAPD, Chief when hired: Parker)

#45

The “King” incident has caused the lowest morale on LAPD in the 21 years I’ve been around. LAPD has gotten no support from the news media or politicians….

(Detective, Male, Caucasian, 42 years old, 21 years PO, 21 years LAPD, Chief when hired: Davis)

#46

I have always been proud & loyal to be a member of LAPD. I have tolerated poor working conditions, poor supervision, sexual harassment and other job hindrances and have still been hard working and proud. I planned to work at least 30 years until the King incident. I am increasingly ashamed of being a member of LAPD and am considering early retirement. Its not all LAPD’s fault—we are good, we do the best with what we have but with the media hype the pubic no longer trusts or respects us. Becoming goody two-shoes social workers will not change this. Doing good police work will.

(Detective, Female, Caucasian, 48 years old, 25 years PO, 25 years LAPD, Chief when hired: Parker)

#47

Our #1 enemy is not the “bad guys” but the news media! They are a business, & show only one side (bad) and very little on the good side. They are definitely not interested in any good we do. If you want the public to like us, all the program’s in the world will not do any good as long as the news media maintains their current policy.

(Police Officer, Male, Caucasian, 44 years old, 21 years PO, 21 years LAPD, Chief when hired: Davis) (Figure 4.2)

#48

… The general public hates and fears us because of how the media portrays us. We are losing the most aggressive & the most innovative police chief in LAPD history because of the power of the media. Chief Gates is popular amongst his troops. It’ll be a major blow when he finally leaves. Because of the public’s misconception and lack of support of us, everything we do on the street is done with added hesitation because of our fear of serious liability.

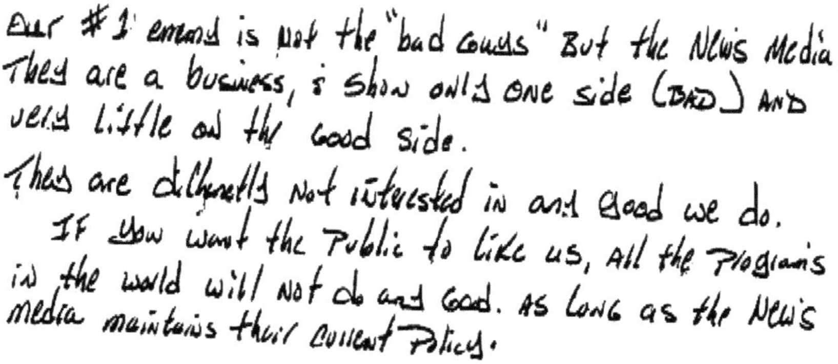

Our #1 enemy is not the "bad guys" But the News Media! They are a business, & show only one side (BAD) AND very little on the good side.
They are definitly not interested in any Good we do.
If you want the Public to like us, All the Program's in the world will not do any Good. As long as the News media maintains their current Policy.

Figure 4.2 Statement Transcription: Our #1 enemy is not the "bad guys" but the news media! They are a business, & show only one side (bad) and very little on the good side. They are definitely not interested in any good we do. If you want the public to like us, all the program's in the world will not do any good as long as the news media maintains their current policy (see Officer Informant statement #47).

(Police Officer, Male, Caucasian, 38 years old, 8 years PO, 8 years LAPD, Chief when hired: Gates)

#49

If these questions were asked before Rodney King you would have had a totally different outlook. The press has screwed us big time.

(Police Officer, Female, Hispanic, 29 years old, 8 years PO, 8 years LAPD, Chief when hired: Gates)

#50

The Rodney King Incident has, without question caused the dept. to over-react because the media and the lawyers wanted you to. Take a lesson from Sherriff Block, there is no doubt who is in charge of the LASD and he won't be pushed around by media, lawyers, and politicians. He will not and can not compromise his Dept., why have you allowed this to happen to us. The lawyers are happy and making money on this City, the politicians are winning elections over this Dept. and the media falsely presents this Dept. to make money, and you, the brass have no supportive response, just over-reaction in the negative. Wake up, before we are mired in political corruption & not just at the higher levels. When this happens, I'm out of here. Do something positive for police ofcrs and morale now or lose the City. Lets not forget the criminal element. Those who kill, rape, rob, steal cars, and block sidewalks and intersections in protest are laughing at how easy it is to manipulate this Dept. and it's management.

(Police Officer, Male, Hispanic, 36 years old, 9 years PO, 9 years LAPD, Chief when hired: Gates)

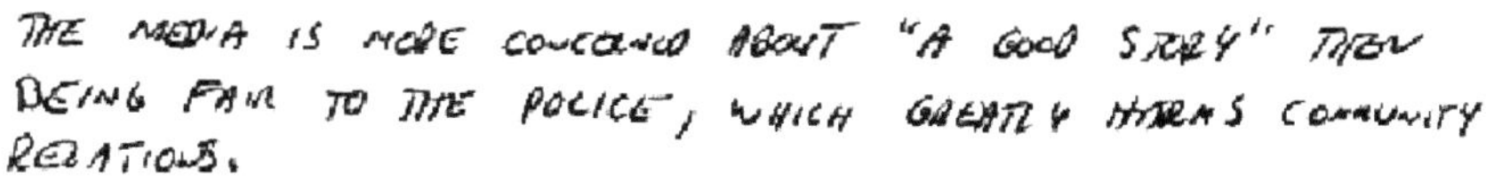
THE MEDIA IS MORE CONCERNED ABOUT "A GOOD STORY" THEN BEING FAIR TO THE POLICE, WHICH GREATLY HARMS COMMUNITY RELATIONS.

Figure 4.3 Statement Transcription: The media is more concerned about "a good story" then being fair to the police, which greatly harms community relations (see Officer Informant statement #51).

#51

… The media is more concerned about "a good story" then being fair to the police, which greatly harms community relations….

(Police Officer, Male Caucasian, 36 years old, 11 years PO, 11 years LAPD, Chief when hired: Gates) (Figure 4.3)

#52

… Officers are being "brow beaten" from every angle. The citizens are brain washed by the news media. Every time I turn on the T.V. it's anti-police. If the news media and citizens think they know how to do police work, then put them in a blk & wht. They are scared to live in LA and are stripping officers of all their resources. Management is succumbing to the "new media" pressure. The citizens will not regain respect for the police until upper management gains respect from the troops. Whatever happened to comraderie?

(Police Officer, Female, Caucasian, 31 years old, 3 years PO, 3 years LAPD, Chief when hired: Gates)

#53

This department is so caught up with how the public views it and the media until it has forgotten about the police officers. We risk our lives every night for the citizens of LA and never receive a thanks. This department does not stand behind it's ofcrs. This causes a lot of stress on us because we know that the department is not going to stand behind us. LAPD officers moral is very low.

(Police Officer, Female, African American, 23 years old, 1 year PO, 1 year LAPD, Chief when hired: Gates)

#54

This Department is more concerned with what the media shows us as and what the public thinks, then the ofcr's who put their life on the line everyday.

(Police Officer, Male, Caucasian, 27 years old, 4 years PO, 4 years LAPD, Chief when hired: Gates)

#55

This dept has to come together. This dept is being run by the media, city council and other wanna be politicians. I believe the dept should be run by a Police Officer not politicians. This dept is running scared.

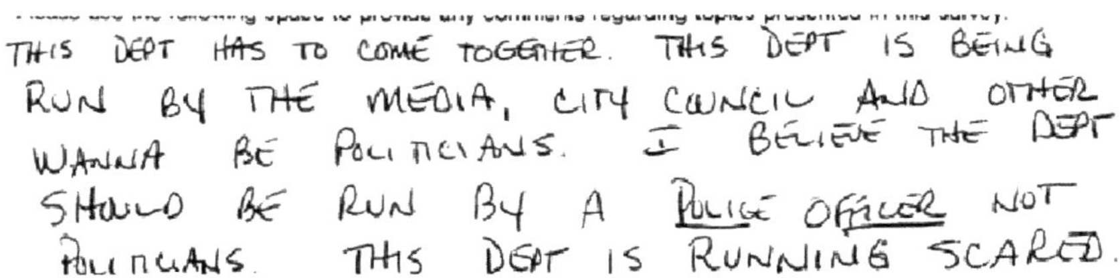
THIS DEPT HAS TO COME TOGETHER. THIS DEPT IS BEING
RUN BY THE MEDIA, CITY COUNCIL AND OTHER
WANNA BE POLITICIANS. I BELIEVE THE DEPT
SHOULD BE RUN BY A POLICE OFFICER NOT
POLITICIANS. THIS DEPT IS RUNNING SCARED.

Figure 4.4 Statement Transcription: This Department has to come together. This Department is being run by the media, city council and other wanna be politicians. I believe the Department should be run by a police officer not politicians. This Department is running scared. After all, we came on this job to be police officers not to sit in an ivory tower worrying about who's spot I'll be taking! (see Officer Informant statement #55).

After all, we came on this job to be police officers not to sit in an ivory tower worrying about who's spot I'll be taking!

(Police Officer, Male, Hispanic, 29 years old, 4 years PO, 4 years LAPD, Chief when hired: Gates) (Figure 4.4)

#56

... As I have watched the political environment since the Rodney King case I am convinced that our detractors have no concept or interest in what is best for the people that live and work in Los Angeles. This means we have a responsibility to hang in and do the right thing and ensure that the community gets what it wants and deserves in the way of police service.

(Lieutenant, Male, Caucasian, 50 years old, 27 years PO 27 years LAPD, Chief when hired: Parker)

#57

It's my personal opinion, that in light of all the negative media attention this department has had you, the administration have failed to defend us against those who are truly responsible for the violence that occurs in the communities that we serve. Rather than make "us" (LAPD) the scapegoat for all the troubles that are prevalent in the city you, the city fathers, and so called "Men of God" should not point fingers at "us" but at yourselves for failing to lead. Now, no one group is alone responsible for today's problems. It falls on everyone of us. But coming back to "us" (LAPD), you the department heads have lost touch with what goes on in the field. The rank and file are not out of control. We are more professional than ever. But there is a serious problem. Our very own people are chipping away at our character and soon there will be nothing left to salvage. I only hope this survey will do something positive. God, knows we need it. Thank you for the opportunity.

(Police Officer, Male, Hispanic, 30 years old, 5 years PO, 5 years LAPD, Chief when hired: Gates)

Theme 2: Unjustified Treatment of Patrol Officers Following the King Incident

The second most prominent theme dealing with the aftermath of the King incident concerned the mistreatment of officers (especially those working patrol and other street level assignments) by supervisors (sergeants, lieutenants, and captains) and by the LAPD upper-level administrators (commanders, deputy chiefs, and assistant chiefs), commonly referred to as the brass or command staff. Specifically, the officers' comments indicate that following the King incident the number of official disciplinary actions taken against patrol officers (referred to as 1.81s or 181s) increased dramatically in both number and harshness. (Briefly, 1.81 is a personnel complaint that accuses an officer of a policy violation that can range from failing to assist citizens in a professional manner to an excessive use of force claim. Once the 1.81 is filed, action taken against the officer for the alleged violation must be initiated by supervisor staff and can result in the officer receiving punishments such as days off without pay, long-term suspension, or even termination of employment with the department.) As will be noted in many of the comments below, there is a general subtheme that patrol officers believed that they were being indiscriminately punished without cause by the department merely as a means to appease the public for what occurred during the King incident. In other words, the unspoken understanding among officers of "I have your back if you have mine," which was instilled by Parker under the professional model, had now been broken by the LAPD supervision and administration as a result of mounting outside pressure over the King incident.

#58

Ofc's are at the end of their rope—not enough space or time avail. to say what I really feel. Uniformed officers are taking the entire brunt of the King Matter, without support from the top. However, it is ironic, that when the top was under fire, the uniformed ofc's gave 100% support to them.

(Sergeant, Male, Caucasian, 54 years old, 24 years PO, 24 years LAPD, Chief when hired: Reddin)

#59

This dept. has always treated ofcrs as children. Sometimes when I come to work, I feel like a 10 year old kid. After the Foothill Incident the mis-trust of ofcrs by upper brass had increased. I'm a 25 year vet & I resent being mis-trusted by anyone.

(Detective, Male, Caucasian, 48 years old, 25 years PO, 25 years LAPD, Chief when hired: Parker)

#60

I loved being a cop and a member of this organization but the events that have transpired during the last year have destroyed my pride and broken my heart. I can only hope that when the current administration retires (all of them) my peers and I can work together to repair the damage that has been done. As with any problem, patrol is the first to be blamed, the first to be criticized, and the first to be punished. Yet we are also the first to be given the mission of correcting the problem. We really are trying to do a good job. Unfortunately, our efforts will be worthless until department managers learn to conduct themselves with the same professionalism and dignity they demand of us.

(Police Officer, Male, Caucasian, 28 years old, 7 years PO, 7 years LAPD, Chief when hired: Gates)

#61

Post Rodney King hysteria in discipline is only being applied to line troops. Recent complaints of misconduct, abuse of authority and discourtesy by supervision (all the way to Capt III) is just covered up, not investigated or just handled as training issues & not 1.81 like would happen to me.

(Police Officer, Male, Caucasian, 41 years old, 15 years PO, 15 years LAPD, Chief when hired: Davis)

#62

One thing that is evident to me over the 19½ years of service on this police dept.—that the Brass governs by "management by crisis"; in other words, the leaders of this dept. are "Reactionaries"—not visionaries. I truly believe that any and all changes now taking place, including this survey, is only the result of Rodney King. It's too bad; all the changes on this dept. have come as a result of an outside pressure and not because of leadership and innovation.

(Detective, Male, Caucasian, 41 years old, 20 years PO, 20 years LAPD, Chief when hired: Davis)

#63

The morale on the dept. is the absolute worst I have seen since coming on the job (and management does not care)! Top management has no concern whatsoever for patrol officers, but only cares about their own careers, advancement and status!! They don't give a damn! I am no longer proud to be with the LAPD!! The dept has totally overreacted to the Rodney King Affair—resulting in needless, unnecessary 1.81s and punishment.

(Police Officer, Male, Caucasian, 35 years old, 8 years PO, 5 years LAPD, Chief when hired: Gates) (Figure 4.5)

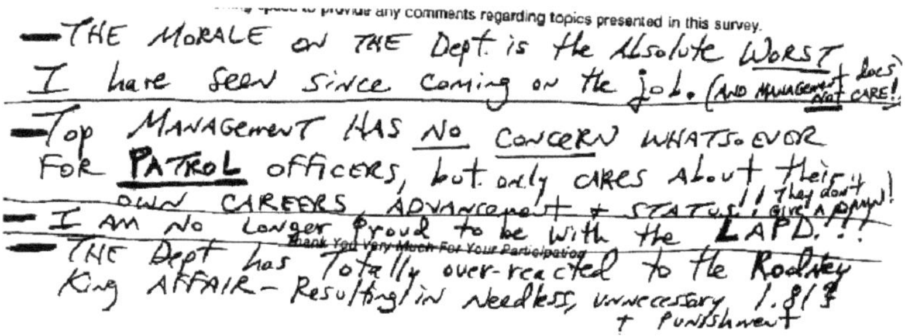
... provide any comments regarding topics presented in this survey.

—THE MORALE ON THE Dept. is the Absolute WORST I have seen since coming on the job. (AND MANAGEMENT does not CARE!)
—Top MANAGEMENT HAS NO CONCERN WHATSOEVER FOR PATROL officers, but only cares about their own CAREERS, ADVANCEMENT + STATUS!! They don't give a damn!
—I AM NO Longer proud to be with the LAPD!!!
Thank You Very Much For Your Participation
—THE Dept has Totally over-reacted to the Rodney King AFFAIR—Resulting in needless, unnecessary 1.81s + Punishment

Figure 4.5 Statement Transcription: The morale on the dept. is the absolute worst I have seen since coming on the job (and management does not care)!) Top management has no concern whatsoever for patrol officers, but only cares about their own careers, advancement and status!! They don't give a damn! I am no longer proud to be with the LAPD!! The Department has totally over-reacted to the Rodney King Affair—resulting in needless, unnecessary 1.81s [personnel complaints against officers] and punishment (see Officer Informant statement #63).

#64

Prior to March of 1991, we were effective as an organization because we had direction and meaning. We are now without a leader, meaning the chief of police and we definitely have no confidence or leadership in our command staff. I used to be extremely proud to be part of this organization. As a late, I am not so sure any more. I have to ask myself a question, and that is, why is morale so poor. Morale starts at the top and its funneling down. The command leadership of this dept is sad & ineffective. Yes I work the streets & always have and always will. After all, every capt, commander and chief did also. But I feel that "they" have forgotten—"the street cop," and the street cop is being thrown to the wolves! Everyone is always saying how important the street cop is. For once, this dept should prove it. By what means this is accomplished I am not certain. The street officer needs to be backed up. Work needs to be done in this area.

(Sergeant, Male, Caucasian, 39 years old, 17 years PO, 17 years LAPD, Chief when hired: Davis)

#65

Stop burning patrol for Rodney King, we were not all there, MDT message investigations have gotten way out of hand, make some changes or a lot of officers will be leaving.

(Police Officer, Male, Caucasian, 30 years old, 8 years PO, 4 years LAPD, Chief when hired: Gates) (Figure 4.6)

#66

Supervisors and command officers have become experts in community relations since March 3, 1991. They placate the press, City Hall, and civil rights groups. They have failed miserably in supporting the

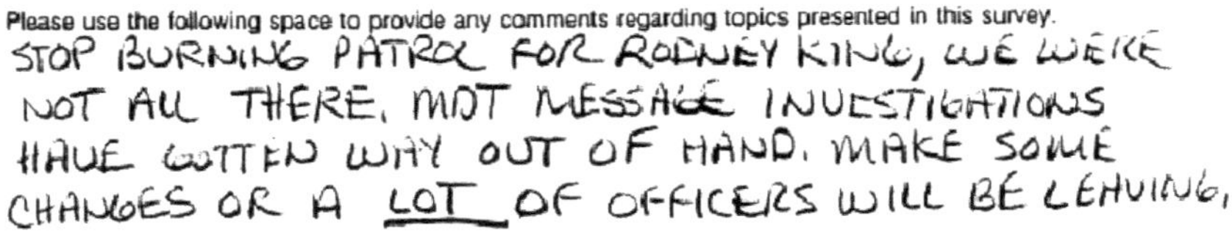

Please use the following space to provide any comments regarding topics presented in this survey.

STOP BURNING PATROL FOR RODNEY KING, WE WERE NOT ALL THERE. MDT MESSAGE INVESTIGATIONS HAVE GOTTEN WAY OUT OF HAND. MAKE SOME CHANGES OR A LOT OF OFFICERS WILL BE LEAVING.

Figure 4.6 Statement Transcription: Stop burning patrol for Rodney King, we were not all there, MDT [Mobile Date Terminal—communication devise located in patrol vehicles] message investigations have gotten way out of hand, make some changes or a lot of officers will be leaving (see Officer Informant statement #65).

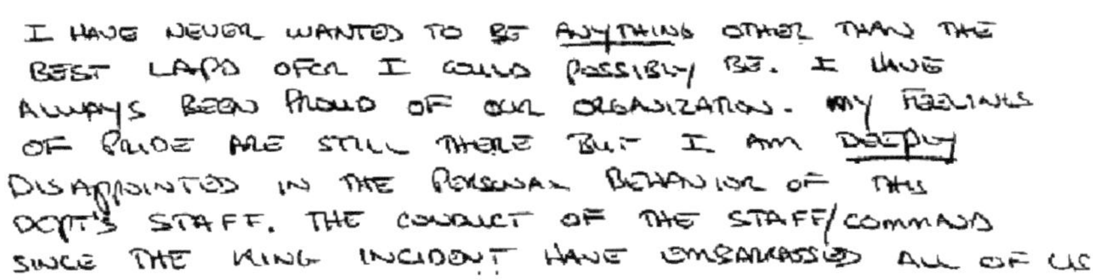

I HAVE NEVER WANTED TO BE ANYTHING OTHER THAN THE BEST LAPD OFCR I COULD POSSIBLY BE. I HAVE ALWAYS BEEN PROUD OF OUR ORGANIZATION. MY FEELINGS OF PRIDE ARE STILL THERE BUT I AM DEEPLY DISAPPOINTED IN THE PERSONAL BEHAVIOR OF THIS DEPT'S STAFF. THE CONDUCT OF THE STAFF/COMMAND SINCE THE KING INCIDENT HAVE EMBARRASSED ALL OF US

Figure 4.7 Statement Transcription: I have never wanted to be anything other than the best LAPD officer I could possibly be. I have always been proud of our organization. My feelings of pride are still there but I am deeply disappointed in the personal behavior of this Department's staff. The conduct of the staff/command [LAPD's upper management] since the King Incident have embarrassed all of us otherwise loyal officers!! (see Officer Informant statement #67).

patrol section—the backbone of the dept. I am a human being. I am not perfect. I have successfully passed a background investigation, yet my work is looked on with doubt compared to that of a convicted felon. Let's learn how to treat the public by treating each other well first!!

(Police Officer, Male, Caucasian, 33 years old, 8 years PO, 2 years LAPD, Chief when hired: Gates)

#67

I have never wanted to be anything other than the best LAPD officer I could possibly be. I have always been proud of our organization. My feelings of pride are still there but I am deeply disappointed in the personal behavior of this Department's staff. The conduct of the staff/command since the King Incident have embarrassed all of us otherwise loyal officers!!

(Lieutenant, Male, Caucasian, 42 years old, 21 years PO, 21 years LAPD, Chief when hired: Davis) (Figure 4.7)

Theme 3: The Rodney King Incident Is LAPD "Business as Usual"

The least prominent subtheme, expressed by the following small group of officers, suggested that the King incident was "nothing new" and that the situation is merely a symptom of long-standing problems of officer aggression and racism that have plagued the department for years—if not decades. Some of the comments below are akin to "whistle blowing" by officers who are attempting to expose the department's physically aggressive style of policing that, in their opinion, resulted in the King incident; obtaining this type of commentary is quite surprising—and extremely rare—because within the LAPD, and in most policing circles, such comments would be considered a violation of the blue code of silence.

#68

The Rodney King incident is only the tip of the ice berg—the whole problem is getting exposed everyday but no one is paying attention. For years now the problems have been evident. The dept is now in a position of disappearing in the way that I know it.

(Police Officer, Male, Hispanic, 43 years old, 20 years PO, 20 years LAPD, Chief when hired: Davis) (Figure 4.8)

#69

Hopefully the city will select a Chief of Police from the outside, if not—do not expect much change. I personally feel the citizens of LA have been getting the short end of the stick. Additionally—incidents like the King matter are not new—It's been prevalent t/o the department for 20+ years. Note: Ten years from now—unless there are some drastic changes most of us that are retired will not even admit were members of the LAPD—sad but true.

(Sergeant, Male, Caucasian, 50 years old, 23 years PO, 23 years LAPD, Chief when hired: Reddin)

#70

I enjoy my job very much. I do feel that we are being forced to "kiss up" to the public to try and make up for Rodney King. I also feel that we are being forced to deal with minorities, especially blacks, in a different and now less forceful manner than we deal with all other persons. People feel that we "pick on" a certain race. It's not our fault

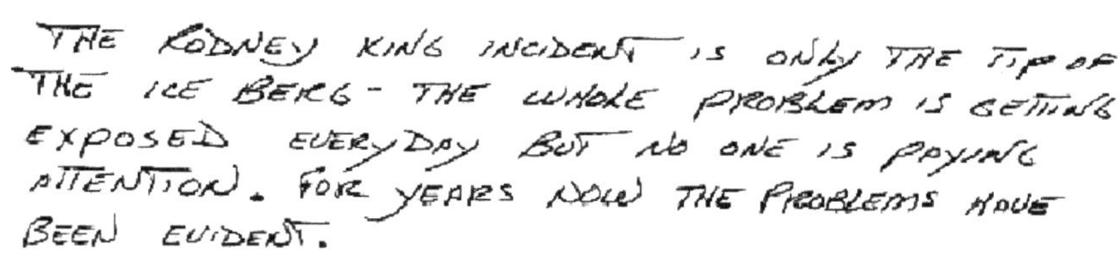
THE RODNEY KING INCIDENT IS ONLY THE TIP OF THE ICE BERG - THE WHOLE PROBLEM IS GETTING EXPOSED EVERYDAY BUT NO ONE IS PAYING ATTENTION. FOR YEARS NOW THE PROBLEMS HAVE BEEN EVIDENT.

Figure 4.8 Statement Transcription: The Rodney King incident is only the tip of the ice berg—the whole problem is getting exposed everyday but no one is paying attention. For years now the problems have been evident (see Officer Informant statement #68).

that 70% of the crime is committed by that race. We don't choose who we arrest, the criminals do that. I'll arrest anyone who commits a crime, I don't care what race they are. So quit showing favoritism both to minority citizens and to ofcrs, but judge on merits, good or bad, and treat persons based on that not skin color or what outside groups say.

(Police Officer, Male, Caucasian, 27 years old, 1 year PO, 1 year LAPD, Chief when hired: Gates)

#71

Top mgt. still believes ofcrs need to go out of roll call with fire in their eyes. The result is 39th & Dalton & Rodney King incident. We still teach & instill the belief that every person an ofcr encounters may kill him. We seem to instill a combination of paranoia and vigilante mentality. The Hammer task forces were an example. Mgt. seemed to believe ofcrs were not aggressive enough, hence the mob mentality and "good" vs. "bad" mentality. We need a change at the top!

(Lieutenant, Male, Caucasian, 45 years old, 24 years PO, 24 years LAPD, Chief when hired: Reddin)

#72

I love this job and would do it for free but I need to eat. The incident only made things better.

(Police Officer, Male, Caucasian, 32 years old, 7 years PO, 7 years LAPD, Chief when hired: Gates)

Theme Analysis

Taken together, there was very little evidence in the above themes to suggest the officers believed the Rodney King incident played a major role in either the LAPD's organizational meltdown or the department's ultimate abandonment of the professional model of policing. Instead, the officers felt that the media, politicians, and other critics of the department were distorting the King affair to create in the public's mind a false negative image of the LAPD as an overly aggressive, out-of-control organization of racist "thugs" who would all react in a manner similar to that seen in the King video. Although none of the officers' comments directly suggested that the methods used by the officers at the King scene were tactically appropriate, it could be argued that the "justified use of force" explanation was supported by this particular theme. In other words, because the majority of officers defended their status (and that of the LAPD) through a denial of the King tape's accuracy, they too may have believed the force used against King may have been justified under LAPD use of force policies.

Second, officers' comments strongly suggested that patrol officers in all LAPD jurisdictions were being punished by their supervisors and by the department's upper administration at an increased rate following the King incident. They felt this was an extremely unfair move by management just to create a public image of street level control over officers following the King incident. This increased level of scrutiny and punishment of patrol officers, according to the study findings, was perceived by the average working officer as totally unjustified and led to extreme feelings of animosity among this group toward the LAPD's supervisory and administrative staff. In a general sense, this finding supports the few bad apples explanation, which contends that the King incident—if not a justified use of force—was perhaps an isolated incident rather than an example of the department's culture of police brutality. Logically speaking, if the officers felt that they would have reacted in a similar way as did the officers at the King scene, they may have not so vehemently opposed the LAPD administration's crackdown on patrol. They may have viewed the punishment as a necessary evil to appease the public until the entire King affair was forgotten, at which time the officers could return to their normal aggressive style of policing. Instead, the few bad apples theme comments are best interpreted as showing that the average patrol officer really did not connect or identify with the situation encountered by officers involved in the King incident and believed that the increased punishment of all patrol officers following the King media frenzy was an extremely unjustified overreaction by the LAPD administration.[7]

The least common viewpoint, yet still considered an independent theme, was in support of the contention that LAPD, through its training and culture, encouraged violent policing tactics like those use by the officers during the King incident. Also, these comments were in agreement with the business as usual explanation for the King affair. Specifically, one of the officer comments expressed concerns that the LAPD organization encouraged patrol officers to handle their law enforcement duties in a highly aggressive manner. Other officers stated that violent police encounters with the public, and in particular racially motivated ones, are not new to the LAPD. Other officers may have possessed similar opinions but were unwilling to express them for fear of being considered disloyal to the department. Quite simply, there is no way of telling how much the blue code of silence effect was present in other officers' comments on the King incident.

Conclusions

Based on the relatively few comments received and the thematic content presented in the foregoing analysis, it can be concluded with relative certainty that the King incident was indeed a cause of the LAPD organizational meltdown and the fall of the professional model—but most likely not a primary cause. Alternatively, this study's findings indicate that the massive amount of attention and criticism brought to the LAPD organization following the King controversy was instead an indirect cause of the department's organizational model and the professional model's demise. That is, the King incident appears to be an initial cause that set into motion other causes that were more directly responsible for the meltdown. In essence, there was an organizational domino effect, with the King domino to be the first to fall. This conclusion begs one new critical research question to be answered by additional study findings: If the King incident wasn't the primary cause of the LAPD organizational meltdown and death of the professional model, what was? In the chapters that follow, additional officer comments will be examined to seek an answer to this vitally important question regarding the practice and theory of modern policing.

References

1. Stacey Koon. *Presumed Guilty: The Tragedy of the Rodney King Affair*. Washington, DC: Regnery Publishing, 1992.
2. Los Angeles Police Department. *Training Manual 1991*. Los Angeles: City of Los Angeles, 1991.
3. Personal interview with anonymous informant. Conducted May 1995.
4. Personal interview with anonymous informant. Conducted May 1995.
5. Personal interview with anonymous informant. Conducted May 1995.
6. Personal interview with anonymous informant. Conducted September 2011.
7. James Lasley. The Impact of the Rodney King Incident on Citizen Attitudes Toward Police. *Policing and Society*, 3, 1995.

Politicians, Special Interest Groups, and Community Influences

5

One of the three major areas identified within the officers' comments as a potential direct cause of the meltdown concerned outside influences on LAPD from politicians, special interest groups, and selected members of the Los Angeles community. Approximately one out of every four comments received contained some mention of these persons/entities adversely affecting the department and their negative impact on the overall functioning of the LAPD organization following the King incident. However, attacks on the department and its adherence to the professional model's aggressive policing style from politicians and the like were by no means new in the city of Los Angeles. In fact, as was noted in Chapter 1, the LAPD endured numerous criticisms of its law enforcement and community relations methods during the years it operated under the professional model. However, during these past occasions of significant political challenge, the department and its officers managed to preserve the organization's integrity and policing style when faced with formidable critics and criticism. Why is it, then, that during the LAPD's post-King era political and special interest group attacks were able to possibly cause such severe and permanent damage to the department and its chief operating model of policing? Answers to the latter question will be explored in the following section.

Possible Explanations

Opponents Got Stronger

One possible explanation is that politicians, special interest groups, and other outside opponents of the LAPD simply got stronger over time in their abilities to affect the organization's policies and policing procedures. This may be especially true regarding the power and influence of the Los Angeles mayor over the position of chief of the LAPD. One of the organizational cornerstones, which may very well have been most critical to the preservation of the professional model, was the early implementation of civil service protection for whoever served in the position of chief at LAPD. Such protection was built into the Los Angeles City Charter as a means of protecting the LAPD chief from political influences—especially those from the mayor's office—that could lead to corruption and other ethical breaches of police services.[1] Unlike most other major cities where the chief of Police SERVED at the will of the mayor, in Los Angeles the chief of LAPD (at the time of this study) could only be removed from office for "good and sufficient cause." In effect, the civil service protection provision of the city charter meant that the LAPD chief could act autonomously of political influences without fear of retaliation or removal from office by the mayor or any other politician so long as his or her actions did not violate the law. Even if the LAPD chief was accused of legal violation constituting a "good and sufficient cause" for removal, the decision to fire the chief had to be made by the Los Angeles Police Commission—which consisted of five civilians who were appointed by the mayor and acted in a part-time capacity to oversee the policies and operations of the LAPD. However, even the police commission's decisions made regarding the LAPD chief's tenure in office were subject to being overridden by the Los Angeles City Council. Thus, all in all, the mayor had virtually no power to interfere with the chief's decisions regarding how to run the LAPD organization.[2]

During the time Parker served as chief, the relationship between the LAPD and the Los Angeles Mayor's Office was cooperative. Although there were some attempts to reform the LAPD by three Los Angeles mayors (Bowron, who appointed Parker in 1950; C. Norris Poulson, who succeeded Bowron; and Sam Yorty, who followed Poulson and was in office during Parker's death in 1966) while Parker served as chief, none of these were serious enough to pierce the organizational veil of the LAPD. It was not until Mayor Tom Bradley was elected in 1973 that political momentum started to gain strength in an attempt to breach the protective organization barrier that separated the LAPD and its chief from attacks by politicians, special interest groups, and outspoken community members. Bradley was the first African American to be elected mayor of Los Angeles and was a former LAPD lieutenant who served with the department for 21 years before leaving to pursue a career in Los Angeles politics. As a police officer and as a politician, he fought to make reforms within the LAPD—many of which were aimed at modifying or abandoning the professional model of policing. Throughout the 1970s and 1980s he made several failed attempts to remove the civil service protection that shielded LAPD's chief from political attacks and oversight by outside government entities.[3] Regarding Bradley's reputation as a former officer and his ultimate political relationship with the department while serving as mayor, there seems to be diametrically opposed opinions generated from his former LAPD colleagues. The following two informants, both former LAPD officers who worked with Bradley during his patrol years, exemplify this observation:

> Pro-Bradley informant: "Bradley was a fine officer. One of the best I've worked with at LAPD. He was always fair as a supervisor and a great mentor for other Black officers who were trying to get ahead at the

department.... He received lots of commendations for his outstanding service and always received the best reviews for his performance while serving as a patrol officer. I believe he quit the department because he felt a need for higher service to the community. He loved the Los Angeles community and did whatever he could to help this LAPD and its officer to do a better job."[4]

Anti-Bradley informant: "Tom Bradley was a racist. He was a true racist in the way he treated black officers and white officers and black Suspects and white Suspects. I know that for a fact from watching him when he was my watch commander. When he was a supervisor he played favorites to black suspects over white suspects. I saw it time and time again, when an officer would bring in a black suspect for a booking approval, especially for DUIs because I was a traffic officer. He would release black suspects and book the white ones. I firmly believe that he always had it out for the department and that everything he did as mayor that affected the LAPD was some sort of payback against us motivated by his racist attitudes. I believe he was a corrupt politician as well ... on the take."[5]

Another key factor is perhaps the contemptuous personal relationship between Mayor Bradley and Chief Daryl Gates, the final LAPD chief to serve under the department's implementation of the professional model. Both Bradley and Gates have a long-standing feud stemming back from their early days at the LAPD. As previously mentioned, Bradley used his executive powers while in position of mayor to not only attempt to reform the LAPD, but also to remove the civil service protection that guarded the LAPD chief from political control. Also, he made numerous attempts to remove Gates from his position as chief—actions that many LAPD observers believed to be motivated by Bradley's extreme disdain for Gates. The following statement from an LAPD informant sheds light on the intensity of the Bradley-Gates feud:

> ... They hated each other. I mean they really hated each other and this went on for a long time. Probably since Bradley was an officer at LAPD. Gates was an adjutant for Chief Parker and he knew everything that went on in Parker's mind. Gates and Parker were very tight. So, I can imagine that Parker didn't like Bradley as well.... Things got so bad between Bradley and Gates that near the last couple years the two attended meetings together they wouldn't talk to each other ... not a word ... in fact, they couldn't even look at each other![6]

The Los Angeles mayor was not the only opponent of the LAPD to get stronger. The American Civil Liberties Union (ACLU) became a veritable watchdog over civil rights violations allegedly perpetrated by the LAPD and its officers during the 1980s. In 1981, the ACLU dealt its strongest legal blow to the department by filing a suit alleging that the LAPD's Public Disorder Intelligence Division (PDID) was being used to spy on LA Mayor Tom Bradley, the California governor, and other elected officials. The lawsuit resulted in the dismantling of the PDID and the end of LAPD's clandestine intelligence gathering efforts aimed at public officials and other persons thought to be enemies of the department. Special interest groups comprised of minority as well as gay and lesbian activists also began taking aim at the LAPD during the 1980s, and their critical allegations of the department's intentional violation of their civil rights began to be featured more prominently in the *Los Angeles Times.*

The LAPD Got Weaker

In addition to the department's opponents getting stronger, the logical inverse of the latter argument is that the LAPD became weaker in its ability to shield itself from outside political influences. In this study, the most accurate measure of a weakness argument is an examination of officers' comments regarding the ability of politicians', special interest groups', and community members' influences to permeate the long-standing organizational barrier established by Parker to isolate the department's interior from this sort of external "contamination." Given the study's time frame (approximately five months after the release of the Christopher Commission report; see Chapter 1), the true test of LAPD's fortitude to resist political influences and perhaps a hostile takeover will be an examination of the officers' comments regarding Mayor Bradley's and the Christopher Commission's demands for reform of the LAPD. These included, among other radical changes to the department, (1) abandoning the professional model in favor of community-based policing, (2) monitoring of officers by civilians outside of the department, (3) oversight of the department by civilian review boards, (4) appointment of the chief of police by the mayor, and (5) the summary removal of Daryl Gates as chief and his replacement with a police executive from outside of the LAPD.

Interestingly, the above test is not new to the present study. Following the 1965 Watts riots, then Los Angeles mayor Sam Yorty assembled the McCone Commission, which served in a very similar capacity to evaluate the policing tactics of the LAPD and Chief Parker's leadership role in handling the riots. Yorty and the commission were specifically concerned with allegations that the LAPD handled the rioters in an overly aggressive manner and that this behavior was a symptom of the department's internal culture of brutality and racism that was fostered by Parker's policing model. When the McCone Commission report was released, it was criticized as a "whitewash" of the LAPD involvement in the riots, the department's organizational culture, and Chief Parker's tactics. In effect, the LAPD and Parker were cleared of all political accusations of wrongdoing during the riots and the professional model survived its first major external attack by political opponents and was left unscathed by the McCone Commission.[7]

Although it is well known at this point that most of the Christopher Commission's recommendations for reform of the LAPD were ultimately adopted and implemented, it remains to be seen how the officers reacted to the report immediately following its release and prior to its later implementation. In other words, was Parker's protective barrier still intact or strong enough to provide officers with a feeling that they would be guarded inside the department against the outside political battering ram being wielded by Mayor Bradley, the Christopher Commission, special interest groups, and others in the community? Or, alternatively, did the officers sense a weakness in the department's past iron-clad protection against attacks by their political nemeses and perhaps an impending doom of the professional model of policing?

Officer Statements and Themes

As will be noted below, two specific general themes were discovered among the officers' comments concerning outside influences on the department. Together, these themes represent the first of three main potential causes of the meltdown as identified after examining the total sample of officer statements contained in this study (see Chapters 6 and 7 for a discussion of the remaining two potential main causes). The majority of these influences were identified as originating from Los Angeles Mayor Tom Bradley, the Christopher Commission, the ACLU, or special interest groups targeting the LAPD. Within each general theme, it was also possible to identify one or more subthemes, which identify more specific ideas or explanations of the officers' attitudes toward a specific outside influence affecting them or the department.

Theme 1: LAPD Is "Running Scared" and "Kowtowing" to Attackers

The following section contains officer comments that share the common theme that LAPD's official response to outside pressure from political and community critics was either to kowtow (or "cowtow" as written by most officers) to their demands or to run scared from them without a fight. These comments suggest that the political affront to the LAPD by Mayor Bradley, the Christopher Commission, special interest groups, and the community at large not only permeated the department's political force field, but also was strongly felt by the patrol officer on the street. In effect, Parker's protective

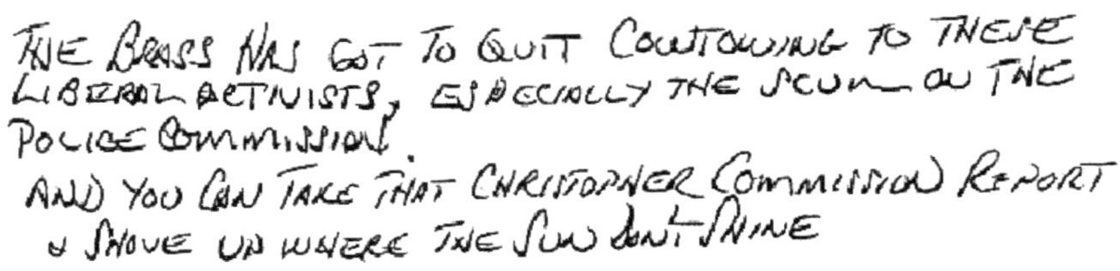
THE BRASS HAS GOT TO QUIT COWTOWING TO THESE LIBERAL ACTIVISTS, ESPECIALLY THE SCUM ON THE POLICE COMMISSION.
AND YOU CAN TAKE THAT CHRISTOPHER COMMISSION REPORT & SHOVE UP WHERE THE SUN DON'T SHINE

Figure 5.1 Statement Transcription: The brass has got to quit cowtowing to these liberal activists, especially the scum on the police commission. And you can take that Christopher Commission Report & shove up where the sun don't shine (see Officer Informant statement #73).

barrier surrounding his troops from attack was apparently broken for the first time by LA politicians, the media, and outspoken community members.

#73

The brass has got to quit cowtowing to these liberal activists, especially the scum on the police commission. And you can take that Christopher Commission Report & shove it up where the sun don't shine.

(Police Officer, Male, Caucasian, 45 years old, 21 years PO, 21 years LAPD, Chief when hired: Davis) (Figure 5.1)

#74

Police ofcrs today no longer are enforcing the laws of society. The service provided is more reactive than proactive. This problem starts with upper management "running scared" from the vocal minority. The criminals know this thus they are not apprehended & in turn the crime rate increases. Man can learn many things from history, some good & some bad. Let the individual officer do their job as they did in the past. Send a message to criminals that the LAPD is back with strength.

(Police Officer, Male, Caucasian, 26 years old, 2 years PO, 2 years LAPD, Chief when hired: Gates)

#75

The LAPD is becoming a political organization kowtowing to every loud mouth politician and refusing to back its own officers. The brass is concerned more about their own image than the Department employees. Patrol has never been the backbone of the Dept (which it should be), its been treated more like the back side of the Dept in terms of caring, promotions and work conditions. We need the Department to "Fight for Us," not use us as a scape-goat.

(Sergeant, Male, Caucasian, 45 years old, 23 years PO, 23 years LAPD, Chief when hired: Reddin)

#76

This department has been flushed down the toilet by liberal, no-nothing politicians, special interest groups, spineless command

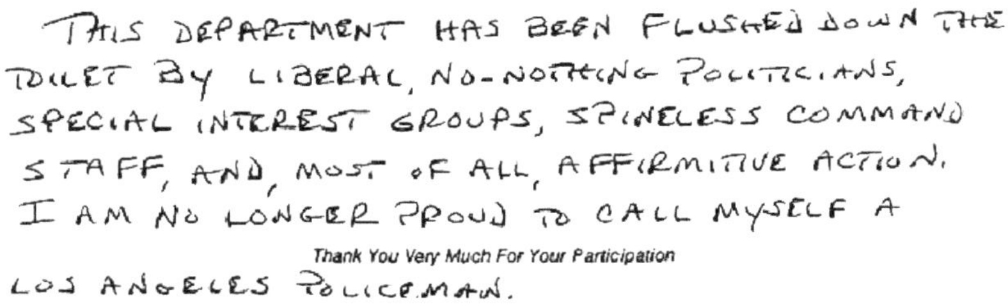
THIS DEPARTMENT HAS BEEN FLUSHED DOWN THE
TOILET BY LIBERAL, NO-NOTHING POLITICIANS,
SPECIAL INTEREST GROUPS, SPINELESS COMMAND
STAFF, AND, MOST OF ALL, AFFIRMITIVE ACTION.
I AM NO LONGER PROUD TO CALL MYSELF A
Thank You Very Much For Your Participation
LOS ANGELES POLICEMAN.

Figure 5.2 Statement Transcription: This department has been flushed down the toilet by liberal, no-nothing politicians, special interest groups, spineless command staff, and, most of all, affirmative action. I am no longer proud to call myself a Los Angeles Policeman (see Officer Informant statement #76).

staff, and, most of all, affirmative action. I am no longer proud to call myself a Los Angeles Policeman.

(Police Officer, Male, Caucasian, 42 years old, 18 years PO, 17 years LAPD, Chief when hired: Davis) (Figure 5.2)

#77

I feel this dept. cares too much about what the citz's have to say and especially what the susps have to say. This dept. wants us (police officers) to work with our hand behind our back. The dept. is creating unnecessary paperwork for us. We do not have enough or proper equipment to work with. This dept is not as strong as they use to be. NO GUTTS!

(Police Officer, Female, Hispanic, 23 years old, 3 years PO, 3 years LAPD, Chief when hired: Gates)

#78

It has been tried, tested and found to fall far short of expectations. We live in a community which views the P.D. as a necessary evil and because of inept Political Leadership and serious doubts as to Dept. Leadership is unwilling to approve measures which would improve the Dept. I am not endorsing the measures suggested by the Christopher Comm. They are a joke, the joke is compounded when you realize that the entire situation is orchestrated by political greed (Mayor Bradley) and media greed.

(Police Officer, Male, Caucasian, 43 years old, 17 years PO, 17 years LAPD, Chief when hired: Davis)

#79

When the Mayor, City Council and Police Commission all get on the same side of the fence as the Police Department (law and order) this community could stand a chance of again being a decent place to live and work. Until then, forget it!

(Detective, Male, Caucasian, 40 years old, 19 years PO, 19 years LAPD, Chief when hired: Davis) (Figure 5.3)

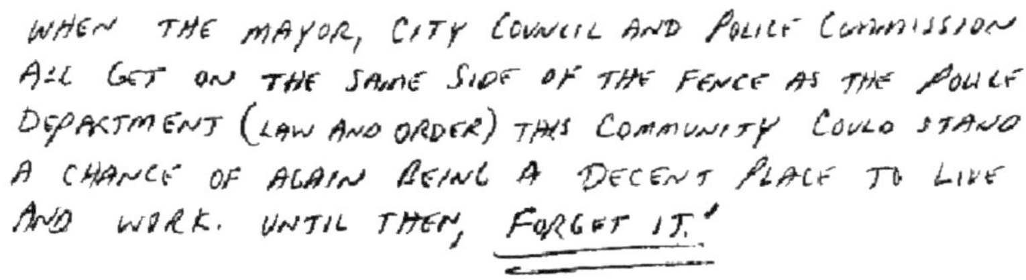
WHEN THE MAYOR, CITY COUNCIL AND POLICE COMMISSION ALL GET ON THE SAME SIDE OF THE FENCE AS THE POLICE DEPARTMENT (LAW AND ORDER) THIS COMMUNITY COULD STAND A CHANCE OF AGAIN BEING A DECENT PLACE TO LIVE AND WORK. UNTIL THEN, FORGET IT!

Figure 5.3 Statement Transcription: When the Mayor, City Council and Police Commission all get on the same side of the fence as the Police Department (law and order) this community could stand a chance of again being a decent place to live and work. Until then, forget it! (see Officer Informant statement #79).

#80

We are under deployed everyday & every watch in every div. We have a worthless lying Mayor for a leader. Crime controls the streets of LA & citzs don't complain because they know we won't solve the problem because we can't. Big mouths (media) complain loudly about what they know nothing about. Citz(s) w/o big mouths don't voice their opinions & they have big problems & solutions & uniform pat knows this, because we are out there every day (alone) w/o citz help or dept help, some backbone of the dept.

(Police Officer, Male, Caucasian, 28 years old, 7 years PO, 7 years LAPD, Chief when hired: Gates)

#81

We need more officers. We need to quit cowtowing down to politicians and liberal left wing groups. We need to quit saying "poor suspect," "bad officer." The brass has to stop punishing the blue suiters in order to placate City Hall and liberal groups.

(Sergeant, Male, Caucasian, 50 years old, 27 years PO, 27 years LAPD, Chief when hired: Parker)

#82

… The Christopher Commission is only a vehicle to speed the process of direction that the department had been headed for years, Thanks to the managers of the department. This whole report was completely off base as to the real issues at hand. But it didn't surprise me because it was written by a handful of lawyers. If management had shown any infinitesimal amount of brains they would have responded. But they couldn't, because they don't know. Their only goal has been only a self-serving mode, only to promote themselves.

(Police Officer, Male, Hispanic, 43 years old, 20 years PO, 20 years LAPD, Chief when hired: Davis)

#83

… A crooked Mayor and his ACLA stooges run the department. Patrol officers are mired in useless paperwork. LAPD is quickly becoming third world and third rate just like the City. I would strongly urge potential recruits against coming on the department. Law enforcement is not the career of the nineties.

(Police Officer, Male, Caucasian, 51 years old, 22 years PO, 22 years LAPD, Chief when hired: Davis)

#84

Two decades ago I joined this department because it was a proud, professional and autonomous organization. In the intervening years it has been besieged by mettling outsiders for self-serving political interests. Today the department is tarnished and impotent. No wonder morale is low and esprit de corps absence. Still, despite all this discouragement, I am proud of what I do and I am proud to be a member of this department. Unfortunately, I am skeptical that this or any other survey will make a difference.

(Detective, Male, Caucasian, 44 years old, 19 years PO, 19 years LAPD, Chief when hired: Davis)

#85

I think the leadership of this dept. below Chief and above Lt. is so concerned with kissing political ass to get the up-coming chief's spot they have lost all concept of what they are really supposed to be doing. Of course that's assuming they ever did know what their job was and were capable of doing it.

(Police Officer, Male, Caucasian, 43 years old, 22 years PO, 22 years LAPD, Chief when hired: Davis)

#86

You pack of clowns can fool some of the ofcrs some of the time, etc. Get a job! Quit sucking political ass!

(Police Officer, Male, Caucasian, 45 years old, 18 years PO, 18 years LAPD, Chief when hired: Davis) (Figure 5.4)

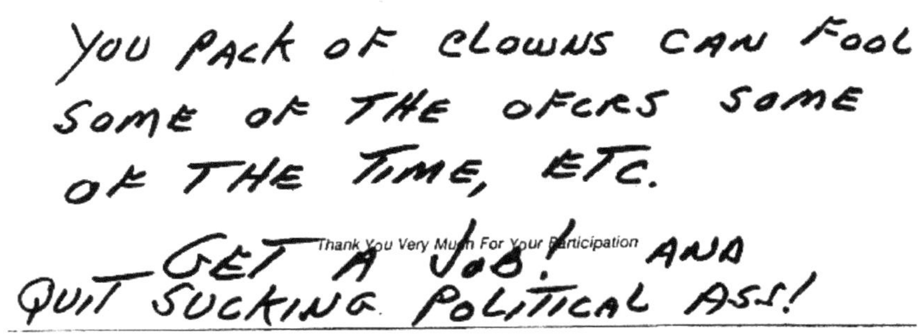
YOU PACK OF CLOWNS CAN FOOL
SOME OF THE OFCRS SOME
OF THE TIME, ETC.
GET A JOB! AND
QUIT SUCKING POLITICAL ASS!

Figure 5.4 Statement Transcription: You pack of clowns can fool some of the ofcrs some of the time, etc. Get a job! Quit sucking political ass! (see Officer Statement #86).

#87

The Dept. seems to more concerned by the threats of public (law suits & 1.81s) than ever before. This has brought moral to an all time low. Everytime we turn around a video camera is pointing at or 1.81 is waiting for us at the station.

(Police Officer, Male, Caucasian, 35 years old, 14 years PO, 14 years LAPD, Chief when hired: Davis)

#88

Presently the Department has no clear goal for its personnel or the community. We still have outstanding people and ethics, however, the on-going political power struggle and pandering to political correctness interests has confused the public and members of the Department. It appears that some decisions are being made to further the interests of individuals and these special interest groups, rather than for the good of the community. I believe many officers are demoralized by this perception. More information must be shared with our field personnel. They are hungry for direction. This survey may help meet that need.

(Detective, Male, Caucasian, 52 years old, 29 years PO, 29 years LAPD, Chief when hired: Parker)

#89

In the final analysis this is a great job that pays well when you take an honest look at the Department (The Christopher Commission did not) we do an outstanding job for the community. We can always improve, however all organizations can. Give the number of people we have and the size of the job of policing Los Angeles we are superstars. We must look beyond our detractors both inside the organization and outside and continue down the road we know is correct. I am confident the community supports us and is in concert with most of our actions. I see the support everyday in the way the community treats my officers and how they appreciate their efforts.

(Lieutenant, Male, Caucasian, 50 years old, 27 years PO, 27 years LAPD, Chief when hired: Parker)

Subtheme 1A: Cops Should Run LAPD, Not Politicians and the Public

As revealed by the comments below, officers felt that the public—and especially politicians—had no business telling the LAPD how best to police the community. Their statements also reinforced Parker's contention, and a guiding principle of the professional model, that police know what is best for the public when it comes to controlling crime.

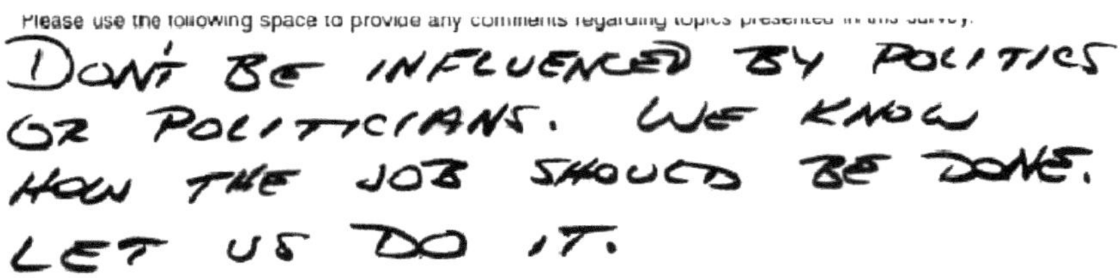
Please use the following space to provide any comments regarding topics presented in this survey.

DON'T BE INFLUENCED BY POLITICS OR POLITICIANS. WE KNOW HOW THE JOB SHOUCD BE DONE. LET US DO IT.

Figure 5.5 Statement Transcription: Don't be influences by politics or politicians. We know how the job should be done. Let us do it (see Officer Informant statement #90).

#90

Don't be influenced by politics or politicians. We know how the job should be done. Let us do it.

(Detective, Male, Caucasian, 43 years old, 15 years PO, 15 years LAPD, Chief when hired: Davis) (Figure 5.5)

#91

In my opinion the reason why I feel that morale is low is because officers don't feel that the media, the mayor, some council members and the police commissioners are supportive of LAPD ofcrs. For example, how can a commissioner who has no formal police training or experience publicly denounce how LAPD K-9s are used to apprehend felony suspects? You gotta be kidding me, give me a break! Maybe he should respond to calls himself since he knows so much about police tactics!

(Police Officer, Male, Hispanic, 31 years old, 11 years PO, 8 years LAPD, Chief when hired: Gates)

#92

I think that we (as a dept), should tell the ACLU where to go. And if they don't know where it is, then we should provide that communist organization with a map. And as far as the mayor & city council members who are against the LAPD as we know it, they should be put in the same boat as the ACLU. Elected officials should not be allowed to have a say so in how the dept is ran.

(Police Officer, Male, African American, 29 years old, 5 years PO, 5 years LAPD, Chief when hired: Gates)

#93

NAACP & Christopher Commission are destroying this dept. These special groups have negative objectives for the dept. They never having anything positive to say about our dept, and it's getting to the point that they are making decisions for our dept.

(Police Officer, Male, Caucasian, 31 years old, 9 years PO, 9 years LAPD, Chief when hired: Gates) (Figure 5.6)

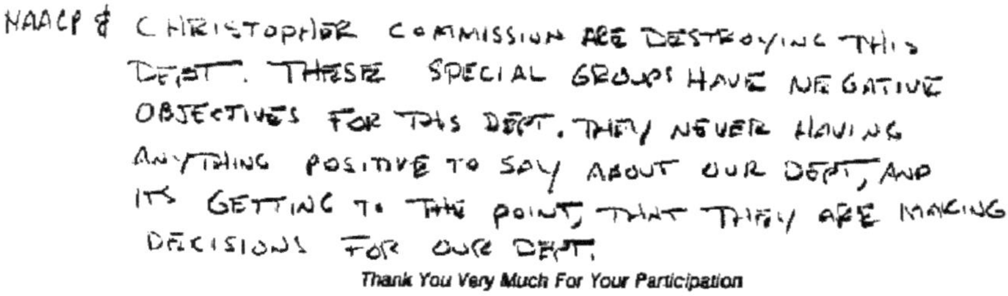
NAACP & CHRISTOPHER COMMISSION ARE DESTROYING THIS
DEPT. THESE SPECIAL GROUPS HAVE NEGATIVE
OBJECTIVES FOR THIS DEPT. THEY NEVER HAVING
ANYTHING POSITIVE TO SAY ABOUT OUR DEPT, AND
ITS GETTING TO THE POINT, THAT THEY ARE MAKING
DECISIONS FOR OUR DEPT.
Thank You Very Much For Your Participation

Figure 5.6 Statement Transcription: NAACP & Christopher Commission are destroying this Department. These special groups have negative objectives for the Department. They never having anything positive to say about our Department, and it's getting to the point that they are making decisions for our Department (see Officer Informant statement #93).

#94

This dept has to come together. This dept is being run by the media, city council and other wanna be politicians. I believe the dept should be run by a Police Officer not politicians. This dept is running scared. After all, we came on this job to be police officers not to sit in an ivory tower worrying about who's spot I'll be taking!

(Police Officer, Male, Hispanic, 29 years old, 4 years PO, 4 years LAPD, Chief when hired: Gates)

Subtheme 1B: Chief Gates Was Targeted and Hit by Political Attacks

According to the following officer comments, an additional casualty of the political attack mounted against the department—and perhaps the most serious one in LAPD's history—is the Office of the Chief of Police. As these statements suggest, Chief Gates himself was clearly targeted and hit by the political onslaught against LAPD.

#95

Learn from your mistakes Chief & don't let the politicians & media push you around.

(Police Officer, Male, Caucasian, 33 years old, 10 years PO, 10 years LAPD, Chief when hired: Gates) (Figure 5.7)

#96

I think the Christopher Commission stinks. I don't know what makes them think they are experts in any field, especially police work. In my opinion when Chief Gates leaves we are in trouble. He is the only one who has guts enough to stand up against all these demonstrators and political activists.

(Police Officer, Male, Caucasian, 47 years old, 21 years PO, 20 years LAPD, Chief when hired: Davis)

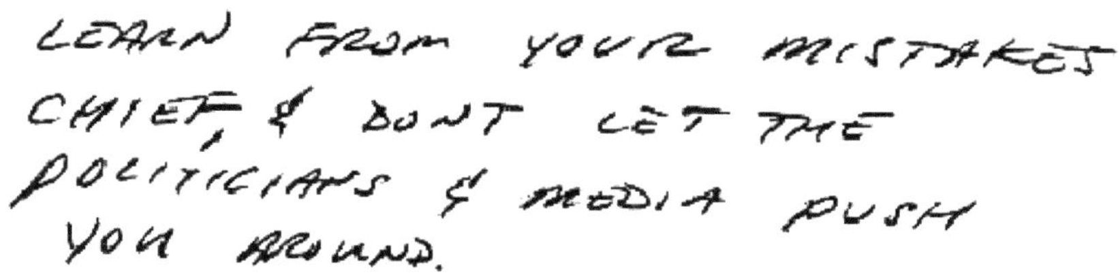
LEARN FROM YOUR MISTAKES CHIEF & DONT LET THE POLITICIANS & MEDIA PUSH YOU AROUND.

Figure 5.7 Statement Transcription: Learn from your mistakes Chief [Gates] & don't let the politicians & media push you around (see Officer Informant statement #95).

#97

With the exception of the Chief of Police, who for political reasons has merely been rendered ineffective, the upper management of the department seems more concerned with promotion/career protection than with the welfare of their people. Their active abuse of ofcrs via the disciplinary system reflects a shameful "cowtow" to the most outrageous & illfounded accusations of the Christopher commission. I no longer feel any professional kinship to these people and feel they are not deserving of the loyalty of any police ofcr of this dept. I am not a racist, brutal incompetent who will violate his public trust given the chance to do so and I resent being treated as such. It is one thing for the public to overreact to a terrible incident; there are no excuses for our upper management.

(Police Officer, Male, Hispanic, 38 years old, 9 years PO, 9 years LAPD, Chief when hired: Gates)

#98

A police chief should be able to act freely when implementing policy or procedure—without influence from those with more self serving interest.

(Police Officer, Male, Hispanic, 42 years old, 20 years PO, 20 years LAPD, Chief when hired: Davis) (Figure 5.8)

#99

Top brass is very weak, they are afraid to make a choice in a tactical decision. The Chief was to quick to convict the Foothill police

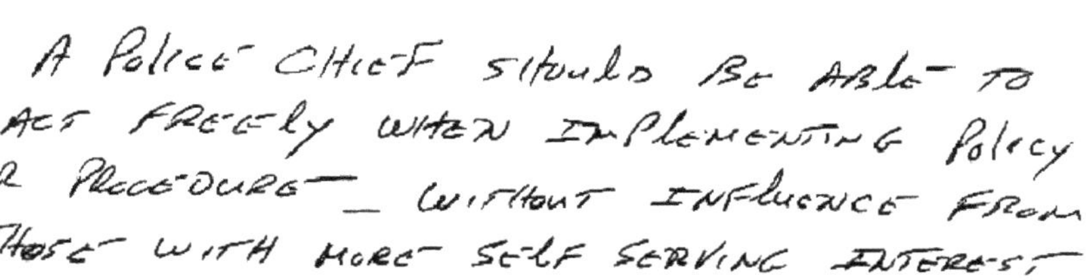
A Police Chief should Be Able to act freely when Implementing Policy or Procedure— without influence from those with more self serving interest

Figure 5.8 Statement Transcription: A police chief should be able to act freely when implementing policy or procedure—without influence from those with more self serving interest (see Officer Informant statement #98).

officers, He folded to the Mayor & the media, he should have fought for his troops like Sherman Block.

(Police Officer, Male, Caucasian, 30 years old, 8 years PO, 8 years LAPD, Chief when hired: Gates)

#100

Have the Chief run for his office with a city wide election this way the political hacks on the city council and in the Mayor's Office won't be able to spoil what once was the department in the country.

(Police Officer, Male, Caucasian, 39 years old, 18 years PO, 18 years LAPD, Chief when hired: Davis)

#101

City council + Mayor have destroyed the most efficient and effective police dept. in the world. They have never responded adequately to our needs to effectively police our growing populous and decaying society. Their priorities are self motivated and not in the best interest of all LA's citizens. The corruption in city government goes on—while we are made the sacrificial lamb for societies ills. Upper mgt. has perpetuated the disease for self-righteous reasons—"looking good" instead of telling a well meaning chief the truth. Chief, you entrusted the fate of the dept you love and are loyal to a group of mgrs loyal only to themselves, with little or no genuine interest in LAPD. They also used us as sacrificial lambs. Chief as your shepherd you entrusted our fate to the wolves. We are a political toy. Lets play the game fair. The demand + need for more police service has never been so great—so the city politicians talk "cut backs"—and we respond with a ploy called community based policing.

(Detective, Male, Caucasian, 56 years old, 33 years PO, 33 years LAPD, Chief when hired: Parker)

#102

It appears that our once proud department is buckling to political pressure from "special interest groups" and politicians trying to gain control in our operations. I never thought I would see the day when groups like Queer Nation could spit on a Los Angeles Police Officer and have that officer's hands tied because of fear by management of political fallout. Chief Gates, don't quit.

(Police Officer, Male, Caucasian, 35 years old, 10 years PO, 10 years LAPD, Chief when hired: Gates)

#103

This department no longer cares for officers or their personal problems. The management (capt & higher) only care about their own careers and personal goals not about the officers that are doing the real work. We are allowing the citizens to control & ruin the community!

(Detective, Male, Caucasian, 34 years old, 11 years PO, 11 years LAPD, Chief when hired: Gates)

Theme 2: If LAPD Buckles to Critics and Enemies, Crooks Will Rule the Streets

The second major theme discovered concerning outside attacks against the LAPD, as suggested by the officer comments, was that if the department should buckle to the demands of politicians and the like, the officer's ability to use aggressive police tactics against hard-core street hoodlums would be greatly compromised. This, in turn, would result in the professional model's thin blue line between law-abiding citizens and predatory criminals to crumble—resulting in rampant crime within the streets of Los Angeles.

#104

> Community racism not LAPD racism has made this dept ineffective in handling the major crime problem today....
>
> (Police Officer, Male, Caucasian, 33 years old, 4 years PO, 4 years LAPD, Chief when hired: Gates) (Figure 5.9)

#105

> We are catering to the squeaky wheel concept of citizen meetings in the Projects & Barrios. The vast majority of honest working stiffs could care less of MTG with police for coffee. They just expect honest police to put bad guys in jail. It could be that after "the special interest groups" have had their way for a few years & crime is running rampant the silent majority will beat on the doors of city hall demanding the return of good aggressive police work to again put the criminals in jail.
>
> (Police Officer, Male, Caucasian, 49 years old, 24 years PO, 24 years LAPD, Chief when hired: Reddin)

#106

> The biggest problem I see with personnel is accountability and fairness. The "doing more with less" system has become ridiculous. We need 2,000 police in uniform on the street or we are going to lose this city! LAPD has lost respect and mostly because upper level managers don't do anything but shuffle paper. Most don't know names of those who work for them because they never get out among them. We

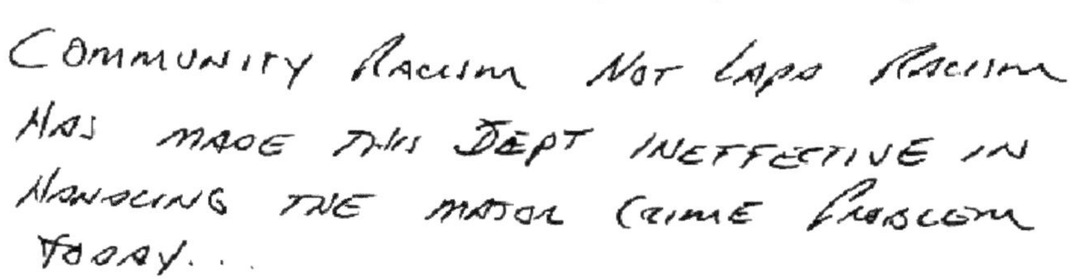

COMMUNITY RACISM NOT LAPD RACISM HAS MADE THIS DEPT INEFFECTIVE IN HANDLING THE MAJOR CRIME PROBLEM TODAY...

Figure 5.9 Statement Transcription: Community racism not LAPD racism has made this dept ineffective in handling the major crime problem today... (see Officer Informant statement #104).

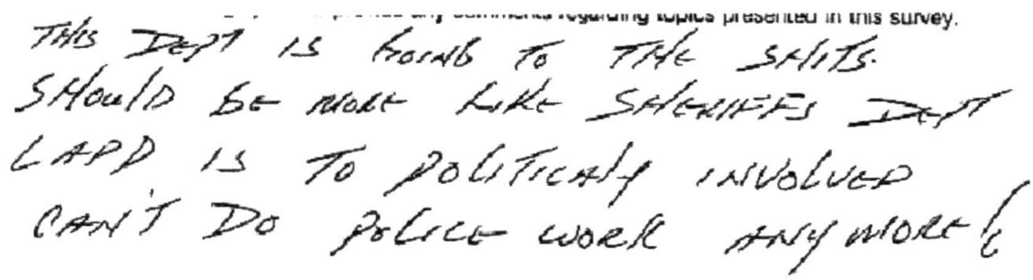
regarding topics presented in this survey.
THIS DEPT IS GOING TO THE SHITS.
SHOULD BE MORE LIKE SHERIFFS DEPT
LAPD IS TO POLITICALY INVOLVED
CAN'T DO POLICE WORK ANYMORE!

Figure 5.10 Statement Transcription: This Department is going to the shits. Should be more like [the Los Angeles] Sheriffs Dept. LAPD is to politically involved can't do police work anymore! (see Officer Informant statement #107).

should keep our standards high and not bow to political pressure. It is not the same as it was 15 years ago and it is going to be our downfall.

(Sergeant, Male, Caucasian, 43 years old, 22 years PO, 19 years LAPD, Chief when hired: Davis)

#107

This Dept is going to the shits. Should be more like Sheriffs Dept. LAPD is to politically involved can't do police work anymore!

(Police Officer, Male, Caucasian, 51 years old, 27 years PO, 27 years LAPD, Chief when hired: Parker) (Figure 5.10)

#108

The community is currently running the Dept & at present, between the "times," special interest groups (ACLU) community leaders & pressure groups, we have abandoned our pro active stance. We have lost Rampart Division. If we continue our present course of action we will become a police dept. like New York or Chicago. I have for 33 years been a proud member of the "thin blue line"! But believe my era is coming to a sad end. No longer is LAPD #1.

(Sergeant, Male, Caucasian, 55 years old, 33 years PO, 33 years LAPD, Chief when hired: Parker)

#109

In the Department's efforts to placate the Police Commission and other groups, it has forgotten that its sworn personnel is also made up of "citizens" who need to be treated fairly, with respect and professionalism. During this period of change, the ofcrs feel abandoned alienated and unjustly accused. Ultimately the public will suffer, but at least the officer who takes the crime report will be a friendly one.

(Police Officer, Male, Hispanic, 42 years old, 8 years PO, 8 years LAPD, Chief when hired: Gates)

#110

I think this dept. is making a big mistake catering to the wants of special interest groups (any groups). Quit trying to please these

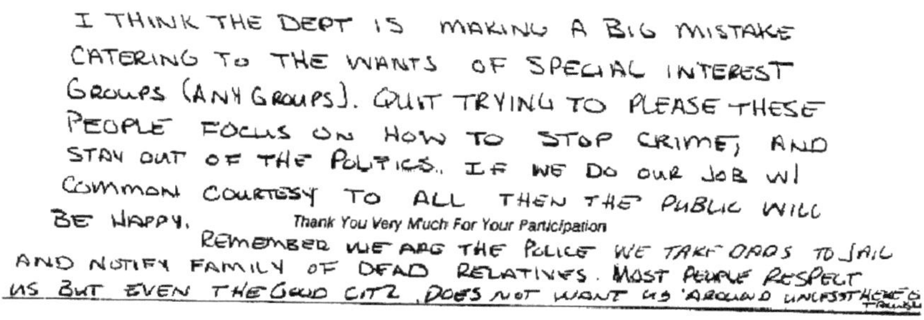
I THINK THE DEPT IS MAKING A BIG MISTAKE
CATERING TO THE WANTS OF SPECIAL INTEREST
GROUPS (ANY GROUPS). QUIT TRYING TO PLEASE THESE
PEOPLE FOCUS ON HOW TO STOP CRIME, AND
STAY OUT OF THE POLITICS. IF WE DO OUR JOB W/
COMMON COURTESY TO ALL THEN THE PUBLIC WILL
BE HAPPY.
Thank You Very Much For Your Participation
REMEMBER WE ARE THE POLICE WE TAKE DADS TO JAIL
AND NOTIFY FAMILY OF DEAD RELATIVES. MOST PEOPLE RESPECT
US BUT EVEN THE GOOD CITZ DOES NOT WANT US AROUND UNLESS THERE IS TROUBLE

Figure 5.11 Statement Transcription: I think this Department is making a big mistake catering to the wants of special interest groups (any groups). Quit trying to please these people. Focus on how to stop crime, and stay out of the politics. If we do our job w/ common courtesy to all then the public will be happy. Remember we are the police. We take dads to jail and notify family of dead relatives. Most people respect us but even the good citizen does not want us around unless there is trouble (see Officer Informant statement #110).

people. Focus on how to stop crime, and stay out of the politics. If we do our job w/ common courtesy to all then the public will be happy. Remember we are the police. We take dads to jail and notify family of dead relatives. Most people respect us but even the good citz does not want us around unless there is trouble.

(Police Officer, Male, Caucasian, 29 years old, 3 years PO, 3 years LAPD, Chief when hired: Gates) (Figure 5.11)

#111

You pack of clowns can fool some of the officers some of the time, etc. Get a job! Quit sucking political ass!

(Police Officer, Male, Caucasian, 40 years old, 18 years PO, 18 years LAPD, Chief when hired: Davis)

#112

Currently management is so worried about political forces and their own ass, they have forgotten about the street officer. Changes only come when they are forces on the Dept. It makes no difference if the proposed changes are good or bad. Why have we watched as LASO and LAPD narcotics officers go to jail and not made any changes? The Dept puts restrictions on vice tours, but not on narcotics positions? Our thinking is behind the times. Thirty years ago vice was the focal point of money. Today narcotics is where the money is. Wake up. This Department is moving to a complacent organization attempting to fight an active group of carrier criminals backed by civil rights activists. Both are going to get what they deserve.

(Sergeant, Male, Caucasian, 47 years old, 20 years PO, 20 years LAPD, Chief when hired: Davis)

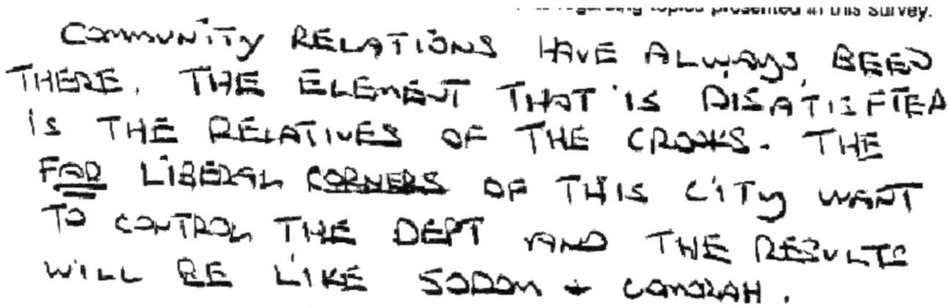
regarding topics presented in this survey.

COMMUNITY RELATIONS HAVE ALWAYS BEED THERE. THE ELEMENT THAT IS DISATISFIEA IS THE RELATIVES OF THE CROOKS. THE FAR LIBERAL CORNERS OF THIS CITY WANT TO CONTROL THE DEPT AND THE RESULTS WILL BE LIKE SODOM + GOMORAH.

Figure 5.12 Statement Transcription: Community relations have always been there. The element that is dissatisfied is the relatives of the crooks. The far liberal corners of this city want to control the dept and the results will be like Sodom & Gomorrah (see Officer Informant statement #113).

#113

Community relations have always been there. The element that is dissatisfied is the relatives of the crooks. The far liberal corners of this city want to control the dept and the results will be like Sodom & Gomorrah.

(Detective, Male, Caucasian, 46 years old, 25 years PO, 25 years LAPD, Chief when hired: Parker) (Figure 5.12)

#114

Our dept policy is becoming "kinder, gentler …" because of public citizen outcry. Some one … press or whoever has to inform bad guys to become kinder & gentler also. We are a reflection of some of societies problems—not the cause as many would like the public to believe.

(Police Officer, Female, Caucasian, 32 years old, 9 years PO, 9 years LAPD, Chief when hired: Gates) (Figure 5.13)

#115

They say that officers have an attitude of "us against them." In my opinion, officers have an attitude of the "police against the criminal element in our society." I can't remember in my 22 years of service with the

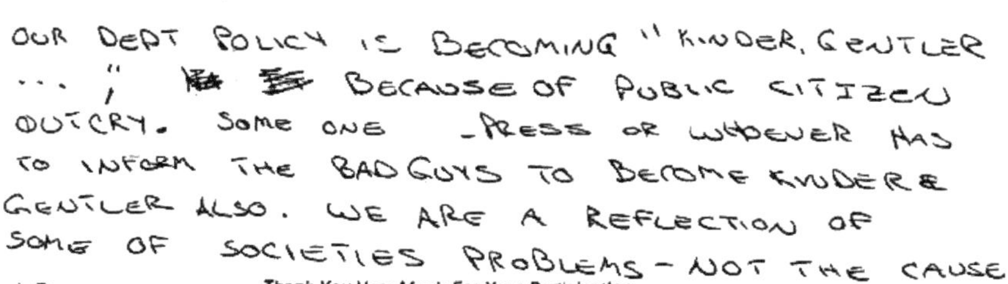
OUR DEPT POLICY IS BECOMING "KINDER, GENTLER ...," BECAUSE OF PUBLIC CITIZEN OUTCRY. SOME ONE -PRESS OR WHOEVER HAS TO INFORM THE BAD GUYS TO BECOME KINDER & GENTLER ALSO. WE ARE A REFLECTION OF SOME OF SOCIETIES PROBLEMS - NOT THE CAUSE AS MANY

Thank You Very Much For Your Participation

Figure 5.13 Statement Transcription: Our Department policy is becoming "kinder, gentler…" because of public citizen outcry. Someone… press or whoever has to inform bad guys to become kinder & gentler also. We are a reflection of some of society's problems—not the cause as many would like the public to believe (see Officer Informant statement #114).

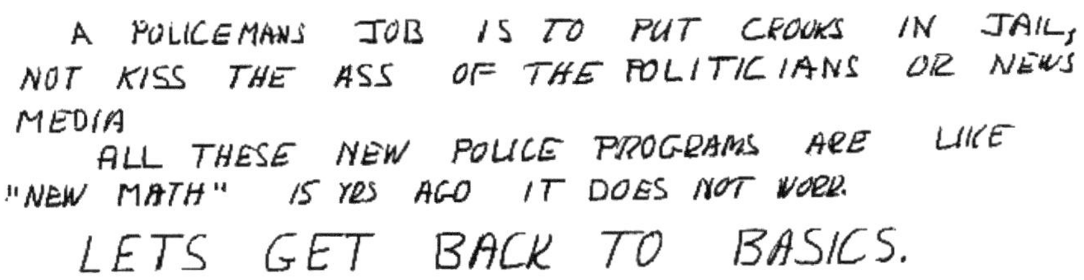
A POLICEMANS JOB IS TO PUT CROOKS IN JAIL,
NOT KISS THE ASS OF THE POLITICIANS OR NEWS
MEDIA
ALL THESE NEW POLICE PROGRAMS ARE LIKE
"NEW MATH" 15 YRS AGO IT DOES NOT WORK.
LETS GET BACK TO BASICS.

Figure 5.14 Statement Transcription: A policeman's job is to put crooks in jail, not kiss the ass of the politicians or new media. All these new police programs are like "new math" 15 years ago it does not work. LET'S GET BACK TO BASICS (see Officer Informant statement #116).

department when I personally felt it was me against the law abiding citizens in this city. However, I do have a problem with the criminal element that makes walking the streets of this city a living hell!!

(Detective, Male, Caucasian, 49 years old, 22 years PO, 22 years LAPD, Chief when hired: Davis)

#116

A policeman's job is to put crooks in jail, not kiss the ass of the politicians or news media. All these new police programs are like "new math" 15 years ago it does not work. LETS GET BACK TO BASICS.

(Police Officer, Female, Caucasian, 47 years old, 23 years PO, 23 years LAPD, Chief when hired: Reddin) (Figure 5.14)

#117

The problem is the dept cares too much about how the public & politicians view us not on what the officers have to deal with on a day by day basis. All the public wants is an officer to respond quickly and efficiently to his emergency call. Not to see the flowers in the station or coffee & donuts. He wants action. The admin of this dept have no idea what patrol officers go through only in books. The reality is in the field not in a book, if you want answers get quality officers, not quantity. And ask the citizens what they want out of our police force and they will tell you the same.

(Police Officer, Male, Hispanic, 26 years old, 13 years PO, 4 years LAPD, Chief when hired: Gates)

#118

There is too much inconsistency with command staff. On one has the guts to make a firm stand with issued concerning this dept. There is too much giving in to these self-appointed community leaders, lets make a stand and get the silent majority (of public) to voice support so we can get these little terrorists (gang members) out of here. It would be nice to go anywhere without worrying about being a victim! Note—lets not punish the whites on the job—lets all earn the position promoted to.

(Police Officer, Male, Caucasian, 27 years old, 7 years PO, 5 years LAPD, Chief when hired: Gates)

#119

LAPD's upper management is bowing to politicians & loud-mouthed prejudiced special interest group's interests & ignoring the safety needs of the patrol officer. Today's street cop has very little control over hard-core criminals due to various policies enacted which limits an office's ability to effectively control suspects & deal with fighting crime. The criminal is winning the war, not the police!

(Police Officer, Female, Asian, 35 years old, 6 years PO, 6 years LAPD, Chief when hired: Gates)

#120

There a few groups that do not want police ofcrs to do their job & that is to put criminals in jail. Those groups want to protect the rights of criminals & not Joe Blow czn. This contributes to job dissatisfaction. Also related is the read & likelihood I will be sued & poss lose everything I worked for because I am trying to do my job, in good faith. How can you expect morale to be high when I can lose my job, be sued & criminals get no time in jail, so why catch them. The City Council does not back us all they look for is their political ratings & don't care how they screw w/ police ofcrs life. Now I have also worry about pay cuts, health benefits cut. Question: Why do the working police ofcrs (patrol, the back-bone w/out us Admin wouldn't have jobs) get day off when Capts. & above don't & they are responsible for our training & acts?

(Police Officer, Male, Caucasian, 28 years old, 2 years PO, 2 years LAPD, Chief when hired: Gates)

#121

At my first opportunity to retire, I intend to do so and leave this cry baby, squabbling city and state. Have fun arguing out issues while society deteriorates from a basic lack of morality.

(Detective, Male, Caucasian, 40 years old, 17 years PO, 17 years LAPD, Chief when hired: Davis) (Figure 5.15)

#122

The Police Department is not the problem. Society is the problem. Society is on a course toward self-destruction. The citizens of the city of LA better wake up to the reality of what is occurring in this city!

(Sergeant, Male, Caucasian, 41 years old, 21 years PO, 21 years LAPD, Chief when hired: Davis)

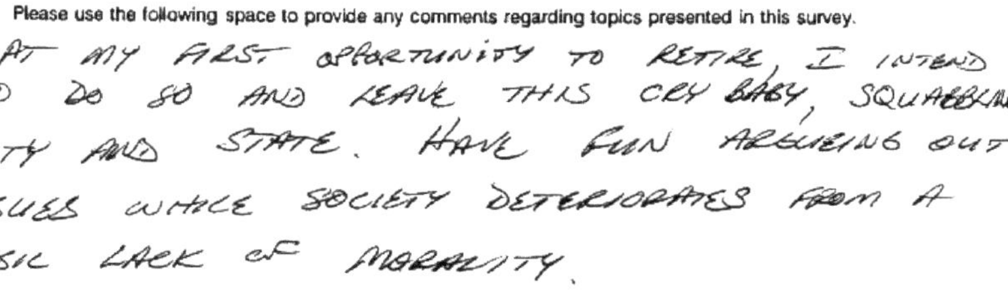
Please use the following space to provide any comments regarding topics presented in this survey.
AT MY FIRST OPPORTUNITY TO RETIRE, I INTEND TO DO SO AND LEAVE THIS CRY BABY, SQUABBLING CITY AND STATE. HAVE FUN ARGUING OUT ISSUES WHILE SOCIETY DETERIORATES FROM A BASIC LACK OF MORALITY.

Figure 5.15 Statement Transcription: At my first opportunity to retire, I intend to do so and leave this cry baby, squabbling city and state. Have fun arguing out issues while society deteriorates from a basic lack of morality (see Officer Informant statement #121).

#123

Most important issue to me: See that the criminal justice system through public outcry "puts away" the hard core criminals & keeps them away—then we can deal with the community issues & support factors cause we'll have the time—Hell! Were catchin the bastards over & over again—that's what is frustrating.

(Detective, Male, Caucasian, 45 years old, 24 years PO, 24 years LAPD, Chief when hired: Reddin) (Figure 5.16)

#124

It is very disturbing to have a relatively few squeaky wheels in the community, who are down on the Department, have so much impact on the Department. To listen to them, we can do nothing right and we are all racist. Obviously, this is not the majority vein. But the majority is silent on the issues and sooner or later begin to believe much of what the rabble rousers profess. The so called hearings on LAPD and LASO are so stacked and bias they are a joke. It is very demoralizing to see these small special interest groups dictate our

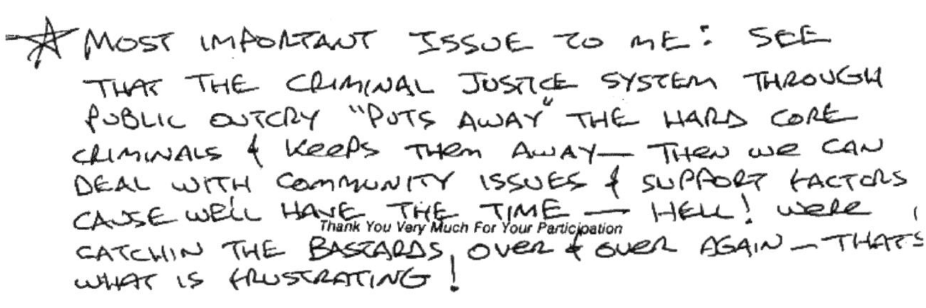
MOST IMPORTANT ISSUE TO ME: SEE THAT THE CRIMINAL JUSTICE SYSTEM THROUGH PUBLIC OUTCRY "PUTS AWAY" THE HARD CORE CRIMINALS & KEEPS THEM AWAY— THEN WE CAN DEAL WITH COMMUNITY ISSUES & SUPPORT FACTORS CAUSE WE'LL HAVE THE TIME — HELL! WERE CATCHIN THE BASTARDS, OVER & OVER AGAIN — THATS WHAT IS FRUSTRATING!
Thank You Very Much For Your Participation

Figure 5.16 Statement Transcription: Most important issue to me: See that the criminal justice system through public outcry "puts away" the hard core criminals & keeps them away—then we can deal with the community issues & support factors cause we'll have the time—Hell! Were catching the bastards over & over again—that's what is frustrating (see Officer Informant statement #123).

direction and destroy our reputation. I am no longer particularly proud to be a LAPD officer.

(Lieutenant, Male, Caucasian, 48 years old, 25 years PO, 25 years LAPD, Chief when hired: Parker)

Subtheme 2A: LAPD Will Become Like Other Large Police Departments

The following section contains a subtheme expressed by officers that if LAPD's style of policing was changed to that of a less aggressive, politically and community controlled model, the result would be changing the LAPD to a police department similar to that of the New York City Police Department or policing agencies in other large cities.

#125

In my 22 years of service, I have seen LAPD service going down the tubes. I feel sorry for the good people in this city. They deserve more. I grew up in New York and saw the decay of that city. I feel LA is going the same way. Politics and police don't mix.

(Detective, Male, Caucasian, 44 years old, 22 years PO, 22 years LAPD, Chief when hired: Davis)

#126

The dept has a freeze on promotions. Community policing is only a hore and pony show. Of course it would help our relations btwn the media & elected officials … we are a police dept, our job is the safety of our czns and ourselves. Not to kiss the butt of someone running for office. I don't want the LAPD to be like NYPD…. "Ofcr there goes the guy who robbed me" "Fine maam sign this report" We don't chase bad guys any more.

(Police Officer, Male, Caucasian, 30 years old, 7 years PO, 7 years LAPD, Chief when hired: Gates) (Figure 5.17)

#127

If this comment gets to anyone who cares, the managements politically motivated in-fighting and back stabbing have been driving this dept. down for several years. The mgmnt lack of emphasis and concern for field ofcrs has never been more evident. This is a very good dept. and your over reaction to every politically sensitive issue contributes more to public dissension than all our field ofcrs combined. Stop allowing the politicians and the media to manipulate you or we will soon become another New York City or Chicago or Miami. They've already lost their cities & they could never hire enough ofcrs to correct it. The City of New York has over 30,000 police ofcrs and they aren't even remotely close to controlling crime problems. This is a

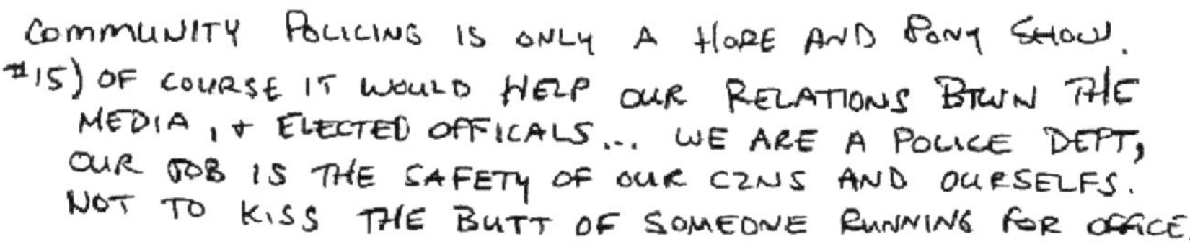
COMMUNITY POLICING IS ONLY A HORE AND PONY SHOW.
#15) OF COURSE IT WOULD HELP OUR RELATIONS BTWN THE MEDIA, & ELECTED OFFICALS... WE ARE A POLICE DEPT, OUR JOB IS THE SAFETY OF OUR CZNS AND OURSELFS. NOT TO KISS THE BUTT OF SOMEONE RUNNING FOR OFFICE.

Figure 5.17 Statement Transcription: Community policing is only a horse and pony show. Of course it would help our relations between the media & elected officials...we are a police Department, our job is the safety of our citizens and ourselves. Not to kiss the butt of someone running for office. I don't want the LAPD to be like NYPD..."Officer there goes the guy who robbed me" "Fine ma'am sign this report" We don't chase bad guys any more (see Officer Informant statement #126).

clear sign of overreaction. What difference is it if you have 8,000 ofcrs or 30,000 ofcrs if they are all handcuffed. My suggestion is fight the people (lawyers, politicians, etc) who choose to take advantage of this dept because you let them force you into over-reacting. Lawyers prompt ridiculous civil suits because the City and Dept. allows it. Politicians att to exploit and manipulate this dept. Management because they can easily force the "brass" into over-reaction. I'm not saying the dept. should not react, just don't over-react…. The lawyers are happy and making money on this City, the politicians are winning elections over this Dept. and the media falsely presents this Dept. to make money, and you, the brass have no supportive response, just over-reaction in the negative…. Special interest and minority groups have caused this dept. to alter policies and procedures and have even forced the dept. into selective non-enforcement of the laws that apply to everyone. What an embarrassing situation for any hard working law enforcement ofcr who wears any uniform, for any city, county or state when special interests are served by mgmnt for political harmony. Where does this special treatment for special interests and groups lead us—into chaos and corruption and dissension. The criminals and protesters alike are laughing at how easy it is to push the right buttons within the LAPD for personal gain. Wake up and stand up and be proud of this dept. because there is a lot to be proud of. Chief Gates, this is to remind you that a street ofcr cares about this dept, and as head of this Dept, wants you to take a stand for all of us.

(Police Officer, Male, Hispanic, 36 years old, 9 years PO, 9 years LAPD, Chief when hired: Gates)

#128

This department seems to have lost its direction & ideals that made it the best in the world. It is too caught up in the political arena.

It wants to please this group and that group instead of doing what it was created for protecting the good people of the city. Now the city wants community based police. Have these people in charge look at this, it does not work. All it does is give the criminals the feeling that police hands are more tied. All the people in charge have to do is look at Houston and New York where crime has increased 700% since they started community police.

(Police Officer, Male, Caucasian, 27 years old, 3 years PO, 3 years LAPD, Chief when hired: Gates)

#129

The community is currently running the Dept & at present, between the "times," special interest groups (ACLU) community leaders & pressure groups, we have abandoned our pro active stance. We have lost Rampart Division. If we continue our present course of action we will become a police dept. like New York or Chicago. I have for 33 years been a proud member of the "thin blue line"! But believe my era is coming to a sad end. No longer is LAPD #1.

(Sergeant, Male, Caucasian, 55 years old, 33 years PO, 33 years LAPD, Chief when hired: Parker)

#130

I see us losing efficiency and pride and sliding into big east coast city mediocrity in future years.

(Lieutenant, Male, Caucasian, 48 years old, 25 years PO, 25 years LAPD, Chief when hired: Parker)

Subtheme 2B: Officers Will Respond to Attacks by Working Less

The following comments, related to the general theme that attempts to change the LAPD's proactive policing style will have a negative impact on the community, suggest that officers may rebel against their attackers and the community by working less aggressively to control criminal activity. In addition, officers believe that they will think twice about making arrests for fear of being punished by the department or sued by suspects for violating new "get tough on cops" policies endorsed by politicians and the community.

#131

Officers don't quit LAPD. They just don't work when dissatisfied!

(Police Officer, Male, Caucasian, 47 years old, 24 years PO, 24 years LAPD, Chief when hired: Reddin) (Figure 5.18)

#132

Please stop being influenced by minority groups & civil right activists. People want protection and police won't enforce & work hard because they are afraid of administrative action. Admin. Action

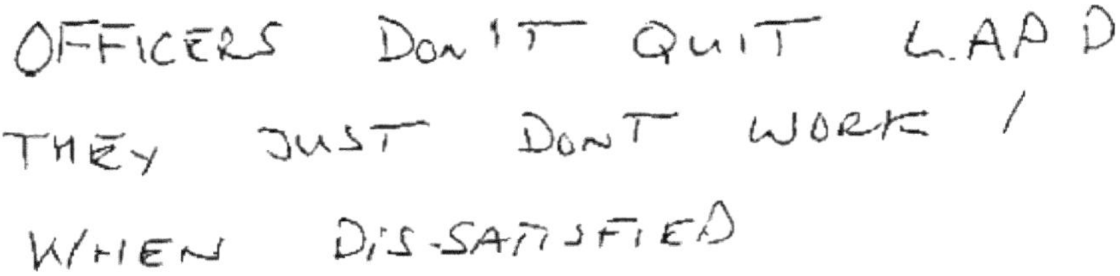
OFFICERS DON'T QUIT L.APD
THEY JUST DON'T WORK /
WHEN DIS-SATISFIED

Figure 5.18 Statement Transcription: Officers don't quit LAPD. They just don't work when dissatisfied! (see Officer Informant statement #131).

results from top management cowering to the press + small groups. This rolls down hill to Sgts + to finally police ofcrs.

(Police Officer, Male, Caucasian, 26 years old, 2 years PO, 2 years LAPD, Chief when hired: Gates)

#133

… Our department is stumbling over itself to please a mayor, council & commission that has no idea of what we're here for. Personal complaints are being taken for stupid things that are causing ofcrs to "pass up" arrests in order to stay out of trouble. We are constantly being second-guessed our experience means nothing. I don't like being in on the death of the once greatest police dept in the world.

(Police Officer, Male, Caucasian, 37 years old, 8 years PO, 8 years LAPD, Chief when hired: Gates)

#134

There a few groups that do not want police ofcrs to do their job & that is to put criminals in jail. Those groups want protect the rights of criminals & not Joe Blow czn. This contributes to job dissatisfaction. Also related is the read & likelihood I will be sued & poss lose everything I worked for because I am trying to do my job, in good faith. How can you expect morale to be high when I can lose my job, be sued & criminals get no time in jail, so why catch them. The City Council does not back us all they look for is their political ratings & don't care how they screw w/ police ofcrs life. Now I have also worry about pay cuts, health benefits cut. Question: Why do the working police ofcrs (patrol, the back-bone w/out us Admin wouldn't have jobs) get day off when Capts. & above don't & they are responsible for our training & acts?

(Police Officer, Male, Caucasian, 28 years old, 2 years PO, 2 years LAPD, Chief when hired: Gates)

#135

This dept discourages proactive police work—(so does the courts). It is easier to just kick back and stay out of trouble than it is to try to "hustle" and stop potential criminals. That only brings law suits for harassment. This dept abandons you when you face civil suits. I disagree w/the way this dept allowed a group (mob) of demonstrators (gay rights) to get out of hand—every officer looked foolish for just standing by. The criminals love the way they can challenge us now they know we're helpless. I've been challenged over twice as much as a year ago.

(Police Officer, Male, Caucasian, 28 years old, 7 years PO, 7 years LAPD, Chief when hired: Gates)

#136

We need to have contact with the community. We need to be sensitive to their needs, but at the same time, they need to be sensitive to ours. Most citizens don't understand what this job entails. We need to communicate with them more & maybe they can understand why we handle situations the way we do. In turn, they may become more satisfied with the LAPD. The more pressure we officers get from supervisors, citizens & the Christopher Commission, the less work we will do. Most ofcrs feel if they get involved & things go sideways, they will receive no support from citizens or the dept. The end result "Don't get involved." Therefore, there is a reduction in good police work.

(Police Officer, Female, Caucasian, 26 years old, 3 years PO, 3 years LAPD, Chief when hired: Gates)

#137

I joined LAPD almost 22 years ago because it was the #1 department and because other people look up and respected the LAPD as a department. Now the tide has changed and we are now the laughing stock of the majority of the citizens I come into contact with. I am constantly asked by the citizens "why we bow to pressure of media and special interest groups"—and asked by officers of other departments why our dept management doesn't back the field troops. LAPD has bowed to pressure by advancing less qualified personnel because of race or sex and putting qualifications on the back burner. This department is quickly falling to the whims of special interest groups and the public in general will be the ones to suffer from this in the long run. The job of being an LAPD officer used to be fun and rewarding—Now it's just the opposite. It's a chore to come to work and I take as much time off as I can so I won't have to be here.

(Police Officer, Male, Caucasian, 44 years old, 22 years PO, 22 years LAPD, Chief when hired: Davis)

#138

The field ofcrs morale is very low. The ofcrs are scared to perform their duties because of the current situation. Give credit to the patrol ofcrs and let the field Supv do their job instead of sitting in the office completing 181s. They need to be in the street making sure the ofcrs are performing their duties....

(Police Officer, Female, African American, 28 years old, 4 years PO, 4 years LAPD, Chief when hired: Gates)

#139

... Ofcrs are scared to work, to get involved & will be in this state until our community realizes that we cannot effectively work until they back off and stop yelling police brutality every time an arrest is made.

(Police Officer, Male, Hispanic, 39 years old, 3 years PO, 3 years LAPD, Chief when hired: Gates)

#140

I know of at least (6) members of LAPD that are or have switched to another police dept due to the work ethic of their fellow officers. Other officers not doing their job specifically in patrol functions.

(Detective, Male, Caucasian, 32 years old, 7 years PO, 7 years LAPD, Chief when hired: Gates)

#141

Imagine you are a fireman sent to Mr. Smith's house. You get there + see flames from the home. As you run up w/your axe & hose Mr. Smith stops you. He tells you you cannot leave mud or ashes on the rug, no water damage, + if you must punch a hole in the roof it cant be over 6" diameter. If, after you've extinguished the fire, Smith finds ashes on the carpet, he tells you he'll complain + suspend you for three days without pay &/or sue you—Has Smith's unreasonable rule done anything to destroy your motivation to put out Smith's fire? Welcome to the LAPD. Community must realize as should administrators remember, that fighting crime is a dirty, messy business. Either allow officers to do the duty, or suffer the consequences. Like sheep, the community must place their trust in the shepherd + dogs. They have no expertise to police themselves. If the sheep don't want us then send in the wolves—they never bothered me!

(Police Officer, Male, Caucasian, 34 years old, 12 years PO, 12 years LAPD, Chief when hired: Gates)

Theme Analysis

Both of the above main themes presented above clearly indicated that the LAPD's normal internal organizational functioning was disrupted by political and other pressures calling for the department's reform following the King incident. Officer statements repeatedly echoed feelings of disdain for and distrust of external critics of the department, such as Mayor Tom Bradley, the Los Angeles City Council members, the ACLU, special interest groups, and outspoken members of the community. Specifically, the officers felt that external efforts to transform the department's proactive policing style into a less aggressive community-based approach were coming to fruition because the LAPD's upper administrators failed to fight back against their political adversaries. Officers also felt that the Christopher Commission's recommendations for the department's reform were misguided and inaccurate. They believed that implementation of the commission's suggested changes would have catastrophic effects on the ability of the LAPD to provide adequate protection for citizen crime and that eventually criminals would gain the upper hand over police. Some officers predicted that they would be less willing to make arrests as a result of recent politically motivated changes affecting the LAPD's ability to function autonomously without external oversight by civilians. Additionally, concerns were expressed over LAPD becoming a larger, more bureaucratic agency similar to those police departments in other major U.S. cities. (Ironically, some officers feared the LAPD would become like NYPD—little did they know that William Bratton from the NYPD would eventually become their chief.)

Perhaps the most significant finding was a subtheme suggesting that LAPD Chief Gates was responding to political pressure from outside of the department. This, more than any other finding, suggested that the LAPD's ability to shield itself from outside influences had indeed weakened. Never before in the history of LAPD's wrangling with political adversaries had the department's chief been "up against the ropes and down for the count." However, in this instance, officer comments suggested that Gates was so overpowered by his opponents that he was willing to make compromises that involved softening the hard-lined policing approach of the professional model. Ostensibly, it appears the answer to the question "Did the LAPD's opponents grow stronger or the department grow weaker?" is most likely twofold: yes, the strength of opponents was greater than in the past; and yes, the department could not defend itself to the degree it had when attacked by politicians in previous years.

Conclusion

It can be concluded with relative certainty that politically motivated attacks from outside of the LAPD were a cause of the organization's meltdown. However, there is reason to believe that this cause was not the only one to produce the department-wide organizational breakdown. In fact, it may not even be the primary cause. However, some preliminary conclusions can be drawn at this stage of the study based on the above findings. Specifically, these can be found by comparing the department's experience with the

McCone Commission under the direction of Chief Parker with that of the Christopher Commission while Chief Gates was in command.

As previously stated, the department stood its political ground against McCone but could not against Christopher. Why did this happen? First, the politicos leading the charge against the LAPD grew much stronger in their methods of attack through building on their past experiences attempting to break through the department's political barrier. Two cases in point support this conclusion: (1) The head of the Christopher Commission (Warren Christopher) played a central role in the preparation of the McCone Commission report some 25 years prior to the King incident; (2) Mayor Tom Bradley was extremely knowledgeable about the LAPD's internal weaknesses based on his two decades of experience as an LAPD police officer. The combined political know-how of these two individuals regarding how to reform the LAPD was quantum leaps beyond that possessed by the entire McCone Commission following the 1965 Watts riots.

Second, it can be concluded that Chief Parker was much more effective than Chief Gates at protecting the LAPD from its political enemies. It is well known that Parker protected the department from political attack by gathering intelligence on politicians. Gates, on the other hand, used a more direct approach by meeting politicians head on in the media. As this study's findings suggest, Gates' strategies to repel political challenges were eventually rendered ineffective. Unlike Parker, who was an unbreakable first line of defense for the LAPD against the McCone Commission, and then LA Mayor Yorty, Gates was unable to "hold the line" against the Christopher Commission and Mayor Tom Bradley. But, was Chief Gates the weak link that caused the organizational meltdown of the LAPD? Likewise, did Gates' inability to maintain the department's long-standing barrier against political intrusion result in the ultimate abandonment of the professional model of policing?

Based on the findings revealed in this chapter, the answers to the above questions must be no, or at least not by himself; in other words, it is here concluded that having a strong chief of police alone (such as Parker) is not enough to insulate a policing agency operating under the professional model from internal meltdown caused by external political challenges. This conclusion is based on the majority of officer comments suggesting that they had their pride in and loyalty to the LAPD organization. For these deep feelings of rejection to occur among police officers, something much greater than a weak chief of police must have been operating within the department's organizational culture. Thus, based on this finding alone, the final conclusion is that although outside politics against the department grew stronger and weaknesses in the department let them pass through to the inside of the organization, some much more potent factor caused the spirit of these external challenges to take root within the LAPD organizational culture and its officers.

References

1. R.J. Sonenshein. *Politics in Black and White: Race and Power in Los Angeles.* Princeton, NJ: Princeton University Press, 1993.
2. Ibid.
3. Christopher Commission. *Report of the Independent Commission of the Los Angeles Police Department.* Los Angeles, CA: LAPD, 1991.
4. Personal interview with anonymous informant. Conducted June 2011.
5. Personal interview with anonymous informant. Conducted August 2011.
6. Telephonic interview with anonymous informant. Conducted December 2011.
7. Robert Fogelson. *Big-City Police.* Cambridge, MA: Harvard University Press, 1977.

6 Hiring, Promotions, and Affirmative Action

It is quite possible that the seeds of LAPD's meltdown and the death of the professional model were planted inside the department over a decade before the King incident. This contention is supported by a second main cause identified within the statements of officers represented in this study: extreme discontent with the department's hiring and promotion practices. The majority of comments addressing this potential cause of the meltdown indicated that the ability of the LAPD to sustain its aggressive policing standards as well as to recruit and promote the most qualified officers had been severely compromised by legal action in the early 1980s that radically altered the department's personnel standards. Specifically, these mandated changes required the LAPD to practice affirmative action in the hiring and promotion of women and minority officers. The primary source of these aforementioned changes was an employment discrimination lawsuit filed against the department by one of its veteran female officers, Sergeant Fanchon Blake.[1]

In 1973, Sergeant Blake filed a civil suit against LAPD alleging that the department's hiring and promotional policies discriminated against women and minorities. Blake's allegations were based on two key arguments. First, the department's height requirement of 5'6" or more for women to be hired as an officer unfairly excluded the majority of women in the U.S. workforce, especially those belonging to certain minority groups. The LAPD counter-defended its need to higher taller women as a necessity for the job of police officer, arguing that shorter females would not be able to see over fences or above crowded areas. The second argument was based on a long-standing promotional policy placing job restrictions on female officers, which stemmed as far back as the Parker era—but was vehemently enforced with Blake by her chief, Ed Davis. The policy prohibited women from promoting above the rank of sergeant and was used to deny Sergeant Blake from sitting for the lieutenants' exam. In addition to limiting promotional opportunities for women, the department did not permit female officers to engage in regular patrol duties and relegated them to duties such as clerical work, communications, jail matrons, and handling juvenile and sex crimes. Gender divisions in the duties of male and female officers were also clearly evident in the officers' uniforms as well. Females wore skirts, heeled shoes, and carried their service revolvers in a purse rather than in a holster. However, the most telling officer gender differences were the LAPD's shield badges: Female officers' badges read "Police Woman" and male officers' badges read "Police Man." These badges were changed in 1974 to the gender-neutral title of "Police Officer" for both men and women. Ironically, this change came just one year after Blake initiated her legal action against the department.[2]

In 1981, approximately 10 years preceding the collection of data for this study, courts handed down a consent decree against the LAPD as the result of Sergeant Blake's lawsuit that was signed by then Chief Gates. (Ex-Chief Davis later commented that he, unlike Gates, would never have signed the decree.) The court order changed the LAPD height requirement to 5' for women and required the department to make various sweeping changes in hiring standards for sworn officers in order to correct for past discriminatory hiring practices against women—and also extended the mandates of the consent decree to minority police recruits. Most profound among these was the new requirement that 20% of LAPD's sworn officers must be women and that the percentages of Latino, African-American, and Asian officers on the force had to match the percentages of these minority groups within the general population of the Los Angeles City workforce. This meant it was necessary to double the number of minority officers serving in the department (from 18% to 31%), and to increase the ranks of female officers by nearly 10 times that of the predecree level (from 2.6% to 20%). To meet these court-imposed hiring quotas, the department was required to embark on an aggressive hiring program to attract and retain women and minority officer recruits.[3] The following statement from an LAPD informant reflects how the Blake consent decree impacted the LAPD's existing hiring practices:

> ... If you were a white male your chances of getting hired after the decree were slim to none. We had no say in who got hired. It was all about meeting the quotas. If you were a minority and a female they were the biggest catch. You could meet two of the quotas, the one for the minority and the one for the female with them. We had all kinds of special programs for them to pass the tests and make sure they stayed on the job. Hell, we basically pinned a badge on them before they went to the academy. On the oral exams, if you were a woman or minority, you could get hired on the spot with a really low score—I think you could get in with a 65 out of 100. If you were a white guy, I think you needed a score something like 115 out of 100. You needed to get a perfect score of 100 on the oral and also needed an extra 15 points for having military experience. It was that bad![4]

In contrast to the above observation, another LAPD informant expressed support for the changes imposed on the department's hiring procedures following the Blake consent decree:

> … The hiring process in this department before [the decree] was extremely selective and "inbred." If you were a woman or not white you had to meet the standards of a particular "mold" the department would have for non-whites or non-males. Women had to be the "men are always first" types and minorities had to be the "yes, sir" types. If you weren't that way when they hired you, you either got that way by them molding you on the job or you were forced to quit the department. The decree is great because it breaks the inbreeding. It forced the department to bring in new blood. The types of recruits that can speak their own voice without being afraid to be shut down by the good ol' boys … the fact that women and minorities were hired with lower scores on orals meant nothing. The oral process is totally subjective, and if you weren't the type of woman or minority they liked, they'd find some reason to give you a low score anyway so they wouldn't have to hire you. This LAPD would have never changed its ways without the decree changing who got hired.[5]

Another change imposed by the Blake decree was the removal of the prior promotional and job restrictions the department had imposed on female officers. This meant that female officers were to be provided full opportunities to promote beyond the rank of sergeant and have work assignments and provisions no different than those afforded to male officers. In addition, certain benefits were afforded to women and minorities in the promotional process by the decree. As the following LAPD informant points out, this provision of the decree might have been the most contentious when it came to the existing (majority male Caucasian) rank-and-file officers' acceptance of the new affirmative action standards placed on the department:

> … The promotional process was totally unfair after the decree. White males got passed up every time for women and other races to get the job. If you were in line for a job competing against them you might as well forget it![6]

Conversely, as the following LAPD minority female officer informant points out, the promotional process prior to the Blake decree was fundamentally flawed and required a serious overhaul as that provided by the court-mandated promotional changes imposed on the department:

> … Could you imagine what it would be like to try and get a fair promotion if you were a minority officer, let alone a woman, after the courts pushed this whole affirmative action hiring rule down the department's throat! No way. They would have hired you all right, but there would be no way that they were going to promote you.[7]

The promotional process following the Blake decree was done by the department in what is referred to as a banding process. When officers are eligible to promote from one rank to the next, they take promotional exams on which they are given a score. Officers are then placed in a band consisting of all other officers obtaining the same exam scores. It is the selection of which officers from a particular band that will ultimately receive a promotion that is the primary point of contention with the promotional process following the Blake decree. Among the factors that could be considered when selecting a particular officer from a specific promotional band would be the officer's level of experience and the officer's gender and race. In an effort to meet quotas established by the Blake decree, under the latter system, it would be possible for a less experienced woman or minority officer to be promoted ahead of a more experienced male nonminority officer. Officers not receiving promotions they felt they deserved, and who did not belong to "protected race and gender classes" under the LAPD's new promotional standards, shared a common belief that such practice was in effect a form of "reverse discrimination."

Possible Explanations

There are two possible explanations or outcomes that were likely to result from the increased hiring of women and minority officers within the LAPD following the Blake consent decree. The first can be referred to as the conformity explanation and the second as the individual identity explanation. These perspectives and their likely relationship to the LAPD organizational meltdown are explained below.

The Conformity Explanation

If the professional model was still well intact during the time period of this study (about 10 years following the Blake decision), the infusion of more "protected class" officers into the existing organizational environment would perhaps have little effect on changing the established LAPD policing culture. In other words, the professional model would serve to socialize these new officers, regardless of their race and gender identities, into conforming to the established methods of policing espoused by the existing organizational culture. Thus, if the hiring and promotional standards of the department were perceived as biased and unfair, this general feeling would be expressed by officers who were both older and newer hires regardless of their gender or race. In other words, officers hired under the special provision of the Blake decree would be expected to refrain from voicing their opinion about the department's employment practices from the viewpoint of their individual identities. Rather, they would speak in one voice along with the older officers who had served as their mentors in learning the LAPD's professional model of policing—in other words, espousing the notion that "all LAPD officers come in only one color, Blue."

The Individual Identity Explanation

Alternatively, the professional model may have been so weakened by radical employment changes introduced inside the department by the Blake decree that it was unable to serve as a socializing agent for new incoming officers hired under race and gender quotas. If this were indeed the case, the individual personal identities of women and minority officers may have remained intact despite efforts made within LAPD's traditional organizational policing to resocialize them. In effect, these officers would show signs of rebellion against the department's old officer guard. Concomitantly, they may also express viewpoints toward the police role that reflect their unique individual identities, which were formulated prior to becoming an LAPD officer, and perhaps create their own officer cliques or subcultures. In regard to changes in promotion and hiring practices, the individual identity explanation would be supported by officer attitudes affirming the need to change the department's employment standards to protect against possible race or gender bias that existed under the traditional LAPD organizational policing culture. However, this explanation also predicts that significant divisions between officers may be created along race and gender lines. In other words, nonminority male officers adhering to the department's older organizational cultural values are likely to be at odds with minority or female officers over the role of affirmative action in the LAPD's post-Blake hiring and promotional standards. In short, officer comments supporting the individual identity explanation would express the general notion that "LAPD officers come in different shades of the color Blue."[8]

Officer Statements and Themes

Rather than identify specific themes among all officers regarding attitudes toward LAPD's hiring and promotional standards, officer statements are presented below separated by race and gender. This was done for two reasons. First, many officers provided comments that expressed multiple themes regarding LAPD's affirmative action policies, making it difficult to place a particular comment within a specific theme category. Second, a comparison of comments in this manner enables a more clear identification of race and gender differences between officers' observations of the department's hiring and promotional practices. The examination of specific themes expressed across all officer interviews provided here will be addressed in the "Theme Analysis" section that follows.

Nonminority Male Officers

#142

Affirmative action is bull!! Hire the best person for the job regardless of color or sex. Requiring one race to have higher oral scores to get into the academy is discriminatory. Lowering the percentage that written test scores will count (so that less deserving people can be given an oral score which will allow them to promote) is unfair….

(Police Officer, Male, Caucasian, 28 years old, 5 years PO, 5 years LAPD, Chief when hired: Gates) (Figure 6.1)

#143

The new consent decree is an insult to the once high standard the LAPD enjoyed. It also sent a message to all non minority officers that the good work that we have done means nothing and that our services are no longer needed. We have lowered our standards to the lowest level and we and the citizens will soon see the proof we will pay for this political foolishness. The top ranks of this Department have rolled over and played dead on this issue and in so doing lost the support of non minority officers. This issue has split the Department into ethnic camps and we will see others getting hurt in the field because of this. We used to say LAPD only came in one color, "Blue," now color and gender matter more than anything else. We let the politicians and the courts destroy years of good work, now we will see a bail out of qualified officers leave this Department because they

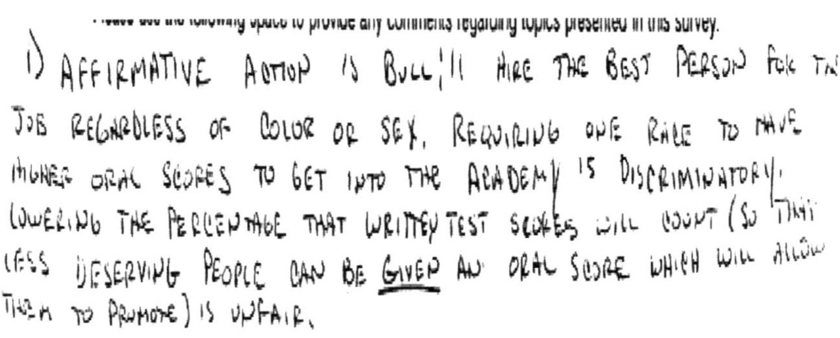

1) AFFIRMATIVE ACTION IS BULL!!! HIRE THE BEST PERSON FOR THE JOB REGARDLESS OF COLOR OR SEX. REQUIRING ONE RACE TO HAVE HIGHER ORAL SCORES TO GET INTO THE ACADEMY IS DISCRIMINATORY. LOWERING THE PERCENTAGE THAT WRITTEN TEST SCORES WILL COUNT (SO THAT LESS DESERVING PEOPLE CAN BE GIVEN AN ORAL SCORE WHICH WILL ALLOW THEM TO PROMOTE) IS UNFAIR.

Figure 6.1 Statement Transcription: Affirmative action is bull!! Hire the best person for the job regardless of color or sex. Requiring one race to have higher oral scores to get into the academy is discriminatory. Lowing the percentage that written test scores will count (so that less deserving people can be given an oral score which will allow them to promote) is unfair (see Officer Informant statement #142).

are ashamed to wear the uniform … they are white males and no longer needed or wanted.

(Sergeant, Male, Caucasian, 39 years old, 14 years PO, 11 years LAPD, Chief when hired: Gates)

#144

Here's a new idea for promotion (this is not a joke Chief Gates). Let's put seniority & affirmative action in an equal standing with job performance/experience instead of Seniority #1…. This dept/city is going to run itself into the ground with their current promotional mentality.

(Detective, Male, Caucasian, 40 years old, 15 years PO, 15 years LAPD, Chief when hired: Davis)

#145

I strongly feel that in our civil service duties that we owe the public the best service available regardless of race or gender. The most qualified should be promoted….

(Detective, Male, Caucasian, 49 years old, 26 years PO, 26 years LAPD, Chief when hired: Parker)

#146

The dept can scrap the stupid & racist affirmative action programs which have degraded the past pride & effectiveness of this dept. The hiring practices of this dept are racist & nonproductive. The leadership of this dept has no guts & seem to spend their time stabbing each other in the back for promotion. The greatest pride in my life is my family & the LAPD. The City is taking my pride in this dept and slowly destroying it. Get rid of the current Mayor.

(Police Officer, Male, Caucasian, 41 years old, 20 years PO, 20 years LAPD, Chief when hired: Davis) (Figure 6.2)

#147

We are hiring ofcrs who are more concerned w/their personal needs than fighting crime. We promote supvs s/ vast admin background, often limited field/special unit experience. We are eliminating proactive, crime fighting units & philosophy for prevention. Prevention is important but should not be the primary focus. Our younger ofcrs are complacent, unprofessional & I'm glad I don't have to work w/ most of them. Racism is destroying our dept; white vs. black and black vs. white. There are many black ofcrs on our dept who are racist.

(Sergeant, Male, Caucasian, 40 years old, 18 years PO, 15 years LAPD, Chief when hired: Davis)

#148

This department is pushing the promotion of minority officers so much that they are the chosen people in this organization. I know several minorities that brag about being sent to specialized management

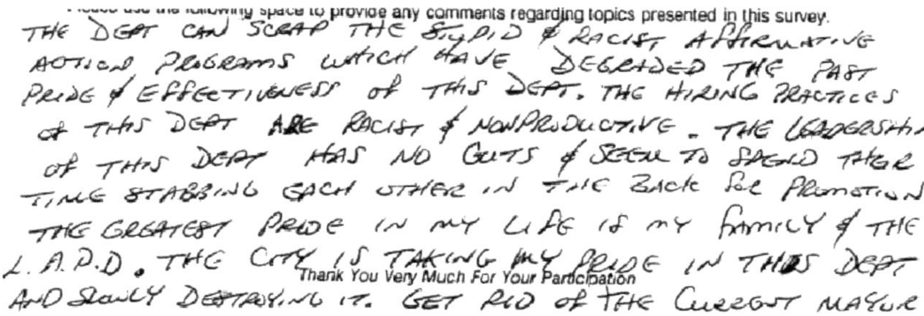
provide any comments regarding topics presented in this survey.
THE DEPT CAN SCRAP THE STUPID & RACIST AFFIRMATIVE
ACTION PROGRAMS WHICH HAVE DEGRADED THE PAST
PRIDE & EFFECTIVENESS OF THIS DEPT. THE HIRING PRACTICES
OF THIS DEPT ARE RACIST & NONPRODUCTIVE. THE LEADERSHIP
OF THIS DEPT HAS NO GUTS & SEEM TO SPEND THEIR
TIME STABBING EACH OTHER IN THE BACK FOR PROMOTION.
THE GREATEST PRIDE IN MY LIFE IS MY FAMILY & THE
L.A.P.D. THE CITY IS TAKING MY PRIDE IN THIS DEPT
Thank You Very Much For Your Participation
AND SLOWLY DESTROYING IT. GET RID OF THE CURRENT MAYOR.

Figure 6.2 Statement Transcription: The Department can scrap the stupid & racist affirmative action programs which have degraded the past pride & effectiveness of this Department. The hiring practices of this Department are racist & nonproductive. The leadership of this Department has not guts & seem to spend their time stabbing each other in the back for promotion. The greatest pride in my life is my family & the LAPD. The City is taking my pride in this dept and slowly destroying it. Get rid of the current Mayor [Bradley] (see Officer Informant statement #146).

school because of their color. White officers are being passed over for specialized assignments because they are white. Unqualified minority officers without qualifications are selected instead. Training officers and the academy are unable to fire unqualified officers particularly minorities because the department is afraid someone will scream racism. This department accepts minorities with very low entrance exam scores and places the people with low scores ahead of people with much higher scores. I'm sick of the attitude of the high management of this department. You've run this job into the ground with the lack of support.

(Detective, Male Caucasian, 38 years old, 18 years PO, 18 years LAPD, Chief when hired: Davis)

#149

P-3 [highest patrol officer pay grade] orals are a joke. The patrol captains know well in advance who they want as P-3! Promotions to P-3 on "Affirm Action" is bull. P-3 promotions stink & are based on favoritism & race. If you're white, forget being promoted. Bilingual pay should stay with the officer upon being transferred. We need more positions! DARE? Its interesting to read about gang violence homicides rising from 200 in 1981 to 700 in 1991. Isn't DARE supposed to be working on reduction of gangs? Crime statistics, civilianize this. We need more cops in uniform in the field. We need better MDTs & rovers! Affirmative action has escalated to the point of reverse discrimination!

(Police Officer, Male, Caucasian, 48 years old, 22 years PO, 22 years LAPD, Chief when hired: Davis)

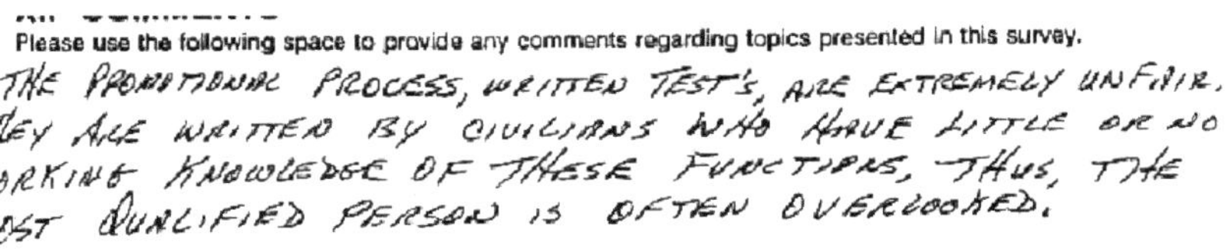
Please use the following space to provide any comments regarding topics presented in this survey.

THE PROMOTIONAL PROCESS, WRITTEN TEST'S, ARE EXTREMELY UNFAIR. THEY ARE WRITTEN BY CIVILIANS WHO HAVE LITTLE OR NO WORKING KNOWLEDGE OF THESE FUNCTIONS, THUS, THE MOST QUALIFIED PERSON IS OFTEN OVERLOOKED.

Figure 6.3 Statement Transcription: The promotional process, written test's, are extremely unfair. They are written by civilians who have little or no working knowledge of these functions, thus, the most qualified person is often overlooked (see Officer Informant statement #150).

#150

The promotional process, written tests, are extremely unfair. They are written by civilians who have little or no working knowledge of these functions, thus, the most qualified person is often overlooked.

(Police Officer, Male, Caucasian, 43 years old, 16 years PO, 16 years LAPD, Chief when hired: Davis) (Figure 6.3)

#151

Morale is bad enough. So why does this department treat its white male officers as evil? Be fair and equal to everyone except white males. Let's strive to treat everyone for any position fairly. The most qualified get the job rather than we don't have a minority so get one. The leadership of this department should stop kissing everyone's ass so everyone will like us. That's not our job. We put bad guys in jail to protect & serve the public, that's our job. So let's stop making excuses to everyone, and do our job.

(Sergeant, Male, Caucasian, 43 years old, 20 years PO, 20 years LAPD, Chief when hired: Davis)

#152

LAPD was born from an agency with good morale and reputation to just another polyglot PD hiring and promoting everyone who alleges to be a minority. Every personnel decision is racially motivated. Good officers see no real chance for promotion….

(Police Officer, Male, Caucasian, 51 years old, 22 years PO, 22 years LAPD, Chief when hired: Davis)

#153

When do you think this department will start hiring people with brains, guts and integrity!!

(Detective, Male, Caucasian, 45 years old, 23 years PO, 23 years LAPD, Chief when hired: Reddin) (Figure 6.4)

#154

This department is not allowing officers to have a sense of humor. The department is not backing the officers in the field as it should.

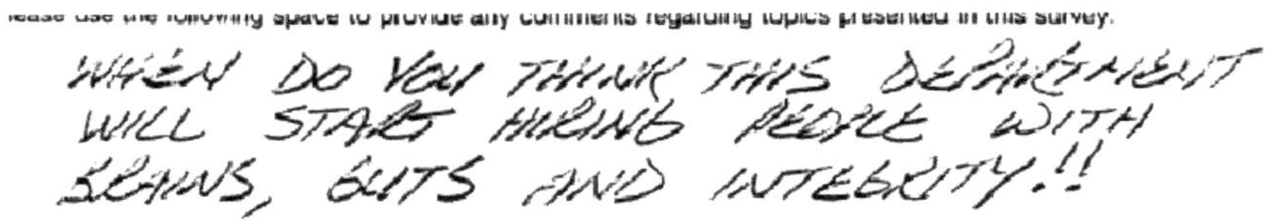
lease use the following space to provide any comments regarding topics presented in this survey.

WHEN DO YOU THINK THIS DEPARTMENT WILL START HIRING PEOPLE WITH BRAINS, GUTS AND INTEGRITY.!!

Figure 6.4 Statement Transcription: When do you think this department will start hiring people with brains, guts and integrity!! (see Officer Informant statement #153).

Everything is becoming a political issue. It's mind over matter—the department doesn't mind & the officer doesn't matter. Affirmative action is reverse discrimination. The hiring practices are favoring minorities. A minority only needs 70% oral to be hired. A male white needs at least a 95% oral. Being passed over for promotion because an officer doesn't speak Spanish is not fair. This is America and the language of this country is English.

(Police Officer, Male, Caucasian, 45 years old, 17 years PO, 17 years LAPD, Chief when hired: Davis)

#155

Crime increase, violence towards officers, lack of support from community & elected officials & gross racial discrimination (towards promotions) increasing against white males is very alarming—will probably cause me to retire sooner than I originally planned—I can see it's going to get a lot worse before it gets better. Also, I see officers not backing-up assisting other officers in dangerous situations, repeatedly.

(Police Officer, Male, Caucasian, 45 years old, 20 years PO, 20 years LAPD, Chief when hired: Davis)

#156

The quality of recruits on the job during the past 5 years has and continues to be going down hill. The department is too concerned with hiring the right amount minorities/women instead of the most qualified person for the job. The news media rpts that we should hire more women since they are "less likely to become aggressive & become involved in excessive force." This is true, but on the other hand—the majority of women patrol ofcrs that I have seen in action fail to take the initiative in most situations that involve 415 [public disturbance/fighting in public] susps. Foot pursuits and situations where it may involve a confrontation of some sort. I've seen it time and time again and its not getting any better. Lets hire the most qualified person, regardless of race or gender.

(Police Officer, Male, Caucasian, 35 years old, 14 years PO, 14 years LAPD, Chief when hired: Davis)

#157

The good news is the LAPD has a mysterious vitality, excellent people, and generally superior management. Chief Gates cares and honestly does what he thinks is best. Despite its problems, the LAPD will survive. The bad news is that the LAPD has fallen under the classic tyranny of the "Big Lie." Affirmative Action is, simply, prejudice given a fancy name. Equal Opportunity (of merit and job quality) cannot and are not co-existing with Affirmative Action. A whole generation of Blacks, Hispanics, and others are being deprived of the satisfaction of being treated as fully able human beings. None can escape the suspicion that their race and/or sex, and not their ability, was the source of success. The benevolent slave-owner mentality is alive and well in the LAPD and the City. Anger, disenchantment, distrust grow on all sides. Not good. Not good. The solution to a wrong has never been—can never be—another wrong.

(Sergeant, Male, Caucasian, 49 years old, 28 years PO, 28 years LAPD, Chief when hired: Parker)

#158

Affirmative Action = Legal Racism. I will be gone from LAPD real soon, if things don't change. It seems like we are becoming the ACLU/NAACP police. Be kind to criminals, and ignore the victs! You can save lives, be a great ofcr with high morals + ethics, but say something rude to a rapist, child molester, etc., and you can get fired. (It almost happened to me.) Seems like you have to be white, to be a racist. I'm sick of hearing that ofcrs (BLK + HISP) are not treated the same. I guess, I am just sick of it!!

(Police Officer, Male, Caucasian, 28 years old, 3 years PO, 3 years LAPD, Chief when hired: Gates) (Figure 6.5)

#159

Working conditions are tragic for Detectives throughout the City. We are 50 years behind the times in working conditions, work space, computers, etc. Promotion based on Affirmative Action is destroying morale! In narcotics clearly unqualified persons are being promoted based on Affirmative Action. This conclusion can only be reached by looking at the recent promotions. 1 female had 1.18 pending [personnel complaint] & has a long history of problems but was promoted to DII [second level detective pay grade] over dozens of more qualified candidates. (I was not affected by this promotion) We must promote on ability & experience. Not Affirmative Action! Brass in the Glass House & Div. Capts need a police background not

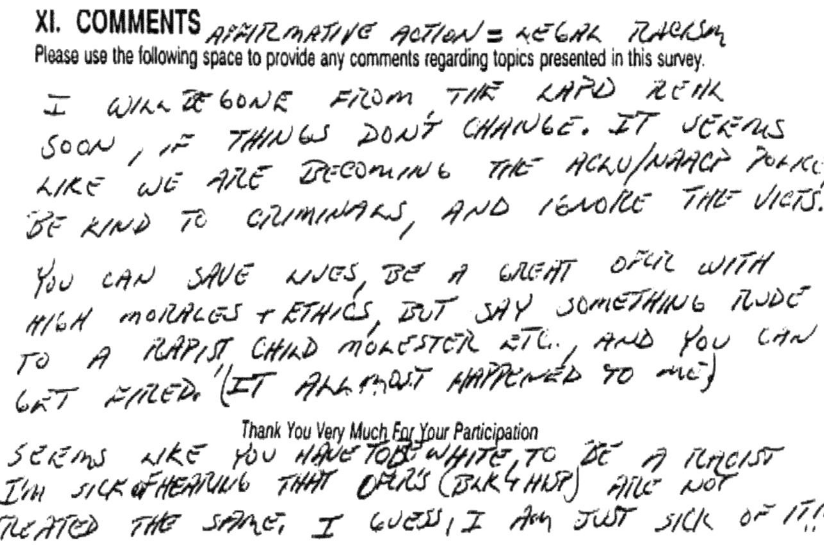
XI. COMMENTS AFFIRMATIVE ACTION = LEGAL RACISM

Please use the following space to provide any comments regarding topics presented in this survey.

I WILL BE GONE FROM THE LAPD REAL SOON, IF THINGS DON'T CHANGE. IT SEEMS LIKE WE ARE BECOMING THE ACLU/NAACP POLICE, BE KIND TO CRIMINALS, AND IGNORE THE VICTS!

YOU CAN SAVE LIVES, BE A GREAT OFCR WITH HIGH MORALES + ETHICS, BUT SAY SOMETHING RUDE TO A RAPIST, CHILD MOLESTER ETC., AND YOU CAN GET FIRED. (IT ALLMOST HAPPENED TO ME)

Thank You Very Much For Your Participation

SEEMS LIKE YOU HAVE TO BE WHITE TO BE A RACIST I'M SICK OF HEARING THAT OFCRS (BLK + HISP) ARE NOT TREATED THE SAME, I GUESS, I AM JUST SICK OF IT!!

Figure 6.5 Statement Transcription: Affirmative Action=Legal Racism. I will be gone from LAPD real soon, if things don't change. It seems like we are becoming the ACLU/NAACP police. Be kind to criminals, and ignore the victims! You can save lives, be a great officer with high morals + ethics, but say something rude to a rapist, child molester, etc., and you can get fired. (It almost happened to me.) Seems like you have to be White to be a racist. I'm sick of hearing that officers (BLK + HISP) are not treated the same. I guess, I am just sick of it!! (see Officer Informant statement (see Officer Informant statement #158).

administrative. They can not evaluate a police ofcrs performance under stress if they have never been there.

(Detective, Male, Caucasian, 43 years old, 20 years PO, 20 years LAPD, Chief when hired: Davis)

#160

Let's get away from bending to special interest groups. They have no real interest in the Depts. operations except to plant seeds of disharmony. Affirmative Action has virtually eliminated qualified candidates from the job and qualifications have taken a back seat to race, sex and ethnic background. Let's get back to basics. Promote and hire the qualified without regard to race, sex or ethnic background. When you settle for less you get exactly what you settle for incompetent officers and supervisors. Stop punishing the proud loyal and productive employee to gain ethnic + sexual balance. We are passing over people more deserving of rewards and instead rewarding incompetence and laziness.

(Police Officer, Male, Caucasian, 43 years old, 20 years PO, 20 years LAPD, Chief when hired: Davis)

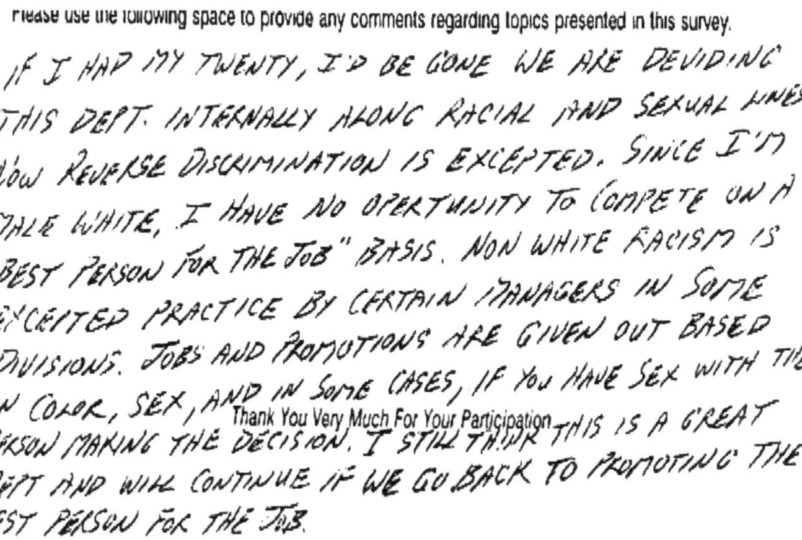
Please use the following space to provide any comments regarding topics presented in this survey.

IF I HAD MY TWENTY, I'D BE GONE WE ARE DEVIDING
THIS DEPT. INTERNALLY ALONG RACIAL AND SEXUAL LINES.
NOW REVERSE DISCRIMINATION IS EXCEPTED. SINCE I'M
MALE WHITE, I HAVE NO OPERTUNITY TO COMPETE ON A
"BEST PERSON FOR THE JOB" BASIS. NON WHITE RACISM IS
EXCEPTED PRACTICE BY CERTAIN MANAGERS IN SOME
DIVISIONS. JOBS AND PROMOTIONS ARE GIVEN OUT BASED
ON COLOR, SEX, AND IN SOME CASES, IF YOU HAVE SEX WITH THE
PERSON MAKING THE DECISION. I STILL THINK THIS IS A GREAT
DEPT AND WILL CONTINUE IF WE GO BACK TO PROMOTING THE
BEST PERSON FOR THE JOB.

Thank You Very Much For Your Participation

Figure 6.6 Statement Transcription: If I had my 20, I'd be gone. We are dividing the Department internally along racial and sexual lines. Now reverse discrimination is accepted. Since I'm male white, I have no opportunity to compete on a "best person for the job" basis. Non White racism is accepted practice by certain managers in some divisions. Jobs and promotions are given out based on color, sex, and in some cases, if you have sex with the person making the decision. I still think this is a great Department and will continue if we go back to promoting the best person for the job (see Officer Informant statement #162).

#161

… Due to the recent consent decree and affirmative action policies, I do not believe I will ever have a fair opportunity to promote because I am white and heterosexual.

(Police Officer, Male Caucasian, 36 years old, 11 years PO, 11 years LAPD, Chief when hired: Gates)

#162

If I had my 20, I'd be gone. We are dividing the Dept. internally along racial and sexual lines. Now reverse discrimination is accepted. Since I'm male white, I have no opportunity to compete on a "best person for the job" basis. Non white racism is accepted practice by certain managers in some divisions. Jobs and promotions are given out based on color, sex, and in some cases, if you have sex with the person making the decision. I still think this is a great dept. and will continue if we go back to promoting the best person for the job.

(Sergeant, Male, Caucasian, 38 years old, 16 years PO, 16 years LAPD, Chief when hired: Davis) (Figure 6.6)

#163

Affirmative Action (Read Reverse Discrimination) will kill this Dept's efficiency. Don't give any special benefits to any group of people. The white male officers will rebel.

(Sergeant, Male, Caucasian, 41 years old, 18 years PO, 18 years LAPD, Chief when hired: Davis)

#164

Affirmative Action is undermining our organization, causing less than qualified personnel to be either hired or promoted. I would like to see the best person get the job, whether it be male/female, black, white, or whatever.

(Police Officer, Male, Caucasian, 27 years old, 6 years PO, 6 years LAPD, Chief when hired: Gates)

#165

The morale of the Dept will continue to erode until something is done about promotions based on Affirmative Action. All tests must be fair in the future or we will be reduced to a second rate police dept.

(Lieutenant, Male, Caucasian, 52 years old, 27 years PO, 27 years LAPD, Chief when hired: Parker) (Figure 6.7)

#166

I believe the hiring practices of this City do not allow us to get the best type of person for this job and the way the scoring of the tests is a way to get certain groups of people promoted not on merit but on their minority status in life. I used to be proud of this job. I don't know what I am now!! No wonder our patrol cops just want to do the basics. No one's willing to back them up against a few loud mouth members of the community looking for political fulfillment.

(Police Officer, Male, Caucasian, 45 years old, 18 years PO, 18 years LAPD, Chief when hired: Davis)

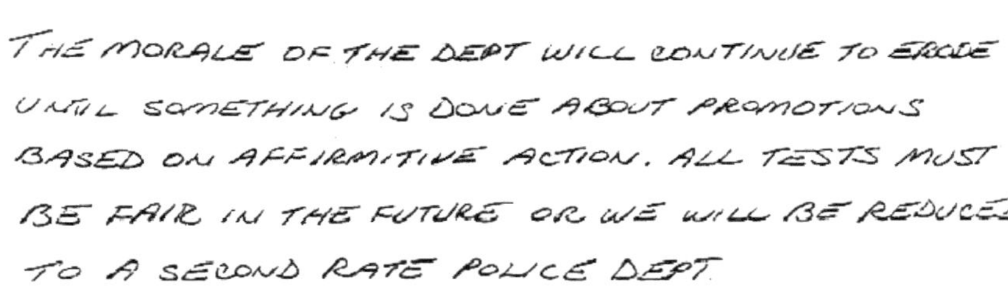

THE MORALE OF THE DEPT WILL CONTINUE TO ERODE
UNTIL SOMETHING IS DONE ABOUT PROMOTIONS
BASED ON AFFIRMITIVE ACTION. ALL TESTS MUST
BE FAIR IN THE FUTURE OR WE WILL BE REDUCED
TO A SECOND RATE POLICE DEPT.

Figure 6.7 Statement Transcription: The morale of the Department will continue to erode until something is done about promotions based on Affirmative Action. All tests must be fair in the future or we will be reduced to a second rate police Department (see Officer Informant statement #165).

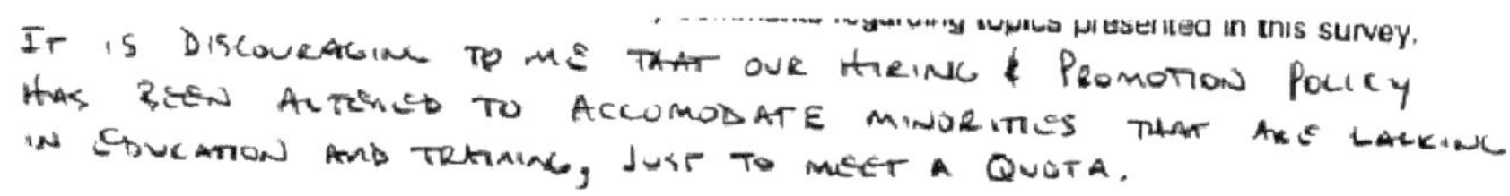
regarding topics presented in this survey.

IT IS DISCOURAGING TO ME THAT OUR HIRING & PROMOTION POLICY HAS BEEN ALTERED TO ACCOMODATE MINORITIES THAT ARE LACKING IN EDUCATION AND TRAINING, JUST TO MEET A QUOTA.

Figure 6.8 Statement Transcription: It is discouraging to me that our hiring & promotion policy has been altered to accommodate minorities that are lacking in education and training, just to meet a quota (see Officer Informant statement #167).

#167

It is discouraging to me that our hiring & promotion policy has been altered to accommodate minorities that are lacking in education and training, just to meet a quota.

(Police Officer, Male, Caucasian, 27 years old, 5 years PO, 5 years LAPD, Chief when hired: Gates) (Figure 6.8)

#168

I am concerned that this survey will be "twisted" by the media. I can see the headlines.... "LAPD SURVEY SHOW PROMOTIONAL SYSTEM UNFAIR" "RANK AND FILE VIEW LAPD AS INEFFICIENT"

(Sergeant, Male, Caucasian, 41 years old, 20 years PO, 20 years LAPD, Chief when hired: Davis)

#169

I love m job and I've had a great career, but I'm sick and tired of minority officers screaming for their rights to promotion. Each group wants immediate representation and I believe extremely unqualified personnel are being promoted to fill percentages. Let's keep the system fair and impartial, and morale will improve.

(Sergeant, Male, Caucasian, 38 years old, 16 years PO, 16 years LAPD, Chief when hired: Davis)

#170

… The new developments in Affirm Action promotions are a joke, allowing individuals with poor performance into positions of great importance. If I was going to have brain surgery, I would want the person who scored high during med school, etc., not a doctor chosen by color or sex. Wake up.

(Police Officer, Male, Caucasian, 30 years old, 3 years PO, 3 years LAPD, Chief when hired: Gates)

#171

In my 20 years, the last five years I've seen more unqualified people get on the job. Promotions are for females & blacks, & hisp. It doesn't make any difference how good you are if you are wht. There are qualified females black & hisp. But there are also qualified whts.

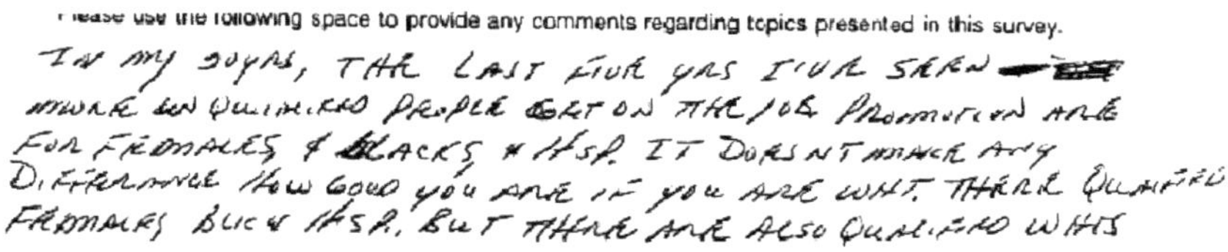
Please use the following space to provide any comments regarding topics presented in this survey.

IN MY 20YRS, THE LAST FIVE YRS I'VE SEEN MORE UNQUALIFIED PEOPLE GET ON THE JOB. PROMOTION ARE FOR FEMALES & BLACKS & HSP. IT DOESN'T MAKE ANY DIFFERENCE HOW GOOD YOU ARE IF YOU ARE WHT. THERE QUALIFIED FEMALES BLACK HSP, BUT THERE ARE ALSO QUALIFIED WHTS

Figure 6.9 Statement Transcription: In my 20 years, the last five years I've seen more unqualified people get on the job. Promotions are for females & Blacks, & Hispanics. It doesn't make any difference how good you are if you are White. There qualified females Blacks & Hispanics. But there are also qualified Whites (see Officer Informant statement #171).

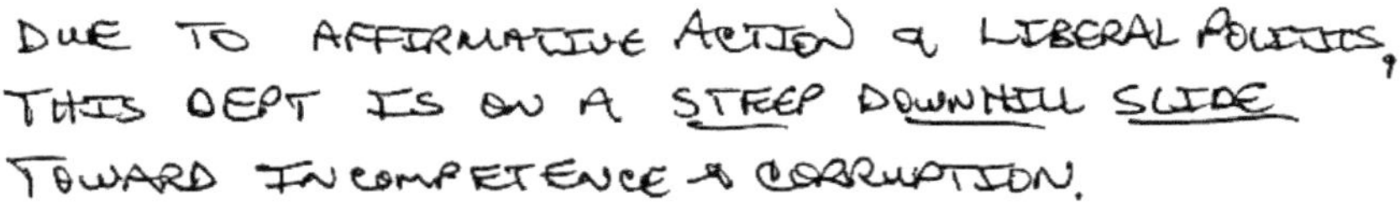
DUE TO AFFIRMATIVE ACTION & LIBERAL POLITICS, THIS DEPT IS ON A STEEP DOWNHILL SLIDE TOWARD INCOMPETENCE & CORRUPTION.

Figure 6.10 Statement Transcription: Due to Affirmative Action & liberal politics, this Department is on a steep downhill slide toward incompetence & corruption. Its administrators are generally incompetent (see Officer Informant statement #172).

(Police Officer, Male, Caucasian, 45 years old, 20 years PO, 20 years LAPD, Chief when hired: Davis) (Figure 6.9)

#172

Due to "Affirmative Action" & liberal politics, this dept is on a steep downhill slide toward incompetence & corruption. Its administrators are generally incompetent.

(Police Officer, Male, Caucasian, 45 years old, 17 years PO, 17 years LAPD, Chief when hired: Davis) (Figure 6.10)

#173

… There is a problem w/race relations between fellow ofcrs due to Affirmative Action policies….

(Police Officer, Male, Caucasian, 25 years old, 1 year PO, 1 year LAPD, Chief when hired: Gates)

#174

… Our promotion potential is drastically reduced under the guise of affirmative action. Long gone are the days when we just hire the best. I couldn't care less if the recipient of a job or promotion is Black, White, Male or Female. How about just the best person for the job, for the best department possible. We are settling for mediocrity and that is a deadly cancer that will serve to cripple this department for years and years to come. No, I'm not bitter. I'm disappointed. Frustrated. Disillusioned.

(Police Officer, Male, Caucasian, 34 years old, 9 years PO, 9 years LAPD, Chief when hired: Gates) (Figure 6.11)

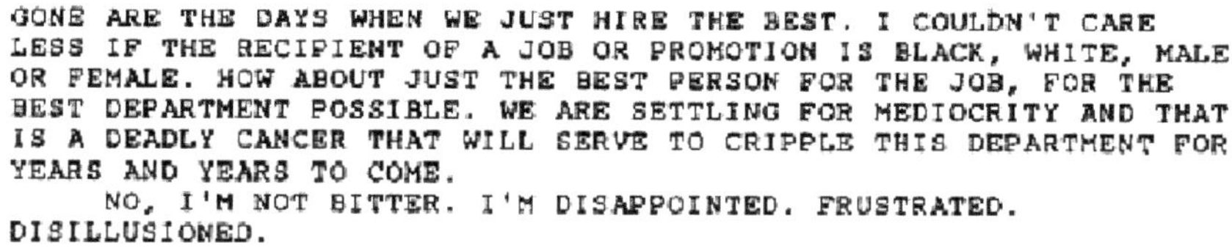
GONE ARE THE DAYS WHEN WE JUST HIRE THE BEST. I COULDN'T CARE LESS IF THE RECIPIENT OF A JOB OR PROMOTION IS BLACK, WHITE, MALE OR FEMALE. HOW ABOUT JUST THE BEST PERSON FOR THE JOB, FOR THE BEST DEPARTMENT POSSIBLE. WE ARE SETTLING FOR MEDIOCRITY AND THAT IS A DEADLY CANCER THAT WILL SERVE TO CRIPPLE THIS DEPARTMENT FOR YEARS AND YEARS TO COME.

NO, I'M NOT BITTER. I'M DISAPPOINTED. FRUSTRATED. DISILLUSIONED.

Figure 6.11 Statement Transcription: Gone are the days when we just hire the best. I couldn't care less if the recipient of a job or promotion is Black, White, Male or Female. How about just the best person for the job, for the best department possible. We are settling for mediocrity and that is a deadly cancer that will serve to cripple this department for years and years to come. No, I'm not bitter. I'm disappointed. Frustrated. Disillusioned (see Officer Informant statement #174).

#175

... The only thing that matters when it comes to promotion on this department is the color of your skin, your sex or sexual preference. When (not if) I am passed over for promotion, because I am white. I promise to file a law suit.

(Police Officer, Male Caucasian, 36 years old, 11 years PO, 11 years LAPD, Chief when hired: Gates)

Minority Male Officers

#176

I think there are some narrow minded bigots on this dept. I think they were that way before they got to the dept. I think they will always be that way and I think therein lies our problem. Attitudes.

(Police Officer, Male, African American, 51 years old, 23 years PO, 23 years LAPD, Chief when hired: Reddin) (Figure 6.12)

#177

... When a supervisor will pick an inferior candidate—and pass over an experienced seasoned ofcr who has paid his dues, to promote a minority, we've lost completely. We've lost the experience and the

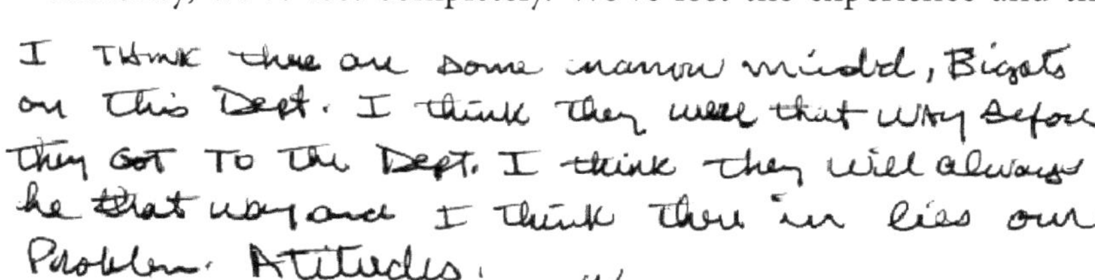
I Think there are some narrow minded, Bigots on this Dept. I think they were that Way Before They GOT To The Dept. I think they will always be that way and I think there in lies our Problem. Attitudes.

Figure 6.12 Statement Transcription: I think there are some narrow minded bigots on this Department. I think they were that way before they got to the Department. I think they will always be that way and I think therein lies our problem. Attitudes (see Officer Informant statement #176).

loyalty of an ofcr who has been threw hell. Management hides behind affirmative action. The police academy is laden with individuals who have no experience in the field, training recruits. This whole scenario is sad to say the least. Patrol is loaded with ofcrs who have years of field experience.

(Police Officer, Male, Hispanic, 43 years old, 20 years PO, 20 years LAPD, Chief when hired: Davis)

#178

Before we can be an effective role in working with citizens and deal with societies ills, we must deal with our internal ills. Relationships between officers are at an all time low & mistrust between all levels within the department is poor. Supervisors are probably the most guilty in fostering this. Before we look at the community & police we should examine ourselves. If we cannot work with one another how can we work with the community?

(Police Officer, Male, African American, 27 years old, 4 years PO, 4 years LAPD, Chief when hired: Gates)

#179

… The ground pounders are always getting hurt, and will continue to be hurt. People are put into positions of leadership not because they are leaders, or possess the qualities, but because they can pass a test or are a minority, and fall within the quota. In the end, the people we swore to "protect and to serve," will receive poor service.

(Police Officer, Male, Hispanic, 26 years old, 3 years PO, 3 years LAPD, Chief when hired: Gates)

#180

Promotions should be based on tenure, experience and ability to adapt to the new position. Not race, education or whether or not you can speak Spanish or pass a test.

(Police Officer, Male, Hispanic, 28 years old, 7 years PO, 7 years LAPD, Chief when hired: Gates) (Figure 6.13)

#181

I know for a fact that a # of my fellow white-male ofcrs have grown to resent the depts affirmative action efforts. I find this very disturbing….

(Police Officer, Male, African American, 33 years old, 9 years PO, 7 years LAPD, Chief when hired: Gates)

#182

… We also need better police ofcr selection. If we can't lure the intelligent & mature individual to come on board, or keep choosing our ofcrs from a pool of designed minorities who cannot even coherently read, write or think, where are we expected to be in 10 years. I'll be surprised if our outcome is not dismal.

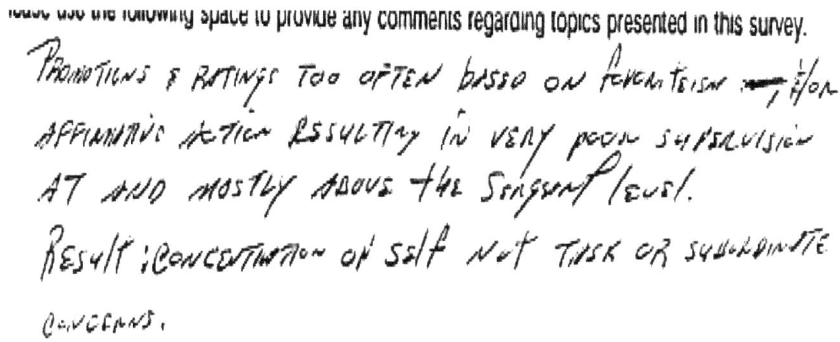
Please use the following space to provide any comments regarding topics presented in this survey.

PROMOTIONS & RATINGS TOO OFTEN BASED ON FAVORITISM &/OR AFFIRMATIVE ACTION RESULTING IN VERY POOR SUPERVISION AT AND MOSTLY ABOVE the Sergeant level.
RESULT: CONCENTRATION OF Self NOT TASK OR SUBORDINATE CONCERNS.

Figure 6.13 Statement Transcription: Promotions & ratings too often based on favoritism &/or affirmative action resulting in very poor supervision at and mostly above the sergeant level. Result: concentration on self not task or subordinate concerns (see Officer Informant statement #184).

(Police Officer, Male, Hispanic, 39 years old, 3 years PO, 3 years LAPD, Chief when hired: Gates)

#183

… I think there should be a more structured procedure for promotions. You should be required to have a certain amount of years on the job before promotions to (P-3) (Sgt) etc. 5 years for P-3, 7-10 years for Sgt or above.

(Police Officer, Male, African American, 30 years old, 4 years PO, 4 years LAPD, Chief when hired: Gates)

#184

Promotions & ratings too often based on favoritism &/or affirmative action resulting in very poor supervision at and mostly above the sergeant level. Result: concentration on self not task or subordinate concerns.

(Police Officer, Male, African American, 28 years old, 6 years PO, 6 years LAPD, Chief when hired: Gates)

#185

This dept has always used the good old boy system for selecting ofcrs to the most wanted jobs. There is no fair system at this time. The Anglo gets the job 99% of the time, no matter if he/she is homosexual or not qualified.

(Detective, Male, Hispanic, 42 years old, 19 years PO, 19 years LAPD, Chief when hired: Davis) (Figure 6.14)

#186

No one cares about the ground pounders!

(Police Officer, Male, Hispanic, 26 years old, 3 years PO, 3 years LAPD, Chief when hired: Gates)

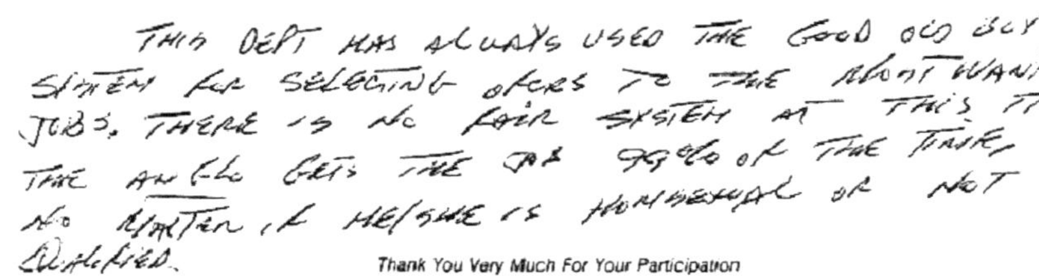
THIS DEPT HAS ALWAYS USED THE GOOD OLD BOY SYSTEM FOR SELECTING OFCRS TO THE MOST WANTED JOBS. THERE IS NO FAIR SYSTEM AT THIS TIME. THE ANGLO GETS THE JOB 99% OF THE TIME, NO MATTER IF HE/SHE IS HOMOSEXUAL OR NOT QUALIFIED.

Thank You Very Much For Your Participation

Figure 6.14 Statement Transcription: This department has always used the good old boy system for selecting officers to the most wanted jobs. There is no fair system at this time. The Anglo gets the job 99% of the time, no matter if he/she is homosexual or not qualified (see Officer Informant statement #185).

Female Officers

#187

Top management is not making a sincere effort to internally change the department's problems—the "changes" are designed to please the public. The "good ole white boy" syndrome is still firmly entrenched with separate racial groups struggling to have their place. There is no LAPD family unless a dept. tragedy occurs, and those feelings are temporary. The bottom line is that top management must recognize the racial/sexist tensions in the department—and do something about it—for the good of the department—not to add to a resume to submit for Chief of Police.

(Sergeant, Female, African American, 36 years old, 12 years PO, 9 years LAPD, Chief when hired: Gates) (Figure 6.15)

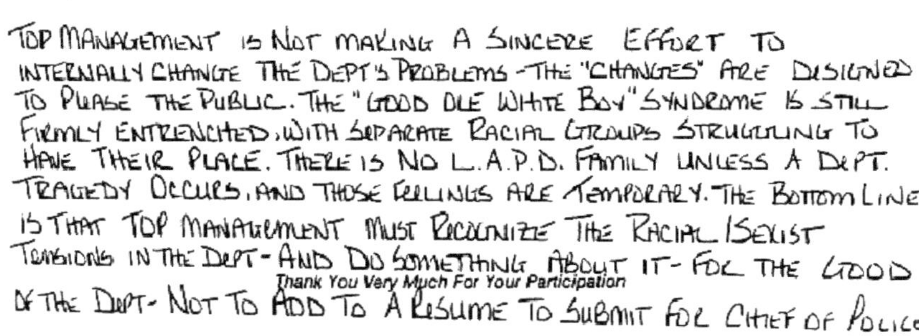
TOP MANAGEMENT IS NOT MAKING A SINCERE EFFORT TO INTERNALLY CHANGE THE DEPT'S PROBLEMS - THE "CHANGES" ARE DESIGNED TO PLEASE THE PUBLIC. THE "GOOD OLE WHITE BOY" SYNDROME IS STILL FIRMLY ENTRENCHED, WITH SEPARATE RACIAL GROUPS STRUGGLING TO HAVE THEIR PLACE. THERE IS NO L.A.P.D. FAMILY UNLESS A DEPT. TRAGEDY OCCURS, AND THOSE FEELINGS ARE TEMPORARY. THE BOTTOM LINE IS THAT TOP MANAGEMENT MUST RECOGNIZE THE RACIAL/SEXIST TENSIONS IN THE DEPT - AND DO SOMETHING ABOUT IT - FOR THE GOOD OF THE DEPT - NOT TO ADD TO A RESUME TO SUBMIT FOR CHIEF OF POLICE

Thank You Very Much For Your Participation

Figure 6.15 Statement Transcription: Top management is not making a sincere effort to internally change the dept's problems—the "changes" are designed to please the public. The "good ole white boy" syndrome is still firmly entrenched with separate racial groups struggling to have their place. There is no LAPD family unless a dept tragedy occurs, and those feelings are temporary. The bottom line is that top management must recognize the racial/sexist tension in the dept—and do something about it—for the good of the dept—not to add to a resume to submit for Chief of Police (see Officer Informant statement #187).

#188

Regardless of it's faults, this department provides the best equal opportunities for all. This is the best department in the world for me. I support the Chief.

(Police Officer, Female, African American, 30 years old, 3 years PO, 3 years LAPD, Chief when hired: Gates)

#189

… Speaking as a female, I resent the implication I need "help" to promote. I am fully capable of studying and passing promotional exams on my own. I dislike the fact that if I promote, my peers think its only because I'm a woman. White males should be allowed to compete equally.

(Police Officer, Female, Caucasian, 33 years old, 7 years PO, 7 years LAPD, Chief when hired: Gates)

#190

If everybody really believed we only come in one color blue we'd be a great department. To much interdepartmental hate going on.

(Police Officer, Female, African American, 29 years old, 7 years PO, 7 years LAPD, Chief when hired: Gates) (Figure 6.16)

#191

… Further, affirmative action "quotas" have impacted our internal standards of excellence.

(Police Officer, Female, Caucasian, 28 years old, 28 years PO, 28 years LAPD, Chief when hired: Parker)

#192

I am a female minority and I do not agree with the new decision on consent decree. Choose me because I'm best qualified, not because I'm female or the color of my skin.

(Police Officer, Female, Hispanic, 33 years old, 11 years PO, 11 years LAPD, Chief when hired: Gates) (Figure 6.17)

#193

The academy is not getting rid of those recruits who are clearly unsuited for police work, resulting in sub-standard, inept & in some cases, dangerous novice police officers. In addition, the ever

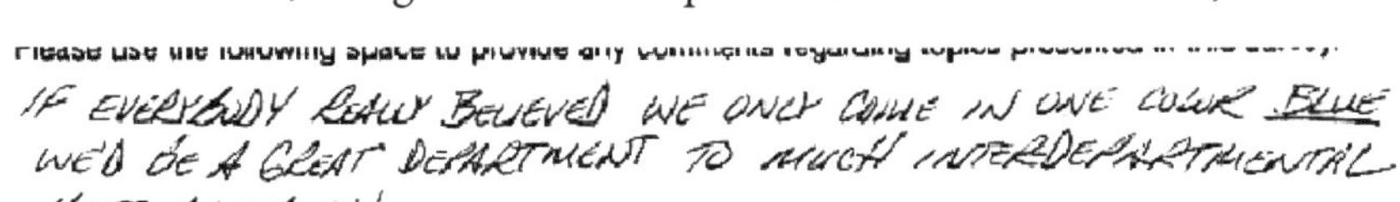
IF EVERYBODY REALLY BELIEVED WE ONLY COME IN ONE COLOR BLUE WE'D BE A GREAT DEPARTMENT TO MUCH INTERDEPARTMENTAL HATE GOING ON.

Figure 6.16 Statement Transcription: If everybody really believed we only come in one color blue we'd be a great department. Too much interdepartmental hate going on (see Officer Informant statement #190).

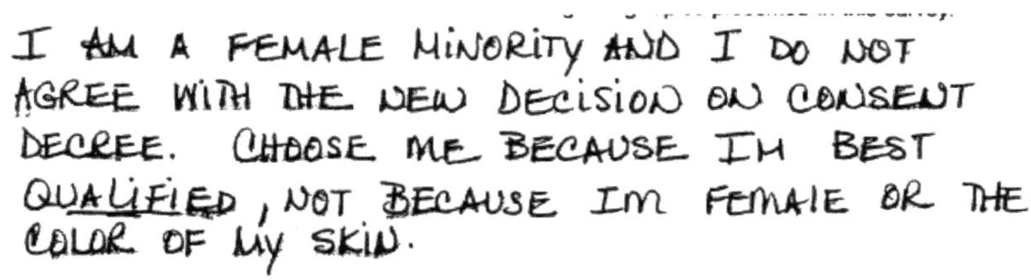
I AM A FEMALE MINORITY AND I DO NOT AGREE WITH THE NEW DECISION ON CONSENT DECREE. CHOOSE ME BECAUSE IM BEST QUALIFIED, NOT BECAUSE IM FEMALE OR THE COLOR OF MY SKIN.

Figure 6.17 Statement Transcription: I am a female minority and I do not agree with the new decision on consent decree. Choose me because I'm best qualified, not because I'm female or the color of my skin (see Officer Informant statement #192).

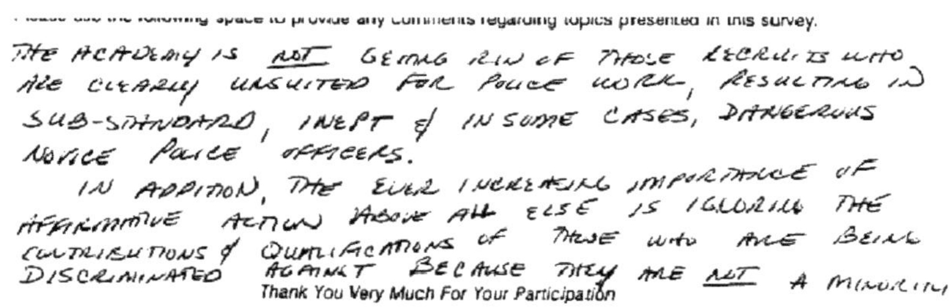
...use the following space to provide any comments regarding topics presented in this survey.

THE ACADEMY IS NOT GETTING RID OF THOSE RECRUITS WHO ARE CLEARLY UNSUITED FOR POLICE WORK, RESULTING IN SUB-STANDARD, INEPT & IN SOME CASES, DANGEROUS NOVICE POLICE OFFICERS.

IN ADDITION, THE EVER INCREASING IMPORTANCE OF AFFIRMATIVE ACTION ABOVE ALL ELSE IS IGNORING THE CONTRIBUTIONS & QUALIFICATIONS OF THOSE WHO ARE BEING DISCRIMINATED AGAINST BECAUSE THEY ARE NOT A MINORITY

Thank You Very Much For Your Participation

Figure 6.18 Statement Transcription: The academy is not getting rid of those recruits who are clearly unsuited for police work, resulting in sub-standard, inept & in some cases, dangerous novice police officers. In addition, the ever increasing importance of affirmative action above all else is ignoring the contributions & qualifications of those who are being discriminated against because they are not a minority (see Officer Informant statement #193).

increasing importance of affirmative action above all else is ignoring the contributions & qualifications of those who are being discriminated against because they are not a minority.

(Detective, Female, Caucasian, 31 years old, 6 years PO, 6 years LAPD, Chief when hired: Gates) (Figure 6.18)

#194

Affirmative Action is going to be a major downfall for this Department. The goal should be the best qualified, i.e., education, experience, seniority, work performance.

(Police Officer, Female, Caucasian, 31 years old, 3 years PO, 3 years LAPD, Chief when hired: Gates)

#195

Promotions: Assessment Center type examinations. Current testing is archaic. Allows for incompetent persons being promoted. Adhere to Affirmative Action procedures. Hire most qualified. If a tie, make Affirmative Action selection.

(Sergeant, Female, Caucasian, 46 years old, 17 years PO, 17 years LAPD, Chief when hired: Davis)

Theme Analysis

The number of officer comments discovered in this study that focused on the department's hiring, promotion, and affirmative action policies was greater than that found for the King incident main theme, yet less in frequency than comments cited as "political and community" causes of the LAPD meltdown (presented in Chapter 5). However, as is easily recognized by examining the tone and tenor of the officer statements included in this chapter, the topic of affirmative action appears to evoke some of the strongest emotional reactions witnessed thus far in the study. This is especially true among male nonminority officers who provided the majority of commentary criticizing the department's hiring and promotional policies following the Blake consent decree.

Perhaps the most salient theme discovered here was that affirmative action had caused the officers to become divided along race and gender lines. Officers representing all ranks, experience, and personal backgrounds suggested that perceived inequality in the department's hiring and promotional practices had "driven a wedge" between minority and nonminority officers as well as between male and female officers. Words such as *racist* and *reverse discrimination* were used by officers, particularly Caucasian males, to describe the department's court-imposed hiring and promotion policies. Bad morale, feelings of hatred, laziness, early retirement, leaving the job, white officer rebellion, poor supervision, field incompetence, and failure to back up other officers were some of the more notable negative side effects associated with the department's imposition of affirmative action. However, the majority of these observations were again made by male nonminority officers. Minority officers, on the other hand, provided relatively few comments about the department's affirmative action policies. In fact, some of the statements provided by both rookie and veteran minority officers claimed that racial tensions within the LAPD organization were high, yet not a new problem to the LAPD organizational culture. Furthermore, they felt that the affirmative action measure would create greater racial and gender equality in hiring and promotional decisions.

Conclusion

Based on the above findings, it can be concluded with some degree of certainty that the professional model's ability to create uniformity among the ranks of all LAPD officers, regardless of race and gender, had been weakened by employment changes introduced into the department by the Blake consent decree. This internal organizational change began to take effect some 10 years before the blitz of media and political attacks impacted the department following the King incident. Was this slow building, yet extremely volatile, situation that changed the racial and gender composition of LAPD officers within the ranks of patrol as well as supervisory positions the precipitating cause of the meltdown? Based on findings presented in this chapter, the best answer to this question is: Yes, affirmative action employment changes that were forced on the department and its officers were a contributing factor to the meltdown, but no, internal conflicts between officers based on race and gender differences were not the main cause of the LAPD's total organizational breakdown.

Judging from the officer comments, and from past experiences such as Sergeant Blake's decision to file an employment discrimination lawsuit against the department, the LAPD has perhaps always suffered from various organizational issues concerning racial and gender tensions among street level officers as well as within supervisory ranks. There is no doubt that these issues were intensified and brought to light by political and media scrutiny of the department following the King incident. However, in the past, the department continued to operate under the professional model despite internal struggles between officers over hiring and promotional issues. It can also be argued that if affirmative action was the main cause of the meltdown, the department would have endured mass organizational confusion and abandoned the professional model long before the King incident—that is, sometime during the 10 years affirmative action policies were in effect at LAPD prior to the community fallout of the King affair. Again, it is here concluded that the problems associated with affirmative action—like those previously identified as potential causes of the meltdown—are merely symptomatic of a much more profound cause that resulted in the department's inability to maintain control over its organizational "demons."

References

1. George T. Felkenes and Peter Unsinger. *Diversity, Affirmative Action and Law Enforcement*. Springfield, IL: Charles C Thomas, 1992.
2. Ibid.
3. Ibid.
4. Personal interview with anonymous informant. Conducted May 1995.
5. Personal interview with anonymous informant. Conducted May 1995.
6. Personal interview with anonymous informant. Conducted May 1995.
7. Personal interview with anonymous informant. Conducted May 1995.
8. James Lasley and George Felkenes. Implications of Hiring Women Police Officers: Police Administrator's Concerns May Not Be Justified. *Policing and Society*, 2, 1992.

7 Management and Administration

By far, the vast majority of officer comments examined in this study concern issues regarding the LAPD's management and administration. These comments target the supervisors and decision makers within all levels of the organization. However, the bulk of commentary is directed at specific reactions of these officers to the organizational meltdown. In order to better understand the officers' comments presented in the following section, it is necessary to have a basic understanding of the LAPD organizational structure and how it relates to the duties of officers who work the street. However, for purposes of this study, it is not necessary to present a detailed description of the department's administrative hierarchy. Rather, it is important to have a working knowledge of the LAPD rank structure and chain of command during the time period this study was executed (see Figure 7.1).

As Figure 7.1 illustrates, the LAPD organizational structure (during the study period) consisted of a chain of command with eight levels or ranks. This structure is almost identical to the paramilitary organizational hierarchy of the department that was operational during the Parker era of the professional policing model. Its design was created to provide the rapid flow of commands from chief of police down to the rank-and-file police officer. Each level or rank descending from the top of the organization (e.g., chief of police) had a well-defined superior-subordinate relationship whereby a "top-down" flow of communication was strictly enforced.

The entire LAPD organizational hierarchy can be broken down into two functional groups: (1) the command staff or staff officers (also referred to herein as the brass) and (2) street level operations. The command staff consisted of Chief Gates, 2 assistant chiefs, 5 deputy chiefs, and 17 commanders. Together, the chief and his staff were responsible for the general management of the LAPD and for establishing all of the department's operational policies. One of the assistant chiefs in charge of the LAPD's Office of Operations oversaw the activities of 84% of the department's sworn personnel. Answering to the assistant chiefs were the deputy chiefs, who had managerial oversight of the four geographic bureaus (Central, South, West, and Valley), which comprised the department's entire operating areas within the LAPD's jurisdiction. The role of commander was to carry out the directives of the deputy chiefs within each of the bureaus, which were broken down into 18 divisions (analogous to a station). In effect, the commander's role was that of a liaison between the

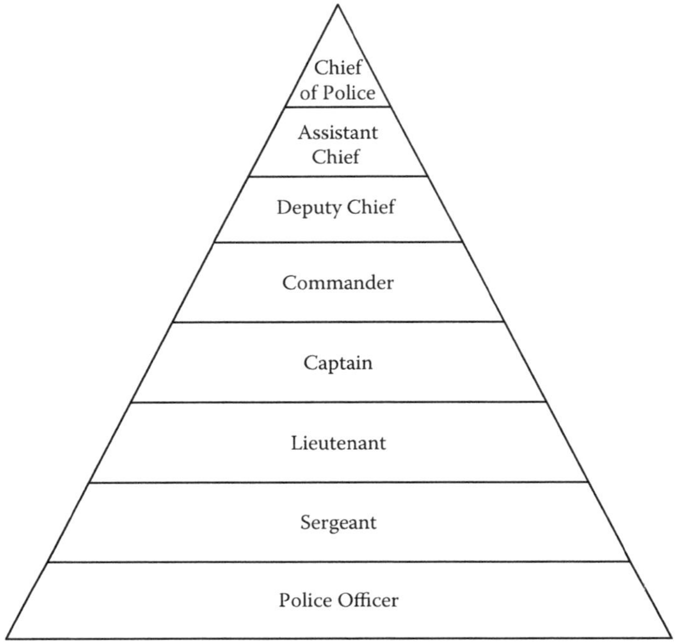

Figure 7.1 Organizational hierarchy (Chain of Command) of the Los Angeles Police Department.

department's policy makers (e.g., the chief and his command staff) and the divisions controlling the majority of activities conducted by patrol officers and detectives. Most of the command staff's directives to street officers were carried out at the LAPD's strategic operational headquarters, Parker Center (or the so-called 6th floor, referring to the location within Parker Center housing the chief's and other members of the command staff's offices).[1]

Policy directives originating within Parker Center were carried out on the street by the head administrator at each of the department's divisions. Each division contained two upper-level managers at the rank of captain who were responsible for ensuring that command staff policy directives were effectively carried out by officers in the streets. However, officers at the lieutenant rank severed as middle-level managers or "watch commanders" to handle administrative tasks at each division on any given shift or watch. Supervising the bulk of field activities were lower-level managers at the rank of sergeant. Officers at this level were primarily responsible for how patrol officers handled enforcement activities and relations with the public. The rank of police officer, which encompassed the bulk of patrol officers, was broken down into three levels: P-I, assigned to officers during their first year of probationary service; P-II, automatically achieved by officers after successfully completing their probationary training; and P-III, achieved through testing and performance evaluations, which could lead to the position of field training officer (FTO), in charge of training newly hired probationary officers. The LAPD's detective branch operated under its own administrative hierarchy. Generally speaking, the lowest-ranking detectives (detective I) were supervised by their own higher-ranking personnel (detectives II and III, which were roughly equivalent in managerial status to lieutenant I and II, respectively).[2]

Possible Explanations

In theory, there are two alternative scenarios that can serve to explain how the LAPD's administration would react to the political and other external pressures placed on the department and its officers to reform or change the professional model of policing. First, and the most likely result based on history, the chief of police and LAPD administrators/managers would use all political and other powers available to them in order to resist change and to preserve the department's traditionally aggressive style of crime fighting. In contrast, the alternative reaction might entail a "duck and cover" organizational response by the chief and LAPD administrators/managers. Such a reaction would, in effect, lower the political barrier imposed by Parker to protect the department and its officers from outside intervention. Without the LAPD's protective barrier against outside intrusion, the entire organization from the Office of Chief to the street level patrol officer could suffer catastrophic consequences in terms of operating autonomously from political and community influences. The latter alternative explanation was first identified, and perhaps most feared, by Chief William Parker himself. Parker predicted that if the professional model of policing should falter, causing the LAPD to lose its war on crime, "it would not be at the hands of an enemy invasion" overpowering his officers on the battlefield. Rather, he prophesized that his mighty department could only be brought down if the great organizational walls surrounding LAPD were to crumble, "allowing the enemy to pour in." This doomsday scenario, which he routinely spoke of during many public appearances, would only come about on the day "when barbarism rotted the moral of supporting timbers" within the LAPD organizational structure.

Officer Statements and Themes

The following set of officer statements and themes provides not only an examination of LAPD's managerial and administrative response during the time of the department's meltdown, but also a test of Parker's prophecy—that the death blow to the professional model of policing would be caused by something or someone inside the LAPD organization, not the result of challenges originating from outside the organization's walls. In all, five specific themes were identified within all officer statements containing the general theme that LAPD's meltdown occurred inside the organization as a result of actions or inactions taken by the department's administration/management in response to outside "enemies" who had organized a coup to topple the professional model of policing. Additionally, the content of this section serves as a test of Parker's prophecy of doom for the professional model should the department falter on its ability to prevent barbarism from rotting the LAPD's internal timbers supporting the morality of the organization's policing culture.

Theme 1: Chief Gates

Numerous comments were received from officers mentioning Chief Gates and his role as guardian of the department against outside influences. As will be noted below, a large number of statements reflected support for the Chief's handling of his outside adversaries and encouraged him to remain in office and fight against the department's enemies. The majority of these officers saw the chief as maintaining strong support for street officers, yet held members of his LAPD administration/management responsible for the department's internal meltdown. Alternatively, a comparatively smaller group of officers suggested that the chief should step down from office, and some officers even blamed the chief for the LAPD's ultimate meltdown.

#196

We need new thinking from Captain to Chief.

(Police Officer, Male, African American, 23 years old, 2 years PO, 2 years LAPD, Chief when hired: Gates) (Figure 7.2)

#197

Chief Gates and XXXX are outstanding officers. Other upper management has proven to be unfaithful to this department. Even immoral. If this Department is in a family there sure is a lot of incest going on. Our morality is disgraceful. It is common practice

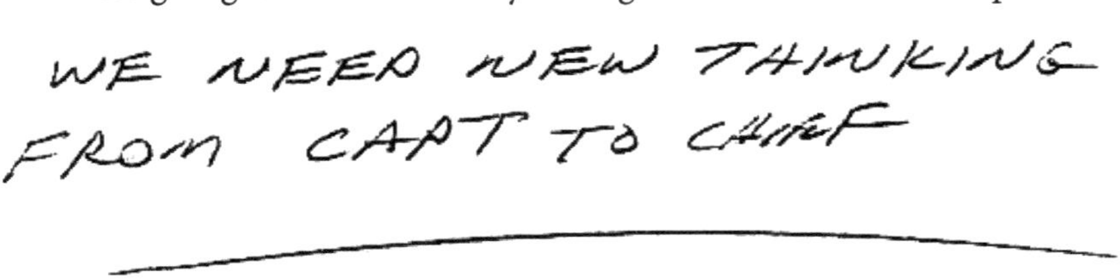

Figure 7.2 Statement Transcription: We need new thinking from Captain to Chief (see Officer Informant statement #196).

daily for our officers to lie to everyone, citizens, supervisors, wives, husbands, etc.

(Police Officer, Male, Caucasian, 30 years old, 11 years PO, 11 years LAPD, Chief when hired: Gates)

#198

Conditions can only improve for the community and LAPD in general when upper level supervision and policy makers can wake up each day and look in the mirror and know that their day work directly affects public safety and the safety of officers working the streets, and then has the clear desire to help those people (community and street officers) be safe. The Chief must demand honesty from all his subordinates especially negative information and not allow boot lickers to "pound sunshine up his ass!" We, at the lower end are thought of as stupid for not promoting. Perhaps it is not as much being stupid as making up for the deficiencies of our policy makers and doing what is necessary to try and keep the streets as safe as possible for everyone's families, yours and mine. Isn't that the basic police job anyway? Leadership is not allowed in the Department!

(Police Officer, Male, Caucasian, 44 years old, 20 years PO, 20 years LAPD, Chief when hired: Davis) (Figure 7.3)

#199

Management has forgotten they are there to help working officers and detectives. They have become self-serving and egotistical (including the Chief!) Changes should start with staff officers in their attitudes before trying to change conditions for working officers and detectives. The 6th Floor has become an Ivory Tower. They need to get out into the community as well as the officers. The Chief should retire now.

(Police Officer, Male, Caucasian, 40 years old, 17 years PO, 17 years LAPD, Chief when hired: Davis)

#200

This dept is too top heavy. The staff has to much freedom in changing things without the knowledge of the chief. The fact that south bureau has the majority of the problem we have less resources and the worst command staff. They also have no common sense when it comes to working relationships with police officers. Their noses are buried too deep in their own career.

(Police Officer, Male, Caucasian, 30 years old, 5 years PO, 5 years LAPD, Chief when hired: Gates)

#201

Dept from the Chief down fail to stand behind the field ofcrs and tend to treat them as bastard children.

(Police Officer, Male, Caucasian, 38 years old, 6 years PO, 6 years LAPD, Chief when hired: Gates) (Figure 7.4)

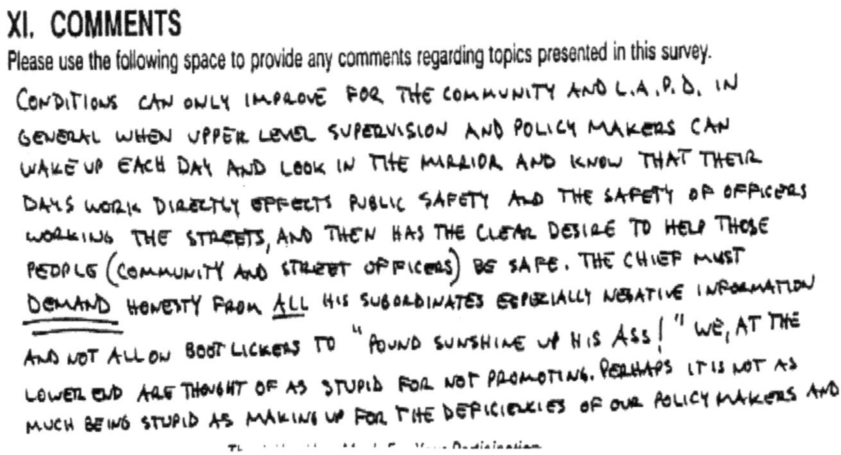

XI. COMMENTS

Please use the following space to provide any comments regarding topics presented in this survey.

CONDITIONS CAN ONLY IMPROVE FOR THE COMMUNITY AND L.A.P.D. IN GENERAL WHEN UPPER LEVEL SUPERVISION AND POLICY MAKERS CAN WAKE UP EACH DAY AND LOOK IN THE MIRROR AND KNOW THAT THEIR DAYS WORK DIRECTLY EFFECTS PUBLIC SAFETY AND THE SAFETY OF OFFICERS WORKING THE STREETS, AND THEN HAS THE CLEAR DESIRE TO HELP THOSE PEOPLE (COMMUNITY AND STREET OFFICERS) BE SAFE. THE CHIEF MUST DEMAND HONESTY FROM ALL HIS SUBORDINATES ESPECIALLY NEGATIVE INFORMATION AND NOT ALLOW BOOT LICKERS TO "POUND SUNSHINE UP HIS ASS!" WE, AT THE LOWER END ARE THOUGHT OF AS STUPID FOR NOT PROMOTING. PERHAPS IT IS NOT AS MUCH BEING STUPID AS MAKING UP FOR THE DEFICIENCIES OF OUR POLICY MAKERS AND

Figure 7.3 Statement Transcription: Conditions can only improve for the community and LAPD in general when upper level supervision and policy makers can wake up each day and look in the mirror and know that their day work directly affects public safety and the safety of officers working the streets, and then has the clear desire to help those people (community and street officers) be safe. The Chief must demand honesty from all his subordinates especially negative information and not allow boot lickers to "pound sunshine up his ass!" We, at the lower end are thought of as stupid for not promoting. Perhaps it is not as much being stupid as making up for the deficiencies of our policy makers and doing what is necessary to try and keep the streets as safe as possible for everyone's families, yours and mine. Isn't that the basic police job anyway? Leadership is not allowed in the Department! (see Officer Informant statement #198).

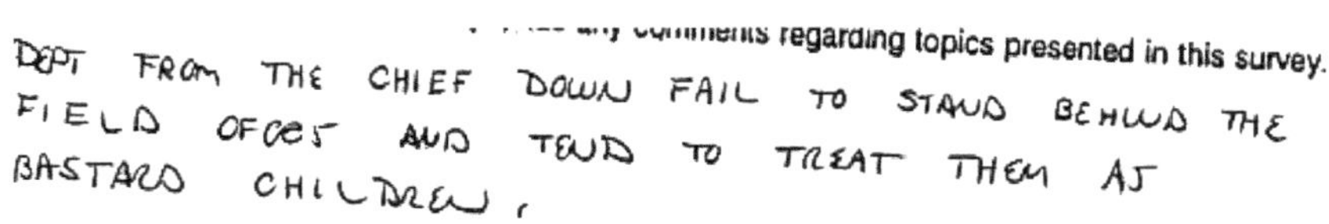

... comments regarding topics presented in this survey.

DEPT FROM THE CHIEF DOWN FAIL TO STAND BEHIND THE FIELD OFCRS AND TEND TO TREAT THEM AS BASTARD CHILDREN,

Figure 7.4 Statement Transcription: Department from the chief down fail to stand behind the field officers and tend to treat them as bastard children (see Officer Informant statement #201).

#202

Admins—Too much information is "Filtered" before it gets to the Chief(s). I hear, "we can't say that" or "we should word that another way." If an officer or Sgt. does staff work because he or she is the expert in that area—that work should go to the brass—not what a Lt. or Captain think the brass wants to see. Training—we are losing the war here! Officers are graduating that should never have been hired. The dept. must regain control of the pre-employee process.

(Detective, Male, Caucasian, 37 years old, 16 years PO, 16 years LAPD, Chief when hired: Davis)

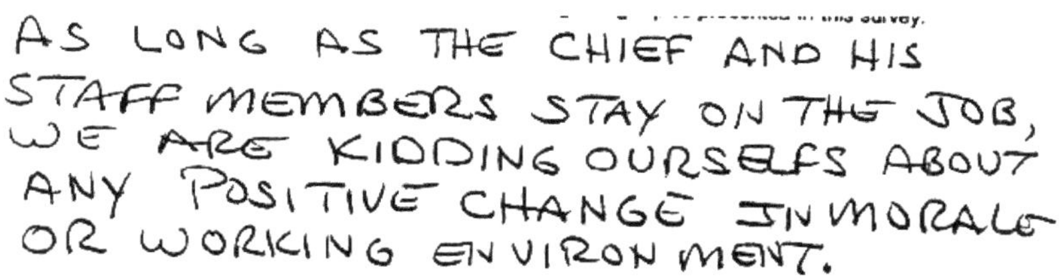
AS LONG AS THE CHIEF AND HIS STAFF MEMBERS STAY ON THE JOB, WE ARE KIDDING OURSELFS ABOUT ANY POSITIVE CHANGE IN MORALE OR WORKING ENVIRONMENT.

Figure 7.5 Statement Transcription: As long as the Chief [Gates] and his staff members stay on the job, we are kidding ourselves about any positive change in morale or working environment (see Officer Informant statement #204).

#203

I love my job, my immediate supervisor and my Chiefs, Booth and Gates—This is and always will be the best Law Enforcement Agency in the world as long as our top administration remains the same.

(Police Officer, Female, Caucasian, 50 years old, 25 years PO, 25 years LAPD, Chief when hired: Parker)

#204

As long as the Chief and his staff members stay on the job, we are kidding ourselves about any positive change in morale or working environment.

(Police Officer, Male, Hispanic, 42 years old, 19 years PO, 19 years LAPD, Chief when hired: Davis) (Figure 7.5)

#205

I came on this job some years ago believing that LAPD was a progressive, proactive, well trained disciplined department that was employee oriented. Now, 8½ years later it appears all of those traits are missing. I am willing to be a team player with a common goal of developing the best department possible, but right now there seems to be no leadership other than a lame duck Chief. Don't get me wrong, I support the Chief but facts are facts….

(Police Officer, Male, Caucasian, 34 years old, 9 years PO, 9 years LAPD, Chief when hired: Gates)

#206

Good luck—we need a new Chief.

(Sergeant, Male, Caucasian, 45 years old, 22 years PO, 22 years LAPD, Chief when hired: Davis) (Figure 7.6)

#207

This dept. needs to be overhauled. Top management is only interested in themselves. There is no togetherness at the top. Management

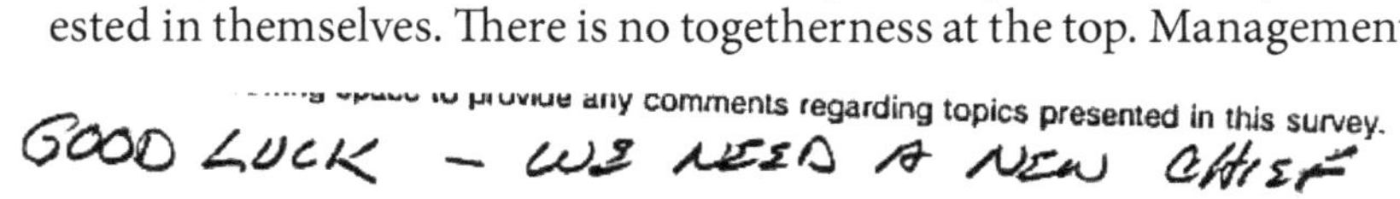
provide any comments regarding topics presented in this survey.

GOOD LUCK – WE NEED A NEW CHIEF

Figure 7.6 Statement Transcription: Good luck—we need a new Chief (see Officer Informant statement #206).

are not the men/women in blue & do not represent the LAPD, only themselves. I love & respect Gates but his management team does not give him a true picture. I've been on the street for my 22 years & I know these things to be true. It's time that management stops listening to each other & listen to the real LAPD, patrol. But that will not happen!!! Good luck.

(Sergeant, Male, Caucasian, 47 years old, 22 years PO, 22 years LAPD, Chief when hired: Davis)

#208

A "few" of our command staff including Chief Gates are people oriented leaders/administrators. Quite a few others need to set their egos aside & be responsive to their people. I'm sure this would except for the dissenters, provide an atmosphere of cooperation, ultimately beneficial to the department and Los Angeles citizens/community.

(Lieutenant, Male, Caucasian, 52 years old, 29 years PO, 29 years LAPD, Chief when hired: Parker)

#209

There is no intent here to case Chief Gates in a bad light or to demean him in any way. He's the finest Chief that I have observed during my tenure. However, the same cannot be said of those staff officers below him.

(Lieutenant, Male, Hispanic, 50 years old, 26 years PO, 26 years LAPD, Chief when hired: Parker)

#210

I believe Chief Gates has done an excellent job as COP. However, I question the judgment and loyalty of some top administrators aspiring to become his successor.

(Detective, Male, African American, 45 years old, 23 years PO, 23 years LAPD, Chief when hired: Reddin) (Figure 7.7)

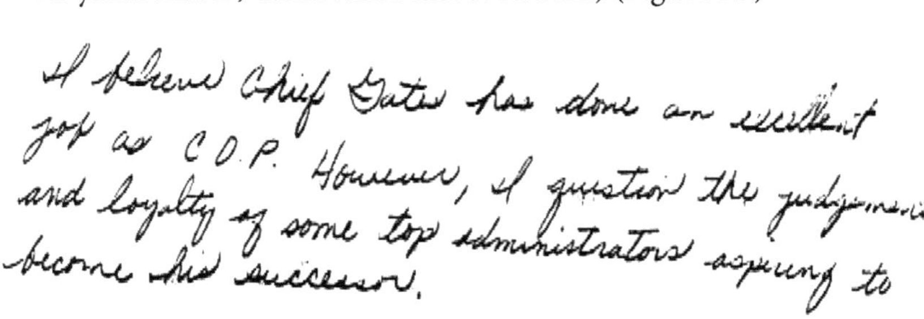
I believe Chief Gates has done an excellent
job as C.O.P. However, I question the judgment
and loyalty of some top administrators aspiring to
become his successor.

Figure 7.7 Statement Transcription: I believe Chief Gates has done an excellent job as COP [Chief of Police]. However, I question the judgment and loyalty of some top administrators aspiring to become his successor (see Officer Informant statement #210).

#211

The problem with management all evolved around the Chief being supportive of imbeciles who make decisions that are completely out of all reality. We have been taken in to believe that we should all be supportive. But at the 1st sign of trouble almost every C.O. went out of their way to stab him in the back, that is loyalty? There are Capts who personally get involved in destroying a policeman's career. The discipline of ofcrs is needed of which I strongly agree, its just that the managers of the whole system have no experience at all to be helpful at what's happening. Loyalty has only flowed one way. The embarrassment of this dept is management not the street policeman—not the detectives.... The dept is now in a position of disappearing in the way that I know it. We're not that effective organization that we once were, thanks to management. We will never be that force again. It's time for an outsider to become Chief only because he would force all the command staff out. This is the only way to restore some faith in management within the dept. I don't think Chief Gates has enough power to remove the middle management of the dept. Most of us see middle management as the problem and until the Chief sees this, nothing will ever improve we're in worse shape now than when Chief Davis left. The effectiveness of middle management can best be described the last few years as a snake who has swallowed their own tail. The Chief is not the problem!

(Police Officer, Male, Hispanic, 43 years old, 20 years PO, 20 years LAPD, Chief when hired: Davis)

#212

A new COP will hopefully give the dept a sense of direction and mission, something it does not have. First problem the dept must tackle is winning back the community.

(Lieutenant, Male, Caucasian, 42 years old, 20 years PO, 20 years LAPD, Chief when hired: Davis)

#213

Top management in the dept is ineffective. Every C/O has his own hidden agenda; looking out for himself instead of the officers he commands. The Assistant and Deputy Chiefs are for the most part a disgrace. It is impossible for a Chief of Police to be effective when so many of his subordinate chiefs are stabbing him in the back.

(Sergeant, Male, Caucasian, 35 years old, 14 years PO, 14 years LAPD, Chief when hired: Davis) (Figure 7.8)

#214

LAPD need someone to back us like (Sherman Block) did for his troops. Not pencil pushers like we have now nobody wants to back us the average patrol cop.

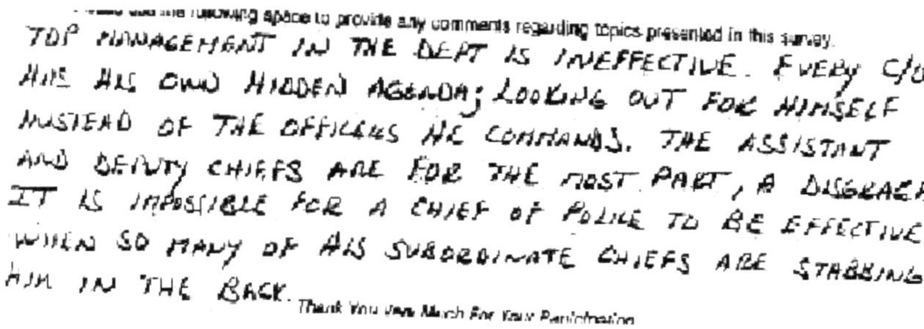
… use the following space to provide any comments regarding topics presented in this survey.

TOP MANAGEMENT IN THE DEPT IS INEFFECTIVE. EVERY C/O HAS HIS OWN HIDDEN AGENDA; LOOKING OUT FOR HIMSELF INSTEAD OF THE OFFICERS HE COMMANDS. THE ASSISTANT AND DEPUTY CHIEFS ARE FOR THE MOST PART, A DISGRACE. IT IS IMPOSSIBLE FOR A CHIEF OF POLICE TO BE EFFECTIVE WHEN SO MANY OF HIS SUBORDINATE CHIEFS ARE STABBING HIM IN THE BACK.

Thank You Very Much For Your Participation

Figure 7.8 Statement Transcription: Top management in the department is ineffective. Every C/O [Commanding officer] has his own hidden agenda; looking out for himself instead of the officers he commands. The Assistant and Deputy Chiefs are for the most part a disgrace. It is impossible for a Chief of Police to be effective when so many of his subordinate chiefs are stabbing him in the back (see Officer Informant statement #213).

(Police Officer, Male, Hispanic, 26 years old, 1 year PO, 1 year LAPD, Chief when hired: Gates)

#215

I believe that Chief Gates has done more for this department than any of the past prior 2 chiefs. I also believe that he would have done more if not for the infighting of the other chiefs. It appears that Chief Gates main concern is our department and its goals. The lesser chiefs appear to be more concerned with their own goals, with the department second.

(Police Officer, Male, Caucasian, 49 years old, 18 years PO, 18 years LAPD, Chief when hired: Davis) (Figure 7.9)

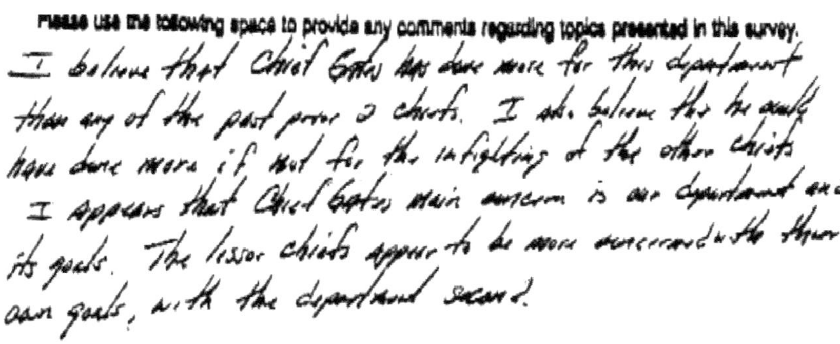
Please use the following space to provide any comments regarding topics presented in this survey.

I believe that Chief Gates has done more for this department than any of the past prior 2 chiefs. I also believe that he would have done more if not for the infighting of the other chiefs. I appears that Chief Gates main concern is our department and its goals. The lessor chiefs appear to be more concerned with their own goals, with the department second.

Figure 7.9 Statement Transcription: I believe that Chief Gates has done more for this department than any of the past prior 2 chiefs. I also believe that he would have done more if not for the infighting of the other chiefs. It appears that Chief Gates main concern is our department and its goals. The lesser chiefs appear to be more concerned with their own goals, with the department second (see Officer Informant statement #215).

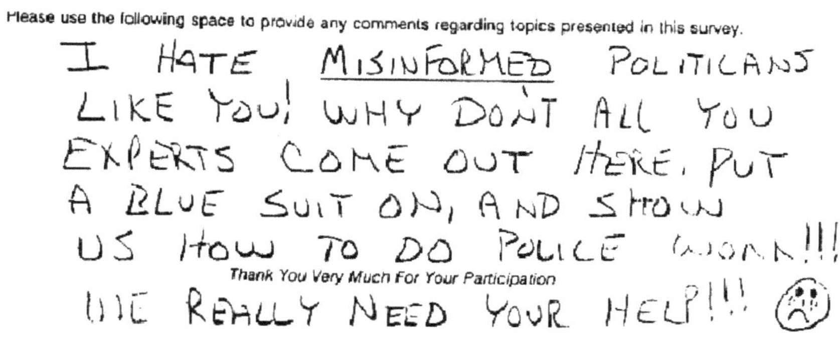

Please use the following space to provide any comments regarding topics presented in this survey.

I HATE MISINFORMED POLITICANS LIKE YOU! WHY DON'T ALL YOU EXPERTS COME OUT HERE, PUT A BLUE SUIT ON, AND SHOW US HOW TO DO POLICE WORK!!!

Thank You Very Much For Your Participation

WE REALLY NEED YOUR HELP!!!

Figure 7.10 Statement Transcription: I hate misinformed politicians like you! [referring to Chief Gates] Why don't all you experts come out here, put a blue suit on, and show us how to do police work!!! We really need your help!!! (see Officer Informant statement #217).

#216

Control your Deputy Chiefs, who are all implementing different programs to look good for the community so they (Deputy Chiefs) could take your duties as Chief of Police. Get back into police work and help patrol officers who are both making you The Chief look good.

(Police Officer, Male, African American, 25 years old, 5 years PO, 5 years LAPD, Chief when hired: Gates)

#217

I hate misinformed politicians like you! [Referring directly to Gates or to the command staff or both] Why don't all you experts come out here, put a blue suit on, and show us how to do police work!!! We really need your help!!! (Officer information not available)

(Figure 7.10)

#218

TOP ADMINISTRATION: I am lucky to be working for a great Staff Officer at the present, however, I am completely dissatisfied with the leadership at the top of the Department. THERE IS NO LEADERSHIP! There is no leadership, acceptance of responsibility or accountability at the upper level. All these characteristics are only required of police officers and sergeants (sometimes lieutenants). Staff officers are not "people oriented," they're "task oriented." Staff is too concerned with "damage assessment" and "damage control" then about caring what the field officers want, need and feel. Loyalty is one-way from the bottom up. The Chief can't find out what's going on because he has a group of people in between that think they know whats best and he doesn't need to be bothered with it. Ego's at the top as well as middle management are destroying this department. The administrators on the sixth floor should remove their doors and start talking to each other. I'm out of room, but if the Chief wants me to continue, I'm Sergeant XXXX.

(Sergeant, Male, Caucasian, 45 years old, 24 years PO, 24 years LAPD, Chief when hired: Reddin)

#219

Top management does not appear to be aware or sensitive to the needs of the front line troops, i.e., patrol & dets. We have inferior equip but are the ones who deal with the citizens on a regular daily basis. Some top mgmt seem more concerned with their own careers than the needs of the "working" officers. Does the Chief have any idea of what's happening out here where the rubber meets the road?

(Detective, Male, Caucasian, 45 years old, 21 years PO, 21 years LAPD, Chief when hired: Davis)

#220

I think the leadership of this dept. below Chief and above Lt. is so concerned with kissing political ass to get the up-coming chief's spot they have lost all concept of what they are really supposed to be doing. Of course that's assuming they ever did know what their job was and were capable of doing it.

(Police Officer, Male, Caucasian, 43 years old, 22 years PO, 22 years LAPD, Chief when hired: Davis)

Theme 2: LAPD Administrators/Managers Don't Care About Street Officers

The following comments, taken together, formulate a theme suggesting that the LAPD's administrators/managers either intentionally or inadvertently turn their backs on the needs and concerns of street officers. Some comments suggest this behavior is arrogance on the part of higher-ranking officers toward lower-ranking officers; other officers blame the lack of concern for patrol and other rank-and-file officers on the general incompetence of the department's administration/management. There is also a general sentiment among officers that they are looked down upon by higher-echelon officers because they prefer to stay working the streets rather than promote up the ranks to a supervisory position.

#221

I think that we have good field supervisors in general. However, I feel that the Administrative people: Captains, other personnel, care more about their careers and kissing butt than about the Department or Field Police Officers.

(Police Officer, Male, Caucasian, 26 years old, 1 year PO, 1 year LAPD, Chief when hired: Gates) (Figure 7.11)

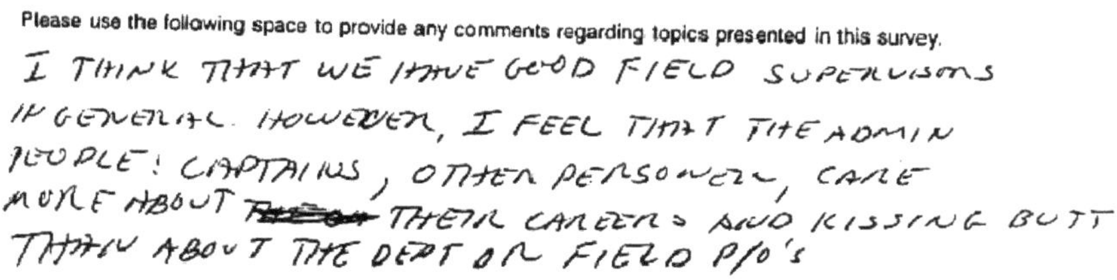

Please use the following space to provide any comments regarding topics presented in this survey.

I THINK THAT WE HAVE GOOD FIELD SUPERVISORS IN GENERAL. HOWEVER, I FEEL THAT THE ADMIN PEOPLE: CAPTAINS, OTHER PERSONNEL, CARE MORE ABOUT ~~THE~~ THEIR CAREERS AND KISSING BUTT THAN ABOUT THE DEPT OR FIELD P/O's

Figure 7.11 Statement Transcription: I think that we have good field supervisors in general. However, I feel that the Administrative people: Captains, other personnel, care more about their careers and kissing butt than about the Department or Field Patrol Officers (see Officer Informant statement #221).

#222

We are lost at sea. The captain of the ship is fighting his crew for control. The Department treats its patrol force poorly. The clear message sent is, if you have no talent, you work patrol. They keep asking those with the least resources to do more. The leadership at Captain on up in general appears to be more concerned with their next promotion than caring about the people who work for them….

(Sergeant, Male, Caucasian, 46 years old, 17 years PO, 17 years LAPD, Chief when hired: Davis) (Figure 7.12)

#223

You people do not give a fuck about the street police officer. You are wasting our time and your time with this fucked up survey.

(Police Officer, Male, Caucasian, 31 years old, 9 years PO, 9 years LAPD, Chief when hired: Gates) (Figure 7.13)

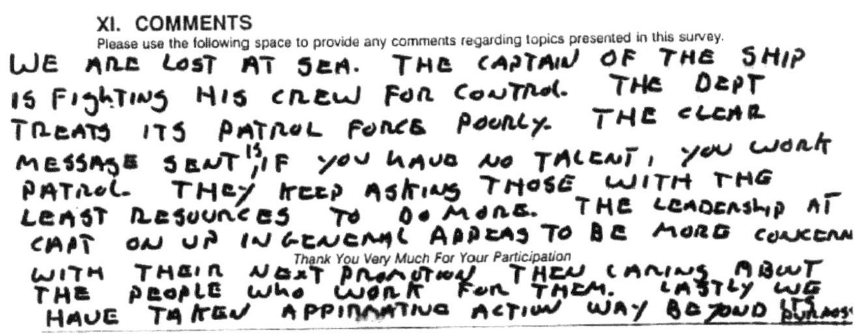

XI. COMMENTS

Please use the following space to provide any comments regarding topics presented in this survey.

WE ARE LOST AT SEA. THE CAPTAIN OF THE SHIP IS FIGHTING HIS CREW FOR CONTROL. THE DEPT TREATS ITS PATROL FORCE POORLY. THE CLEAR MESSAGE SENT IS, IF YOU HAVE NO TALENT, YOU WORK PATROL. THEY KEEP ASKING THOSE WITH THE LEAST RESOURCES TO DO MORE. THE LEADERSHIP AT CAPT ON UP IN GENERAL APPEAS TO BE MORE CONCERN WITH THEIR NEXT PROMOTION THEN CARING ABOUT THE PEOPLE WHO WORK FOR THEM. LASTLY WE HAVE TAKEN AFFIRMATIVE ACTION WAY BEYOND ITS PURPOSE

Thank You Very Much For Your Participation

Figure 7.12 Statement Transcription: We are lost at sea. The captain of the ship is fighting his crew for control. The Department treats its patrol force poorly. The clear message sent is that if you have no talent you work patrol. They keep asking those with the least resources to do more. The leadership at Captain on up in general appear to be more concerned with their next promotion than caring about the people who work for them. Lastly, we have taken affirmative action way beyond its purpose (see Officer Informant statement #222).

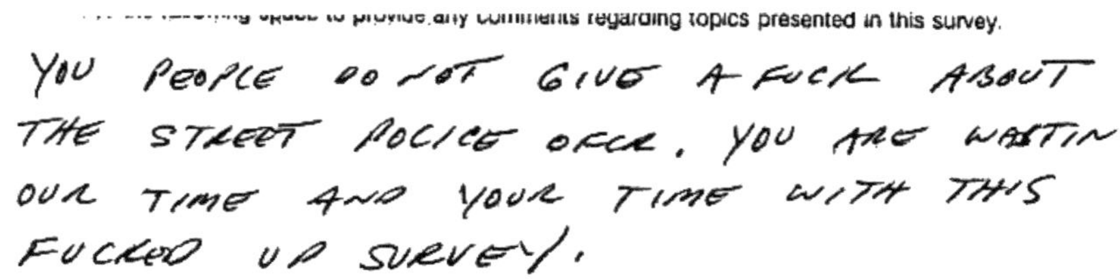
provide any comments regarding topics presented in this survey.

YOU PEOPLE DO NOT GIVE A FUCK ABOUT THE STREET POLICE OFCR. YOU ARE WASTING OUR TIME AND YOUR TIME WITH THIS FUCKED UP SURVEY/.

Figure 7.13 Statement Transcription: You people do not give a fuck about the street police officer. You are wasting our time and your time with this fucked up survey (see Officer Informant statement #223).

#224

I feel that most of management (SGT'S & above) are mainly concerned with self promotion & have lost touch with officers and their needs. Most of upper management want to kiss ass with politicians & high ranking officials than take into consideration w/ the need of ofcrs—morale is low but ofcrs are still getting the job done.

(Police Officer, Male, Caucasian, 26 years old, 1 year PO, 1 year LAPD, Chief when hired: Gates)

#225

The dept still puts more emphasis on promotion than on effective street police work. If you're not promoting you're a moron. The major aim seems to be, transfer and promote, be minimally effective at a lot of things and promote. "Staying on the street is only for the stupid" is the message being transmitted from the top.

(Police Officer, Male, Caucasian, 40 years old, 18 years PO, 15 years LAPD, Chief when hired: Davis)

#226

... I feel prepared to deal with everything on this job except trivial, nitpicking rules overly enforced without reasonableness, and the low esteem patrol is held in on this department, from day one its, "if you want to promote, get out of patrol" This is wrong and counter productive!

(Police Officer, Male, African American, 36 years old, 10 years PO, 2 years LAPD, Chief when hired: Gates)

#227

Commanding officers should immediately identify the top ofcrs within the division and listen to their ideas and input. Those ofcrs that wish to work hard should be given the opportunity to work on their ideas to combat crime. At this time there is no incentive for anyone in patrol to any more then the biggest malcontent drone, except personal pride. Many ofcrs have major knowledge about crime problems and/or suspects in their division. But no one ever lets those ofcrs loose to do what they do best. Crime in LA is going to get a lot worse and the same old tired tactics cannot cope. We need new and imaginative techniques. Don't expect commanders, captains, sgts etc to solve crime. They either don't care or don't know. Turn the right cops loose! And get them out of cars that look like police cars! Try something tricky!

(Police Officer, Male, Caucasian, 42 years old, 19 years PO, 19 years LAPD, Chief when hired: Davis)

#228

This department has always been responsive to the community needs within our job functions. We are not a social agency. Our duties are crime suppression/apprehension & the enforcement of state & local laws. In general, the community members that are dissatisfied with our dept are the same that have been targeted for enforcement at one time or another. The overall morale on this dept is negative. The ofcrs in the field feel management has turned its back. We are losing qualified ofcrs in droves as a result of managements refusal to accept responsibility for existing policies.

(Detective, Male, Caucasian, 31 years old, 8 years PO, 8 years LAPD, Chief when hired: Gates)

#229

The top brass has to commit themselves to helping the patrol ofcrs perform their everyday functions rather than self promotion—today—patrol has been forgotten and looked upon as nonpromoters—when they are what this department is all about. Immediate police service to the community.

(Detective, Male, Caucasian, 30 years old, 7 years PO, 7 years LAPD, Chief when hired: Gates) (Figure 7.14)

#230

This will have no positive results. Like all other paper work it will be filed & forgotten. The staff ofcrs of the department are too busy playing politics (and they are terrible at it) to care about field ofcrs. If you can't do something right gentlemen you should go to (political) training. The staff ofcrs don't care about the department but they expect rank & file to—loyalty should work both ways not for only staff capt. & above.

(Police Officer, Male, Caucasian, 36 years old, 8 years PO, 8 years LAPD, Chief when hired: Gates)

#231

Staff ofcrs are out of touch with patrol. Many staff ofcrs only care about their success. Patrol is always looked down on. Patrol is what makes this dept. Patrol sgts & lts should be adv pay grades. Not someone at a bureau crime for periods etc. Patrol ofcrs worry about

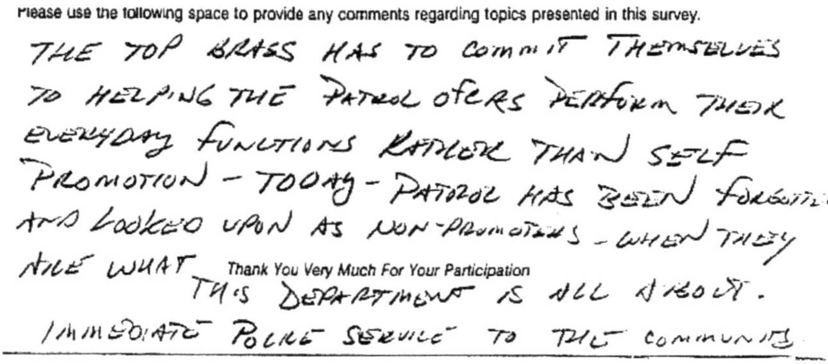
Please use the following space to provide any comments regarding topics presented in this survey.

THE TOP BRASS HAS TO COMMIT THEMSELVES TO HELPING THE PATROL OFCRS PERFORM THEIR EVERYDAY FUNCTIONS RATHER THAN SELF PROMOTION - TODAY - PATROL HAS BEEN FORGOTTEN AND LOOKED UPON AS NON-PROMOTERS - WHEN THEY ARE WHAT THIS DEPARTMENT IS ALL ABOUT. IMMEDIATE POLICE SERVICE TO THE COMMUNITY

Thank You Very Much For Your Participation

Figure 7.14 Statement Transcription: The top brass has to commit themselves to helping the patrol officers perform their everyday functions rather than self promotion—today—patrol has been forgotten and looked upon as nonpromoters—when they are what this department is all about. Immediate police service to the community (see Officer Informant statement #229).

181s Patrol officers don't have time to study on duty. Staff posit do study on duty and succeed. That is not the way it should be.

(Sergeant, Male, Caucasian, 43 years old, 21 years PO, 21 years LAPD, Chief when hired: Davis)

#232

To Staff: "Do unto others as you …"

(Sergeant, Male, Caucasian, 48 years old, 22 years PO, 18 years LAPD, Chief when hired: Davis)

#233

I am a very loyal dedicated employee who likes to work but my experience with the dept in sick or injury cases is you are just a number. You have no name or face & are replaceable at anything. This non-caring attitude for the employee has caused some employees to develop an attitude of "Why should I care for the Public, the City or Dept. doesn't care for me." Ask yourself this, when was the last time you received a Xmas present, bonus or a tip for an above & beyond the call of duty situation. We are the most needed city service but the least rewarded or liked for our services.

(Police Officer, Male, Caucasian, 45 years old, 23 years PO, 23 years LAPD, Chief when hired: Reddin)

#234

I am as proud to be a member of the Los Angeles Police Dept. as I was when sworn in 7 years ago. My loyalty is the same. I must say, however, that as a patrol ofcr, serving all 7 years in patrol, I as well as others have continually felt unappreciated by the public, immediate

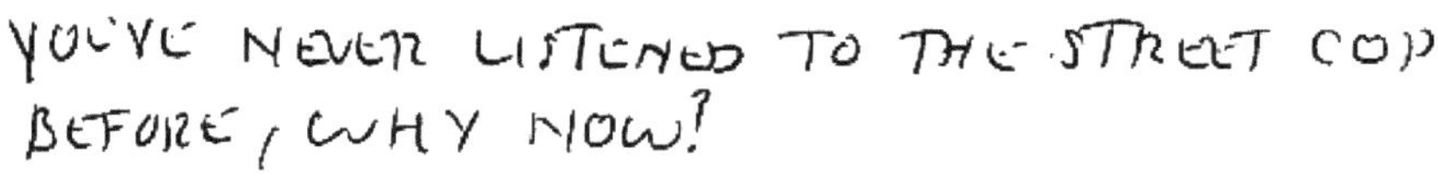

Figure 7.15 Statement Transcription: You've never listened to the street cop before, why now? (see Officer Informant statement #235).

supervision and the dept. management. Patrol ofcrs are what makes or breaks this dept's image of greatness. Those who serve it in its proudest and grandest tradition deserve to have recognition not continuous negativity in roll calls. Let someone speak up for all the good we do out there everyday that goes unseen by management, but leaves the citizen with a good feeling and his or her dignity. Please do not overlook how low the morale of the majority of patrol ofcrs has become.

#235

You've never listened to the street cop before, why now?

(Police Officer, Male, Caucasian, 40 years old, 15 years PO, 15 years LAPD, Chief when hired: Davis) (Figure 7.15)

#236

Admin needs to be more responsive to ofcrs. Admin still remains the biggest stress factor in an ofcr's life. Some incentive for patrol is needed!

(Police Officer, Male, Caucasian, 33 years old, 5 years PO, 5 years LAPD, Chief when hired: Gates)

Theme 3: LAPD's Administrators/Managers Are Out of Touch With the Street

Related to the above theme are the general comments presented in the following theme that upper management of the LAPD is out of touch with the realities of police work. Specifically, many officers included in this section felt that the LAPD's administrators/managers constructed policing policies that were either antiquated or unrealistic. Comments, as will be noted below, refer to the department's policy-making headquarters (Parker Center) as the Ivory Tower, suggesting that the LAPD's center for policy making is far removed from the real world of policing. Some officers also suggested that administrators and managers should have mandatory field duty to see what it was really like for patrol officers on the streets.

#237

I believe that the upper command (i.e. Captain & above) has lost sight of what is occurring on the streets of our city, drugs, guns,

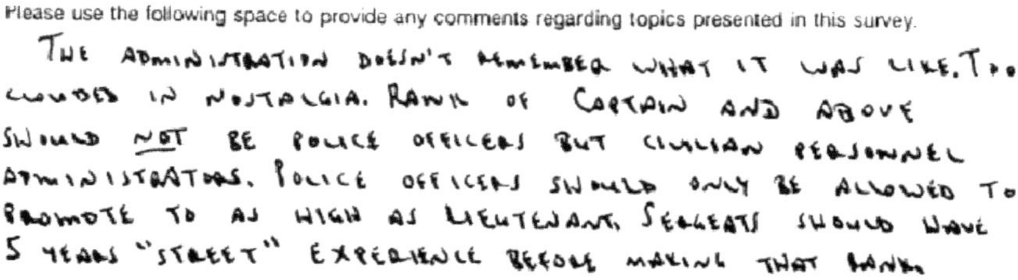
Please use the following space to provide any comments regarding topics presented in this survey.

THE ADMINISTRATION DOESN'T REMEMBER WHAT IT WAS LIKE. TOO CLOUDED IN NOSTALGIA. RANK OF CAPTAIN AND ABOVE SHOULD NOT BE POLICE OFFICERS BUT CIVILIAN PERSONNEL ADMINISTRATORS. POLICE OFFICERS SHOULD ONLY BE ALLOWED TO PROMOTE TO AS HIGH AS LIEUTENANT. SERGEANTS SHOULD HAVE 5 YEARS "STREET" EXPERIENCE BEFORE MAKING THAT RANK.

Figure 7.16 Statement Transcription: Top administration doesn't remember what it was like. Too clouded by nostalgia. Rank of Captain and above should not be police officers but civilian personnel administrators. Police officers should only be allowed to promote to as high as Lieutenant. Sergeants should have 5 years "street" experience before making that rank (see Officer Informant statement #238).

gangs & even traffic control. I believe that all Captains and above (Chiefs included) should have a mandatory field working day a month. They must actually work in a patrol unit.

(Police Officer, Male, Caucasian, 28 years old, 3 years PO, 3 years LAPD, Chief when hired: Gates)

#238

Top administration doesn't remember what it was like. Too clouded by nostalgia. Rank of Captain and above should not be police officers but civilian personnel administrators. Police officers should only be allowed to promote to as high as Lieutenant. Sergeants should have 5 years "street" experience before making that rank.

(Police Officer, Male, Caucasian, 45 years old, 17 years PO, 17 years LAPD, Chief when hired: Davis) (Figure 7.16)

#239

You should place management (Lt's-Capt's-Commanders, etc) twice a week in patrol so they know what is a police officer. You should train management not to be complete liars, racist and cowards. Promotions should be based on knowledge and not who says "Yes Sir Master." Back up your officer and reduce stupid 181s. Go back to basic police work … etc., etc., etc.…

(Police Officer, Male, Hispanic, 45 years old, 16 years PO, 16 years LAPD, Chief when hired: Davis) (Figure 7.17)

#240

Revamp upper management. You must have 5–10 years for P-3 (LAPD's most advanced level of patrol officer) plus patrol experience. Supervisor 10+ years—with 8+ years in the field. You have ill trained, non-functional P-3s & Supervisors with 1–2 years on the job, maybe 3 years patrol. They don't know anything.

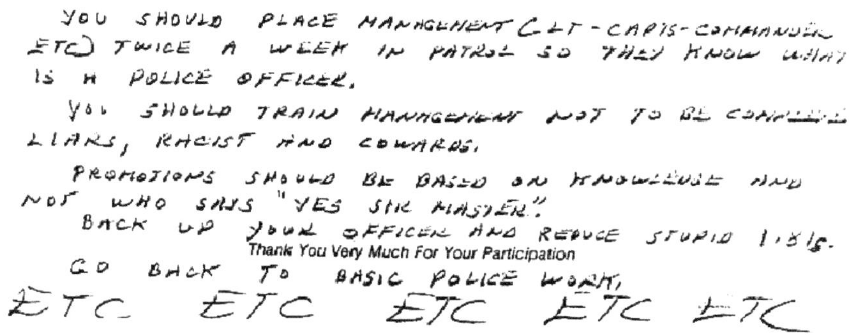
YOU SHOULD PLACE MANAGEMENT (LT-CAPTS-COMMANDER ETC) TWICE A WEEK IN PATROL SO THEY KNOW WHAT IS A POLICE OFFICER.
YOU SHOULD TRAIN MANAGEMENT NOT TO BE COMPLETE LIARS, RACIST AND COWARDS.
PROMOTIONS SHOULD BE BASED ON KNOWLEDGE AND NOT WHO SAYS "YES SIR MASTER".
BACK UP YOUR OFFICER AND REDUCE STUPID 1.81s.
Thank You Very Much For Your Participation
GO BACK TO BASIC POLICE WORK,
ETC ETC ETC ETC ETC

Figure 7.17 Statement Transcription: You should place management (Lieutenants-Captains-Commanders, etc) twice a week in patrol so they know what is a police officer. You should train management not to be complete liars, racist and cowards. Promotions should be based on knowledge and not who says "Yes Sir Master." Back up your officer and reduce stupid 181s [personnel complaints against officers]. Go back to basic police work…etc., etc., etc… (see Officer Informant statement #239).

(Police Officer, Female, Caucasian, Age: N/A, 15 years PO, 15 years LAPD, Chief when hired: Davis)

#241

In general I'm satisfied with my job, but we need more supervisors with "street knowledge." Many supervisors today are nothing but "pencil pushing nobodies who don't know the difference between left or right"!!!!

(Police Officer, Male, Hispanic, 32 years old, 1 year PO, 1 year LAPD, Chief when hired: Gates) (Figure 7.18)

#242

Our biggest and foremost problem is our upper management they are completely out of touch with patrol. Patrol is the most important job and we get treated the worst in the area of promotion, training and pay.

(Police Officer, Male, Caucasian, 29 years old, 6 years PO, 6 years LAPD, Chief when hired: Gates)

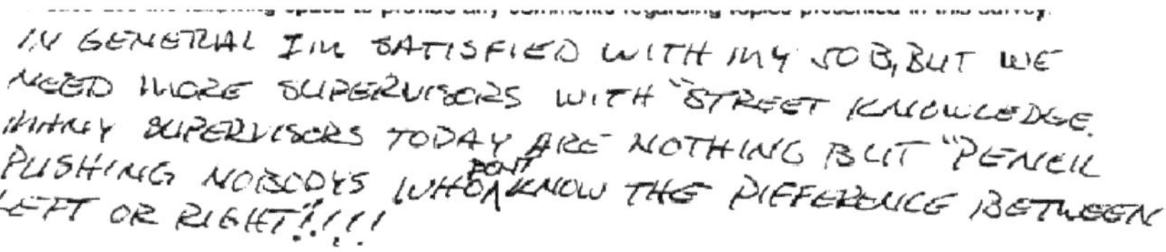
IN GENERAL I'M SATISFIED WITH MY JOB, BUT WE NEED MORE SUPERVISORS WITH "STREET KNOWLEDGE. MANY SUPERVISORS TODAY ARE NOTHING BUT "PENCIL PUSHING NOBODYS WHO DON'T KNOW THE DIFFERENCE BETWEEN LEFT OR RIGHT!!!!

Figure 7.18 Statement Transcription: In general I'm satisfied with my job, but we need more supervisors with "street knowledge." Many supervisors today are nothing but "pencil pushing nobodies who don't know the difference between left or right!!!! (see Officer Informant statement #241).

#243

Service to Public: "For years this department has been selling the public an 'image' without substance." Upper Management has taken every media opportunity to convince the public that we have a handle on gangs, narcotics, and violent crimes. This misrepresentation has caused mistrust in the community where these crimes occur because the citizens wonder if we really know what's going on. Upper management deals in "image" Not substance!

(Detective, Male, Hispanic, 39 years old, 18 years PO, 18 years LAPD, Chief when hired: Davis)

#244

I can handle almost any situation in the field and deal with it with a minimal amount of stress. I feel the biggest problem and where officers get 99% of the stress is from management or (mismanagement).

(Police Officer, Male, Caucasian, 32 years old, 9 years PO, 9 years LAPD, Chief when hired: Gates)

#245

I can't believe there is no common sense anymore, children know what is right & wrong but no one else, I think upper management should get their butts out of the bldgs & into the front line so they can open their eyes.

(Police Officer, Male, Caucasian, 35 years old, 8 years PO, 8 years LAPD, Chief when hired: Gates) (Figure 7.19)

#246

We have a very specific problem at LAPD—individuals who are at the top of the management level, are making decisions and policies that directly effect the rank and file. Normally this would not be a problem; however these individuals obviously lack the knowledge, experience and proper education to make intelligent command decisions.

(Police Officer, Male, Caucasian, 43 years old, 13 years PO, 13 years LAPD, Chief when hired: Davis) (Figure 7.20)

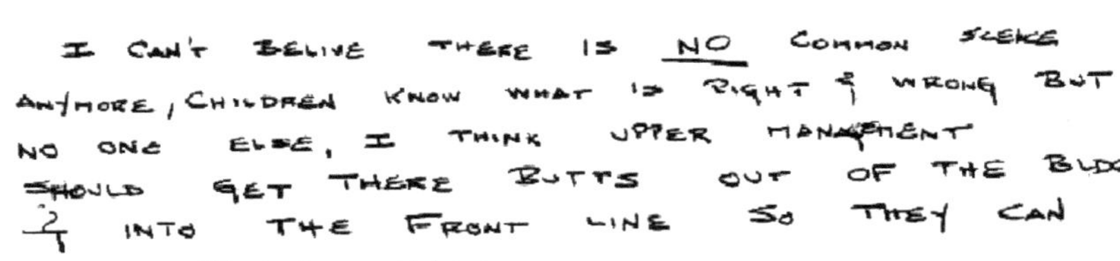
I CAN'T BELIVE THERE IS NO COMMON SENSE
ANYMORE, CHILDREN KNOW WHAT IS RIGHT & WRONG BUT
NO ONE ELSE, I THINK UPPER MANAGEMENT
SHOULD GET THERE BUTTS OUT OF THE BLDGS
& INTO THE FRONT LINE SO THEY CAN
OPEN THEIR EYES.

Figure 7.19 Statement Transcription: I can't believe there is no common sense anymore, children know what is right & wrong but no one else, I think upper management should get there butts out of the bldgs & into the front line so they can open their eyes (see Officer Informant statement #245).

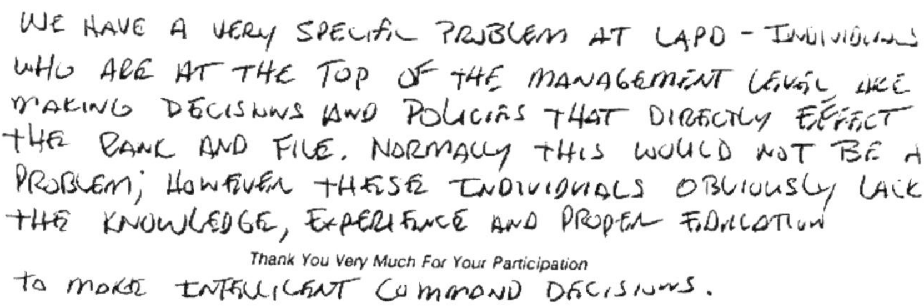
WE HAVE A VERY SPECIFIC PROBLEM AT LAPD - INDIVIDUALS
WHO ARE AT THE TOP OF THE MANAGEMENT LEVEL ARE
MAKING DECISIONS AND POLICIES THAT DIRECTLY EFFECT
THE RANK AND FILE. NORMALLY THIS WOULD NOT BE A
PROBLEM; HOWEVER THESE INDIVIDUALS OBVIOUSLY LACK
THE KNOWLEDGE, EXPERIENCE AND PROPER EDUCATION
Thank You Very Much For Your Participation
TO MAKE INTELLIGENT COMMAND DECISIONS.

Figure 7.20 Statement Transcription: We have a very specific problem at LAPD—individuals who are at the top of the management level, are making decisions and policies that directly affect the rank and file. Normally this would not be a problem; however these individuals obviously lack the knowledge, experience and proper education to make intelligent command decisions (see Officer Informant statement #246).

#247

Supervisors like XXXX who are out of touch with his subordinates. The Dept is too concerned about public image and doesn't care about its officers. Negative rules + regulations are always spotlighted. Nothing positive. Every day there's more paper work and guidelines. We have poor equipment, and are grossly undermanned. During 1.81 investigations, the dept. is more likely to believe the susp who just killed three victs than the officer who arrested him. Care about your men, or you won't have any to care about.

(Police Officer, Male, Asian, 29 years old, 3 years PO, 3 years LAPD, Chief when hired: Gates)

#248

There are many discrepancies from div to div and bureau to bureau. Field ofcrs should be involved in management decisions. Chief XXXX is destroying the XXXX community. He is not sensitive to the needs of the area. He is out of touch with the violent nature of the community. Don't care about ofcrs.

(Police Officer, Male, African American, 34 years old, 10 years PO, 10 years LAPD, Chief when hired: Gates)

Theme 4: LAPD's Administrators/Managers Used Street Officers as Scapegoats

Many officer statements expressed the theme that lower-ranking street officers, especially those working patrol, were being used as scapegoats by the department's administrators/managers in an effort create the illusion that (1) LAPD's street cops were out of control, as suggested by the Christopher Commission report, and (2) administrators and managers were "cracking down" and punishing these officers to correct the problem. Street officers in this theme contend that punishments against them (181 personnel complaints) were being administered indiscriminately or without cause by micromanaging administrators and managers who were attempting to deflect the public's scrutiny from them to the LAPD's patrol force.

#249

There is a feeling among Ptrl Ofcrs that we, as the individuals most likely to make contact with the public, are being used as the dept's scape goats. There is a pervasive distrust of anyone above the rank of sgt-1. By the way, how are we going to make community based policing work with only 8,000 officers?

(Police Officer, Male, Caucasian, 29 years old, 4 years PO, 4 years LAPD, Chief when hired: Gates)

#250

After 20 years of service in LAPD police officers are more afraid of supervisors and 181 then criminals in the streets. I live in N/E div I know that too many criminal/gang members get away with anything they want because police officers are not aggressive and don't believe the courts, brass and don't give a dam. Soon the citz of LA will feel the same way! You don't make things better for the street cop. You just promote each other.

(Police Officer, Male, Hispanic, 42 years old, 20 years PO, 20 years LAPD, Chief when hired: Davis)

#251

Ofcrs feel like they are being told to go out there and do the job with one hand tied behind their back. You can't do aggressive police work (and generate the recap demanded by supervision) without generating 181s & use of force; management is going to have to tolerate lower recap, or tolerate uof [use of force] incidents as a necessary job occurance & not a "pattern of misconduct."

(Police Officer, Male, Caucasian, 38 years old, 8 years PO, 8 years LAPD, Chief when hired: Gates) (Figure 7.21)

#252

How can you expect officers to feel confident about job when they are not backed up. One must wonder if one should back up a Capt or staff in the field because of tendency to neg scrutinize the ofc to point of dysfunction. It is like you don't back me up so why should I back up?

(Police Officer, Male, Caucasian, 47 years old, 25 years PO, 25 years LAPD, Chief when hired: Parker) (Figure 7.22)

#253

The upper management (Captain & above) are dinosaurs. They are too quick to jump on the working bees for every little thing. I took a 5 day

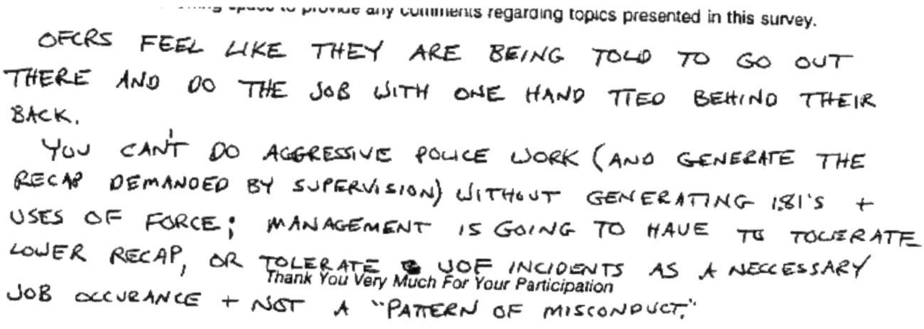
...regarding topics presented in this survey.

OFCRS FEEL LIKE THEY ARE BEING TOLD TO GO OUT THERE AND DO THE JOB WITH ONE HAND TIED BEHIND THEIR BACK.

YOU CAN'T DO AGGRESSIVE POLICE WORK (AND GENERATE THE RECAP DEMANDED BY SUPERVISION) WITHOUT GENERATING 181'S + USES OF FORCE; MANAGEMENT IS GOING TO HAVE TO TOLERATE LOWER RECAP, OR TOLERATE UOF INCIDENTS AS A NECCESSARY JOB OCCURANCE + NOT A "PATTERN OF MISCONDUCT."

Thank You Very Much For Your Participation

Figure 7.21 Statement Transcription: Officers feel like they are being told to go out there and do the job with one hand tied behind their back. You can't do aggressive police work (and generate the recap [daily summary of police officer activities] demanded by supervision) without generating 181's [personnel complain against officers] & use of force; management is going to have to tolerate lower recap, or tolerate uof [use of force] incidents as a necessary job occurance & not a "pattern of misconduct." (see Officer Informant statement #251).

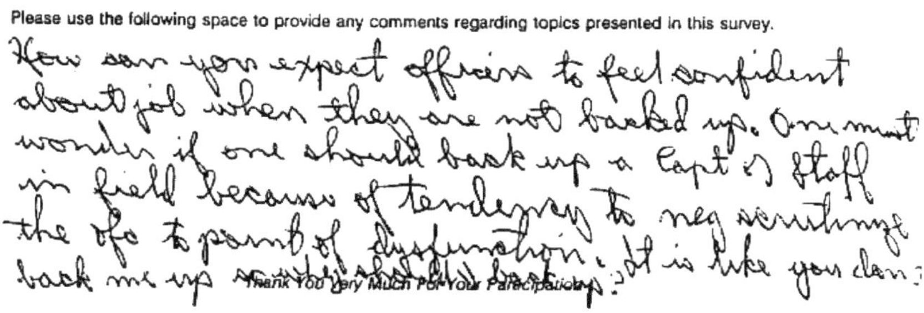
Please use the following space to provide any comments regarding topics presented in this survey.

How can you expect officers to feel confident about job when they are not backed up. One must wonder if one should back up a Capt or staff in field because of tendency to neg scrutinize the ofc to point of dysfunction. It is like you don't back me up ... ?

Thank You Very Much For Your Participation

Figure 7.22 Statement Transcription: How can you expect officers to feel confident about job when they are not backed up. One must wonder if one should back up a Captain or staff in the field because of tendency to negatively scrutinize the officers to point of dysfunction. It is like you don't back me up so why should I back up? (see Officer Informant statement #252).

suspension and my partner who had 22 years on the job at the time took 10 days for the horrible crime of stopping to have a piece of pie without asking permission. The department stresses promotion entirely too much. It takes an attitude that if you are happy being a police officer then you are either lazy, stupid or crooked. The upper management is full of self serving hypocritical individuals who have one concern and that is how can they achieve the next level. We are grossly understaffed and under paid (no cash for overtime). We should be on a 4–10 plan or 3–12 plan [4–10 officers work 4 days per week, 10 hours; 3–12, three days per week, 12 hours]. That would eliminate a great deal of the stress. We should go to a civilian body for disciplinary decisions.

(Police Officer, Male, Hispanic, 37 years old, 10 years PO, 10 years LAPD, Chief when hired: Gates) (Figure 7.23)

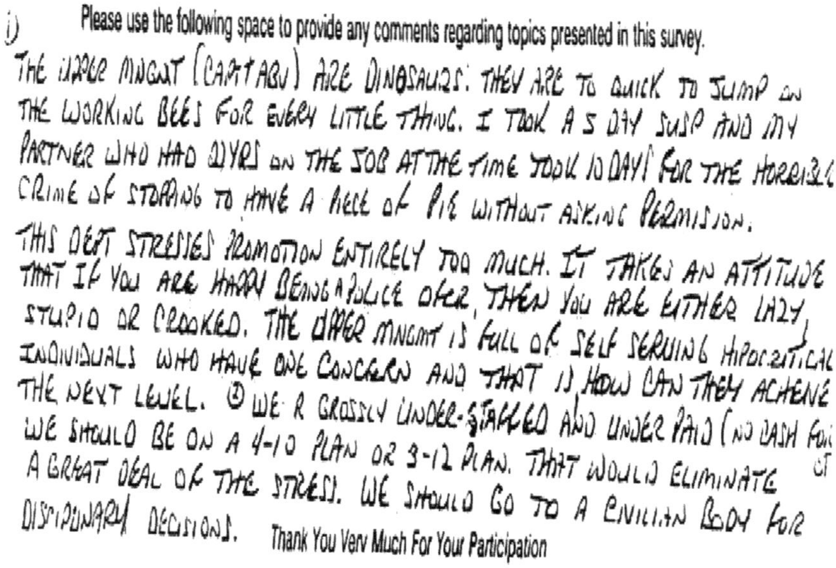
i) Please use the following space to provide any comments regarding topics presented in this survey.

THE UPPER MNGMT (CAPTAIN) ARE DINOSAURS. THEY ARE TO QUICK TO JUMP ON THE WORKING BEES FOR EVERY LITTLE THING. I TOOK A 5 DAY SUSP AND MY PARTNER WHO HAD 22 YRS ON THE JOB AT THE TIME TOOK 10 DAYS FOR THE HORRIBLE CRIME OF STOPPING TO HAVE A PIECE OF PIE WITHOUT ASKING PERMISION.

THIS DEPT STRESSES PROMOTION ENTIRELY TOO MUCH. IT TAKES AN ATTITUDE THAT IF YOU ARE HAPPY BEING A POLICE OFCR, THEN YOU ARE EITHER LAZY, STUPID OR CROOKED. THE UPPER MNGMT IS FULL OF SELF SERVING HIPOCRITICAL INDIVIDUALS WHO HAVE ONE CONCERN AND THAT IS HOW CAN THEY ACHEIVE THE NEXT LEVEL. ③ WE R GROSSLY UNDER-STAFFED AND UNDER PAID (NO CASH FOR OT) WE SHOULD BE ON A 4-10 PLAN OR 3-12 PLAN. THAT WOULD ELIMINATE A GREAT DEAL OF THE STRESS. WE SHOULD GO TO A CIVILIAN BODY FOR DISCIPLINARY DECISIONS.

Thank You Very Much For Your Participation

Figure 7.23 Statement Transcription: The upper management (Captain & above) are dinosaurs. They are too quick to jump on the working bees for every little thing. I took a 5 day suspension and my partner who had 22 yrs. on the job at the time took 10 days for the horrible crime of stopping to have a piece of pie without asking permission. The department stresses promotion entirely too much. It takes an attitude that if you are happy being a police officer then you are either lazy, stupid or crooked. The upper management is full of self serving hypocritical individuals who have one concern and that is how can they achieve the next level. We are grossly understaffed and under paid (no cash for overtime). We should be on a 4-10 plan or 3-12 plan (4-10 officer work 4 days per week 10 hours/ 3-12, three days per week 12 hours). That would eliminate a great deal of the stress. We should go to a civilian body for disciplinary decisions (see Officer Informant statement #253).

#254

Upper Management (Capt's & above) is the most poorly appointed positions on this dept & in most cases are a true embarrassment to our dept than those lower grade ofcrs. whom they punish daily for misconduct they commit but is swept under the table by their peers.

(Police Officer, Male, Hispanic, 45 years old, 18 years PO, 18 years LAPA, Chief when hired: Davis) (Figure 7.24)

#255

There is no unity in this organization. There is a double standard and duplicity throughout the department. Management has no realistic idea how to effectively manage the organization. Each commander and deputy chief has their own agenda with no concern for the department. There is too much micro management

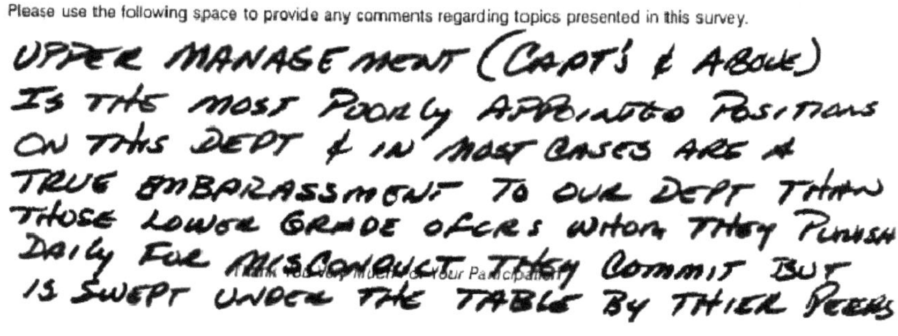

Please use the following space to provide any comments regarding topics presented in this survey.

UPPER MANAGEMENT (CAPT'S & ABOVE) IS THE MOST POORLY APPOINTED POSITIONS ON THIS DEPT & IN MOST CASES ARE A TRUE EMBARRASSMENT TO OUR DEPT THAN THOSE LOWER GRADE OFCRS WHOM THEY PUNISH DAILY FOR MISCONDUCT THEY COMMIT BUT IS SWEPT UNDER THE TABLE BY THIER PEERS

Figure 7.24 Statement Transcription: Upper management (Captains & above) is the most poorly appointed positions on this department & in most cases are a true embarrassment to our department than those lower grade officers whom they punish daily for misconduct they commit but is swept under the table by their peers (see Officer Informant statement #254).

at the bureau level. Captains and above do not have a clue what proper and effective discipline is. Some people are disciplined when they should not be and some are not disciplined when they should be. Some discipline is unfairly based on sex and race. Ideas from senior supervisors are not sought. There is a very low feeling about the department at this time. I have never seen it this bad in my 28 years.

(Sergeant, Male, Caucasian, 50 years old, 28 years PO, 28 years LAPD, Chief when hired: Parker)

#256

It's my personal opinion, that in light of all the negative media attention this department has had you, the administration have failed to defend us against those who are truly responsible for the violence that occurs in the communities that we serve. Rather than make "us" (LAPD) the scapegoat for all the troubles that are prevalent in the city you, the city fathers, and so called "Men of God" should not point fingers at "us" but at yourselves for failing to lead. Now, no one group is alone responsible for today's problems. It falls on everyone of us. But coming back to "us" (LAPD), you the department heads have lost touch with what goes on in the field. The rank and file are not out of control. We are more professional than ever. But there is a serious problem. Our very own people are chipping away at our character and soon there will be nothing left to salvage. I only hope this survey will do something positive. God, knows we need it. Thank you for the opportunity.

(Police Officer, Male, Hispanic, 30 years old, 5 years PO, 5 years LAPD, Chief when hired: Gates)

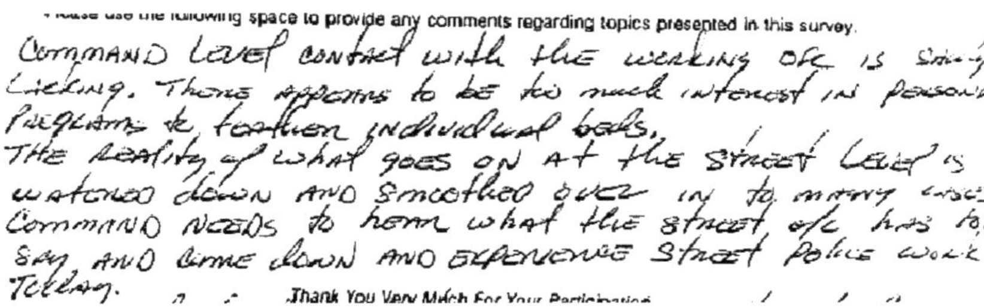

Figure 7.25 Statement Transcription: Command level contact with the working officer is sadly lacking. There appears to be too much interest in personal programs and feathering individual beds. The reality of what goes on at the street level is watered down and smoother over in too many cases. Command needs to hear what the street officer has to say and come down and experience police work today. (See Appendix #254a.)

Theme 5: LAPD's Administration/Management Is Self-Serving

Perhaps most critical of the LAPD's administration/management's reaction to the department's organizational meltdown are the following officer comments, which suggested some of these officers neglected their duties to constructively defend the department against outside adversaries and instead used the meltdown as an opportunity to further their own careers in a possible bid for promotions by "selling out" the LAPD to its enemies.

#257

Captains/staff/command ofcrs need to put on a blue suit and get out in the field. They're the ones who need "in service" training and get their heads out of the clouds. They appear to be brain washed spineless worms attempting to make a name for themselves, no matter what the cost.

(Police Officer, Male, Caucasian, 33 years old, 7 years PO, 7 years LAPD, Chief when hired: Gates)

#258

Fuck Management.

(Detective, Male, Caucasian, 47 years old, 26 years PO, 26 years LAPD, Chief when hired: Parker) (Figure 7.26)

Figure 7.26 Statement Transcription: Fuck Management (see Officer Informant statement #258).

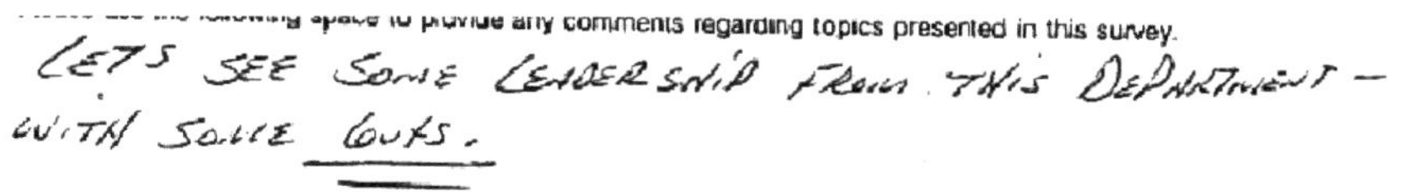
provide any comments regarding topics presented in this survey.
LETS SEE SOME LEADERSHIP FROM THIS DEPARTMENT —
WITH SOME GUTS.

Figure 7.27 Statement Transcription: Let's See Some Leadership From This Department—With Some Guts (see Officer Informant statement #260).

#259

In my opinion the Command Staff on this dept are more preoccupied with promoting & making themselves look good than considering the needs of the policeman working the street. These particular individuals (command staff) cannot make a decision for fearing how it will affect their career, thus they don't make any decisions. There is too much back biting & self service. When you have this attitude in the command staff you have a do nothing attitude among the police rank working the street because no one will back up the working policeman.

(Police Officer, Male, Hispanic, 44 years old, 22 years PO, 22 years LAPD, Chief when hired: Davis)

#260

Let's see some leadership from this department—with some guts.

(Male, Caucasian, 48 years old, 23 years PO, 23 years LAPD, Chief when hired: Reddin) (Figure 7.27)

#261

The staff from capt & above are nothing but back stabbing, self serving thiefs. This deps need to get rid of more than ½ of these do nothing people. They think they are Gods & don't know what the streets are like and don't care. They care nothing about the citizens of LA & don't care. All they want is their own power & making themselves jobs where no one knows what they are doing from capt. up. Why do you need two capts of the Divisions. You will have answers which say nothing. (Officer information not available)

#262

It appears that the brass & upper management is out for their own glory & benefit. Do what is good for them at the expense of the troops and working class.

(Sergeant, Male, Caucasian, 57 years old, 32 years PO, 32 years LAPD, Chief when hired: Parker) (Figure 7.28)

#263

In regards to morale, the reason that it is so low in the patrol ranks, which is supposed to be the "backbone of the Department," is the strong feelings that the upper management people are not concerned about the field officers and are only involved in taking Chief Gates

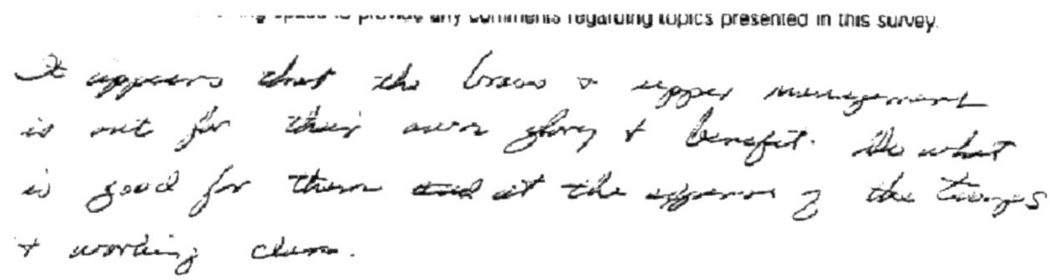
...g space to provide any comments regarding topics presented in this survey.

It appears that the brass & upper management is out for their own glory & benefit. Do what is good for them and at the expense of the troops & working class.

Figure 7.28 Statement Transcription: It appears that the brass & upper management is out for their own glory & benefit. Do what is good for them at the expense of the troops and working class (see Officer Informant statement #262).

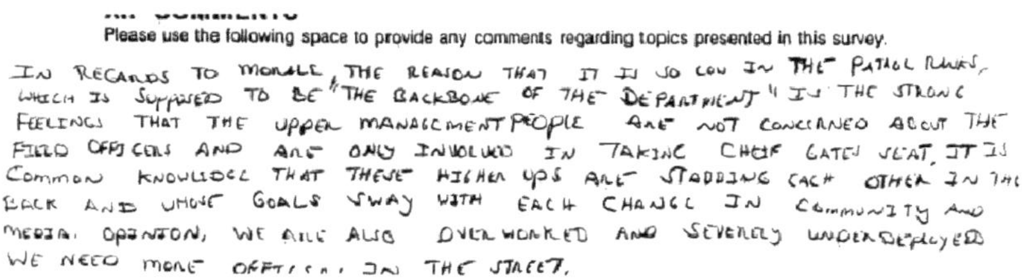
Please use the following space to provide any comments regarding topics presented in this survey.

IN REGARDS TO MORALE, THE REASON THAT IT IS SO LOW IN THE PATROL RANKS, WHICH IS SUPPOSED TO BE "THE BACKBONE OF THE DEPARTMENT" IS THE STRONG FEELINGS THAT THE UPPER MANAGEMENT PEOPLE ARE NOT CONCERNED ABOUT THE FIELD OFFICERS AND ARE ONLY INVOLVED IN TAKING CHIEF GATES SEAT. IT IS COMMON KNOWLEDGE THAT THESE HIGHER UPS ARE STABBING EACH OTHER IN THE BACK AND WHOSE GOALS SWAY WITH EACH CHANGE IN COMMUNITY AND MEDIA. OPINION, WE ARE ALSO OVERWORKED AND SEVERELY UNDERDEPLOYED WE NEED MORE OFFICERS IN THE STREET.

Figure 7.29 Statement Transcription: In regards to morale, the reason that it is so low in the patrol ranks, which is supposed to be the "backbone of the Department," is the strong feelings that the upper management people are not concerned about the field officers and are only involved in taking Chief Gates seat. It is common knowledge that these higher ups are stabbing each other in the back and whose goals sway with each change in the community and media. Opinion, we are also overworked and severely under deployed. We need more officers in the street (see Officer Informant statement #263).

seat. It is common knowledge that these higher ups are stabbing each other in the back and whose goals sway with each change in the community and media. Opinion, we are also overworked and severely under deployed. We need more officers in the street.

(Police Officer, Male, Caucasian, 32 years old, 11 years PO, 11 years LAPD, Chief when hired: Gates) (Figure 7.29)

#264

I have seen through my contact with other officers the nearly complete lack of confidence in the loyalty of the department's middle to upper management. A great number of junior officers are looking for new jobs.

(Police Officer, Male, Caucasian, 34 years old, 5 years PO, 4 years LAPD, Chief when hired: Gates)

#265

Brass has no balls.

(Police Officer, Male, Caucasian, 31 years old, 10 years PO, 10 years LAPD, Chief when hired: Gates) (Figure 7.30)

BRASS HAS NO BALLS

Figure 7.30 Statement Transcription: Brass has no balls (see Officer Informant statement #265).

Theme 6: LAPD's Administration/Management Failed to Support the Professional Model

Perhaps most detrimental to the life of the professional model of policing within the LAPD, and a factor of organizational change feared most by the model's architect, Chief Parker, is the department's internal failure to justify and support its professional policing style in the face of outside criticism. Parker's fears are brought to light in the following theme, which contains officer comments suggesting that LAPD's administrators/managers were willing to abandon the professional model's aggressive crime-fighting style in favor of a more passive community-based policing model. Central to community-based policing is the assumption that police practices must incorporate the desires of community members and politicians alike. Accepting the principles of this new policing model meant that LAPD's administration/management was, as Parker warned, "allowing the department's internal moral timbers to rot." For decades in the past, these timbers were protected by LAPD's administration/management, and they had provided organizational support for the professional model. As the following officer comments indicate, the vast majority of street officers resisted this change in policing style, which was endorsed by many of the Department's administrators and managers following the organizational meltdown.

#266

I find the department leaning toward being a social agency rather than concentrating on crime prevention

(Detective, Male, Caucasian, 53 years old, 28 years PO, 28 years LAPD, Chief when hired: Parker) (Figure 7.31)

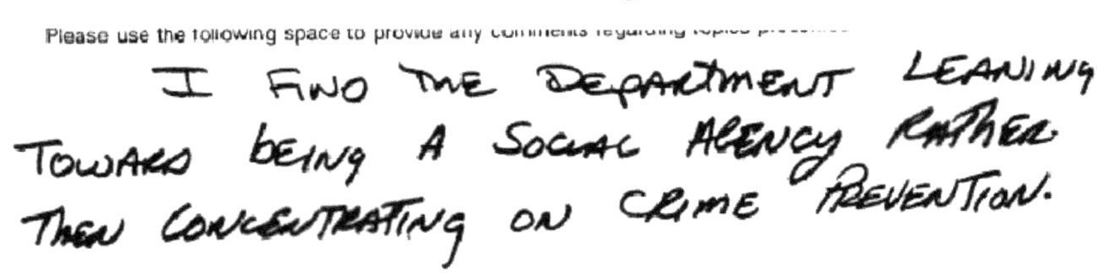
Please use the following space to provide any

I FIND THE DEPARTMENT LEANING TOWARD BEING A SOCIAL AGENCY RATHER THEN CONCENTRATING ON CRIME PREVENTION.

Figure 7.31 Statement Transcription: I find the department leaning toward being a social agency rather than concentrating on crime prevention (see Officer Informant statement #266).

#267

This department needs to return to basics. Trendy programs with cute names won't replace good street cops. Relations with the community is an important part of police work as long as you have knowledgeable, aggressive "street wise" loyal officers. Affirmative action has divided this dept and no survey is going to mend the wounds. This dept places no emphasis on arrests/convictions/expertise in the patrol force. To say that a patrol ofcr is generally qualified in this period of time, is a joke!

(Detective, Male, Caucasian, 39 years old, 16 years PO, 16 years LAPD, Chief when hired: Davis)

#268

Community based policing is extremely important. However, it appears the dept is forgetting force is absolutely necessary at times & should not discourage the use of it. An ofcr is going to get seriously hurt or killed because of the doubts the admin has set up. If we reach out to the community & explain our actions & do role playing it's guaranteed to change attitudes about what is excessive force & what's necessary force. I would like nothing better than to be proud again to be a Los Angeles Police ofcr. What happened to our backbone?

(Police Officer, Female, Caucasian, 32 years old, 8 years PO, 8 years LAPD, Chief when hired: Gates)

#269

The LAPD is in Full Retreat from the criminal elements in our once beautiful city! Unless the LAPD reassumes its once aggressive, no nonsense & professional stance, we will continue our decline into the depths of apathy, foolishness, & social chaos.

(Police Officer, Male, Caucasian, 26 years old, 3 years PO, 3 years LAPD, Chief when hired: Gates) (Figure 7.32)

#270

Community policing while in theory may sound good, will eventually offer no significant positive results in combating crime. As long as officers are used as scapegoats for societies' inability to deal with criminals, we will continue to see ineffective policing in our communities. Tying police officers hands and taking away proven tools in combating crime will only lead to more crime and apathy in the dept.

(Police Officer, Male, Caucasian, 33 years old, 8 years PO, 8 years LAPD, Chief when hired: Gates)

#271

Get the street back for the citizens of LA and put the fear back into the susps. Try and give the citizens a sense of security in knowing that we can protect them to some degree.

(Police Officer, Male, Caucasian, 44 years old, 22 years PO, 22 years LAPD, Chief when hired: Davis)

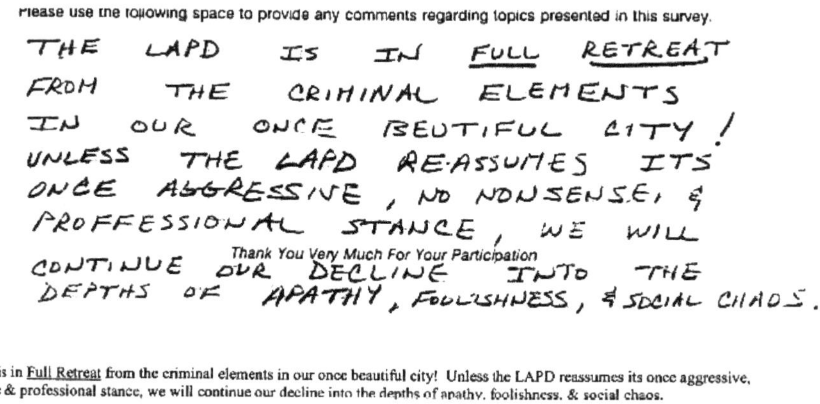
Please use the following space to provide any comments regarding topics presented in this survey.

THE LAPD IS IN FULL RETREAT
FROM THE CRIMINAL ELEMENTS
IN OUR ONCE BEUTIFUL CITY!
UNLESS THE LAPD RE-ASSUMES ITS
ONCE AGGRESSIVE, NO NONSENSE, &
PROFFESSIONAL STANCE, WE WILL
CONTINUE OUR DECLINE INTO THE
DEPTHS OF APATHY, FOOLISHNESS, & SOCIAL CHAOS.

Thank You Very Much For Your Participation

› is in Full Retreat from the criminal elements in our once beautiful city! Unless the LAPD reassumes its once aggressive,
se & professional stance, we will continue our decline into the depths of apathy, foolishness, & social chaos.

Figure 7.32 Statement Transcription: The LAPD is in Full Retreat from the criminal elements in our once beautiful city! Unless the LAPD reassumes its once aggressive, no nonsense & professional stance, we will continue our decline into the depths of apathy, foolishness, & social chaos (see Officer Informant statement #269).

#272

A policeman's job is to put crooks in jail, not kiss the ass of the politicians or news media. All these new police programs are like "new math" 15 years ago it does not work. LETS GET BACK TO BASICS.

(Police Officer, Female, Caucasian, 47 years old, 23 years PO, 23 years LAPD, Chief when hired: Reddin)

#273

… Someone should realize that we are not selling bedsheets at a white sale at Nordstroms. Until you separate the vict & susp the service satisfaction issue will never fly. I didn't spend twenty years on the street to kiss the ass of some robber or burglar. I could care less if the child molester is satisfied with the service.

(Sergeant, Male, Caucasian, 45 years old, 20 years PL, 20 years LAPD, Chief when hired: Davis)

#274

The recruiting at the Acad. is structured so that recruits go out in the field ill-prepared for how susp. will treat them. Instructors are too easy on them on the P.T. field. If they can't handle stress in the academy then let them quit & good riddance to them. They can be trained to be polite but firm. This dept. seems like it doesn't want to hire anyone that may look too intimidating to the public. The brass on this dept. doesn't care if they humiliate us, especially at a demonstration. Show some balls! Handle all demonstrators the same. The queer nation doesn't deserve special treatment. My bureau commander is a good example. I'm running out of room.

(Police Officer, Male, Caucasian, 43 years old, 22 years PO, 22 years LAPD, Chief when hired: Davis)

#275

My opinion is that the high brass (Sgt's & above) forget what patrol is all about. So they want to burn people (ofcrs) for any little citizen complaint (181) so that they will promote faster. Now as a patrol officer, you go out to the streets & you won't get respect from suspects, gang members, etc…. They will come right up to you & say "Fuck You" … Now what do we do? Nothing because we don't have a backbone like LASO-Sheriff Block!!! You want community based policing … that's Bullshit, just ask New York PD and look at their crime rate. C-YA.

(Police Officer, Male, Hispanic, 22 years old, 2 years PO, 2 years LAPD, Chief when hired: Gates) (Figure 7.33)

#276

The focus of attention has shifted and the main goal in the street has shifted. Change takes time. We've always had good ofcrs. When I came on 20 years ago, the emphasis was on running things with a strong hand and public opinion was secondary. Now community involvement is primary and the "battering ram" is unacceptable. It'll work out for the best.

(Sergeant, Male, Hispanic, 45 years old, 21 years PO, 21 years LAPD, Chief when hired: Davis)

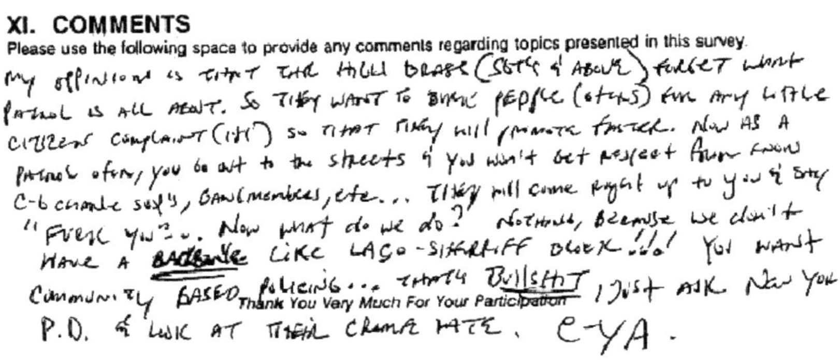
XI. COMMENTS

Please use the following space to provide any comments regarding topics presented in this survey.

My opinion is that the high brass (Sgt's & above) forget what patrol is all about. So they want to burn people (ofcrs) for any little citizen complaint (181) so that they will promote faster. Now as a patrol ofcr, you go out to the streets & you won't get respect from suspects, gang members, etc... They will come right up to you & say "Fuck You"... Now what do we do? Nothing, because we don't have a backbone like LASO-Sheriff Block!!! You want community based policing... that's Bullshit, just ask New York P.D. & look at their crime rate. C-YA.

Thank You Very Much For Your Participation

Figure 7.33 Statement Transcription: My opinion is that the high brass (Sergeants & above) forget what patrol is all about. So they want to burn people (officers) for any little citizen complaint (181) so that they will promote faster. Now as a patrol officer, you go out to the streets & you won't get respect from suspects, gang members, etc…They will come right up to you & say "Fuck You" … Now what do we do? Nothing because we don't have a backbone like LASO [Los Angeles Sheriffs Office]-Sheriff Block!!! You want community based policing…that's Bullshit, just ask New York PD and look at their crime rate. C-YA (see Officer Informant statement #275).

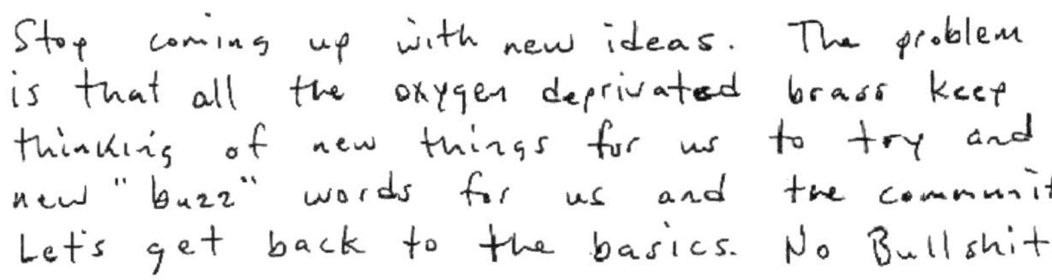
Stop coming up with new ideas. The problem is that all the oxygen deprivated brass keep thinking of new things for us to try and new "buzz" words for us and the community. Let's get back to the basics. No Bullshit.

Figure 7.34 Statement Transcription: Stop coming up with new ideas. The problem is that all the oxygen deprivated brass keep thinking of new things for us to try and new "buzz" words for us and the community. Let's get back to the basics. No bullshit (see Officer Informant statement #277).

#277

Stop coming up with new ideas. The problem is that all the oxygen deprivated brass keep thinking of new things for us to try and new "buzz" words for us and the community. Let's get back to the basics. No bullshit.

(Sergeant, Male, Caucasian, 30 years old, 9 years PO, 9 years LAPD, Chief when hired: Gates) (Figure 7.34)

#278

This is a start toward building a better dept. Hopefully mgmt will not crumble in the face of individual political goals, as we are seeing actually happen today. Let's not lose sight of our goal to have a crime free community, rather than a bend over backwards weak dept that gives in to the concept of leaving all persons smiling. We can't make everyone happy all the time, and I really don't think we should make criminals happy about LAPD.

(Police Officer, Male, Caucasian, 37 years old, 12 years PO, 8 years LAPD, Chief when hired: Gates)

#279

Community-based policing, though a great concept, will never work in a city as diverse and transient as Los Angeles. It looks like the bad guys have won and the decent citizens will suffer the consequences. The squeaky wheel got the grease while the bike as a whole fell apart!

(Police Officer, Male, Hispanic, 25 years old, 7 years PO, 4 years LAPD, Chief when hired Gates)

#280

Community based policing is a good idea. But we are a police dept. and need to remain in an "aggressive arrest mode." This is the priority of the LAPD I joined. Help out patrol. We love to work, we just need some help from the administrators when it comes to supporting us. Please don't sell out LAPD to the liberals.

(Police Officer, Male, Hispanic, 25 years old, 4 years PO, 4 years LAPD, Chief when hired: Gates) (Figure 7.35)

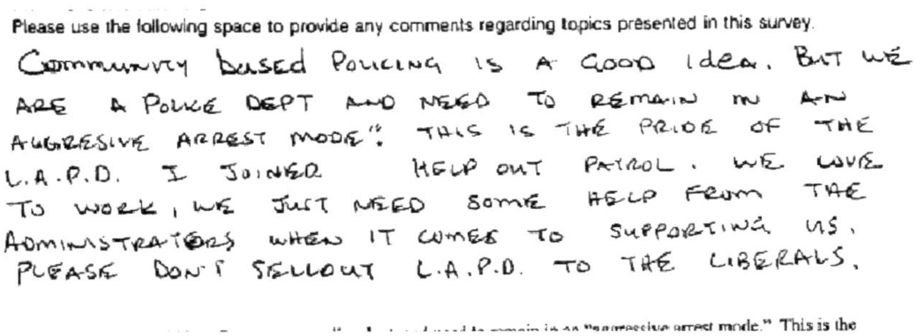
Please use the following space to provide any comments regarding topics presented in this survey.

COMMUNITY BASED POLICING IS A GOOD IDEA. BUT WE ARE A POLICE DEPT AND NEED TO REMAIN IN AN AGGRESIVE ARREST MODE". THIS IS THE PRIDE OF THE L.A.P.D. I JOINED HELP OUT PATROL. WE LOVE TO WORK, WE JUST NEED SOME HELP FROM THE ADMINISTRATORS WHEN IT COMES TO SUPPORTING US. PLEASE DON'T SELLOUT L.A.P.D. TO THE LIBERALS.

Figure 7.35 Statement Transcription: Community-based policing, though a great concept, will never work in a city as diverse and transient as Los Angeles. It looks like the bad guys have won and the decent citizens will suffer the consequences. The squeaky wheel got the grease while the bike as a whole fell apart! (see Officer Informant statement #279).

#281

Community based policing is proven ineffective. Keep LAPD the way it was.

(Police Officer, Male, Filipino, 29 years old, 4 years PO, 4 years LAPD, Chief when hired: Gates)

#282

I do not think we should become a Department that is not enforcement orientated. We should be involved with the community we serve but we should not give up putting crooks in jail.

(Detective, Male, Caucasian, 43 years old, 20 years PO, 20 years LAPD, Chief when hired: Davis)

#283

We should give the public the service they need, not bullshit them with coffee & tea.

(Police Officer, Male, Caucasian, 37 years old, 10 years PO, 3 years LAPD, Chief when hired: Gates) (Figure 7.36)

#284

More decisions need to be made by officers who are sincere about the welfare of patrol officers, and not by the officers downtown sitting around playing "Monday Morning Quarterback." The majority of people making the rules do not and have not worked in the streets in years. A lot of these changes that have been implemented

Please use the following space to provide any comments regarding topics presented in this survey.

WE SHOULD GIVE THE PUBLIC THE SERVICE THEY NEED, NOT BULLSHIT THEM WITH COFFEE & TEA

Figure 7.36 Statement Transcription: We should give the public the service they need, not bullshit them with coffee and tea (see Officer Informant statement #283).

are going to cause officers to get hurt second guessing themselves because they're thinking about what the pencil pushers will think later, much later. This department was not formed to be a dept of psychologists. We are people just like everyone else. We are not sponges to soak up the frustration of the community. We are here to stop, prevent and catch criminal activity. The public as a whole still support the police. The criminals and those people who have never been victims of crimes and/or have lived sheltered lives are the people so bent on change. Granted, some things should be changed. But making officers more sensitive to everyone who may be a little different than the rest just magnifies their difference. Training people (recruits) to be nice in a society where more & more criminals are arising is somewhat CRAZY!!

(Police Officer, Male, African American, 27 years old, 4 years PO, 4 years LAPD, Chief when hired: Gates)

Theme Analysis

Of the six separate themes presented in this chapter, it is difficult to say which is most prominent in the officers' minds as a potential cause of the LAPD organizational meltdown. Logically speaking, each of the themes points to the same internal problem within the department: a fundamental lack of unity within the ranks of LAPD's administration/management to support the department and its officers in a time of dire organizational crisis. Furthermore, the officers contend that this breach of loyalty on the part of these officers resulted in the ability of outside influences to defeat the department's protective barrier, which shielded and protected the professional model from political compromise.

Themes presented here suggested that officers felt the LAPD's administration/management to be more concerned with their own reputations and promotional opportunities than with the development of policies designed to improve the functioning and efficiency of street level enforcement activities. Many officers continued to support Chief Gates throughout the meltdown period, suggesting that his efforts to save the professional model were thwarted by disloyal members of the department's administration/management who viewed the meltdown as an opportunity to gain support from LAPD detractors (especially the media and politicians) for personal career advancement. In addition, officers stated that administrators/managers unfairly punished them for using established and accepted aggressive methods of policing to control violent crime. These officers, on the other hand, believed such punishments were merely a ploy by administrators to make patrol officers scapegoats for real or imaginary departmental problems they played no part in.

Conclusion

Of all the main potential causes of the LAPD organizational meltdown, the one presented in this chapter is most profound. For the most part, the above officer statements suggested the presence of a large and strong disconnect between the LAPD's administrators/managers and street level operations. The result of this disconnect was a weakness in the department's ability to isolate its internal organizational culture from outside intervention. In effect, a divide and conquer situation existed between the upper and lower ranks within the LAPD at the time of the meltdown. Quite simply, the bulk of LAPD's street level officers felt that their leaders and managers (with the exception of Chief Gates) "did not have their backs" during a time when support for them and the department was needed most. Many patrol officers, on the other hand, stated that they had always "had the backs" of LAPD's administrators/managers when they came under fire and needed help from the troops. Thus, this feeling of betrayal appeared to create a rebellion ("why should I have your back when you don't have mine") among the rank and file against the department's management and leadership ranks.

If there is one primary cause of the LAPD meltdown and the fall of the professional model, it is most likely the "dissension among the ranks" of the department's administrators and managers, and according to officers, especially those composing the brass. This is the one direct cause that had the potential to allow all other indirect causes (i.e., the King incident; attacks from politicians, special interest groups, and the media; and affirmative action) to become firmly rooted within the LAPD organizational culture. There is no telling from the findings of this study if the meltdown could have been avoided had Chief Gates and LAPD's administration/management staff and the street level officers taken a unified stand against the wave of public and political criticism directed at the department following the King incident. Chief Parker predicted decades before the King incident or affirmative action that strong internal moral fortitude within the LAPD organization was necessary to preserve the professional model. He also predicted that should the department become internally weak, the professional model's organizational thin blue line would be broken. Using this study's findings as a test of Parker's claims, it can be concluded with relative certainty that outside influences did indeed penetrate the walls of the LAPD organization due to internal organizational weaknesses—and the department did indeed melt down, and the fall of the professional model occurred soon thereafter.

References

1. Los Angeles Police Department. *Training Manual 1991.* Los Angeles: City of Los Angeles, 1991.
2. Ibid.

Quantitative Analyses

8

In this chapter, various quantitative analyses are used to provide further clarification of qualitative research findings presented in earlier sections of this study.* The purpose of performing these statistical examinations is to explore "numeric" differences that may help to explain which aspects of the LAPD meltdown were most or least important to specific types of officers. Specifically, limited background data gathered from each officer are used as a predictor (or independent variable) of the specific cause of the meltdown (or dependent variable) they identified as most important to them. Five officer characteristics are utilized in these statistical tests: gender, race, age, length of time employed by LAPD, and the chief of police when hired. As identified by previous qualitative study findings, the four major causes of the LAPD meltdown examined here are: (1) the Rodney King incident (see Chapter 4); (2) politicians, special interest groups, and community influences (see Chapter 5); (3) hiring, promotions, and affirmative action (see Chapter 6); and (4) management and administration (see Chapter 7). Again, it should be noted that all findings presented here are extremely exploratory in nature and should be interpreted with caution due to possible limitations of the study data that may produce biased statistical estimates.

The Total Sample

Prior to examining specific causes of the LAPD meltdown by officer characteristics, an analysis of the entire officer sample was conducted to show the overall percentage distribution of study responses. Figure 8.1 presents percentages of the entire officer sample within categories of the four major meltdown causes: the King incident (hereafter King); politicians, special interest groups, and community influences (hereafter politicians); hiring, promotions, and affirmative action (hereafter affirmative action); and management and administration (hereafter management).

As Figure 8.1 reveals, the majority of officers stated that the meltdown was caused by management influences (37%; $N = 87$), followed in importance by causes relating to politicians (29%; $N = 69$), affirmative action

* For a more detailed discussion of this analytical transformation procedure, see N.K. Denzin and Y.S. Lincoln, *Handbook of Qualitative Research* (2nd ed.), Thousand Oaks, CA: Sage Publications, 2000.

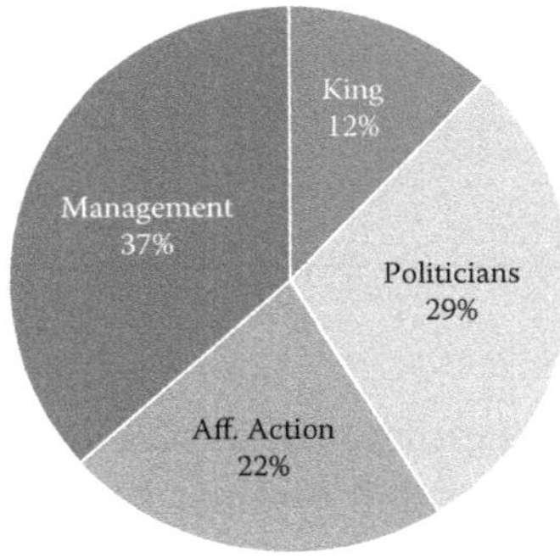

Figure 8.1 The above chart indicates that the majority of officers (37%) believed that LAPD's management was in some way responsible for the Department's meltdown, followed by Political Influences, Affirmative Action and the Rodney King Incident.

(22%; $N = 53$), and King (12%; $N = 29$). These findings support earlier conclusions that the King incident was the least influential major cause and that LAPD's management/administration was, by comparison, most influential. Another way of interpreting the above findings is to examine the relative importance of causes that were predominantly internal or external to the LAPD organization. It can logically be assumed that King and politicians had more external effects on the meltdown and management and affirmative action were mostly internal in their effects on the department. Figure 8.2 shows a percentage breakdown of internal and external causes resulting from the aforementioned regrouping of the major meltdown categories. Ostensibly, the overall internal effects were judged by officers as more important for explaining the meltdown, as evidenced by the nearly two out of every three responses falling within this category. However, the relative importance of individual major meltdown factors composing both the internal and external causes examined in the sections that follow will build on this preliminary finding. Specifically, it will be determined which of the internal and external major causes of the meltdown are most important to groups of officers when separated by personal background and organizational characteristics.

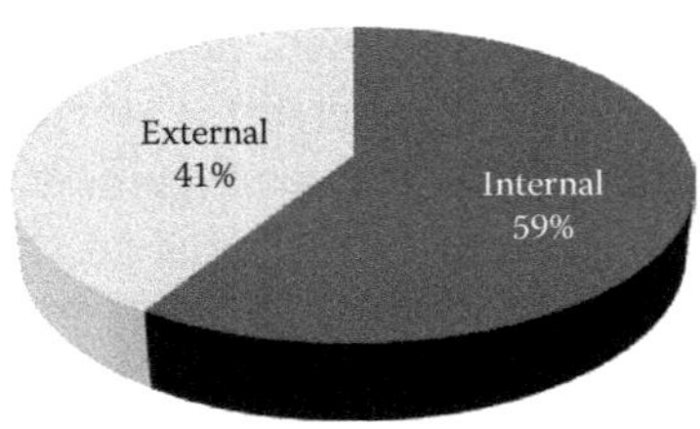

Figure 8.2 Data in the above chart suggest that the majority of officers (59%) blamed the LAPD meltdown on events/factors which were internal to the LAPD organization.

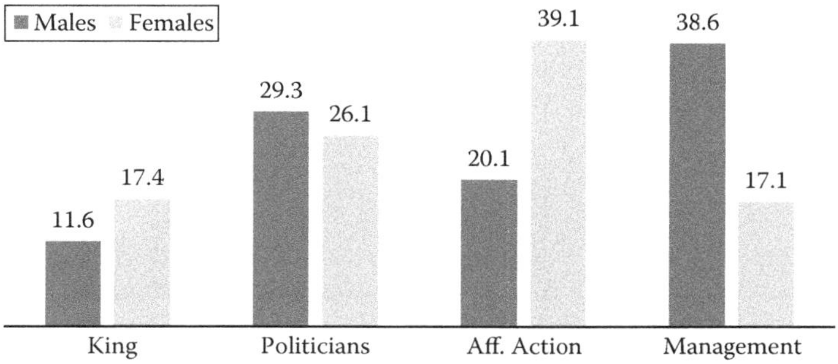

Figure 8.3 As the above chart shows, Male officers (38.6%) were most likely to indicate that the Department's meltdown was caused by LAPD's management whereas Female officers (39.1%) were most likely to indicate that Affirmative Action policies were a primary cause of the meltdown.

Officer Gender

Figure 8.3 presented results for analyses examining the effects of officer gender on each of the four major meltdown causes. As discovered among the written officer narratives, King was perceived as a relatively minor cause for both male and female officers (11.6 and 17.4%, respectively). For the politicians cause, both males (29.3%) and females (26.1%) had quite similar opinions. Furthermore, both genders considered politicians to be the second most important cause of the meltdown. However, for the affirmative action and management factors there were several gender effects discovered. First, female officers rated gender as their most important meltdown cause (39.1%); on the other hand, males rated this factor as third most in importance (20.1%). Second, in almost a mirror image of the latter findings for females, male officers rated management as their top choice (38.6%) for explaining the meltdown. In addition, these findings suggest that both genders place the epicenter of the meltdown within the LAPD organization rather than blaming external causes (i.e., King and politicians).

Females may have favored affirmative action causes much more so than males due to recent changes within the department directly relating to the Blake consent decree. It may be recalled that some of the female officers' comments regarding affirmative action changes resulting from Blake were positive and others were negative. On the positive side, women may consider internal conflict within the department as a necessary evil to support their newly acquired equal policing status with males. In other words, the meltdown was an inevitable reaction to their power struggle with males, which also brought minority officers in on the organizational infighting over departmental hiring and promotional policies. Other statements from females, however, were not supportive of the changes produced by the Blake

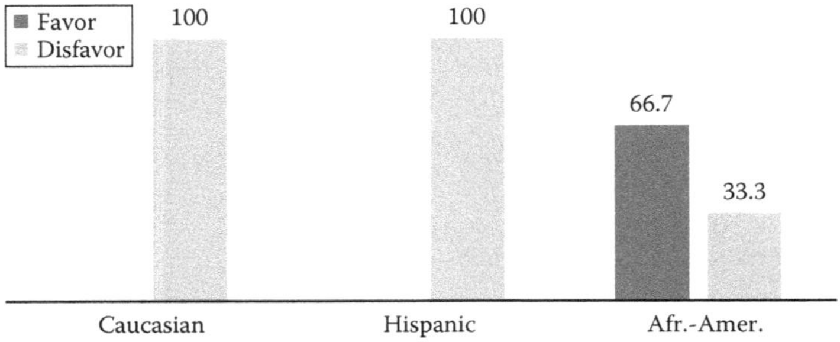

Figure 8.4 Data presented in the above chart suggests that African-American female officers were more likely than Caucasian or Hispanic female officers to favor the LAPD's affirmative action hiring programs.

decree. Among these comments were female officers who expressed disdain for the notion of being hired and promoted because of their gender. In short, these women found affirmative action yet another unnecessary source of conflict between their male coworkers and a major disruptive factor for the well-being of the LAPD organization.

In order to further clarify this conclusion, Figure 8.4 shows results of an analysis comparing Caucasian, Hispanic, and African-American female officers' attitudes toward affirmative action policies. These results are based on an interpretation of the officers' comments as either favoring or disfavoring hiring and promotional policies within LAPD resulting from affirmative action changes. (These findings must be interpreted with caution due to the small number of women officers included in the analysis: $N = 9$.)

Among male officers, as previously stated, affirmative action did not appear to be a primary concern regarding the meltdown. Instead, most of the blame for LAPD's troubled organization was, according to these officers, to be placed squarely on the shoulders of the LAPD management and administration. The finding is best interpreted as a reaction on the part of male officers to the management's handling of problems such as affirmative action, politicians, and King. In effect, they perhaps did not consider these other factors as major direct causes of the meltdown. Rather, they may have felt that these other threats could have and should have been solved by the LAPD managers and administrators in a way that would have preserved the integrity of the LAPD organization.

Officer Race

Related to the above analyses for gender are the following findings for analyses of the officer race data (see Figure 8.5). That is, both women and minority officers' presence and status within the LAPD were equally impacted by the

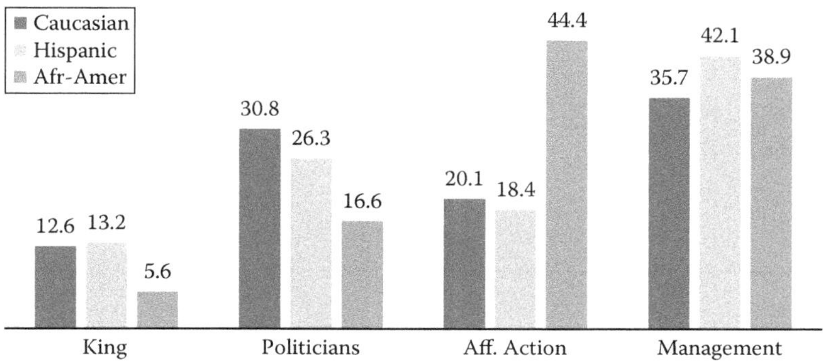

Figure 8.5 The above chart indicates that LAPD's management was perceived as a major cause of the Department's meltdown by Caucasian and Hispanic officers; however, African-American officers were most likely to claim the Department's affirmative action policies were the primary cause.

Blake decree's imposition in the early 1980s. The first obvious result for these findings is that King was again one of the least important major causes, as it was in the earlier analysis performed for officer gender. Especially surprising was the fact that not only did African-American officers rate King as their lowest possible cause of the meltdown, but also that their percentage of comments concerning King (5.6%) was far below that of Hispanic (13.2%) and Caucasian (12.6%) officers. Prior studies have shown that the King incident was particularly race specific in that African-American citizens were more likely than those of other races to be critical of the police following the incident's media coverage. However, this effect did not appear to hold true among African-American officers in this study. Ironically, the data show that they were in fact the least sensitive out of all officer races to the impact of King on the department.

Various commonalties between Caucasian and Hispanic officers were observed in the race analyses. First, both racial groups rated management as the primary major cause of the LAPD meltdown. Second, Caucasians and Hispanics each felt that politicians were the second most important cause. And last, both rated affirmative action as the third choice for explaining the meltdown. However, this observed racial parity for Caucasians and Hispanics was in sharp contrast to similar results specific to African-American officers. Specifically, African-American officers—like female officers—rated affirmative action as their top priority for explaining the LAPD's organizational distress. Management and politicians were their second and third choices, respectively. Taken together, these results suggest that African-American officers, similar to female officers, may have perceived themselves to be at odds with other officer groups—namely, Caucasians and Hispanics—with regard to hiring and promotional standards. Further supporting this conclusion is

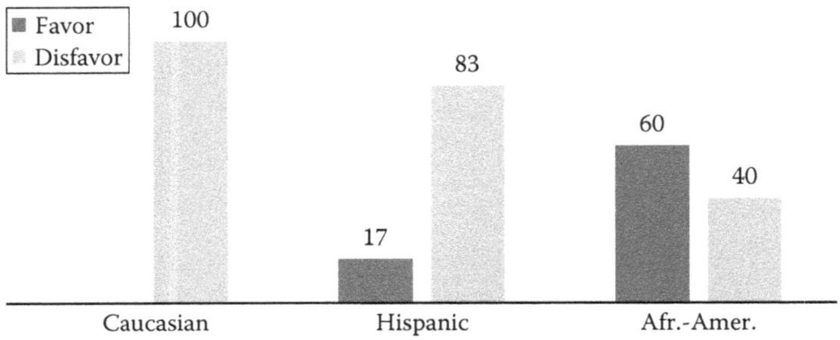

Figure 8.6 The above data suggest that African-American male officers were more likely to favor LAPD's affirmative action hiring policies than their Caucasian or Hispanic officer coworkers. Similar analyses reported for female officers revealed nearly identical findings.

the fact that during the time of this study women officers comprised approximately 12% of the LAPD's sworn force; in addition, African-American officers were the least represented race (13%) within the ranks of male officers as well. In comparison, Caucasians comprised 64% of all LAPD's officers and Hispanic officers 20%.

Figure 8.6 presents results from an analysis comparing minority officers' attitudes toward affirmative action to those obtained from nonminority officers. The results show similar patterns to findings discovered for a similar analysis performed for female officer data. That is, Caucasian and Hispanic officers shared similar, nearly unanimous disfavor of affirmative action policing within LAPD, while African-American officers were split in their attitudes—with 60% favoring and 40% disfavoring LAPD's post-Blake decree hiring and promotional standards. Based on this and the above findings for officer race, it does not appear that all minorities within the ranks of the LAPD viewed affirmative action in the same way, regarding it as a probable cause of the meltdown. In fact, evidence presented here suggests that the viewpoint held by Hispanic males (and perhaps females) was significantly different from that held by all African Americans regardless of gender.

Officer Age

Most research on policing suggests that officer age is a significant factor in predicting how officers perform in field duties, but also how they view the organization in which they work. In regard to field performance, for example, older officers tend to make fewer arrests than their younger counterparts, but the number of arrestee convictions associated with older officers significantly exceeds that of officers who are more youthful. In addition to on-the-job performance changes, older officers tend to be more cynical about their role as a

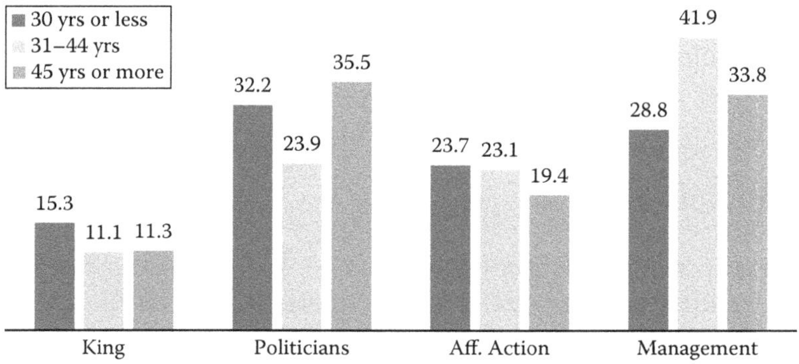

Figure 8.7 The above chart indicates that the youngest (30 yrs or less) and oldest (45 yrs or more) officers viewed political influences as a major cause of the LAPD meltdown, while the majority of middle-age-range officers (31–44 yrs) believed the major cause was the Department's management.

police officer and the organizational environment in which they work. Most studies of police cynicism suggest that as officers age, they generally become less satisfied with their job and the employment policies of their workplace. This is especially true where upper-level management is concerned. It is well established in the policing research that older officers who choose to spend their career on the street rather than promote to higher ranks experience much higher levels of work-related stress from their managers than from street level duties.

Results presented in Figure 8.7 indicate mild support for the age and cynicism relationship discussed above, suggesting that older officers' reactions to the meltdown was not merely a function of becoming more cynical toward management over age. In fact, the elderly officers (ages 45 years or more) rated politicians (35.5%) as the primary cause of the meltdown and management as the second most recognized cause (33.8%). In a normal police organizational setting, it would not be expected for politics to be on the same page as management in the minds of the senior officers. Generally speaking, the oldest and youngest (age 30 years or younger) officer groups shared a similar outlook toward the meltdown, with both groups stating politicians as their first major cause (35.5 and 32.2%, respectively) and management as the second (33.38 and 28.8%, respectively).

Differing from the youngest and oldest officers in their outlooks toward the meltdown were seasoned officers representing the middle age range of 31 to 44 years. In particular, this group identified management as their first choice for explaining the LAPD's organizational collapse. Not only was the percentage of these intermediate-aged officers approximately 8 to 12 percentage points higher than those of all other officers, but they were nearly two times more likely to identify management issues with the meltdown than problems relating to either affirmative action or politicians. Among officers of all ages, affirmative action was rated as the third most important major factor relating to the meltdown, and King was rated least important.

Officer Experience

Officer experience in this study is highly associated with an officer's age, so it would be expected that percentage distributions for both the age and the experience factors would be quite similar. As results presented in Figure 8.8 indicate, the latter prediction was in fact true, with a few notable exceptions. First, any differences between results from the age and experience analyses may simply be an artifact of the data; that is, the data cut points for both analyses may not exactly correspond with one another and result in a greater number of younger officers represented in higher experience levels or older officers in lower experience categories. However, the effects of data manipulation can be ruled out; the results presented in Figure 8.8 suggest that experience did in fact have an effect on officers' perceptions of the meltdown that was above and beyond that evidence for age.

In support of the above interpretation are the findings representing the least and most experienced officers groups. When these results are compared to those discovered in the age analysis a near mirror image reversal in attitudes is discovered among the youngest officer group for both the politicians and management causes. Specifically, in the age analysis these officers identified politicians as their primary cause of the meltdown. However, the least experienced officers, regardless of their age, identified management as the top cause of the meltdown. In contrast, the most experienced and oldest

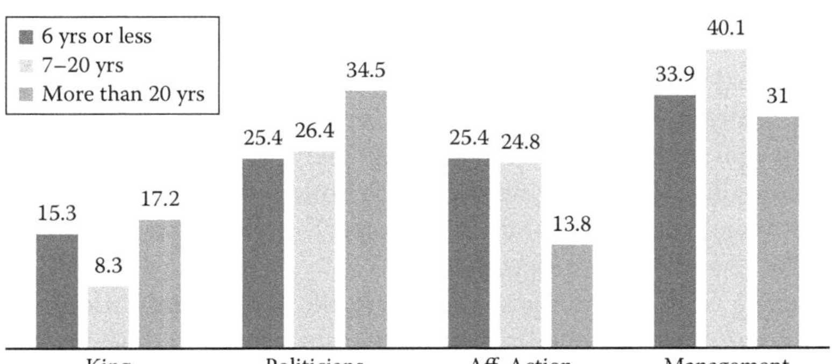

Figure 8.8 The above chart reveals that the most veteran officers on the LAPD blamed political influences for the Department's meltdown, while the rookie and mid-career officers believed that the meltdown was most likely brought on by LAPD's management.

officers as well as the officers categorized within middle age and experience groups did not evidence any change in their identification of top causes. Thus, taking these findings at face value, it appears age and experience functioned to condition certain younger officers' perceptions of the meltdown. One possible explanation for this result is perhaps that less experienced officers who are younger are most apt to be influenced by their more experienced peers and thus share their negative outlooks toward the LAPD's management. Conversely, some older less experienced officers may be more independent in their thinking and more resistant to the opinions of older more experienced officers regarding the meltdown's primary cause.

Chief at the Time of Hire (or the Chief Effect)

Fortunately, this present analysis captures officers representing all of the major eras of the LAPD, in terms of chiefs of police, during the life of the professional model at LAPD. As previously mentioned, these are the Parker, Davis, and Gates eras. (The decision was made to group the Reddin and Parker data due to the small number of officers hired during Reddin's tenure and due to the time proximity of these two chiefs.) Again, it would be expected that the measure of an officer's "chief at the time of hire" would produce highly similar results to those found for officer age and experience—considering the older and most experienced officers would have been hired by Chief Parker, and less experienced and younger by Davis, and so on. However, there is also reason to perform such an analysis in order to search for what might be termed a chief effect, that is, the unique influence that each specific chief might have had on the LAPD organization and his officers working for him.

Specifically, the Parker era marks a generation where the professional model was at its purest state within the LAPD organization. The Davis era is highlighted by a continuation of the Parker leadership method, but is perhaps a less pure version of the professional model due to Chief Davis' introduction of community relations into the department's policing style during the 1970s. The professional model, although still alive, was most challenged during the Gates era and perhaps least potent within the LAPD policing culture during the final days of Gates' tenure as chief.

Figure 8.9 presents the results examining the chief effect. These findings show some distinct differences between officers' attitudes toward the meltdown and the chief of the LAPD at the time they were hired. Clearly, officers representing the Parker era felt that the outside influence of the politicians factor was the most important causal factor. This result was also discovered in the previous analyses for officers who were most experienced and advanced in age. In contrast, officers representing the Davis era blamed the meltdown

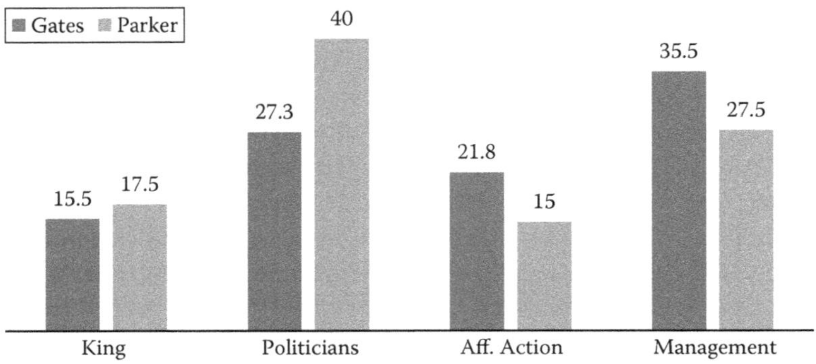

Figure 8.9 Data in the above chart indicate that officers hired during the Parker era were most likely to blame the meltdown on political influences and those hired during the Gates era were most likely to believe the meltdown was caused by the Department's management.

on management factors. This result, too, was discovered in earlier age and experience analyses that were likely representative of officer groups who had hired and served under Chief Davis. Gates era officers, like those representing the Davis era, also identified management as their primary cause for LAPD's organizational collapse. However, prior analyses for younger officers likely hired and serving under Gates suggested that the politicians and management factors played a significant role in how they viewed the meltdown's major cause.

In sum, these finding suggest that attitudes toward the cause of the LAPD meltdown could have been conditioned somehow by organizational culture imposed by a specific chief of police during his period of leadership within the LAPD. This influence, or the chief effect, is assumed to have its most influential impact on officers during the time of their initial hire and training as an LAPD officer. Supporting this theoretical assumption are prior research study findings suggesting that the most crucial time for rookie officers to formulate job perceptions is during their initial training period. Also during this time, they are oriented to their department's policing culture by their training officers. Thus, it stands to reason that a particular LAPD chief, and his particular orientation to the police culture and training, could have produced a lasting effect on officers that is reflected in this analysis.

Applying the chief effect logic to the immediate findings, the emphasis of Parker era officers on the politicians cause is perhaps a product of their socialization into Parker's no-nonsense policing culture, which effectively resisted the challenges of politicians, special interest groups, and the media. Likewise, the Davis era officers' emphasis on the management factor may have been evoked by their socialization into an LAPD policing culture that advocated the use of strong managers to overcome internal departmental challenges to the professional model. Last, the Gates era officers who were exposed to an LAPD culture experiencing both internal and external challenges never before seen in the department's history may not have possessed the same strong LAPD cultural underpinnings of leadership and management possessed by the two generations of officers before them. In short, the Gates era officers—who witnessed their chief being overpowered by lawsuits and the department's managers unable to respond effectively against their adversaries—may not have been socialized into a policing culture that enabled them to effectively discern whether the falling professional model was the result of weak management or strong outside political attacks or both.

Conclusion

Findings from the quantitative analyses performed in this chapter are summarized in Table 8.1. The table includes rank scores based on the relative importance of each major meltdown cause as reflected by percentage difference discovered in the above findings for each officer group. For example, the ranking of 4 for King associated with male officers means that the lowest percentage (i.e., 11.6%; see Figure 8.5) of officers in this group identified the King incident as the major cause of the LAPD meltdown. Likewise, the ranking of 1 in this same category indicates that the highest percentage (i.e., 38.6%; see Figure 8.5) of male officers identified King as the major cause. It is possible to determine the overall importance of each major meltdown cause, as reflected by all officer groups, by examining the most frequently occurring rank (or rank mode) within each of the major cause columns.

The summary findings presented in Table 8.1 are congruent with earlier findings reporting percentage breakdowns of the four major meltdown cause categories for the entire sample (see Figure 8.1). As the table indicates, management was identified by the majority of officer groups as the number 1 cause of the meltdown. This finding was supported by 57.1% (mode = 8) of the officer groups. Second in overall importance was politicians, which was found to be rated most frequently as the number 2 cause (mode = 8 or 57.1%). Third in importance was affirmative action (mode = 9 or 63.3%), receiving the largest number of 3 rankings. The least important cause among all officer groups, receiving the most frequent number of 4 rankings (mode = 11 or 78.6%), was the King incident.

Overall, the findings revealed in this chapter based on quantitative measures of content contained in the officer statements corroborate the earlier qualitative study findings. Taken together, both sets of findings support the general conclusion that if indeed there was a main cause of the LAPD meltdown, it most likely originated from the inside rather than the outside of the organization. Specifically, preexisting organizational turmoil between officers

Table 8.1 Rankings of Major Meltdown Causes Within Officer Groups

	King	Politicians	Affirmative Action	Management
		Gender		
Male	4	2	3	1
Female	3	1	2	4
		Race		
Caucasian	4	2	3	1
Hispanic	4	2	3	1
African American	4	1	3	2
		Age		
≤30 years	4	1	3	2
31–44 years	4	2	3	1
≥45 years	4	1	3	2
		Experience		
≤6 years	4	2[a]	2[a]	1
7–20 years	4	2	3	1
≥21 years	3	1	4	2
		Chief		
Parker	3	1	4	2
Davis	4	2[a]	2[a]	1
Gates	4	2	3	1
Modal Rank	4	2	3	1
Mode (*N*)	(11)	(8)	(9)	(8)
%	(78.6%)	(57.1%)	(64.3%)	(57.1%)

[a] Denotes within rank ties.

(i.e., affirmative action), coupled with a growing wave of anti-LAPD sentiments outside of the organization (i.e., the King incident; attacks from politicians, special interest groups, the media; and the community in general), was somehow allowed to take root inside of the department. This was an occurrence that had never before happened in the history of the LAPD. According to most officers' observations contained in this study, the primary explanation for why these organization seeds of destruction grew and gradually overtook the department's policing culture lies somewhere in the inability of LAPD's managers and leaders—the caretakers of the professional model—"to protect and to serve" the legacy of Chief Parker's thin blue line.

Conclusions and Policy Recommendations: Reconstructing the Meltdown

9

From a practical standpoint, the most valuable information contained within this study concerns results from the individual analyses that enable a causal reconstruction of the LAPD organizational meltdown. These results, comprised of the four major causes and their relationships to one another, can be arranged to show the organizational dynamics of the meltdown and probable stages in which it occurred. Figure 9.1 illustrates the model that is here assumed to best explain or fit the study findings. By examining the model from left to right it is possible to order or sequence the major meltdown causes and their relationship to one another. Among the causes that lie outside of the organization, the King incident is believed to be the first event to occur and set the other causes in motion. The next reaction was composed of a flurry of outside effects emanating from politicians, special interest groups, the media, and the community. Thus, the King incident—according to the study results—was a direct cause of these potent outside effects, yet it was an indirect cause of the meltdown (contrary to popular belief). From an organizational standpoint, if the latter proposition was indeed true, there is a possibility that the professional model could have survived the King incident and its political fallout had other internal causes not occurred inside of the LAPD organization.

If there was a death blow to the professional model it was caused by external forces directly penetrating the LAPD's organizational wall, which since the model's inception by Parker repelled would-be outside challenges to the organization's operational autonomy and policing culture. As hypothesized in Figure 9.1, the outside political and related forces touched off by the King incident, which were perhaps no more potent than past major challenges to the department, such as those posed by the Watts riots, penetrated the LAPD protective barrier and passed through to the organization's interior. As the study results suggest, these causes did not directly affect the rank-and-file officers, but rather directly impacted the functioning of LAPD's administration/management. It was most likely the reaction at this level of the LAPD organizational hierarchy to this permeation of outside causes or forces that triggered the meltdown. More specifically, it is assumed that the actions, inactions, or both occurring among the department's administrators/managers set into motion a chain reaction of events between the supervisory and street level officers that even a strong chief such as Gates could not control.

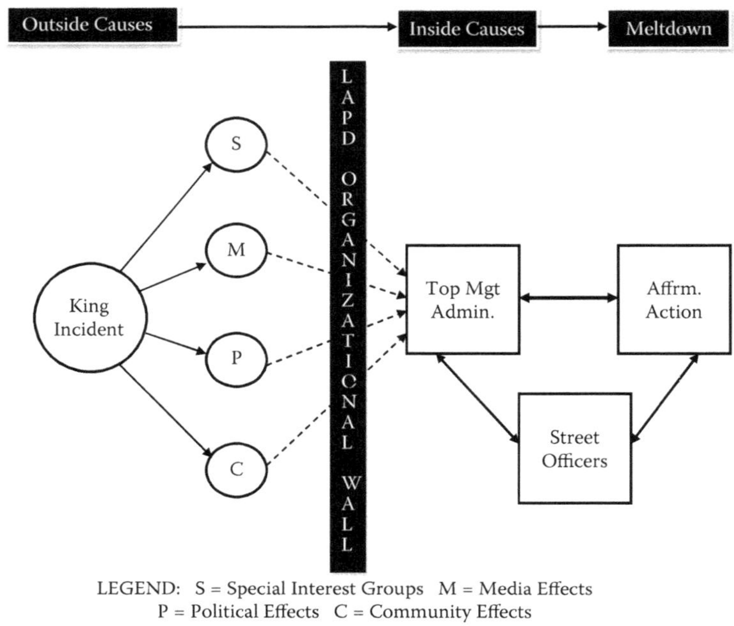

Figure 9.1 The above chart suggests the causal relationship between the 4 major causes of the meltdown identified in the study. From left to right: (1) The meltdown began with the King Incident triggering various outside criticism of the LAPD; (2) These effects permeated the LAPD organizational barrier setting off a series of reactions from LAPD's top management (e.g., Affirmative Action and Street Officer enforcement policy changes) which, in combination, spiraled out of control triggering the Department's internal meltdown.

Adding fuel to the internal organizational flames causing the meltdown were the tensions created between officers relating to the hiring and promotional policies resulting from affirmative action policies. These tensions, although present within the organization for some time, did not appear to be, by themselves, potent enough to cause mass internal organizational disruption. Rather, their effects were similar to that of a dormant powder keg ready to ignite when exposed to a flame. The fire for this flame, in this case, was the friction between the upper administrative and street officer levels of the LAPD organization. The explosive result was the meltdown.

What Went Wrong?

The key to discovering what went wrong within the LAPD organizational culture is to closely examine, through the eyes of the witnessing officers, the department's administrative and managerial reactions in response to the meltdown. By way of analogy, and as suggested by several officers, the

LAPD was a ship in distress—lost at sea—and it was up to the captain and his crew to coordinate a plan to save it from destruction. Thus, with the chief at the helm and his administrators/managers responsible for the department's navigation through dangerous waters, what caused the ship to ultimately capsize and sink? Listed below are various propositions based on content of the officers' statements that attempt to explain how the LAPD lost managerial control of the ship and perhaps caused the department's meltdown as well as the fall of the professional model.

1. Acquiescence to Outside Forces

First and foremost, and creating the opportunity for the meltdown to occur within the walls of the LAPD organization, was the lack of an immediate, strong, and most of all unified defensive response on the part of administrators/managers to defend the department's reputation against outside attackers. Many of the officers commented that the department's administrators and managers were "running scared" from their political, media, and special interest group opponents. This was an atypical reaction of the LAPD top administration compared to past political and media confrontations. Historically speaking, the department was vehemently defended by the likes of Chiefs Parker and Davis, whose top administrators perhaps reacted in unison with their chief to meet their political opponents head on in their organizational battles. The end result of a running scared reaction to the meltdown left the organization to be defended only by Chief Gates, who many officers commented was doing his best to hold the "thin blue organizational line." But with the chief unable to hold the line, the organizational walls were breached by outside attackers. As a result, the reputations of every street officer came under attack as well. Officers' comments suggested they felt betrayed by the lack of effort on the part of the department's administrators and managers to defend their reputation as professionals in the public's eye. Instead, they were labeled by outside critics as out-of-control "thugs" who were finally exposed by the King incident. In short, by acquiescing to outside forces, the LAPD's administrators/managers had violated the most important organizational rule of the professional model: Always have the other officer's back. As one officer noted: "We have always had your backs (meaning administrators/managers) now when we (meaning the street officers) need you, you don't have our backs." And as another officer noted: "Do unto others as [you would have them do to you]."

2. Punishing Aggressive Enforcement

The hallmark of the professional policing model is an aggressive stance toward criminal activity. This, in effect, is the real thin blue line of the LAPD as conceived by Chief Parker. According to Parker, and his concept of the model, the perception of an aggressive street response to crime by police is a necessary form of deterrence that keeps serious crime and predatory offenders separated from law-abiding citizens. Should the police not be able to maintain the thin blue line through aggressive proactive policing, society would be thrown into a state of chaos by crime and criminals running rampant in the streets—a prediction espoused by Parker.[1] At the time of the meltdown, the LAPD policing culture was still fully operational under the professional model and the average street officer had been socialized to believe in the Parker prophecy; that is, aggressive policing is a necessary and appropriate response to handling criminal situations. Conversely, a soft approach to dealing with criminals at the time of the meltdown would be viewed within the LAPD's culture as not only ineffective policing, but also a "slack job" done by an officer who was living up to his or her promise to protect the community. However, the immediate response to the meltdown by LAPD managers and administrators was to step up the punishment of street officers (e.g., 181 personnel complaints) for aggressive policing. In effect, the department's management began instantly punishing officers "today" for policing behavior that was rewarded by the department "yesterday." It stands to reason that such inconsistencies and contradictions in the use of punishment would throw any organizational culture into a state of meltdown. As many officers commented: "How are we expected to fight the bad guys when the administration has tied one of our hands behind our backs by threatening us with punishment every time we use force?"

3. Heeding Enforcement ADVICE From the Community

Under the professional model it is assumed that the police know best how to control crime and enforce the law. The model does not permit the community to take an active role in dictating a police agency's internal policies or enforcement activities. In short, as Parker believed, the police—not the public—know what's best to keep the streets safe. This is not to say the professional model has no place for community relations. To the contrary, the model operates on the belief that public support is essential to the survival of any policing agency. A case in point: Parker spent countless hours making public appearances during which he made speeches to the community in order to gain the public's support for the LAPD and its officers.[2] During the meltdown, however, LAPD's top administrators made concessions to community members regarding their ability to provide the department with policy guidance over their enforcement practices—thus violating another essential component of the professional model. It may be recalled that Chief Gates instituted a 10-point plan (part of which was the present study) that promised to identify citizen priorities for the operation of the LAPD and incorporate them into the department's operations. This plan was ultimately commandeered by Mayor Bradley and underwent a political metamorphosis that eventually resulted in the Christopher Commission report. The report's recommendations for sweeping changes in the LAPD's implementation of the professional model, most of which were eventually adopted by the department, represented a loss of the autonomy from public interference in policing that Parker believed was so essential to effective crime control.[3]

4. Forcing "Friendship" on the Streets

The professional model is fact-driven policing, as is exemplified in the television show *Dragnet* by Sergeant Joe Friday's famous "just the facts, ma'am" warning to witnesses when they become too personal or emotional in their reporting of a crime to officers. Parker believed that emotion not only clouded police officers' decision-making capabilities, but also was a catalyst for police corruption.[4] Quite simply, under the professional model, there was no legitimate purpose served by an officer's being friends on a personal level with the public. One of the first reactions to the meltdown by LAPD's administrators/managers was to urge, if not force, street officers to show their personal side to the community—another rule violation of the professional model. Sensitivity training sessions, interpersonal awareness seminars, and even lectures from customer satisfaction experts representing the high-end retail department store Nordstrom's were some of the retraining tactics used on street officers in order to increase their people skills when interacting with civilians during the course of their duties. Several officers commented about this forced change in their street attitudes, such as "we are not social workers," "we are not selling bed sheets at a sale," or "people want us to catch criminals not have coffee and tea with us."

5. Removing the "Force Multiplier" of Patrol

In regard to controlling crime, the force multiplier effect refers to the ability of a policing agency to maximize the crime control potential of its officer force by discovering ways to maximize the efficiency of its officers working the streets. Throughout its history under Chiefs Parker, Davis, and Gates, the LAPD was noted for having the smallest number of sworn officers of any large metropolitan policing agency. At the time data for this study were gathered, the LAPD sworn officer force was roughly 8,800, compared to 12,000 for Chicago and some 30,000 for New York City. In addition, these officers were responsible for policing some 450 square miles around the clock. It was not unusual, according to some patrol officer informants, that there were only 350 patrol units on the streets to cover all calls for service throughout LAPD's entire jurisdiction. However, it was Parker's contention that the department should remain intentionally small relative to other large city agencies. This size limitation, he reasoned, would have several force multiplier effects in the form of organizational efficiency, namely, quick flow of communication from top management to rank-and-file officers on the streets and increased organizational flexibility for rapid officer deployment.

At the street level, LAPD relied heavily on directed and random patrol patterns in order to transform the department's slimmed-down organizational hierarchy and smaller sworn officer population into what they believed to be a force multiplier effect. The first of these, directed patrol, refers to time spent by officers in a patrol unit driving though specific areas (in particular, high-crime hot spots) to prevent or observe criminal activities. Random patrol involved creating the illusion of police omnipresence by patrol units appearing unpredictably in various geographic areas. The majority of LAPD officers' shifts was spent behind the wheel of a patrol unit engaging in these preventive patrol activities. However, the endorsement of community-based policing by LAPD's administrators/managers following the meltdown, in concurrence with the Christopher Commission recommendations, meant that officers would spend less time patrolling the streets looking for would-be offenders, and more time on their shift engaging in nondirected patrol activities such as "meet and greets" with citizens and community groups.[5]

Many officers' comments suggested that the meltdown may have been caused, in part, over serious concerns regarding the street level ramification of this change in patrol strategy. In particular, officers were concerned that the professional model's organizational strategy of an intentionally undersized police force would collapse under the new time demands for non-crime-fighting activities under the community-based policing model. On this subject, officers commented: The department's idea of doing more with less won't work. We need more officers. How are we expected to spend our patrol time getting to know citizens when we already don't have enough time to respond to all of our calls for service? In short, many officers felt that moves by LAPD's administrators and managers to take them out of their patrol vehicles and require them to spend their time interacting with citizens was not only a potential threat to the public's as well as their own safety, but also, according to the opinion of street officers, a clear sign that the "brass" was out of touch with modern-day demands placed on officers who worked the streets.

6. Failure to Address Morale Issues

Perhaps the most prevalent issue discovered among all themes created to explain the meltdown was that concerning officer bad morale within the LAPD organization, with many veteran officers stating they had never before seen worse morale in the department. "Looking for other police jobs," "early retirement," and even "making fewer arrests" were some of the stated side effects of the poor officer morale following the meltdown. One of the number one reasons cited by most officers as the cause of bad morale within the department appeared to be conflict between officers of different genders and race based on feelings that hiring and promotional decisions were handled unfairly due to affirmative action policies.

Ironically, Parker maintained that building high moral, or a strong esprit de corps, among officers was an essential cornerstone of the professional model's success. Furthermore, he assumed that internal organizational fortitude among officers created a "fighting spirit" that galvanized officers at all levels into forgetting their individual differences and focusing on the LAPD's common goal of fighting crime.[6] However, it is clear from the officers' comments that such an esprit de corps did not exist prior to and during the meltdown. Many officers blamed the LAPD's administration/management for mismanaging the department's hiring and promotional practices in order to quickly fill gender and racial quotas with un- or underqualified officers.

Some officers who were the subject of these employment quotas were, in turn, resentful of top management's handling of affirmative action standards as well. In particular, they felt their true abilities qualifying them for employment and promotion as a police officer were not recognized by other officers as a result of the effort to fill the department's race and gender quotas. Although it is not assumed here that affirmative action changes imposed on the LAPD were not a direct result of the meltdown, it appears as though officers had recognized the need for the department's administrators and managers to correct long-standing problems relating to the department's affirmative action standards long before the major organizational collapse occurred. In effect, failure to address the interdepartmental turmoil between officers stemming from affirmative action appears to have led to the crippling lack of LAPD's esprit de corps, which is essential to fostering office unity while operating under the professional model.

7. Dissension Among the Ranks

Under the professional model dissension among the ranks or a lack of loyalty to the department's leader is a sure formula for disaster. Officers' comments suggested that such a condition might have existed between Chief Gates and his administrators and managers during the time of the LAPD meltdown. Various statements suggested that some administrators/managers did "not have the chief's back" when the department's breakdown occurred, but rather were in a state of organizational mutiny motivated by their own desire to be promoted to higher ranks. "Backstabbing," "self-serving," and "spineless worms" were some of the words used by officers to describe the behavior of some administrators/managers and their reactions to the meltdown. If indeed the department's administrators/managers did perceive the internal disruption of the department as an opportunity to further their own careers rather than a threat to the chief and the department's reputation in the community, it is quite possible that this reaction alone served to short-circuit the entire organizational inner workings of the professional model within LAPD.

Assessing the Manner of Death

The above discussion outlines just some of the main probable causes of the meltdown, and perhaps the death of the professional model within the LAPD organization. Undoubtedly, there are many more possible additional causes that can be gleaned from further examinations of the officer comments obtained for this study (see appendix or the downloadable full version of officer comments). In a sense, the discovery of these primary causes of the meltdown is analogous to performing an organizational autopsy of the LAPD during the post "organizational" mortem phase of the professional model's life within the department. However, just like a pathological examination, autopsy results must determine the manner of death in addition to its cause. For every cause of death there are usually five possible outcomes explaining the circumstances or manner in which the death took place: death by natural causes, accident, suicide, homicide, or undetermined causes. This manner of death classification can also be applied to the results of the LAPD organizational autopsy:

1. Natural death: Death occurred as the result of natural causes associated with the LAPD, and was not at the hands of another. The most likely explanation here is that the professional model died of old age. Simply put, the idea of aggressive enforcement tactics focusing on crime control was no longer an acceptable policing model within the changing community in which LAPD operated.
2. Accidental death: Death occurred as the result of an accident, possibly by an act committed by the organization itself or at the hands of another, and was unintended by the LAPD. If the professional model died as the result of an accident, the causes of the organizational meltdown would have been unforeseen and unintentional by those committing the acts that ultimately led to the department's internal collapse.
3. Suicidal death: Death occurred as the result of an intentional act committed by the LAPD, and not at the hands of another (i.e., the organization did not experience an "assisted suicide"). In this case, the LAPD would have produced the meltdown intentionally to rid the department of the professional model.

4. Homicidal death: Death occurred intentionally and at the hands of another. This manner of organizational death implies that some person(s) or entity outside of the LAPD organization, perhaps possessing malicious intent, willfully took the life of the professional model by causing its death within the department.
5. Undetermined death: Death occurred for unknown reasons. For this conclusion to be drawn, the results of the organizational autopsy would not allow a clear manner of death to be determined from the observed causes of the LAPD organizational meltdown.

Typically, the manner of death is determined by process of elimination; that is, each possible manner is excluded before reaching a final conclusion. By applying this process to the LAPD organizational autopsy, the following manner of death conclusions regarding the professional model of policing can be reached:

1. The manner of death should not be classified as undetermined. As the evidence in this study clearly shows, there were distinct causes of the meltdown, both internal and external to the LAPD organization.
2. The manner of death should not be classified as suicide. The study evidence does not support the conclusion that the meltdown was intentionally triggered by persons within the LAPD organization in an attempt to kill the professional model and to perhaps replace it with the community-based policing model. Quite to the contrary, most of the officers within the organization appeared willing to use organizational life support in an effort to save the professional model as the LAPD's key operating style.
3. The manner of death should not be classified as natural. In other words, was the manner of death due to the fact that the professional model became outmoded in the increasingly diverse Los Angeles community and those who administered the model were in fact "dinosaurs," as was suggested by some of the officer comments? Based on evidence present in this study, this manner of death should be ruled out in favor of another. Again, most of the officers were in favor of preserving the professional model at LAPD. In fact, most felt that the model was the only way to curb the growing threat of increasingly hard-core criminality in the streets. However, did the community members outside of LAPD reject the professional model? If they did, and the attacks on the LAPD from outside of the organization were intended to "take out the model" by hostile means, then the manner of death associated with these actions would have to be classified as homicide.

4. The manner of death could be classified as homicide. As mentioned above, intentional actions from the community—especially those originating from politicians and special interest groups—may have killed the professional model. A history of political battles between LA Mayor Bradley and the LAPD suggests that there may have been many prior political attempts to take the professional model's life within the department. But was it the bullet shot by the LAPD's adversaries that really caused the meltdown and then the model's abandonment within the organization? If the answer to this question is yes, then the manner of death should be classified as homicide. Alternatively, there is another scenario worth considering. Could it be that the bullet fired by politicians and other outsiders at the LAPD was in fact a "shot in the dark." That is, the political bullet was fired but the intended outcome was not the death of the professional model. If this were the case, it could be argued that the same political battles between certain segments of the Los Angeles community and the LAPD merely resurfaced and intensified after the King incident, yet for some unintended reason, this time they hit the department in such a way that the model's death occurred.
5. The manner of death should be classified as accidental. Most of the evidence in this study suggests the death of the professional model was accidental. First, the study findings show that the officers' reaction to fallout over the King incident itself was not anything out of the ordinary compared to prior outside attacks against the department. In fact, their reaction to the imposition of affirmative action may have been more intense, judging from the officer statements. Although the Christopher Commission and other political entities claim responsibility for promoting the organizational change within the LAPD, this study suggests that without preexisting internal disruptions within the department, outside efforts to reform the professional model may have been successfully repelled had the "thin blue organizational wall" been maintained through proper managerial fortification. Thus, it must here be concluded that the weakness in the wall that was intentionally caused by LAPD's top administrators/managers allowed the potentially deadly effects of outside attackers to impact all levels of the department—and especially the majority of street officers. But if the top intent of the department's administrators/managers was to weaken the organization for purposes of organizational change—that is, removing the professional model—then the manner of death should be classified as suicide by top administration.

However, this did not appear to be true. Rather, according to officer observations, the administrators/managers utilized the meltdown as an opportunity to advance their own careers, and in doing so may have intentionally failed to join the chief and lower-level officers in a unified effort to fortify the department's organizational exterior from penetration by outside attackers. Most likely, some of the department's administrators/managers felt that by implementing their own internal reforms (e.g., punishing officers, changing patrol methods) they would be supported by politicians and other influential outsiders in their bid for a higher-level position in the department following the removal and replacement of Chief Gates as their leader. However, it is also here assumed that they never suspected that their actions would have produced the entire department's meltdown and the accidental death of the professional model. Thus, it is here concluded, based on an overall assessment of the study findings, that the professional model was abandoned within the LAPD organization—and perhaps throughout the world—as the result of what may be the worst organizational accident in the history of modern policing.

Rethinking the History of Policing

The findings from this study also have relevance to current thought regarding the evolution of policing within the United States. Present historical accounts suggest that three distinct periods or models of modern policing have been used in major U.S. cities since the model, succeeded by the profession model, which was the predecessor to the community-based policing model. History also suggests that the transition from one model to the next has resulted from some type of critical event. Two of these critical events have taken place at the LAPD: The first was the fall of the political model at the hands of scandal and corruption within the LAPD, leading to the imposition of the "corruption resistant" professional model; the second fall was the subject of this study, leading to the rejection of the professional model in favor of the community-based policing model. Ironically, allegations of corruption and scandal—all occurring within the LAPD—were associated in policing history with the evolution of American modern policing.[7]

Figure 9.2 shows how the policing literature currently explains the evolution of modern policing. Thus, as the pattern of events in the figure indicates, the current understanding of how policing models have evolved assumes a linear transition. That is, as one model is abandoned it is replaced by another. In effect, the older model dies or becomes extinct through this evolutionary process. However, based on this study's findings for the professional model,

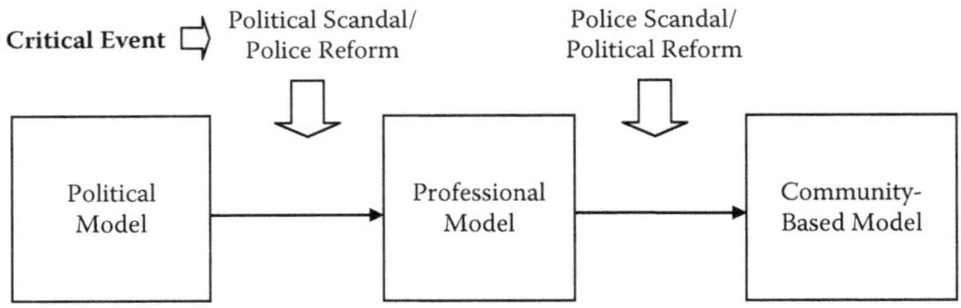

Figure 9.2 The currently accepted model of police reform, as depicted in the above illustration, suggests that a linear progression has resulted in the death of existing police models and their replacement with new models based on police reform measures. As the above model suggests, the demise of the earliest policing model (the Political Model) resulted in the adoption of the LAPD Professional Model. Likewise, the death of the Professional Model ushered in the adoption of its replacement—the Community-Based Model.

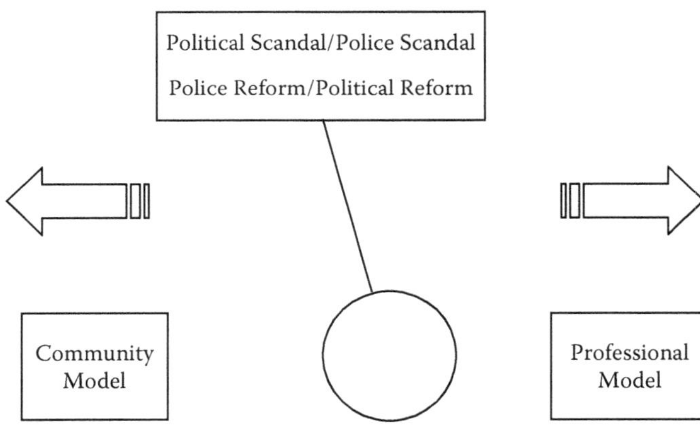

Figure 9.3 The above illustration, based on the study findings, suggests that changes in policing models over time are best conceived as a "pendulum" shift between community-based and professional policing rather than the traditional linear model which assumes that old methods of policing become obsolete and "die" when they are replaced with new ones. For example, the community-based Political Model was replaced by the non-community based Professional model following a series of political/police scandals; in turn, the Professional model was replaced by Community-based Policing following similar scandal/reform activities.

it is possible to rethink the current position within the policing literature regarding how policing models have evolved. Figure 9.3 presents an alternative way of understanding this relationship.

The method of change for policing models hypothesized in the figure reflects a fluid rather than linear progression from one model to the next. In other words, rather than assuming that models change and become obsolete (or die) over time, the alternative assumption outlined above is that methods of policing in America represent a continuum that spans from a pure community model to a pure professional model. History provides support for this proposition. The community was a central component of America's first modern model of policing (the political model), and it is also a key factor of community-based policing, which is the preferred model of today's policing world.[8] Political scandal may have caused the policing pendulum to swing away from the earlier politically based community model toward a less politically oriented professional policing model. When the more police-based model fell out of favor, perhaps the policing pendulum swung back to a more community-based approach. The primary takeaway from this alternative explanation is that rather than assuming (as does the current policing literature) that the professional model has been replaced and died, it may in fact still be alive and merely dormant. Furthermore, when the time and place calls for a change to the next approach for policing, the pendulum may swing back to the professional model.

Lessons Learned for the Future

It is beyond the scope of this study to provide a detailed discussion of specific methods of organizational management and design that could have been used by LAPD to prevent its organizational meltdown or to prevent the fall of the professional model. Generally speaking, all administrative, managerial, and operational components required to create a properly functioning police agency operating under the professional model are basically the same as those recommended for any organization that is highly centralized in structure. But should the professional model be called upon as a viable policing organizational framework in the future, there are several lessons learned from this study that would be useful for its successful implementation:

1. Preserve autonomy. The most vital organizational component of the professional model appears to be its autonomy from political influences. When lost, the model is subject to internal contamination of its culture that can amplify preexisting internal organizational problems. As originally constructed, the professional model provided autonomy for political and other outside influences by providing the chief of police with civil service protection. However, as was demonstrated in this study, even civil service protection was not enough to protect the model from outside intrusion. Aside from breakdowns in the department's resistance to political challenges, the political operating environment of the model was not optimum for preserving autonomy. Namely, the process whereby departmental policies were dictated by the police commission, whose members were appointed

by the mayor, provided a direct linkage between city politics and the LAPD. A political environment best suited for operating a professional policing model is that which operates under a city manager system of government. Under this system of government, the city manager, who typically hires the chief of police and oversees police operations, does not usually serve at the will of city politicians, thus breaking the direct linkage between politics and policing.

2. Don't mix models. The study findings suggest that creating a hybrid model consisting of community-based methods, such as allowing community input to steer policing policies, mixed with the professional model's aggressive enforcement methods does not work. This was evident during the meltdown at LAPD when efforts were made "to get officers out of their patrol car and on the street making friends with citizens." This and similar policy changes trading enforcement activities for community-based activities were clearly not accepted by officers operating under the professional model. Again, community support is a necessary component of the model, but aggressive crime control must be emphasized over community interaction.
3. Unity of leadership. Aside from autonomy from outside influences, the third most important factor in operating a successful professional model is unity among all leaders in the organization. It has always been assumed, dating back from the Parker era, that having a strong chief of police as an organizational leader was enough to preserve the model. As shown in this study, that assumption is clearly wrong. As demonstrated by the political overpowering of Chief Gates, who by some officer accounts was as strong as or stronger than Chiefs Parker and Davis, a strong chief alone is not enough. Surprisingly, and not a known fact prior to discovery in this study, the collective leadership power, LAPD's top administrators immediately subordinate to the chief, appears to be vital to the department's functioning under the professional model. In effect, these leaders serve to galvanize the leadership of the chiefs to the ranks of the department's middle- and lower-level managers as well as to the rank-and-file officers on the street. Unity of leadership must be instilled in these top administrative officers. Any sign that these officers are lacking unity in the form of loyalty, due diligence, and esprit de corps should be addressed immediately and corrected to ensure the professional model's continuing successful operation.

If nothing else is learned from the findings of this study, one thing should be remembered regarding the LAPD meltdown and the fall of the professional model. This relates to an initial question posed by Chief Gates at the outset of this study (also presented in Chapter 2): "Could the LAPD have been saved from the meltdown?" This study suggests that the appropriate answer to Chief Gates would have been maybe. The one thing that policing administrators and managers should take away from this study is that any police agency operating under the professional model cannot allow a potential "divide and conquer" situation to persist within its department's organizational culture. The end result will be a meltdown similar to that experienced by LAPD. On the other hand, if appropriate corrective measures are taken in time to fix a divided organizational culture, the professional model may prove to be resilient to "internal rotting" of the organization's "moral timbers," as predicted by Chief William Parker over a half century ago. The following final officer observation supports this conclusion and the overall study conclusions:

#285

> I feel that our Department has lost sight of its mission. With upper level administrators thinking more of their individual reputations & political aspirations, they seem to have the tendency to cower down to the liberal politicians and various ad hoc committees instead of backing the very working force that keeps them in their various administrative kingdoms. This Department is dying & it is not being destroyed from the outside.
>
> (Police Officer, Male, Hispanic, 43 years old, 22 years LAPD, Chief when hired: Davis)

References

1. Orlando Wilson and William H. Parker. *Parker on Police*. Springfield, IL: Charles C Thomas, 1957.
2. Ibid.
3. Christopher Commission. *Report of the Independent Commission of the Los Angeles Police Department*. Los Angeles: LAPD, 1991.
4. Sarah Alisa Kramer. *William H. Parker and the Thin Blue Line: Politics, Public Relations and Policing in Postwar Los Angeles* [PhD dissertation]. Washington, DC: American University, 2007.
5. Michael Hooper. Commission on Peace Officer Standards and Training. Telephonic interview conducted June 2011.
6. James Gazell. William H. Parker, Police Professionalization and the Public: An Assessment. *Journal of Police Science and Administration*, 4(1), 1976.
7. Stephen D. Mastrofski. What Does Community Policing Mean for Daily Police Work? *National Institute of Justice Journal*, 225, 1992.
8. Ibid.

Appendix: Officer Statements

#1

It's been a rough year but, we will bounce back. We all need to work together. Service is #1 that's why we are all here—I think that is the general feeling among uniformed ofc's (90%). Mang. needs to lighten up or we are going to lose some of our most outstanding ofc's/workers—then it will truly be the citz that suffer.

(Police Officer, Male, Hispanic, 24 years old, 2 years PO, 2 years LAPD, Chief when hired: Gates)

#2

We should be careful not to over react to criticism from the uninformed or those who are historically anti-LAPD. We should continue to have faith in the Depts. goals and procedures. That is not to say that we can't improve. But to say that if there is not clear evidence that change is needed lets not!

(Lieutenant, Male, Caucasian, 54 years old, 31 years PO, 29 years LAPD, Chief when hired: Parker)

#3

In the final analysis this is a great job that pays well when you take an honest look at the Department (The Christopher Commission did not) we do an outstanding job for the community. We can always improve, however all organizations can. Given the number of people we have and the size of the job of policing Los Angeles we are superstars. We must look beyond our detractors both inside the organization and outside and continue down the road we know is correct. I am confident the community supports us and is in concert with most of our actions. I see the support everyday in the way the community treats my officers and how they appreciate their efforts. As I have watched the political environment since the Rodney King case I am convinced that our detractors have no concept or interest in what is best for the people that live and work in Los Angeles. This means we have a responsibility to hang in and do the right thing and ensure that the community gets what it wants and deserves in the way of police service.

(Lieutenant, Male, Caucasian, 50 years old, 27 years PO, 27 years LAPD, Chief when hired: Parker)

#4

After careful consideration, I have decided to include a portion of my personal work on law enforcement reform. Read it: If you dare. It will make a difference; here or somewhere else.

Background

Although I have only limited time on this earth, I have been a "people watcher" a good portion of that time. I have been a law enforcement officer since I was eighteen years old and an emergency dispatcher before that. I have served three difference agencies: all of which I am proud—not even Chief Gates can say that. I lose sleep at night because the LAPD I love is taking a beating by some of its very own members and many don't even realize it. I am going to talk about people here and I want to put in a disclaimer that I believe there is a minority of officers and employees negatively impacting the Department. We can clean it up.

Job Satisfaction

I am a strong believer in the saying "We can do more with less." I am proud that our current administration has resisted accepting applicants who have experimented with cocaine and other narcotics. It is decisions like that which offer me a sense of security from bodily harm. When this practice finally falls, the Department will suffer.

It is not the stationhouse or facility which makes a Division—People make a Division. Although I am an Air Force Man, I once had the misfortune to stay in a dormitory (of sorts) on the Biggs Army Air Field at Fort Bliss Texas. Until then, I had never slept in a crab-infested rat-hole. The building was no doubt worse than our 77th Station. As a "life of luxury"—Air Force man, I was in shock. But after two weeks of this hell and a bottle or two of that unmistakable blue-green crab shampoo, our misplaced Air Force unit was stronger in morale and ready war-making capability than ever before. I am not suggesting that we scrap plans to build new stationhouses; I am saying that without a doubt one does not make something smooth by rubbing something soft against it. Quite the opposite is true. A block of wood, like a person, takes shape, becomes smooth, and can in some cases be reduced to dust by rubbing something rough against it.

If it wasn't for my house payment, I would be willing to take a pay cut. In return I believe that "has beens," the people "in it for the money," and the people experiencing "delusions of grandeur" would leave. Unfortunately, we are so drastically undermanned and doing so much with less that many officers are doing the work of two or three. Some are working harder than that. A few are not working at all. But when a police force of 8000 officers is doing the work of 20,000 officers you couldn't pay them enough if you doubled their salaries.

Supervision and Job Performance

The only item I wish to address under this heading is LAPD promotions. I recently attended the Supervisory Development Course. It was great training; mostly because it showed me how I will be received as a young Sergeant. Although I respect the field experience of a particular new Sergeant he suggested that field training officers should have a minimum of five years patrol experience, Sergeants an additional five years of field training and so on. BALONEY!

If we ever intend to promote a Chief of Police from within our own organization, we can never adopt such a plan. By the time someone will qualify to be the Chief, she or he would be dead or close to it.

In this country we are obsessed with this notion that age and time in a position is the sole determiner of competence. (e.g., 16 years old to drive a car, 18 years old to buy spray paint, and 21 years old to drink). Were it not for the political fallout, I would suggest that we carry "IQ cards"—(e.g., IQ 100 you may drive a car, IQ 120 you may own a gun, etc). I offer that example here as light hearted humor, but don't miss the point—One can be in a position for five years and be less qualified for promotion than a first day recruit at the Academy. Another point is that some things can be attained (e.g., skill and experience) and others cannot (e.g., IQ).

Working With Other Divisions

Near the very top of my list titled "Things Wrong) is the way we treat each other. If there is anything that gives me a clue about how the public is being treated, it is how we treat each other. Once I called my duty station on a day off. A detective happened to answer the phone. He seemed to be doing whatever he could to avoid giving me simple information and that was after I identified myself.

I suggest that we monitor how we treat each other a little closer. For this particular problem, we should force the attitude that if you ever pick up an LAPD phone you are responsible for following through to see that the problem we solved or a proper transfer was made. A program must have some teeth to it. A person should be used to make "wrong number" calls for service. If the person answering the phone does not attempt to help the caller, then a notice to correct should follow—the first time. We are worse than the old DMV. The DMV didn't change by building a new facility or by getting new equipment. The new DMV's are new because they realized that they were no longer service oriented and decided to hold people accountable. I know that Chief Gates believes that "holding people accountable" is a throw-away term. BALONEY! It is a throw-away term only if you don't put teeth in the program.

At the very top of my list of "Things Wrong" are the delusions of grandeur experienced by some and perhaps many police officers. We may be entering police service for the wrong reasons (e.g., we are hard-core unemployables, we want to feel powerful, we are arrogant, and some want to feel superior to the public). Many have lost the SERVANT attitude and some never had it. We are not "watch dogs" over the public; we are servants. This is ruining our Department. Many people are "coat tailing" on the achievements of the men and women who are now retired or retiring. We need to revitalize the servant attitude in a big and meaningful way and then build our own legacy.

One way to find out who some of the people are who feel superior to the public is to require that officers earn the right or articulate the need to carry an off-duty firearm. At my Academy Class graduation party there were many loaded firearms. One-day police officers carrying guns to a drinking party—delusions of grandeur? Or the servants attitude? The system could require two years of unblemished service to carry an off-duty firearm. Exception could include to and from work or court and specific exceptions by the Chief.

If you are thinking "too harsh" or "it will never work" YOU could be part of the problem. We have to really find out why people are here and make them earn the privileges. If we don't grab hold of the things that mean something to the officers, we too will be responsible when someone proposes a bill and a procedure like the one I described becomes a law. Remember, we don't make something smooth by rubbing something soft against it, we make it smooth by rubbing something rough against it. Make them earn the privilege.

This idea may not be a viable alternative because of the violent society in which we live. But, we must earn our privileges so that we will be more careful about losing them—no more easy-come easy-go.

If we lose our K-9 corp I believe we will have lost a good thing. However, I believe that K-9 handlers are among the most susceptible to the delusions of grandeur which I have been talking about. Before the courts mandate that we employ only non-attack dogs, perhaps we should do it ourselves. This is my half-serious idea:

Employ Poodles or Beagles as a K-9 training Corp at the bureau or divisional level. Then Metropolitan Division could recruit from the best divisional handlers. This one or two year "low priority search" K-9 training program would weed out the officers who seek the immediate gratification of handling German Shepherds and injuring people. Offer no additional pay and the anti-status of a scroungy dog and you WILL draw the service-minded officer most of the time.

Personnel Involvement

I am particularly concerned about the delusions of grandeur possessed by a particular deputy chief. Recently, a program was developed in an attempt to standardize use of force reporting. The program was subjected to the standard review process. An assistant chief and the Chief of Police apparently decided to pilot the program in two Areas. One of the Areas was in a bureau headed by this chief. He is effectively killing the project by doing exactly what the project is trying to prevent. We need standardization; we are not 18 different departments. If an assistant chief and the Chief himself decide to try something, even a subordinate deputy chief should follow the rules. The Department Manual is clear on what is a "use of force" yet some division captains and some bureau chiefs feel compelled to set up their own standards (more or less restrictive). I'm sure there is a reason why the Chief doesn't redirect this deputy chief's energy, but I just can't see it. This particular deputy chief is known for his intelligence and his ability to read everything that hits his desk. Unfortunately that is where my IQ theory hits the skids; because, this high IQ deputy chief is interjecting his standards on only a portion of the Department. When a bureau officer perceives that she/he cannot get a job because of 10 or 12 uses of force based on the bureau standard, morale suffers. I don't even work for the guy and my morale is suffering because I perceive the lack of standardization. I think it's okay to try new and unusual programs; but not in the area of use of force. The community and the Department seems to be demanding equal treatment no matter where in the City you may be.

Perceptions should be investigated and addressed. Perceptions are more important than some people realize. For example, if we lose our K-9s based on a perception that we abuse them, we it be comforting to know that the perception was not true? If someone perceives that a police officer is stealing, in that person's mind it is as if the officer was stealing whether or not he did. We have to address the perceptions. If it turns out to be true that some deputy chiefs are enacting policy over an existing Department standard the Chief should reel them in. If I were the chief I would give out more than a "talking to."

The Organization

I am proud to be a Los Angeles Police Officer. I will be a sergeant soon. I have been offered work outside law enforcement and I have resisted the temptations. I know I cannot change the world alone but dadgumit if I'm not going to change a part of it—alone or with help.

We have the potential to be number one but I don't think it means much to be "self proclaimed number one." If we work hard our status will return; overall, we don't deserve the number ranking today.

The Community and the Police

We need to be respectful whenever possible. We are not "watch dogs" over the public; we are servants. When I hear officers and sergeants say "Who do they think we are social workers?" I cringe because we are merely the paid police force and we will do and be what and who the public want. If that means teaching school, painting walls, public speaking, disaster rescue, or medical worker we should have a willing spirit. If we do what the community wants, then I believe that they will realize how undermanned we really are and respond to that need.

Enforcement Functions

We need to keep up the good work. We also need to address the perceived problems when they arise (e.g., excessive force and the different levels of service between the Valley and South Central Los Angeles). Remember a perceived problem is as good as a real one if we don't address it.

Training

We claim that our training is great but based on my recent experience in Sergeant School this is not true. Our training has good intentions; but, Department instructors teach personal philosophies without Department monitoring and a type of INBREED occurs.

In one class a sergeant taught a philosophy regarding gay and lesbian officers which is blatantly illegal. A captain suggested several ways to squash a personnel complaint. The ideas seemed very innovative and included giving a transient a dollar bill which he had claimed an officer took. These may have been okay except a day or two before the Captain of Internal Affairs Division had explained a new more rigid policy on taking the personnel complaint. The contradictions were not many but significant.

We should be careful in selecting the staff officer to teach ethics class. This class needs a serious tone. While I appreciate getting out of class a little early now and then, going home two hours early from ethics class is inappropriate.

Here again, we have the potential to be great

Thank you for your consideration

(Police Officer, Male, Hispanic, 27 years old, 9 years PO, 4 years LAPD, Chief when hired: Gates)

#5

This ship is dead in the water….

(Police Officer, Male, Caucasian, 45 years old, 22 years PO, 22 years LAPD, Chief when hired: Davis)

#6

There is no unity in this organization. There is a double standard and duplicity throughout the department. Management has no realistic idea how to effectively manage the organization. Each commander and deputy chief has their own agenda with no concern for the department. There is too much micro management at the bureau level. Captains and above do not have a clue what proper and effective discipline is. Some people are disciplined when they should not be and some are not disciplined when they should be. Some discipline is unfairly based on sex and race. Ideas from senior supervisors are not sought. There is a very low feeling about the department at this time. I have never seen it this bad in my 28 years.

(Sergeant, Male, Caucasian, 50 years old, 28 years PO, 28 years LAPD, Chief when hired: Parker)

#7

Why don't you people get out of your Ivory Offices and back on the street so you can see the Deep "Shit" this Department is really in.

(Police Officer, Male, Caucasian, 43 years old, 16 years PO, 16 years LAPD, Chief when hired: Davis)

#8

This department is so caught up with how the public views it and the media until it has forgotten about the police officers. We risk our lives every night for the citizens of LA and never receive a thanks. This department does not stand behind it's ofcrs. This causes a lot of stress on us because we know that the department is not going to stand behind us. LAPD officers moral is very low.

(Police Officer, Female, African American, 23 years old, 1 year PO, 1 year LAPD, Chief when hired: Gates)

#9

I am unhappy with the function of the entire dept. But, I am thankful to have a job.

(Police Officer, Male, African American, 25 years old, 3 years PO, 3 years LAPD, Chief when hired: Gates)

#10

At this time I am looking for work with a different police dept. I strongly feel this dept is becoming an unfavorable place to work. The good people of LA will suffer in the end from all the radical changes this dept. is going through.

(Police Officer, Male, Hispanic, 27 years old, 4 years PO, 4 years LAPD, Chief when hired: Gates)

#11

Personally, I feel the problems plaguing the LAPD are so serious and so abundant that there is no hope for restoring this organization to what it once was. Frankly, I can longer care. It used to be fun to come to work. I couldn't wait for the next day. I never wanted to go home. No longer! I can't wait for my 20. I'm out of here. What's really unfortunate about this is that at one time I cared; I'm very good at what I do. I squarely place the blame on the shoulder of the depts. top administrators. You have no idea what we have to put up with. If you do you should be fired for inaction.

(Detective, Male, Caucasian, 41 years old, 18 years PO, 18 years LAPD, Chief when hired: Davis)

#12

It's not like it was, Backstabbing—laziness, supervisors who don't want to get involved "Cover You Ass" mentality. Officers brag about being Do-Nothings.

(Police Officer, Male, Caucasian, 44 years old, 22 years PO, 22 years LAPD, Chief when hired: Davis)

#13

There's not enough time to list everything & it will take 15–20 years to turn it around if they start now. We have already promoted too many Bozo's that have a lot of years left with the LAPD. Good Luck. Glad I'm leaving, maybe I can get my blood pressure down when I have to constantly think about how fucked up we are.

(Sergeant, Male, Caucasian, 50 years old, 28 years PO, 28 years LAPD, Chief when hired: Parker)

#14

Two decades ago I joined this department because it was a proud, professional and autonomous organization. In the intervening years it has been besieged by mettling outsiders for self-serving political interests. Today the department is tarnished and impotent. No wonder morale is low and esprit de corps absence. Still, despite all this discouragement, I am proud of what I do and I am proud to be a member of this department. Unfortunately, I am skeptical that this or any other survey will make a difference.

(Detective, Male, Caucasian, 44 years old, 19 years PO, 19 years LAPD, Chief when hired: Davis)

#15

We have lost control. Its evident in that the majority of the ofcrs are dissatisfied with work. I believe that command staff has lost sight of the goals of the ultimate goal of any police dept.—to jail the bad guy and have a positive effect and outcome on crime. Ofcrs are scared to work, to get involved & will be in this state until our community realizes that we cannot effectively work until they back off and stop yelling police brutality every time an arrest is made. Community based policing is good if directed at the good people of our community. Vermin still need to be put in jail. I did not come here for the $—I earned 10+K more/year elsewhere. We also need better police ofcr selection. If we cant lure the intelligent & mature individual to come on board, or keep choosing our ofcrs from a pool of designed minorities who cannot even coherently read, write or think, where are we expected to be in 10 years. I'll be surprised if our outcome is not dismal.

(Police Officer, Male, Hispanic, 39 years old, 3 years PO, 3 years LAPD, Chief when hired: Gates)

#16

If these questions were asked before Rodney King you would have had a totally different outlook. The press has screwed us big time.

(Police Officer, Female, Hispanic, 29 years old, 8 years PO, 8 years LAPD, Chief when hired: Gates)

#17

One thing that is evident to me over the 19½ years of service on this police dept.—that the Brass governs by "management by crisis"; in other words, the leaders of this dept. are "Reactionaries"—not visionaries. I truly believe that any and all changes now taking place, including this survey, is only the result of Rodney King. It's too bad; all the changes on this dept. have come as a result of an outside pressure and not because of leadership and innovation.

(Detective, Male, Caucasian, 41 years old, 20 years PO, 20 years LAPD, Chief when hired: Davis)

#18

How secure are the people of this city in their homes, neighborhoods, places of business? Have these liberal commissions go into the neighborhoods and ask. The answer may surprise them, but not those of us who deal with the victim & others affected by crime & drugs. The entire elected establishment & media went to extremes to slam this dept. for the "King" incident. Pick any weekend of the year and count the gang drive-by shootings alone. Count the dead bodies. Ask the surviving relatives if they want a kinder & gentler dept, or do they want us to do our job of maintaining law and order. I have seen an unbelievable deterioration in our ability to control the streets of this city. It's getting worse. We need more officers, many more to fight crime.

(Detective, Male, Caucasian, 47 years old, 26 years PO, 26 years LAPD, Chief when hired: Parker)

#19

Just more lip service. The same problems exist now as 25 years ago. Nothing has been done. The complaints have been ignored.

(Sergeant, Male, Caucasian, 47 years old, 25 years PO, 25 years LAPD, Chief when hired: Parker)

#20

In my 22 years of service, I have seen LAPD service going down the tubes. I feel sorry for the good people in this city. They deserve more. I grew up in New York and saw the decay of that city. I feel LA is going the same way. Politics and police don't mix.

(Detective, Male, Caucasian, 44 years old, 22 years PO, 22 years LAPD, Chief when hired: Davis)

#21

Narcotics Div. of LAPD is totally corrupt & ineffective! The people of LA are getting ripped off by the calls for service which are horrible! We need more uniform cops and the department is so top heavy I am surprised it hadn't collapsed! The morale of troops in the field is in the basement which is reflective onto the citizens! A new Chief is not the answer it is a major overhaul of the specialized units which will never happen because of corruption! Ad vice, Ad Narc Totally good ol' boys corrupt.

(Police Officer, Male, Caucasian, 35 years old, 8 years PO, 8 years LAPD, Chief when hired: Gates)

#22

I believe the hiring practices of this City do not allow us to get the best type of person for this job and the way the scoring of the tests is a way to get certain groups of people promoted not on merit but on their minority status in life. I used to be proud of this job. I don't know what I am now!! No wonder our patrol cops just want to do the basics. No one's willing to back them up against a few loud mouth members of the community looking for political fulfillment.

(Police Officer, Male, Caucasian, 45 years old, 18 years PO, 18 years LAPD, Chief when hired: Davis)

#23

I know for a fact that a # of my fellow white-male ofcrs have grown to resent the depts affirmative action efforts. I find this very disturbing. My feelings about this dept have deteriorated greatly over the past several years. Upper-level mgt cares only about themselves and almost nothing about those who are out there putting their lives & reputations on the line for this dept daily. My greatest fear is that once Gates retires our next Chief will seek to appease every ctz group etc. & he too will show little concern & respect for "The Little Guy" He too will over react as has been done for years.

(Police Officer, Male, African American, 33 years old, 9 years PO, 7 years LAPD, Chief when hired: Gates)

#24

Morale is bad enough. So why does this department treat its white male officers as evil? Be fair and equal to everyone except white males. Let's strive to treat everyone for any position fairly. The most qualified get the job rather than we don't have a minority so get one. The leadership of this department should stop kissing everyone's ass so everyone will like us. That's not our job. We put bad guys in jail to protect & serve the public, that's our job. So let's stop making excuses to everyone, and do our job.

(Sergeant, Male, Caucasian, 43 years old, 20 years PO, 20 years LAPD, Chief when hired: Davis)

#25

I have 2½ years as a uniform sergeant but I am currently a detective. I waited over a year to attend sergeant's school after I was promoted. Poor police service which I rec. while living in Foothill Div (as a police officer) was a major consideration in moving my family out of the City of Los Angeles to Ventura County.

(Detective, Male, Caucasian, 37 years old, 12 years PO, 12 years LAPD, Chief when hired: Gates)

#26

There is a piss poor training at the academy. What's this stuff about everybody makes it. The City Attorney's office has let this City down.

(Police Officer, Male, Hispanic, 34 years old, 11 years PO, 11 years LAPD, Chief when hired: Gates)

#27

In regard to academy training, I feel my entire 6mts in academy was mostly useless. Shooting, tactics and radio communications was most important. The field is completely different then the academy. Community relations is important however officer safety overrides everything else.

(Police Officer, Female, African American, 23 years old, 1 year PO, 1 year LAPD, Chief when hired: Gates)

#28

Training at the academy is a waste of time & manpower. Academy training is set up to last 3 days, when it could be done in one.

(Police Officer, Male, Caucasian, 49 years old, 25 years PO, 25 years LAPD, Chief when hired: Parker)

#29

Allow any ofcr who want to go to extra training the opportunity. I have signed up for many training schools including drivers, gang, narco and have not gone to any because of only 5–6 a division can go. Fine, but don't overlook that 50 ofcrs signed up. Not because they see it as a day off (some do) but because they desperately want to be trained. Give them the knowledge they are hungry for!! Be strong enough in leadership to recognize the task ofcrs are given. Which is solve the problem!!! If you put the pressure on ofcrs to solve problems then support them when they make a mistake. Don't ignore the mistake, of course, but "burn and learn" is wrong. If that is what it takes to right a mistake then you have the wrong type of ofcrs. A supervisor of respect can do more to change and enlighten misguided ofcrs than 2 days off. That increases the bitterness to the dept and public. Also be strong enough to tell a "hot head" or stubborn ofcr they ar wrong then supervisors who know THEM by increasing contact between Sgts & ofcrs.

(Police Officer, Male, Caucasian, 30 years old, 7 years PO, 7 years LAPD, Chief when hired: Gates)

#30

If the Dept. would spend more time in training officers in self defense, they would raise the confidence level of ofcrs and, reduce the percentage of out of policy shootings. Promotions. I think there should be a more structured procedure for promotions. You should be required to have a certain amount of years on the job before promotions to (P-3) (Sgt) etc. 5 years for P-3, 7-10 years for Sgt or above.

(Police Officer, Male, African American, 30 years old, 4 years PO, 4 years LAPD, Chief when hired: Gates)

#31

Should be more self-defense training for ofcrs after 1 year.

(Police Officer, Male, African American, 53 years old, 22 years PO, 22 years LAPD, Chief when hired: Davis)

#32

Captains/staff/command ofcrs need to put on a blue suit and get out in the field. They're the ones who need "in service" training and get their heads out of the clouds. They appear to be brain washed spineless worms attempting to make a name for themselves, no matter what the cost.

(Police Officer, Male, Caucasian, 33 years old, 7 years PO, 7 years LAPD, Chief when hired: Gates)

#33

This is by no means the dept. I joined nearly 20 years ago. We've bent over backwards for some and ignored many. The double standard that exists between brass and sgts, dets and ofcrs is a pity. It's just now being exposed now more than ever before. The people in the mainstream of the dept will go nowhere unless connected to the brass or a particular group. We need to promote the police profession and those dedicated people who carry on despite obstacles from the police executives, politicians, and the misguided public. Despite my feeling I will always be faithful to the public I serve and my chosen profession—law enforcement.

(Detective, Male, Caucasian, 42 years old, 20 years PO, 20 years LAPD, Chief when hired: Davis)

#34

This dept. has always treated ofcrs as children. Sometimes when I come to work, I feel like a 10 year old kid. After the Foothill Incident the mis-trust of ofcrs by upper brass had increased. I'm a 25 year vet & I resent being mis-trusted by anyone.

(Detective, Male, Caucasian, 48 years old, 25 years PO, 25 years LAPD, Chief when hired: Parker)

#35

The staff from capt & above are nothing but back stabbing, self serving thiefs. This dept needs to get rid of more than ½ of these do nothing people. They think they are Gods & don't know what the streets are like and don't care. They care nothing about the citizens of LA & don't care. All they want is their own power & making themselves jobs where no one knows what they are doing from capt. up. Why do you need two capts of the Divisions. You will have answers which say nothing. (Officer information not available)

#36

For the most part, anyone above Lt. rank could be replaced by a manager at McDonald's restaurant. Politics—pleasing vocal groups—is too important on this dept, but probably the same everywhere else.

(Police Officer, Male, Caucasian, 44 years old, 22 years PO, 22 years LAPD, Chief when hired: Davis)

#37

You forgot Air Support! We're not surprised. We can tell by the way everyone is concerned how we feel about what kind of Helicopter we fly. Our management does not speak for the line pilots + (observers), especially our deceased ones. We could even save you money!

(Police Officer, Male, Caucasian, 39 years old, 16 years PO, 16 years LAPD, Chief when hired: Davis)

#38

I work a small specialized unit. We can't get enough cars, radios and other equipment to properly do our jobs. We use our own pagers, mobile phones, and whatever else we can borrow just to make it thru the day. Our supervision is fantastic, it's our administration that lacks good judgment. This is generally caused by refusing to listen to middle MGRS. (SGTs, Det-3s, LT's, ETC).

(Detective, Male, N/A, 40 years old, 15 years PO, 15 years LAPD, Chief when hired: Davis)

#39

Working conditions are tragic for Detectives throughout the City. We are 50 years behind the times in working conditions, work space, computers, etc. Promotion based on Affirmative Action is destroying morale! In narcotics clearly unqualified persons are being promoted based on Affirmative Action. This conclusion can only be reached by looking at the recent promotions. 1 female had 1.18 pending & has a long history of problems but was promoted to DII over dozens of more qualified candidates. (I was not affected by this promotion) We must promote on ability & experience. Not Affirmative Action! Brass in the Glass House & Div. Capts need a police background not administrative. They can not evaluate a police ofcrs performance under stress if they have never been there.

(Detective, Male, Caucasian, 43 years old, 20 years PO, 20 years LAPD, Chief when hired: Davis)

#40

II. Job Satisfaction

1. Our police facilities are terrible. They are dirty, uncomfortable and loaded with safety and health hazards. There is never enough equipment (cars, rovers, computers or even reports) to do the job and station security does not exist.
2. Supervision (Sergeants) on this Department is generally good but they are forced to comply with too many administrative orders. There is far too much micro management on this department. A guy does his time in the field, studies and is deemed qualified to make decisions. LET HIM MAKE THOSE DECISIONS.
3. We could all use more pay but our health benefits are good. Paid medical for retirees would be nice and so would no cost of living cap.
4. I get along well with my supervisors, peers and the community but the civilian employees on this department treat officers like dirt.
5. No Comment
6. I have no faith or confidence in the top management of this department. Why can't they be discreet in their personal affairs and beliefs and stay out of the papers? They just give the media more things to criticize us about. They are completely out of touch with the community and officers because they never talk to us. They give conflicting signals and messages, depending on the latest political fad, and have destroyed morale.

7. Due to the recent consent decree and affirmative action policies, I do not believe I will ever have a fair opportunity to promote because I am white and heterosexual.
8. We are told to do work, when to show up and how to handle virtually every situation. This department has stripped us of all freedom, decision making power and even our right to free speech. According to the Human Relation Handbook, I'm not even allowed to harbor the thought that homosexuality is wrong because I might offend one.
9. I have been associated with this department for 7 years, and can say that I was satisfied with my job up until the last year.
10. It [morale] wasn't too bad six months ago.
11. I used to be proud to be a Los Angeles Police Officer.

III. Supervision and Job Performance

1. No Comment
2. This question infers that I (we) have a problem dealing with the community we serve. I don't think so. I have never had a problem communicating with citizens and I don't let my personal feelings interfere with my job. I am polite and I care about the people I work for. This very question and its inference has just created more stress than any citizen contact. How dare you!
3. The only thing that matters when it comes to promotion on this department is the color of your skin, your sex or sexual preference. When (not if) I am passed over for promotion, because I am white. I promise to file a law suit.
4. As I've said before, line supervision is not a problem on this department.

IV. Working With Other Divisions

My only complaint with other divisions is that civilians forget they're supposed to provide support functions and they treat us with little or no respect.

V. Personnel Involvement

Patrol has no say, opinion or input.

VI. The Organization

I used to be proud to be a member of this department, now I am ashamed and embarrassed. Enough said.

VII. The Community and Police

It would probably be beneficial to form closer contacts with the public but not under the current circumstances. We don't have enough officers to spend time talking to people, we have to get to the next four calls.

VIII. Enforcement Functions

It depends on the latest political fad. Whatever that is, be it drugs, response time, the homeless … we do a great job considering our limited resources.

IX. Training

Our training is fine, both academy and in-service

X. In General

I loved being a cop and a member of this organization but the events that have transpired during the last year have destroyed my pride and broken my heart. I can only hope that when the current administration retires (all of them) my peers and I can work together to repair the damage that has been done. As with any problem, patrol is the first to be blamed, the first to be criticized, and the first to be punished. Yet we are also the first to be given the mission of correcting the problem. We really are trying to do a good job. Unfortunately, our efforts will be worthless until department managers learn to conduct themselves with the same professionalism and dignity they demand of us.

(Police Officer, Male, Caucasian, 28 years old, 7 years PO, 7 years LAPD, Chief when hired: Gates)

#41

1. Re-instate the choke hold
2. New MDT'S Rovers; comm. System
3. Cages in veh's; spotlights on veh's (dual) Upright shotgun racks; put one-piece plastic (hard) seats in rear of veh's.
4. Adopt a semi-auto hi-capacity shotgun (modern) or a dual operation (i.e., super 90 M1 or M3) w/a tac light forearm.
5. Adopt a cloth badge for outerwear (foul/inclement weather)
6. Revamp all combat/hand-to-hand (dangerously inefficient)
7. Allow use of Glock; Sig-Saur etc 9mm

(Police Officer, Male, Caucasian, 25 years old, 2 years PO, 2 years LAPD, Chief when hired: Gates)

#42

LAPD does an outstanding job with the resources we have available. One of our main problems is lack of personnel and adequate equipment. We have a 25,000 person problem and are trying to solve it with 8,000 people. In 20 years we have only marginally increased the department size in the light of an enormous increase in crime and complexity of service. We are inundated with requests for service and are simply overloaded. Patrol division personnel and detectives are burning out. In addition, upper managements lack of direction is contributing to low morale. We need 1. More people 2. Better equipment 3. Better facilities 4. Better upper management leadership. I could write 20 pages easily on this topic—out of room.

(Sergeant, Male, Caucasian, 44 years old, 23 years PO, 23 years LAPD, Chief when hired: Reddin)

#43

I'm sick and tired of hearing about "poor Rodney King!"

(Police Officer, Male, Hispanic, 30 years old, 5 years PO, 5 years LAPD, Chief when hired: Gates)

#44 (see #18)

#45

The "King" incident has caused the lowest morale on LAPD in the 21 years I've been around. LAPD has gotten no support from the news media or politicians. I don't trust, nor do I have support of my captain, commander or deputy chief. I do trust Gates, Parks & Kroeker!

(Detective, Male, Caucasian, 42 years old, 21 years PO, 21 years LAPD, Chief when hired: Davis)

#46

I have always been proud & loyal to be a member of LAPD. I have tolerated poor working conditions, poor supervision, sexual harassment and other job hindrances and have still been hard working and proud. I planned to work at least 30 years until the King incident. I am increasingly ashamed of being a member of LAPD and am considering early retirement. Its not all LAPD's fault—we are good, we do the best with what we have but with the media hype the pubic no longer trusts or respects us. Becoming goody two-shoes social workers will not change this. Doing good police work will.

(Detective, Female, Caucasian, 48 years old, 25 years PO, 25 years LAPD, Chief when hired: Parker)

#47

Our #1 enemy is not the "bad guys" but the news media! They are a business, & show only one side (bad) and very little on the good side. They are definitely not interested in any good we do. If you want the public to like us, all the program's in the world will not do any good as long as the news media maintains their current policy.

(Police Officer, Male, Caucasian, 44 years old, 21 years PO, 21 years LAPD, Chief when hired: Davis)

#48

We are very thin in terms of manpower, our equipment is outdated. In terms of recruitment, we are turning away quality individuals to fulfill some pathetic quota. The general public hates and fears us because of how the media portrays us. We are losing the most aggressive & the most innovative police chief in LAPD history because of the power of the media. Chief Gates is popular amongst his troops. It'll be a major blow when he finally leaves. Because of the public's misconception and lack of support of us, everything we do on the street is done with added hesitation because of our fear of serious liability.

(Police Officer, Male, Caucasian, 38 years old, 8 years PO, 8 years LAPD, Chief when hired: Gates)

#49 (see #16)

#50

If this comment gets to anyone who cares, the managements politically motivated in-fighting and back stabbing have been driving this dept. down for several years. The mgmnt lack of emphasis and concern for field ofcrs has never been more evident. This is a very good dept. and your over reaction to every politically sensitive issue contributes more to public dissension than all our field ofcrs combined. Stop allowing the politicians and the media to manipulate you or we will soon become another New York City or Chicago or Miami. They've already lost their cities & they could never hire enough ofcrs to correct it. The City of New York has over 30,000 police ofcrs and they aren't even remotely close to controlling crime problems. This is a clear sign of overreaction. What difference is it if you have 8,000 ofcrs or 30,000 ofcrs if they are all handcuffed. My suggestion is fight the people (lawyers, politicians, etc) who choose to take advantage of this dept because you let them force you into over-reacting. Lawyers prompt ridiculous civil suits because the City and Dept. allows it. Politicians att to exploit and manipulate this dept. Management because they can easily force the "brass" into over-reaction. I'm not saying the dept. should not react, just don't over-react. The Rodney King Incident has, without question caused the dept. to over-react because the media and the lawyers wanted you to. Take a lesson from Sherriff Block, there is no doubt who is in charge of the LASD and he won't be pushed around by media, lawyers, and politicians. He will not and can not compromise his Dept., why have you allowed this to happen to us. The lawyers are happy and making money on this City, the politicians are winning elections over this Dept. and the media falsely presents this Dept. to make money, and you, the brass have no supportive response, just over-reaction in the negative. Wake up, before we are mired in political corruption & not just at the higher levels. When this happens, I'm out of here. Do something positive for police ofcrs and morale now or lose the City. Lets not forget the criminal element. Those who kill, rape, rob, steal cars, and block sidewalks and intersections in protest are laughing at how easy it is to manipulate this Dept. and it's management. Special interest and minority groups have caused this dept. to alter policies and procedures and have even forced the dept. into selective non-enforcement of the laws that apply to everyone. What an embarrassing situation for any hard working law enforcement ofcr who wears any uniform, for any city, county or state when special interests are served by mgmnt for political harmony. Where does this special treatment for special interests and groups lead us—into chaos and corruption and dissension. The criminals and protesters alike are laughing at how easy it is to push the right buttons within the LAPD for personal gain. Wake up and stand up and be proud of this dept. because there is a lot to be proud of. Chief Gates, this is to remind you that a street ofcr cares about this dept, and as head of this Dept, wants you to take a stand for all of us.

(Police Officer, Male, Hispanic, 36 years old, 9 years PO, 9 years LAPD, Chief when hired: Gates)

#51

Too few officers to do the job. The media is more concerned about "a good story" then being fair to the police, which greatly harms community relations. Out dated equipment (radios, cars, etc.) no PKG & a small station does not help job satisfaction.

(Police Officer, Male Caucasian, 36 years old, 11 years PO, 11 years LAPD, Chief when hired: Gates)

#52

Affirmative Action is going to be a major downfall for this Department. The goal should be the best qualified, i.e., education, experience, seniority, work performance. Officers are being "brow beaten" from every angle. The citizens are brain washed by the news media. Every time I turn on the T.V. it's anti-police. If the news media and citizens think they know how to do police work, then put them in a blk & wht. They are scared to live in LA and are stripping officers of all their resources. Management is succumbing to the "new media" pressure. The citizens will not regain respect for the police until upper management gains respect from the troops. Whatever happened to comraderie?

(Police Officer, Female, Caucasian, 31 years old, 3 years PO, 3 years LAPD, Chief when hired: Gates)

#53 (see #8)

#54

This Department is more concerned with what the media shows us as and what the public thinks, then the ofcr's who put their life on the line everyday.

(Police Officer, Male, Caucasian, 27 years old, 4 years PO, 4 years LAPD, Chief when hired: Gates)

#55

This dept has to come together. This dept is being run by the media, city council and other wanna be politicians. I believe the dept should be run by a Police Officer not politicians. This dept is running scared. After all, we came on this job to be police officers not to sit in an ivory tower worrying about who's spot I'll be taking!

(Police Officer, Male, Hispanic, 29 years old, 4 years PO, 4 years LAPD, Chief when hired: Gates)

#56 (see #3)

#57

It's my personal opinion, that in light of all the negative media attention this department has had you, the administration have failed to defend us against those who are truly responsible for the violence that occurs in the communities that we serve. Rather than make "us" (LAPD) the scapegoat for all the troubles that are prevalent in the city you, the city fathers, and so called "Men of God" should not point fingers at "us" but at yourselves for failing to lead. Now, no one group is alone responsible for today's problems. It falls on everyone of us. But coming back to "us" (LAPD), you the department heads have lost touch with what goes on in the field. The rank and file are not out of control. We are more professional than ever. But there is a serious problem. Our very own people are chipping away at our character and soon there will be nothing left to salvage. I only hope this survey will do something positive. God, knows we need it. Thank you for the opportunity.

(Police Officer, Male, Hispanic, 30 years old, 5 years PO, 5 years LAPD, Chief when hired: Gates)

#58

Ofc's are at the end of their rope—not enough space or time avail. to say what I really feel. Uniformed officers are taking the entire brunt of the King Matter, without support from the top. However, it is ironic, that when the top was under fire, the uniformed ofc's gave 100% support to them.

(Sergeant, Male, Caucasian, 54 years old, 24 years PO, 24 years LAPD, Chief when hired: Reddin)

#59 (see #34)

#60 (see #40)

#61

Post Rodney King hysteria in discipline is only being applied to line troops. Recent complaints of misconduct, abuse of authority and discourtesy by supervision (all the way to Capt III) is just covered up, not investigated or just handled as training issues & not 1.81 like would happen to me.

(Police Officer, Male, Caucasian, 41 years old, 15 years PO, 15 years LAPD, Chief when hired: Davis)

#62 (see #17)

#63

The morale on the dept. is the absolute worst I have seen since coming on the job (and management does not care)! Top management has no concern whatsoever for patrol officers, but only cares about their own careers, advancement and status!! They don't give a damn! I am no longer proud to be with the LAPD!! The dept has totally overreacted to the Rodney King Affair—resulting in needless, unnecessary 1.81s and punishment.

(Police Officer, Male, Caucasian, 35 years old, 8 years PO, 5 years LAPD, Chief when hired: Gates)

#64

Prior to March of 1991, we were effective as an organization because we had direction and meaning. We are now without a leader, meaning the chief of police and we definitely have no confidence or leadership in our command staff. I used to be extremely proud to be part of this organization. As a late, I am not so sure any more. I have to ask myself a question, and that is, why is morale so poor. Morale starts at the top and its funneling down. The command leadership of this dept is sad & ineffective. Yes I work the streets & always have and always will. After all, every capt, commander and chief did also. But I feel that "they" have forgotten—"the street cop," and the street cop is being thrown to the wolves! Everyone is always saying how important the street cop is. For once, this dept should prove it. By what means this is accomplished I am not certain. The street officer needs to be backed up. Work needs to be done in this area.

(Sergeant, Male, Caucasian, 39 years old, 17 years PO, 17 years LAPD, Chief when hired: Davis)

#65

Stop burning patrol for Rodney King, we were not all there, MDT message investigations have gotten way out of hand, make some changes or a lot of officers will be leaving.

(Police Officer, Male, Caucasian, 30 years old, 8 years PO, 4 years LAPD, Chief when hired: Gates)

#66

It is quite apparent that the department is making a great effort to improve relations with the community and to reach out in particular to minority communities. The department however has in exchange for this improved relationship with the community sunk to an all time low in employee relations. In the past we had problems with excessive force and now we have problems with excessive discipline against officers. The same administrative managers who accepted excessive force as an everyday part of police work are now implementing an unbearable and unfair system of discipline. Before we were too tough, now we are too easy. Before we were too conservative and now we're too liberal. Somehow, we never have been able to find a happy median. We have thrown the baby out with the bath. Since we have compared our future as being like "Nordstroms" Dept Store where the customer is always right, we can only achieve good customer satisfaction when we first achieve quality employee satisfaction. This system of extreme "negative discipline" has had a tremendous effect on morale, the crime rate, and community trust in this dept. Supervisors and command officers have become experts in community relations since March 3, 1991. They placate the press, City Hall, and civil rights groups. They have failed miserably in supporting the patrol section—the backbone of the dept. I am a human being. I am not perfect. I have successfully passed a background investigation, yet my work is looked on with doubt compared to that of a convicted felon. Let's learn how to treat the public by treating each other well first!!

(Police Officer, Male, Caucasian, 33 years old, 8 years PO, 2 years LAPD, Chief when hired: Gates)

#67

I have never wanted to be anything other than the best LAPD officer I could possibly be. I have always been proud of our organization. My feelings of pride are still there but I am deeply disappointed in the personal behavior of this Department's staff. The conduct of the staff/command since the King Incident have embarrassed all of us otherwise loyal officers!!

(Lieutenant, Male, Caucasian, 42 years old, 21 years PO, 21 years LAPD, Chief when hired: Davis)

#68

The problem with management all evolved around the Chief being supportive of imbeciles who have make a decisions that are completely out of all reality. We have been taken in to believe that we should all be supportive. But at the 1st sign of trouble almost every C.O. went out of their way to stab him in the back, that is loyalty? There are Capts who personally get involved in destroying a policeman's career. The discipline of ofcrs is needed of which I strongly agree, its just that the managers of the whole system have no experience at all to be helpful at what's happening. Loyalty has only flowed one way. The embarrassment of this dept is management not the street policeman—not the detectives. When a supervisor will pick an inferior candidate—and pass over an experienced seasoned ofcr who has paid his dues, to promote a minority, we've lost completely. We've lost the experience and the loyalty of an ofcr who has been threw hell. Management hides behind affirmative action. The police academy is laden with individuals who have no experience in the field, training recruits. This whole scenario is sad to say the least. Patrol is loaded with ofcrs who have years of field experience. The Christopher Commission is only a vehicle to speed the process of direction that the department had been headed for years, Thanks to the managers of the department. This whole report was completely off base as to the real issues at hand. But it didn't surprise me because it was written by a handful of lawyers. If management had shown any infinitesimal amount of brains they would have responded. But they couldn't, because they don't know. Their only goal has been only a self-serving mode, only to promote themselves. And who has really suffered—the whole dept. The Rodney King incident is only the tip of the ice berg—the whole problem is getting exposed everyday but no one is paying attention. For years now the problems have been evident. The dept is now in a position of disappearing in the way that I know it. We're not that effective organization that we once were, thanks to management. We will never be that force again. It's time for an outsider to become Chief only because he would force all the command staff out. This is the only way to restore some faith in management within the dept. I don't think Chief Gates has enough power to remove the middle management of the dept. Most of us see middle management as the problem and until the Chief sees this, nothing will ever improve we're in worse shape now than when Chief Davis left. The effectiveness of middle management can best be described the last few years as a snake who has swallowed their own tail. The Chief is not the problem!

(Police Officer, Male, Hispanic, 43 years old, 20 years PO, 20 years LAPD, Chief when hired: Davis)

#69

Hopefully the city will select a Chief of Police from the outside, if not—do not expect much change. I personally feel the citizens of LA have been getting the short end of the stick. Additionally—incidents like the King matter are not new—It's been prevalent t/o the department for 20+ years. Note: Ten years from now—unless there are some drastic changes most of us that are retired will not even admit were members of the LAPD—sad but true.

(Sergeant, Male, Caucasian, 50 years old, 23 years PO, 23 years LAPD, Chief when hired: Reddin)

#70

I enjoy my job very much. I do feel that we are being forced to "kiss up" to the public to try and make up for Rodney King. I also feel that we are being forced to deal with minorities, especially blacks, in a different and now less forceful manner than we deal with all other persons. People feel that we "pick on" a certain race. It's not our fault that 70% of the crime is committed by that race. We don't choose who we arrest, the criminals do that. I'll arrest anyone who commits a crime, I don't care what race they are. So quit showing favoritism both to minority citizens and to ofcrs, but judge on merits, good or bad, and treat persons based on that not skin color or what outside groups say.

(Police Officer, Male, Caucasian, 27 years old, 1 year PO, 1 year LAPD, Chief when hired: Gates)

#71

Top mgt. still believes ofcrs need to go out of roll call with fire in their eyes. The result is 39th & Dalton & Rodney King incident. We still teach & instill the belief that every person an ofcr encounters may kill him. We seem to instill a combination of paranoia and vigilante mentality. The Hammer task forces were an example Mgt. seemed to believe ofcrs were not aggressive enough, hence the mob mentality and "good" vs. "bad" mentality. We need a change at the top!

(Lieutenant, Male, Caucasian, 45 years old, 24 years PO, 24 years LAPD, Chief when hired: Reddin)

#72

I love this job and would do it for free but I need to eat. The incident only made things better.

(Police Officer, Male, Caucasian, 32 years old, 7 years PO, 7 years LAPD, Chief when hired: Gates)

#73

The brass has got to quit cowtowing to these liberal activists, especially the scum on the police commission. And you can take that Christopher Commission Report & shove it up where the sun don't shine.

(Police Officer, Male, Caucasian, 45 years old, 21 years PO, 21 years LAPD, Chief when hired: Davis)

#74

Police ofcrs today no longer are enforcing the laws of society. The service provided is more reactive than proactive. This problem starts with upper management "running scared" from the vocal minority. The criminals know this thus they are not apprehended & in turn the crime rate increases. Man can learn many things from history, some good & some bad. Let the individual officer do their job as they did in the past. Send a message to criminals that the LAPD is back with strength.

(Police Officer, Male, Caucasian, 26 years old, 2 years PO, 2 years LAPD, Chief when hired: Gates)

#75

The LAPD is becoming a political organization kow-towing to every loud mouth politician and refusing to back its own officers. The brass is concerned more about their own image than the Department employees. Patrol has never been the backbone of the Dept (which it should be), its been treated more like the back side of the Dept in terms of caring, promotions and work conditions. We need the Department to "Fight for Us," not use us as a scape-goat.

(Sergeant, Male, Caucasian, 45 years old, 23 years PO, 23 years LAPD, Chief when hired: Reddin)

#76

This department has been flushed down the toilet by liberal, no-nothing politicians, special interest groups, spineless command staff, and, most of all, affirmative action. I am no longer proud to call myself a Los Angeles Policeman.

(Police Officer, Male, Caucasian, 42 years old, 18 years PO, 17 years LAPD, Chief when hired: Davis)

#77

I feel this dept. cares too much about what the citz's have to say and especially what the susps have to say. This dept. wants us (police officers) to work with our hand behind our back. The dept. is creating unnecessary paperwork for us. We do not have enough or proper equipment to work with. This dept is not as strong as they use to be. NO GUTTS!

(Police Officer, Female, Hispanic, 23 years old, 3 years PO, 3 years LAPD, Chief when hired: Gates)

#78

It has been tried, tested and found to fall far short of expectations. We live in a community which views the P.D. as a necessary evil and because of inept Political Leadership and serious doubts as to

Dept. Leadership is unwilling to approve measures which would improve the Dept. I am not endorsing the measures suggested by the Christopher Comm. They are a joke, the joke is compounded when you realize that the entire situation is orchestrated by political greed (Mayor Bradly) and media greed.

(Police Officer, Male, Caucasian, 43 years old, 17 years PO, 17 years LAPD, Chief when hired: Davis)

#79

When the Mayor, City Council and Police Commission all get on the same side of the fence as the Police Department (law and order) this community could stand a chance of again being a decent place to live and work. Until then, forget it!

(Detective, Male, Caucasian, 40 years old, 19 years PO, 19 years LAPD, Chief when hired: Davis)

#80

We are under deployed everyday & every watch in every div. We have a worthless lying Mayor for a leader. Crime controls the streets of LA & citzs don't complain because they know we won't solve the problem because we can't. Big mouths (media) complain loudly about what they know nothing about. Citz(s) w/o big mouths don't voice their opinions & they have big problems & solutions & uniform pat knows this, because we are out there every day (alone) w/o citz help or dept help, some backbone of the dept.

(Police Officer, Male, Caucasian, 28 years old, 7 years PO, 7 years LAPD, Chief when hired: Gates)

#81

We need more officers. We need to quit cowtowing down to politicians and liberal left wing groups. We need to quit saying "poor suspect," "bad officer." The brass has to stop punishing the blue suiters in order to placate City Hall and liberal groups.

(Sergeant, Male, Caucasian, 50 years old, 27 years PO, 27 years LAPD, Chief when hired: Parker)

#82 (see #68)

#83

LAPD has bone from an agency with good morale and reputation to just another polyglot PD hiring and promoting everyone who alleges to be a minority. Every personnel decision is racially motivated. Good officers see no real chance for promotion. A crooked Mayor and his ACLA stooges run the department. Patrol officers are mired in useless paperwork. LAPD is quickly becoming third world and third rate just like the City. I would strongly urge potential recruits against coming on the department. Law enforcement is not the career of the nineties.

(Police Officer, Male, Caucasian, 51 years old, 22 years PO, 22 years LAPD, Chief when hired: Davis)

#84 (see #14)

#85

I think the leadership of this dept. below Chief and above Lt. is so concerned with kissing political ass to get the up-coming chief's spot they have lost all concept of what they are really supposed to be doing. Of course that's assuming they ever did know what their job was and were capable of doing it.

(Police Officer, Male, Caucasian, 43 years old, 22 years PO, 22 years LAPD, Chief when hired: Davis)

#86

You pack of clowns can fool some of the ofcrs some of the time, etc. Get a job! Quit sucking political ass!

(Police Officer, Male, Caucasian, 45 years old, 18 years PO, 18 years LAPD, Chief when hired: Davis)

#87

The Dept. seems to more concerned by the threats of public (law suits & 1.81s) than ever before. This has brought moral to an all time low. Everytime we turn around a video camera is pointing at or 1.81 is waiting for us at the station.

(Police Officer, Male, Caucasian, 35 years old, 14 years PO, 14 years LAPD, Chief when hired: Davis)

#88

Presently the Department has no clear goal for its personnel or the community. We still have outstanding people and ethics, however, the on-going political power struggle and pandering to political correctness interests has confused the public and members of the Department. It appears that some decisions are being made to further the interests of individuals and these special interest groups, rather than for the good of the community. I believe many officers are demoralized by this perception. More information must be shared with our field personnel. They are hungry for direction. This survey may help meet that need.

(Detective, Male, Caucasian, 52 years old, 29 years PO, 29 years LAPD, Chief when hired: Parker)

#89 (see #3)

#90

Don't be influenced by politics or politicians. We know how the job should be done. Let us do it.

(Detective, Male, Caucasian, 43 years old, 15 years PO, 15 years LAPD, Chief when hired: Davis)

#91

In my opinion the reason why I feel that morale is low is because officers don't feel that the media, the mayor, some council members and the police commissioners are supportive of LAPD ofcrs. For example, how can a commissioner who has no formal police training or experience publicly denounce how LAPD K-9s are used to apprehend felony suspects? You gotta be kidding me, give me a break! Maybe he should respond to calls himself since he knows so much about police tactics!

(Police Officer, Male, Hispanic, 31 years old, 11 years PO, 8 years LAPD, Chief when hired: Gates)

#92

I think that we (as a dept), should tell the ACLU where to go. And if they don't know where it is, then we should provide that communist organization with a map. And as far as the mayor & city council members who are against the LAPD as we know it, they should be put in the same boat as the ACLU. Elected officials should not be allowed to have a say so in how the dept is ran.

(Police Officer, Male, African American, 29 years old, 5 years PO, 5 years LAPD, Chief when hired: Gates)

#93

NAACP & Christopher Commission are destroying this dept. These special groups have negative objectives for the dept. They never having anything positive to say about our dept, and it's getting to the point that they are making decisions for our dept.

(Police Officer, Male, Caucasian, 31 years old, 9 years PO, 9 years LAPD, Chief when hired: Gates)

#94 (see #55)

#95

Learn from your mistakes Chief & don't let the politicians & media push you around.

(Police Officer, Male, Caucasian, 33 years old, 10 years PO, 10 years LAPD, Chief when hired: Gates)

#96

I think the Christopher Commission stinks. I don't know what makes them think they are experts in any field, especially police work. In my opinion when Chief Gates leaves we are in trouble. He is the only one who has guts enough to stand up against all these demonstrators and political activists.

(Police Officer, Male, Caucasian, 47 years old, 21 years PO, 20 years LAPD, Chief when hired: Davis)

#97

With the exception of the Chief of Police, who for political reasons has merely been rendered ineffective, the upper management of the department seems more concerned with promotion/career protection than with the welfare of their people. Their active abuse of ofcrs via the disciplinary system reflects a shameful "kowtow" to the most outrageous & illfounded accusations of the Christopher commission. I no longer feel any professional kinship to these people and feel they are not deserving of the loyalty of any police ofcr of this dept. I am not a racist, brutal incompetent who will violate his public trust given the chance to do so and I resent being treated as such. It is one thing for the public to overreact to a terrible incident; there are no excuses for our upper management.

(Police Officer, Male, Hispanic, 38 years old, 9 years PO, 9 years LAPD, Chief when hired: Gates)

#98

A police chief should be able to act freely when implementing policy or procedure—without influence from those with more self serving interest.

(Police Officer, Male, Hispanic, 42 years old, 20 years PO, 20 years LAPD, Chief when hired: Davis)

#99

Top brass is very weak, they are afraid to make a choice in a tactical decision. The Chief was too quick to convict the Foothill police officers, He folded to the Mayor & the media, he should have fought for his troops like Sherman Block.

(Police Officer, Male, Caucasian, 30 years old, 8 years PO, 8 years LAPD, Chief when hired: Gates)

#100

Have the Chief run for his office with a city wide election this was the political hacks on the city council and in the Mayor's Office won't be able to spoil what once was the department in the country.

(Police Officer, Male, Caucasian, 39 years old, 18 years PO, 18 years LAPD, Chief when hired: Davis)

#101

City council + Mayor have destroyed the most efficient and effective police dept. in the world. They have never responded adequately to our needs to effectively police our growing populous and decaying society. Their priorities are self motivated and not in the best interest of all LA's citizens. The corruption in city government goes on—while we are made the sacrificial lamb for societies ills. Upper mgt. has perpetuated the disease for self ritious reasons—"looking good" instead of telling a well meaning chief the truth. Chief, you entrusted the fate of the dept you love and are loyal to to a group of mgrs loyal only to themselves, with little or no genuine interest in LAPD. They also used us as sacrificial lambs. Chief as your shepherd you entrusted our fate to the wolves. We are a political toy. Lets play the game fair. The demand + need for more police service has never been so great—so the city politicians talk "cut backs"—and we respond with a ploy called community based policing.

(Detective, Male, Caucasian, 56 years old, 33 years PO, 33 years LAPD, Chief when hired: Parker)

#102

It appears that our once proud department is buckling to political pressure from "special interest groups" and politicians trying to gain control in our operations. I never thought I would see the day when groups like Queer Nation could spit on a Los Angeles Police Officer and have that officers hands tied because of fear by management of political fallout. Chief Gates, don't quit.

(Police Officer, Male, Caucasian, 35 years old, 10 years PO, 10 years LAPD, Chief when hired: Gates)

#103

This department no longer cares for officers or their personal problems. The management (capt & higher) only care about their own careers and personal goals not about the officers that are doing the real work. We are allowing the citizens to control & ruin the community!

(Detective, Male, Caucasian, 34 years old, 11 years PO, 11 years LAPD, Chief when hired: Gates)

#104

Community racism not LAPD racism has made this dept ineffective in handling the major crime problem today….

(Police Officer, Male, Caucasian, 33 years old, 4 years PO, 4 years LAPD, Chief when hired: Gates)

#105

We are catering to the squeaky wheel concept of citizen meetings in the Projects & Barrios. The vast majority of honest working stiffs could care less of MTG with police for coffee. They just expect honest police to put bad guys in jail. It could be that after "the special interest groups" have had their way for a few years & crime is running rampant the silent majority will beat on the doors of city hall demanding the return of good aggressive police work to again put the criminals in jail.

(Police Officer, Male, Caucasian, 49 years old, 24 years PO, 24 years LAPD, Chief when hired: Reddin)

#106

The biggest problem I see with personnel is accountability and fairness. The "doing more with less" system has become ridiculous. We need 2,000 police in uniform on the street or we are going to lose this city! LAPD has lost respect and mostly because upper level managers don't do anything but shuffle paper. Most don't know names of those who work for them because they never get out among them. We should keep our standards high and not bow to political pressure. It is not the same as it was 15 years ago and it is going to be our downfall.

(Sergeant, Male, Caucasian, 43 years old, 22 years PO, 19 years LAPD, Chief when hired: Davis)

#107

This Dept is going to the shits. Should be more like Sheriffs Dept. LAPD is to politically involved can't do police work anymore!

(Police Officer, Male, Caucasian, 51 years old, 27 years PO, 27 years LAPD, Chief when hired: Parker)

#108

The community is currently running the Dept & at present, between the "times," special interest groups (ACLU) community leaders & pressure groups, we have abandoned our pro active stance. We have lost Rampart Division. If we continue our present course of action we will become a police dept. like New York or Chicago. I have for 33 years been a proud member of the "thin blue line"! But believe my era is coming to a sad end. No longer is LAPD #1.

(Sergeant, Male, Caucasian, 55 years old, 33 years PO, 33 years LAPD, Chief when hired: Parker)

#109

In the Department's efforts to placate the Police Commission and other groups, it has forgotten that its sworn personnel is also made up of "citizens" who need to be treated fairly, with respect and professionalism. During this period of change, the ofcrs feel abandoned alienated and unjustly accused. Ultimately the public will suffer, but at least the officer who takes the crime report will be a friendly one.

(Police Officer, Male, Hispanic, 42 years old, 8 years PO, 8 years LAPD, Chief when hired: Gates)

#110

I think this dept. is making a big mistake catering to the wants of special interest groups (any groups). Quit trying to please these people. Focus on how to stop crime, and stay out of the politics. If we do our job w/ common courtesy to all then the public will be happy. Remember we are the police. We take dads to jail and notify family of dead relatives. Most people respect us but even the good citz does not want us around unless there is trouble.

(Police Officer, Male, Caucasian, 29 years old, 3 years PO, 3 years LAPD, Chief when hired: Gates)

#111 (see #86)

#112

Currently management is so worried about political forces and their own ass, they have forgotten about the street officer. Changes only come when they are forces on the Dept. It makes no difference if the proposed changes are good or bad. Why have we watched as LASO and LAPD narcotics officers go to jail and not made any changes? The Dept puts restrictions on vice tours, but not on narcotics positions? Our thinking is behind the times. Thirty years ago vice was the focal point of money. Today narcotics is where the money is. Wake up. This Department is moving to a complacent organization attempting to fight an active group of carrier criminals backed by civil rights activists. Both are going to get what they deserve.

(Sergeant, Male, Caucasian, 47 years old, 20 years PO, 20 years LAPD, Chief when hired: Davis)

#113

Community relations have always been there. The element that is dissatisfied is the relatives of the crooks. The far liberal corners of this city want to control the dept and the results will be like Sodom & Gomorrah.

(Detective, Male, Caucasian, 46 years old, 25 years PO, 25 years LAPD, Chief when hired: Parker)

#114

Our dept policy is becoming "kinder, gentler …" because of public citizen outcry. Some one … press or whoever has to inform bad guys to become kinder & gentler also. We are a reflection of some of societies problems—not the cause as many would like the public to believe.

(Police Officer, Female, Caucasian, 32 years old, 9 years PO, 9 years LAPD, Chief when hired: Gates)

#115

They say that officers have an attitude of "us against them." In my opinion, officers have an attitude of the "police against the criminal element in our society." I can't remember in my 22 years of service with the department when I personally felt it was me against the law abiding citizens in this city. However, I do have a problem with the criminal element that makes walking the streets of this city a living hell!!

(Detective, Male, Caucasian, 49 years old, 22 years PO, 22 years LAPD, Chief when hired: Davis)

#116

A policeman's job is to put crooks in jail, not kiss the ass of the politicians or new media. All these new police programs are like "new math" 15 years ago it does not work. LETS GET BACK TO BASICS.

(Police Officer, Female, Caucasian, 47 years old, 23 years PO, 23 years LAPD, Chief when hired: Reddin)

#117

The problem is the dept cares too much about how the public & politicians view us not on what the officers have to deal with on a day by day basis. All the public wants is an officer to respond quickly and efficiently to his emergency call. Not to see the flowers in the station or coffee & donuts. He wants action. The admin of this dept have no idea what patrol officers go through only in books. The reality is in the field not in a book, if you want answers get quality officers, not quantity. And ask the citizens what they want out of our police force and they will tell you the same.

(Police Officer, Male, Hispanic, 26 years old, 13 years PO, 4 years LAPD, Chief when hired: Gates)

#118

There is too much inconsistency with command staff. On one has the guts to make a firm stand with issues concerning this dept. There is too much giving in to these self-appointed community leaders, lets make a stand and get the silent majority (of public) to voice support so we can get these little terrorists (gang members) out of here. It would be nice to go anywhere without worrying about being a victim! Note—lets not punish the whites on the job—lets all earn the position promoted to.

(Police Officer, Male, Caucasian, 27 years old, 7 years PO, 5 years LAPD, Chief when hired: Gates)

#119

LAPD's upper management is bowing to politicians & loud-mouthed prejudiced special interest group's interests & ignoring the safety needs of the patrol officer. Today's street cop has very little control over hard-core criminals due to various policies enacted which limits an office's ability to effectively control suspects & deal with fighting crime. The criminal is winning the war, not the police!

(Police Officer, Female, Asian, 35 years old, 6 years PO, 6 years LAPD, Chief when hired: Gates)

#120

There a few groups that do not want police ofcrs to do their job & that is to put criminals in jail. Those groups want to protect the rights of criminals & not Joe Blow czn. This contributes to job dissatisfaction. Also related is the read & likelihood I will be sued & poss lose everything I worked for because I am trying to do my job, in good faith. How can you expect morale to be high when I can lose my job, be sued & criminals get no time in jail, so why catch them. The City Council does not back us all they look for is their political ratings & don't care how they screw w/ police ofcrs life. Now I have also worry about pay cuts, health benefits cut. Question: Why do the working police ofcrs (patrol, the back-bone w/out us Admin wouldn't have jobs) get day off when Capts. & above don't & they are responsible for our training & acts?

(Police Officer, Male, Caucasian, 28 years old, 2 years PO, 2 years LAPD, Chief when hired: Gates)

#121

At my first opportunity to retire, I intend to do so and leave this cry baby, squabbling city and state. Have fun arguing out issues while society deteriorates from a basic lack of morality.

(Detective, Male, Caucasian, 40 years old, 17 years PO, 17 years LAPD, Chief when hired: Davis)

#122

The Police Department is not the problem. Society is the problem. Society is on a course toward self-destruction. The citizens of the city of LA better wake up to the reality of what is occurring in this city!

(Sergeant, Male, Caucasian, 41 years old, 21 years PO, 21 years LAPD, Chief when hired: Davis)

#123

Most important issue to me: See that the criminal justice system through public outcry "puts away" the hard core criminals & keeps them away—then we can deal with the community issues & support factors cause we'll have the time—Hell! Were catchin the bastards over & over again—that's what is frustrating.

(Detective, Male, Caucasian, 45 years old, 24 years PO, 24 years LAPD, Chief when hired: Reddin)

#124

It is very disturbing to have a relatively few squeaky wheels in the community, who are down on the Department, have so much impact on the Department. To listen to them, we can do nothing right and we are all racist. Obviously, this is not the majority vein. But the majority is silent on the issues and sooner or later begin to believe much of what the rabble rousers profess. The so called hearings on LAPD and LASO are so stacked and bias they are a joke. It is very demoralizing to see these small special interest groups dictate our direction and destroy our reputation. I am no longer particularly proud to be a LAPD officer. I see us losing efficiency and pride and sliding into big east coast city mediocrity in future years.

(Lieutenant, Male, Caucasian, 48 years old, 25 years PO, 25 years LAPD, Chief when hired: Parker)

#125

In my 22 years of service, I have seen LAPD service going down the tubes. I feel sorry for the good people in this city. They deserve more. I grew up in New York and saw the decay of that city. I feel LA is going the same way. Politics and police don't mix.

(Detective, Male, Caucasian, 44 years old, 22 years PO, 22 years LAPD, Chief when hired: Davis)

#126

The dept has a freeze on promotions. Community policing is only a hore and pony show. Of course it would help our relations btwn the media & elected officials … we are a police dept, our job is the safety of our czns and ourselves. Not to kiss the butt of someone running for office. I don't want the LAPD to be like NYPD…. "Ofcr there goes the guy who robbed me" "Fine maam sign this report" We don't chase bad guys any more.

(Police Officer, Male, Caucasian, 30 years old, 7 years PO, 7 years LAPD, Chief when hired: Gates)

#127 (see #50)

#128

This department seems to have lost its direction & ideals that made it the best in the world. It is too caught up in the political arena. It wants to please this group and that group instead of doing what it was created for protecting the good people of the city. Now the city wants community based police. Have these people in charge look at this, it does not work. All it does is give the criminals the feeling that police hands are more tied. All the people in charge have to do is look at Houston and New York where crime has increased 700% since they started community police.

(Police Officer, Male, Caucasian, 27 years old, 3 years PO, 3 years LAPD, Chief when hired: Gates)

#129 (see #108)

#130 (see #124)

#131

Officers don't quit LAPD. They just don't work when dissatisfied!

(Police Officer, Male, Caucasian, 47 years old, 24 years PO, 24 years LAPD, Chief when hired: Reddin)

#132

Please stop being influenced by minority groups & civil right activists. People want protection and police won't enforce & work hard because they are afraid of administrative action. Admin. Action results from top management cowering to the press + small groups. This rolls down hill to Sgts + to finally police ofcrs.

(Police Officer, Male, Caucasian, 26 years old, 2 years PO, 2 years LAPD, Chief when hired: Gates)

#133

1 year ago I couldn't wait to go to work each night. Today, I would do something else if I could find it. The main problem is supervision that doesn't give a damn about their people & an administration that doesn't care about our mission—protecting the public from predators of society. Our department is stumbling over itself to please a mayor, council & commission that has no idea of what we're here for. Personal complaints are being taken for stupid things that are causing ofcrs to "pass up" arrests in order to stay out of trouble. We are constantly being second-guessed our experience means nothing. I don't like being in on the death of the once greatest police dept in the world.

(Police Officer, Male, Caucasian, 37 years old, 8 years PO, 8 years LAPD, Chief when hired: Gates)

#134 (see #120)

#135

This dept discourages proactive police work—(so does the courts). It is easier to just kick back and stay out of trouble than it is to try to "hustle" and stop potential criminals. That only brings law suits for harassment. This dept abandons you when you face civil suits. I disagree w/the way this dept allowed a group (mob) of demonstrators (gay rights) to get out of hand—every officer looked foolish for just standing by. The criminals love the way they can challenge us now they know we're helpless. I've been challenged over twice as much as a year ago.

(Police Officer, Male, Caucasian, 28 years old, 7 years PO, 7 years LAPD, Chief when hired: Gates)

#136

We need to have contact with the community. We need to be sensitive to their needs, but at the same time, they need to be sensitive to ours. Most citizens don't understand what this job entails. We need to communicate with them more & maybe they can understand why we handle situations the way we do. In turn, they may become more satisfied with the LAPD. The more pressure we officers get from supervisors, citizens & the Christopher Commission, the less work we will do. Most ofcrs feel if they get involved & things go sideways, they will receive no support from citizens or the dept. The end result "Don't get involved." Therefore, there is a reduction in good police work.

(Police Officer, Female, Caucasian, 26 years old, 3 years PO, 3 years LAPD, Chief when hired: Gates)

#137

I joined LAPD almost 22 years ago because it was the #1 department and because other people look up and respected the LAPD as a department. Now the tide has changed and we are now the laughing stock of the majority of the citizens I come into contact with. I am constantly asked by the citizens "why we bow to pressure of media and special interest groups"—and asked by officers of other departments why our dept management doesn't back the field troops. LAPD has bowed to pressure by advancing less qualified personnel because of race or sex and putting qualifications on the back burner. This department is quickly falling to the whims of special interest groups and the public in general will be the ones to suffer from this in the long run. The job of being an LAPD officer used to be fun and rewarding—Now it's just the opposite. It's a chore to come to work and I take as much time off as I can so I won't have to be here.

(Police Officer, Male, Caucasian, 44 years old, 22 years PO, 22 years LAPD, Chief when hired: Davis)

#138

The field ofcrs morale is very low. The ofcrs are scared to perform their duties because of the current situation. Give credit to the patrol ofcrs and let the filed Supv do their job instead of sitting in the office completing 181s. They need to be in the street making sure the ofcrs are performing their duties....

(Police Officer, Female, African American, 28 years old, 4 years PO, 4 years LAPD, Chief when hired: Gates)

#139 (see #15)

#140

I know of at least (6) members of LAPD that are or have switched to another police dept due to the work ethic of their fellow officers. Other officers not doing their job specifically in patrol functions.

(Detective, Male, Caucasian, 32 years old, 7 years PO, 7 years LAPD, Chief when hired: Gates)

#141

Imagine you are a fireman sent to Mr. Smith's house. You get there + see flames from the home. As you run up w/your axe & hose Mr. Smith stops you. He tells you you cannot leave mud or ashes on the rug, no water damage, + if you must punch a hole in the roof it cant be over 6" diameter. If, after you've extinguished the fire, Smith finds ashes on the carpet, he tells you he'll complain + suspend you for three days without pay &/or sue you—Has Smith's unreasonable rule done anything to destroy your motivation to put out Smith's fire? Welcome to the LAPD. Community must realize as should administrators remember, that fighting crime is a dirty, messy business. Either allow officers to do the duty, or suffer the consequences. Like sheep, the community must place their trust in the shepherd + dogs. They have no expertise to police themselves. If the sheep don't want us then send in the wolves—they never bothered me!

(Police Officer, Male, Caucasian, 34 years old, 12 years PO, 12 years LAPD, Chief when hired: Gates)

#142

Affirmative action is bull!! Hire the best person for the job regardless of color or sex. Requiring one race to have higher oral scores to get into the academy is discriminatory. Lowering the percentage that written test scores will count (so that less deserving people can be given an oral score which will allow them to promote) is unfair. Get us back the choke hold.... The top brass should not be coddling these militant special interest groups. Let us do our jobs!!! The street cops have lost faith in this dept's top brass....

(Police Officer, Male, Caucasian, 28 years old, 5 years PO, 5 years LAPD, Chief when hired: Gates)

#143

The new consent decree is an insult to the once high standard the LAPD enjoyed. It also sent a message to all non minority officers that the good work that we have done means nothing and that our services are no longer needed. We have lowered our standards to the lowest level and we and the citizens will soon see the proof we will pay for this political foolishness. The top ranks of this Department have rolled over and played dead on this issue and in so doing lost the support of non minority officers. This issue has split the Department into ethnic camps and we will see others getting hurt in the field because of this. We used to say LAPD only came in one color, "Blue," now color and gender matter more than anything else. We let the politicians and the courts destroy years of good work, now we will see a bail out of qualified officers leave this Department because they are ashamed to wear the uniform. Fortunately, they are white males and no longer needed or wanted.

(Sergeant, Male, Caucasian, 39 years old, 14 years PO, 11 years LAPD, Chief when hired: Gates)

#144

Here's a new idea for promotion (this is not a joke Chief Gates). Let's put seniority & affirmative action in an equal standing with job performance/experience instead of Seniority #1 Affirmative Action #2 Ability—mildly interesting. This dept/city is going to run itself into the ground with their current promotional mentality.

(Detective, Male, Caucasian, 40 years old, 15 years PO, 15 years LAPD, Chief when hired: Davis)

#145

I strongly feel that in our civil service duties that we owe the public the best service available regardless of race or gender. The most qualified should be promoted and our affirmative action....

(Detective, Male, Caucasian, 49 years old, 26 years PO, 26 years LAPD, Chief when hired: Parker)

#146

The dept can scrap the stupid & racist affirmative action programs which have degraded the past pride & effectiveness of this dept. The hiring practices of this dept are racist & nonproductive. The leadership of this dept has no guts & seem to spend their time stabbing each other in the back for promotion. The greatest pride in my life is my family & the LAPD. The City is taking my pride in this dept and slowly destroying it. Get rid of the current Mayor.

(Police Officer, Male, Caucasian, 41 years old, 20 years PO, 20 years LAPD, Chief when hired: Davis)

#147

We are hiring ofcrs who are more concerned w/their personal needs than fighting crime. We promote supvs w/vast admin background, often limited field/special unit experience. We are eliminating proactive, crime fighting units & philosophy for prevention. Prevention is important but should not be the primary focus. Our younger ofcrs are complacent, unprofessional & I'm glad I don't have to work w/ most of them. Racism is destroying our dept; white vs. black and black vs. white. There are many black ofcrs on our dept who are racist.

(Sergeant, Male, Caucasian, 40 years old, 18 years PO, 15 years LAPD, Chief when hired: Davis)

#148

This department is pushing the promotion of minority officers so much that they are the chosen people in this organization. I know several minorities that brag about being sent to specialized management school because of their color. White officers are being passed over for specialized assignments because they are white. Unqualified minority officers without qualifications are selected instead. Training officers and the academy are unable to fire unqualified officers particularly minorities because the department is afraid someone will scream racism. This department accepts minorities with very low entrance exam scores and places the people with low scores ahead of people with much higher scores. I'm sick of the attitude of the high management of this department. You've run this job into the ground with the lack of support.

(Detective, Male Caucasian, 38 years old, 18 years PO, 18 years LAPD, Chief when hired: Davis)

#149

P-3 orals are a joke. The patrol captains know well in advance who they want as P-3! Promotions to P-3 on "Affirm Action" is bull. P-3 promotions stink & are based on favoritism & race. If you're white, forget being promoted. Bilingual pay should stay with the officer upon being transferred. We need more positions! DARE? Its interesting to read about gang violence homicides rising from 200 in 1981 to 700 in 1991. Isn't DARE supposed to be working on reduction of gangs? Crime statistics, civilianize this. We need more cops in uniform in the field. We need better MDTs & rovers! Affirmative action has escalated to the point of reverse discrimination!

(Police Officer, Male, Caucasian, 48 years old, 22 years PO, 22 years LAPD, Chief when hired: Davis)

#150

The promotional process, written tests, are extremely unfair. They are written by civilians who have little or no working knowledge of these functions, thus, the most qualified person is often overlooked.

(Police Officer, Male, Caucasian, 43 years old, 16 years PO, 16 years LAPD, Chief when hired: Davis)

#151 (see #24)

#152 (see #83)

#153

When do you think this department will start hiring people with brains, guts and integrity!!

(Detective, Male, Caucasian, 45 years old, 23 years PO, 23 years LAPD, Chief when hired: Reddin)

#154

This department is not allowing officers to have a sense of humor. The department is not backing the officers in the field as it should. Everything is becoming a political issue. It's mind over matter—the department doesn't mind & the officer doesn't matter. Affirmative action is reverse discrimination. The hiring practices are favoring minorities. A minority only needs 70% oral to be hired. A male white needs at least a 95% oral. Being passed over for promotion because an officer doesn't speak Spanish is not fair. This is America and the language of this country is English.

(Police Officer, Male, Caucasian, 45 years old, 17 years PO, 17 years LAPD, Chief when hired: Davis)

#155

Crime increase, violence towards officers, lack of support from community & elected officials & gross racial discrimination (towards promotions) increasing against white males is very alarming—will probably cause me to retire sooner than I originally planned—I can see it's going to get a lot worse before it gets better. Also, I see officers not backing-up assisting other officers in dangerous situations, repeatedly.

(Police Officer, Male, Caucasian, 45 years old, 20 years PO, 20 years LAPD, Chief when hired: Davis)

#156

The quality of recruits on the job during the past 5 years has and continues to be going down hill. The department is too concerned with hiring the right amount minorities/women instead of the most qualified person for the job. The news media rpts that we should hire more women since they are "less likely to become aggressive & become involved in excessive force." This is true, but on the other hand—the majority of women patrol ofcrs that I have seen in action fail to take the initiative in most situations that involve 415 susps. Foot pursuits and situations where it may involve a confrontation of some sort. I've seen it time and time again and its not getting any better. Lets hire the most qualified person, regardless of race or gender.

(Police Officer, Male, Caucasian, 35 years old, 14 years PO, 14 years LAPD, Chief when hired: Davis)

#157

The good news is the LAPD has a mysterious vitality, excellent people, and generally superior management. Chief Gates cares and honestly does what he thinks is best. Despite its problems, the LAPD will survive. The bad news is that the LAPD has fallen under the classic tyranny of the "Big Lie." Affirmative Action is, simply, prejudice given a fancy name. Equal Opportunity (of merit and job quality) cannot and are not co-existing with Affirmative Action. A whole generation of Blacks, Hispanics, and others are being deprived of the satisfaction of being treated as fully able human beings. None can escape the suspicion that their race and/or sex, and not their ability, was the source of success. The benevolent slave-owner mentality is alive and well in the LAPD and the City. Anger, disenchantment, distrust grow on all sides. Not good. Not good. The solution to a wrong has never been—can never be—another wrong.

(Sergeant, Male, Caucasian, 49 years old, 28 years PO, 28 years LAPD, Chief when hired: Parker)

#158

Affirmative Action = Legal Racism. I will be gone from LAPD real soon, if things don't change. It seems like we are becoming the ACLU/NAACP police. Be kind to criminals, and ignore the victs! You can save lives, be a great ofcr with high morals + ethics, but say something rude to a rapist, child molester, etc., and you can get fired. (It almost happened to me.) Seems like you have to be white, to be a racist. I'm sick of hearing that ofcrs (BLK + HISP) are not treated the same. I guess, I am just sick of it!!

(Police Officer, Male, Caucasian, 28 years old, 3 years PO, 3 years LAPD, Chief when hired: Gates)

#159 (see #39)

#160

Let's get away from bending to special interest groups. They have no real interest in the Depts. operations except to plant seeds of disharmony. Affirmative Action has virtually eliminated qualified candidates from the job and qualifications have taken a back seat to race, sex and ethnic background. Let's get back to basics. Promote and hire the qualified without regard to race, sex or ethnic background. When you settle for less you get exactly what you settle for incompetent officers and supervisors. Stop punishing the proud loyal and productive employee to gain ethnic + sexual balance. We are passing over people more deserving of rewards and instead rewarding incompetence and laziness.

(Police Officer, Male, Caucasian, 43 years old, 20 years PO, 20 years LAPD, Chief when hired: Davis)

#161

... Due to the recent consent decree and affirmative action policies, I do not believe I will ever have a fair opportunity to promote because I am white and heterosexual.

(Police Officer, Male Caucasian, 36 years old, 11 years PO, 11 years LAPD, Chief when hired: Gates)

#162

If I had my 20, I'd be gone. We are dividing the Dept. internally along racial and sexual lines. Now reverse discrimination is accepted. Since I'm male white, I have no opportunity to compete on a "best person for the job" basis. Non white racism is accepted practice by certain managers in some divisions. Jobs and promotions are given out based on color, sex, and in some cases, if you have sex with the person making the decision. I still think this is a great dept. and will continue if we go back to promoting the best person for the job.

(Sergeant, Male, Caucasian, 38 years old, 16 years PO, 16 years LAPD, Chief when hired: Davis)

#163 (see #51)

#164

Affirmative Action is undermining our organization, causing less than qualified personnel to be either hired or promoted. I would like to see the best person get the job, whether it be male/female, black, white, or whatever.

(Police Officer, Male, Caucasian, 27 years old, 6 years PO, 6 years LAPD, Chief when hired: Gates)

#165

The morale of the Dept will continue to erode until something is done about promotions based on Affirmative Action. All tests must be fair in the future or we will be reduced to a second rate police dept.

(Lieutenant, Male, Caucasian, 52 years old, 27 years PO, 27 years LAPD, Chief when hired: Parker)

#166 (see #22)

#167

It is discouraging to me that our hiring & promotion policy has been altered to accommodate minorities that are lacking in education and training, just to meet a quota.

(Police Officer, Male, Caucasian, 27 years old, 5 years PO, 5 years LAPD, Chief when hired: Gates)

#168

I am concerned that this survey will be "twisted" by the media. I can see the headlines.... "LAPD SURVEY SHOW PROMOTIONAL SYSTEM UNFAIR" "RANK AND FILE VIEW LAPD AS INEFFICIENT"

(Sergeant, Male, Caucasian, 41 years old, 20 years PO, 20 years LAPD, Chief when hired: Davis)

#169

I love m job and I've had a great career, but I'm sick and tired of minority officers screaming for their rights to promotion. Each group wants immediate representation and I believe extremely unqualified personnel are being promoted to fill percentages. Lets keep the system fair and impartial, and morale will improve.

(Sergeant, Male, Caucasian, 38 years old, 16 years PO, 16 years LAPD, Chief when hired: Davis)

#170

Training for patrol should be more diverse with guest speakers from specialized units coming to roll call on a reg. basis. The new developments in Affirm Action promotions are a joke, allowing individuals with poor performance into positions of great importance. If I was going to have brain surgery, I would want the person who scored high during med school, etc., not a doctor chosen by color or sex. Wake up.

(Police Officer, Male, Caucasian, 30 years old, 3 years PO, 3 years LAPD, Chief when hired: Gates)

#171

In my 20 years, the last five years I've seen more unqualified people get on the job. Promotions are for females & blacks, & hisp. It doesn't make any difference how good you are if you are wht. There are qualified females black & hisp. But there are also qualified whts.

(Police Officer, Male, Caucasian, 45 years old, 20 years PO, 20 years LAPD, Chief when hired: Davis)

#172

Due to "Affirmative Action" & liberal politics, this dept is on a steep downhill slide toward incompetence & corruption. Its administrators are generally incompetent.

(Police Officer, Male, Caucasian, 45 years old, 17 years PO, 17 years LAPD, Chief when hired: Davis)

#173

Ofcrs see instability at admin positions. There is a problem w/race relations between fellow ofcrs due to Affirmative Action policies. Ofcrs do not trust their supv's.

(Police Officer, Male, Caucasian, 25 years old, 1 year PO, 1 year LAPD, Chief when hired: Gates)

#174

I came on this job some years ago believing that LAPD was a progressive, proactive, well trained disciplined department that was employee oriented. Now, 8½ years later it appears all of those traits are missing. I am willing to be a team player with a common goal of developing the best department possible, but right now there seems to be no leadership other than a lame duck Chief. Don't get me wrong, I support the Chief but facts are facts. I feel that we allow outside loudmouths to determine our policy and don't stand up for ourselves. Some issues that are being attacked by the media and whomever are things that have been developed to protect officers in an increasingly hostile environment. They are not meant to be demeaning, they are meant to promote officer safety. People want society to be a peaceful, caring environment. None more so than police officers. But Goddamnit I want to go home too. I believe we do a good job with the best intentions and yet we are constantly preyed on and subjected to unfair and distorted scrutiny unimagined by civilians. Then, our promotion potential is drastically reduced under the guise of affirmative action. Long gone are the days when we just hire the best. I couldn't care less if the recipient of a job or promotion is Black, White, Male or Female. How about just the best person for the job, for the best department possible. We are settling for mediocrity and that is a deadly cancer that will serve to cripple this department for years and years to come. No, I'm not bitter. I'm disappointed. Frustrated. Disillusioned.

(Police Officer, Male, Caucasian, 34 years old, 9 years PO, 9 years LAPD, Chief when hired: Gates)

#175 (see #40)

#176

I think there are some narrow minded bigots on this dept. I think they were that way before they got to the dept. I think they will always be that way and I think therein lies our problem. Attitudes.

(Police Officer, Male, African American, 51 years old, 23 years PO, 23 years LAPD, Chief when hired: Reddin)

#177 (see #68)

#178

Before we can be an effective role in working with citizens and deal with societies ills, we must deal with our internal ills. Relationships between officers are at an all time low & mistrust between all levels within the department is poor. Supervisors are probably the most guilty in fostering this. Before we look at the community & police we should examine ourselves. If we cannot work with one another how can we work with the community?

(Police Officer, Male, African American, 27 years old, 4 years PO, 4 years LAPD, Chief when hired: Gates)

#179

This survey, as all others, will most probably be another waste of time, and money. The ground pounders are always getting hurt, and will continue to be hurt. People are put into positions of leadership not because they are leaders, or possess the qualities, but because they can pass a test or are a minority, and fall within the quota. In the end, the people we swore to "protect and to serve," will receive poor service. No one cares about the ground pounders!

(Police Officer, Male, Hispanic, 26 years old, 3 years PO, 3 years LAPD, Chief when hired: Gates)

#180

Promotions should be based on tenure, experience and ability to adapt to the new position. Not race, education or whether or not you can speak Spanish or pass a test.

(Police Officer, Male, Hispanic, 28 years old, 7 years PO, 7 years LAPD, Chief when hired: Gates)

#181 (see #23)

#182 (see #15)

#183 (see #30)

#184

Promotions & ratings too often based on favoritism &/or affirmative action resulting in very poor supervision at and mostly above the sergeant level. Result: concentration on self not task or subordinate concerns.

#185

This dept has always used the good old boy system for selecting ofcrs to the most wanted jobs. There is no fair system at this time. The Anglo gets the job 99% of the time, no matter if he/she is homosexual or not qualified.

(Detective, Male, Hispanic, 42 years old, 19 years PO, 19 years LAPD, Chief when hired: Davis)

#186 (see #179)

#187

Top management is not making a sincere effort to internally change the dept's problems—the "changes" are designed to please the public. The "good ole white boy" syndrome is still firmly entrenched with separate racial groups struggling to have their place. There is no LAPD family unless a dept. tragedy occurs, and those feelings are temporary. The bottom line is that top management must recognize the racial/sexist tension in the dept—and do something about it—for the good of the dept—not to add to a resume to submit for Chief of Police.

(Female, African American, 32 years old, 8 years LAPD, Chief when hired: Gates)

#188

Regardless of it's faults, this department provides the best equal opportunities for all. This is the best department in the world for me. I support the Chief.

(Police Officer, Female, African American, 30 years old, 3 years PO, 3 years LAPD, Chief when hired: Gates)

#189

We are an outstanding law enforcement agency; however, due to extreme media exposure, the department has backed away from its primary responsibility of protecting the citizens of this city. Street officers and anyone who is actively arresting susps must think twice for fear of spurious law suits and/or criminal charges. The upper echelon of this department had abandoned the average police ofcr/detectives to the whimsey of a vocal minority. No one will step forward and clearly tell the citizens that their safety is being jeopardized by a department that refuses to back up its employees when needed. Additionally, I feel that the top officers of this department are so busy back stabbing each other and trying to lay blame on the Chief for their failure to address problems and find adequate solution. Along with the problems generated in the aftermath of Rodney King, the blatant unfairness of the promotion process is another factor as low morale. Speaking as a female, I resent the implication I need "help" to promote. I am fully capable of studying and passing promotional exams on my own. I dislike the fact that if I promote, my peers think its only because I'm a woman. White males should be allowed to compete equally. To make matters worse, we now have upholstered chairs free food/drink at the lobby. This is not a bad idea—citizens should be comfortable while waiting. But the contrast between the plush atmosphere of the lobby and the dingy rooms and (where existent!) dilapidated equipment provided to the officers is simply untenable. It is amazing to me that the employees of this department do the outstanding job they do in the deplorable conditions they are forced to work in.

(Police Officer, Female, Caucasian, 33 years old, 7 years PO, 7 years LAPD, Chief when hired: Gates)

#190

If everybody really believed we only come in one color blue we'd be a great department. To much interdepartmental hate going on.

(Police Officer, Female, African American, 29 years old, 7 years PO, 7 years LAPD, Chief when hired: Gates)

#191

The Department has changed radically. I personally feel that we were at our most effective level of service to the community when "they" (the public) respected our professionalism as opposed to liking and approving of us on a personal level. Further, affirmative action "quotas" have impacted our internal standards of excellence.

(Police Officer, Female, Caucasian, 28 years old, 5 years PO, 5 years LAPD, Chief when hired: Parker)

#192

I am a female minority and I do not agree with the new decision on consent decree. Choose me because I'm best qualified, not because I'm female or the color of my skin.

(Police Officer, Female, Hispanic, 33 years old, 11 years PO, 11 years LAPD, Chief when hired: Gates)

#193

The academy is not getting rid of those recruits who are clearly unsuited for police work, resulting in sub-standard, inept & in some cases, dangerous novice police officers. In addition, the ever increasing importance of affirmative action above all else is ignoring the contributions & qualifications of those who are being discriminated against because they are not a minority.

(Detective, Female, Caucasian, 31 years old, 6 years PO, 6 years LAPD, Chief when hired: Gates)

#194 (see #52)

#195

Promotions: Assessment Center type examinations. Current testing is archaic. Allows for incompetent person being promoted. Adhere to Affirmative Action procedures. Hire most qualified. If a tie, make Affirmative Action selection.

(Sergeant, Female, Caucasian, 46 years old, 17 years PO, 17 years LAPD, Chief when hired: Davis)

#196

We need new thinking from Captain to Chief.

(Police Officer, Male, African American, 23 years old, 2 years PO, 2 years LAPD, Chief when hired: Gates)

#197

Chief Gates + XXXX are outstanding officers. Other upper management has proven to be unfaithful to this department. Even immoral. If this Department is in a family there sure is a lot of incest going on. Our morality is disgraceful. It is common practice daily for our officers to lie to everyone, citizens, supervisors, wives, husbands, etc. Tactical knowledge and knowledge of policies should constantly be evaluated and tested by those who use them.

(Police Officer, Male, Caucasian, 30 years old, 11 years PO, 11 years LAPD, Chief when hired: Gates)

#198

Conditions can only improve for the community and LAPD in general when upper level supervision and policy makers can wake up each day and look in the mirror and know that their day work directly affects public safety and the safety of officers working the streets, and then has the clear desire to help those people (community and street officers) be safe. The Chief must demand honesty from all his subordinates especially negative information and not allow boot lickers to "pound sunshine up his ass!" We, at the lower end, are thought of as stupid for not promoting. Perhaps it is not as much being stupid as making up for the deficiencies of our policy makers and do what is necessary to try and keep the streets as safe as possible for everyone's families, yours and mine. Isn't that the basic police job anyway? Leadership is not allowed in the Department!

(Police Officer, Male, Caucasian, 44 years old, 20 years PO, 20 years LAPD, Chief when hired: Davis)

#199

Management has forgotten they are there to help working officers and detectives. They have become self-serving and egotistical (including the Chief!) Changes should start with staff officers in their attitudes before trying to change conditions for working officers and detectives. The 6th Floor has become an Ivory Tower. They need to get out into the community as well as the officers. The Chief should retire now.

(Police Officer, Male, Caucasian, 40 years old, 17 years PO, 17 years LAPD, Chief when hired: Davis)

#200

This dept is too top heavy. The staff has to much freedom in changing things without the knowledge of the chief. The fact that south bureau has the majority of the problem we have less resources and the worst command staff. They also have no common sense when it comes to working relationships with police officers. Their noses are buried too deep in their own career.

(Police Officer, Male, Caucasian, 30 years old, 5 years PO, 5 years LAPD, Chief when hired: Gates)

#201

Dept from the chief down fail to stand behind the field ofcrs and tend to treat them as bastard children.

(Police Officer, Male, Caucasian, 38 years old, 6 years PO, 6 years LAPD, Chief when hired: Gates)

#202

Admins—Too much information is "Filtered" before it gets to the Chief(s). I hear, "we can't say that" or "we should word that another way." If an officer or Sgt. does staff work because he or she is the expert in that area—that work should go to the brass—not what a Lt. or Captain think the brass wants to see. Training—we are losing the war here! Officers are graduating that should never have been hired. The dept. must regain control of the pre-employee process.

(Detective, Male, Caucasian, 37 years old, 16 years PO, 16 years LAPD, Chief when hired: Davis)

#203

I love my job, my immediate supervisor and my Chiefs, Booth and Gates—This is and always will be the best Law Enforcement Agency in the world as long as our top administration remains the same.

(Police Officer, Female, Caucasian, 50 years old, 25 years PO, 25 years LAPD, Chief when hired: Parker)

#204

As long as the Chief and his staff members stay on the job, we are kidding ourselves about any positive change in morale or working environment.

(Police Officer, Male, Hispanic, 42 years old, 19 years PO, 19 years LAPD, Chief when hired: Davis)

#205 (see #174)

#206

Good luck—we need a new Chief.

(Sergeant, Male, Caucasian, 45 years old, 22 years PO, 22 years LAPD, Chief when hired: Davis)

#207

This dept. needs to be overhauled. Top management is only interested in themselves. There is no togetherness at the top. Management are not the men/women in blue & do not represent the LAPD, only themselves. I love & respect Gates but his management team does not give him a true picture. I've been on the street for my 22 years & I know these things to be true. It's time that management stops listening to each other & listen to the real LAPD, patrol. But that will not happen!!! Good luck.

(Sergeant, Male, Caucasian, 47 years old, 22 years PO, 22 years LAPD, Chief when hired: Davis)

#208

A "few" of our command staff including Chief Gates are people oriented leaders/administrators. Quite a few others need to set their egos aside & be responsive to their people. I'm sure this would except for the dissenters, provide an atmosphere of cooperation, ultimately beneficial to the department and Los Angeles citizens/community.

(Lieutenant, Male, Caucasian, 52 years old, 29 years PO, 29 years LAPD, Chief when hired: Parker)

#209

There is no intent here to case Chief Gates in a bad light or to demean him in any way. He's the finest Chief that I have observed during my tenure. However, the same cannot be said of those staff officers below him.

(Lieutenant, Male, Hispanic, 50 years old, 26 years PO, 26 years LAPD, Chief when hired: Parker)

#210

I believe Chief Gates has done an excellent job as COP. However, I question the judgment and loyalty of some top administrators aspiring to become his successor.

(Detective, Male, African American, 45 years old, 23 years PO, 23 years LAPD, Chief when hired: Reddin)

#211 (see #68)

#212

A new COP will hopefully give the dept a sense of direction and mission, something it does not have. First problem the dept must tackle is winning back the community.

(Lieutenant, Male, Caucasian, 42 years old, 20 years PO, 20 years LAPD, Chief when hired: Davis)

#213

Top management in the dept is ineffective. Every C/O has his own hidden agenda; looking out for himself instead of the officers he commands. The Assistant and Deputy Chiefs are for the most part a disgrace. It is impossible for a Chief of Police to be effective when so many of his subordinate chiefs are stabbing him in the back.

(Sergeant, Male, Caucasian, 35 years old, 14 years PO, 14 years LAPD, Chief when hired: Davis)

#214

LAPD need someone to back us like (Sherman Block) did for his troops. Not pencil pushers like we have now nobody wants to back us the average patrol cop.

(Police Officer, Male, Hispanic, 26 years old, 1 year PO, 1 year LAPD, Chief when hired: Gates)

#215

I believe that Chief Gates has done more for this department than any of the past prior 2 chiefs. I also believe that he would have done more if not for the infighting of the other chiefs. It appears that Chief Gates main concern is our department and its goals. The lesser chiefs appear to be more concerned with their own goals, with the department second.

(Police Officer, Male, Caucasian, 49 years old, 18 years PO, 18 years LAPD, Chief when hired: Davis)

#216

Control your Deputy Chiefs, who are all implementing different programs to look good for the community so they (Deputy Chiefs) could take your duties as Chief of Police. Get back into police work and help patrol officers who are both making you The Chief look good.

(Police Officer, Male, African American, 25 years old, 5 years PO, 5 years LAPD, Chief when hired: Gates)

#217

I hate misinformed politicians like you! Why don't all you experts come out here, put a blue suit on, and show us how to do police work!!! We really need your help!!! (Officer information not available)

#218

TOP ADMINISTRATION: I am lucky to be working for a great Staff Officer at the present, however, I am completely dissatisfied with the leadership at the top of the Department. THERE IS NO LEADERSHIP! There is no leadership, acceptance of responsibility or accountability at the upper level. All these characteristics are only required of police officers and sergeants (sometimes lieutenants). Staff officers are not "people oriented," they're "task oriented." Staff is too concerned with "damage assessment" and "damage control" than about caring what the field officers want, need and feel. Loyalty is one-way from the bottom up. The Chief can't find out what's going on because he has a group of people in between that think they know whats best and he doesn't need to be bothered with it. Ego's at the top as well as middle management are destroying this department. The administrators on the sixth floor should remove their doors and start talking to each other. I'm out of room, but if the Chief wants me to continue, I'm Sergeant X.

(Sergeant, Male, Caucasian, 45 years old, 24 years PO, 24 years LAPD, Chief when hired: Reddin)

#219

Top management does not appear to be aware or sensitive to the needs of the front line troops, i.e., patrol & dets. We have inferior equip but are the ones who deal with the citizens on a regular daily basis. Some top mgmt seem more concerned with their won careers than the needs of the "working" officers. Does the Chief have any idea of what's happening out here where the rubber meets the road?

(Detective, Male, Caucasian, 45 years old, 21 years PO, 21 years LAPD, Chief when hired: Davis)

#220 (see #85)

#221

I think that we have good field supervisors in general. However, I feel that the Administrative people: Captains, other personnel, care more about their careers and kissing butt than about the Department or Field Patrol Officers.

(Police Officer, Male, Caucasian, 26 years old, 1 year PO, 1 year LAPD, Chief when hired: Gates)

#222 (see #149)

#223

You people do not give a fuck about the street police officer. You are wasting our time and your time with this fucked up survey.

(Police Officer, Male, Caucasian, 31 years old, 9 years PO, 9 years LAPD, Chief when hired: Gates)

#224

I feel that most of management (SGT'S & above) are mainly concerned with self promotion & have lost touch with officers and their needs. Most of upper management with to kiss ass with politicians & high ranking officials than take into consideration w/ the need of ofcrs—morale is low but ofcrs are still getting the job done.

(Police Officer, Male, Caucasian, 26 years old, 1 year PO, 1 year LAPD, Chief when hired: Gates)

#225

The dept still puts more emphasis on promotion than on effective street police work. If you're not promoting you're a moron. The major aim seems to be, transfer and promote, be minimally effective at a lot of things the study and promote. "Staying on the street is only for the stupid" is the message being transmitted from the top.

(Police Officer, Male, Caucasian, 40 years old, 18 years PO, 15 years LAPD, Chief when hired: Davis)

#226

The pressure and stress on this job come from brass reacting to the media. Not from the public. I feel prepared to deal with everything on this job except trivial, nitpicking rules overly enforced without reasonableness, and the low esteem patrol is held in on this department, from day one its, "if you want to promote, get out of patrol" This is wrong and counter productive!

(Police Officer, Male, African American, 36 years old, 10 years PO, 2 years LAPD, Chief when hired: Gates)

#227

Commanding officers should immediately identify the top ofcrs within the division and listen to their ideas and input. Those ofcrs that wish to work hard should be given the opportunity to work on their ideas to combat crime. At this time there is no incentive for anyone in patrol to any more then the biggest malcontent drone, except personal pride. Many ofcrs have major knowledge about crime problems and/or suspects in their division. But no one ever lets those ofcrs loose to do what they do best. Crime in LA is going to get a lot worse and the same old tired tactics cannot cope. We need new and imaginative techniques. Don't expect commanders, captains, sgts etc to solve crime. They either don't care or don't know. Turn the right cops loose! And get them out of cars that look like police cars! Try something tricky!

(Police Officer, Male, Caucasian, 42 years old, 19 years PO, 19 years LAPD, Chief when hired: Davis)

#228

This department has always been responsive to the community needs within our job functions. We are not a social agency. Our duties are crime suppression/apprehension & the enforcement of state & local laws. In general, the community members that are dissatisfied with our dept are the same that have been targeted for enforcement at one time or another. The overall morale on this dept is negative. The ofcrs in the field feel management has turned its back. We are losing qualified ofcrs in droves as a result of managements refusal to accept responsibility for existing policies.

(Detective, Male, Caucasian, 31 years old, 8 years PO, 8 years LAPD, Chief when hired: Gates)

#229

The top brass has to commit themselves to helping the patrol ofcrs perform their everyday functions rather than self promotion—today—patrol has been forgotten and looked upon as nonpromoters—when they are what this department is all about. Immediate police service to the community.

(Detective, Male, Caucasian, 30 years old, 7 years PO, 7 years LAPD, Chief when hired: Gates)

#230

This will have no positive results. Like all other paper work it will be filed & forgotten. The staff ofcrs of the department are too busy playing politics (and they are terrible at it) to care about field ofcrs. If you can't do something right gentlemen you should go to (political) training. The staff ofcrs don't care about the department but they expect rank &file to—loyalty should work both ways not for only staff capt. & above.

(Police Officer, Male, Caucasian, 36 years old, 8 years PO, 8 years LAPD, Chief when hired: Gates)

#231

Staff ofcrs are out of touch with patrol. Many staff ofcrs only care about their success. Patrol is always looked down on. Patrol is what makes this dept. Patrol sgts & lts should be adv pay grades. Not someone at a bureau crime for periods etc. Patrol ofcrs worry about 181s Patrol officers don't have time to study on duty. Staff posit do study on duty and succeed. That is not the way it should be.

(Sergeant, Male, Caucasian, 43 years old, 21 years PO, 21 years LAPD, Chief when hired: Davis)

#232

To Staff: "Do unto others as you …"

(Sergeant, Male, Caucasian, 48 years old, 22 years PO, 18 years LAPD, Chief when hired: Davis)

#233

I am a very loyal dedicated employee who likes to work but my experience with the dept in sick or injury cases is you are just a number. You have no name or face & are replaceable at anything. This non-caring attitude for the employee has caused some employees to develop an attitude of "Why should I care for the Public, the City or Dept. doesn't care for me." Ask yourself this, when was the last time you received a Xmas present, bonus or a tip for an above & beyond the call of duty situation. We are the most needed city service but the least rewarded or liked for our services.

(Police Officer, Male, Caucasian, 45 years old, 23 years PO, 23 years LAPD, Chief when hired: Gates)

#234

I am as proud to be a member of the Los Angeles Police Dept. as I was when sworn in 7 years ago. My loyalty is the same. I must say, however, that as a patrol ofcr, serving all 7 years in patrol, I as well as others have continually felt unappreciated by the public, immediate supervision and the dept. management. Patrol ofcrs are what makes or breaks this dept's image of greatness. Those who serve it in its proudest and grandest tradition deserve to have recognition not continuous negativity in roll calls. Let someone speak up for all the good we do out there everyday that goes unseen by management, but leaves the citizen with a good feeling and his or her dignity. Please do not overlook how low the morale of the majority of patrol ofcrs has become.

(Police Officer, Female, Caucasian, 28 years old, 7 years PO, 7 years LAPD, Chief when hired: Gates)

#235

You've never listened to the street cop before, why now?

(Police Officer, Male, Caucasian, 40 years old, 15 years PO, 15 years LAPD, Chief when hired: Davis)

#236

Admin needs to be more responsive to ofcrs. Admin still remains the biggest stress factor in an ofcr's life. Some incentive for patrol is needed!

(Police Officer, Male, Caucasian, 33 years old, 5 years PO, 5 years LAPD, Chief when hired: Gates)

#237 (see #205)

#238

Top administration doesn't remember what it was like. Too clouded by nostalgia. Rank of Captain and above should not be police officers but civilian personnel administrators. Police officers should only be allowed to promote to as high as Lieutenant. Sergeants should have 5 years "street" experience before making that rank.

(Police Officer, Male, Caucasian, 45 years old, 17 years PO, 17 years LAPD, Chief when hired: Davis)

#239

You should place management (Lt's-Capt's-Commanders, etc) twice a week in patrol so they know what is a police officer. You should train management not to be complete liars, racist and cowards. Promotions should be based on knowledge and not who says "Yes Sir Master." Back up your officer and reduce stupid 181s. Go back to basic police work … etc., etc., etc.…

(Police Officer, Male, Hispanic, 45 years old, 16 years PO, 16 years LAPD, Chief when hired: Davis)

#240

Revamp upper management. You must have 5–10 years for P-3 (LAPD's most advanced level of patrol officer) plus patrol experience. Supervisor 10+ years—with 8+ years in the field. You have ill trained, non-functional P-3s & Supervisors with 1–2 years on the job, maybe 3 years patrol. They don't know anything.

(Police Officer, Female, Caucasian, Age: N/A, 15 years PO, 15 years LAPD, Chief when hired: Davis)

#241

In general I'm satisfied with my job, but we need more supervisors with "street knowledge." Many supervisors today are nothing but "pencil pushing nobodies who don't know the difference between left or right"!!!!

(Police Officer, Male, Hispanic, 32 years old, 1 year PO, 1 year LAPD, Chief when hired: Gates)

#242

Our biggest and foremost problem is our upper management they are completely out of touch with patrol. Patrol is the most important job and we get treated the worst in the area of promotion, training and pay.

(Police Officer, Male, Caucasian, 29 years old, 6 years PO, 6 years LAPD, Chief when hired: Gates)

#243

Service to Public: "For years this department has been selling the public an 'image' without substance." Upper Management has taken every media opportunity to convince the public that we have a handle on gangs, narcotics, and violent crimes. This misrepresentation has caused mistrust in the community where these crimes occur because the citizens wonder if we really know what's going on. Upper management deals in "image" Not substance!

(Detective, Male, Hispanic, 39 years old, 18 years PO, 18 years LAPD, Chief when hired: Davis)

#244

I can handle almost any situation in the field and deal with it with a minimal amount of stress. I feel the biggest problem and where officers get 99% of the stress is from management or (mismanagement).

(Police Officer, Male, Caucasian, 32 years old, 9 years PO, 9 years LAPD, Chief when hired: Gates)

#245

I can't believe there is <u>no</u> common sense anymore, children know what is right & wrong but no one else, I think upper management should get there butts out of the bldgs & into the front line so they can open their eyes.

(Police Officer, Male, Caucasian, 35 years old, 8 years PO, 8 years LAPD, Chief when hired: Gates)

#246

We have a very specific problem at LAPD—individuals who are at the top of the management level, are making decisions and policies that directly effect the rank and file. Normally this would not be a problem; however these individuals obviously lack the knowledge, experience and proper education to make intelligent command decisions.

(Police Officer, Male, Caucasian, 43 years old, 13 years PO, 13 years LAPD, Chief when hired: Davis)

#247

Supervisors like XXXX who are out of touch with his subordinates. The Dept is too concerned about public image and doesn't care about its officers. Negative rules + regulations are always spotlighted. Nothing positive. Every day there's more paper work and guidelines. We have poor equipment, and are grossly undermanned. During 1.81 investigations, the dept. is more likely to believe the susp who just killed three victs than the officer who arrested him. Care about your men, or you won't have any to care about.

(Police Officer, Male, Asian, 29 years old, 3 years PO, 3 years LAPD, Chief when hired: Gates)

#248

There are many discrepancies from div to div and bureau to bureau. Field ofcrs should be involved in management decisions. Chief XXXX is destroying the XXXX community. He is not sensitive to the needs of the area. He is out of touch with the violent nature of the community. Don't care about ofcrs.

(Police Officer, Male, African American, 34 years old, 10 years PO, 10 years LAPD, Chief when hired: Gates)

#249

There is a feeling among Ptrl Ofcrs that we, as the individuals most likely to make contact with the public, are being used as the dept's scape goats. There is a pervasive distrust of anyone above the rank of sgt-1. By the way, how are we going to make community based policing work with only 8,000 officers?

(Police Officer, Male, Caucasian, 29 years old, 4 years PO, 4 years LAPD, Chief when hired: Gates)

#250

After 20 years of service in LAPD police officers are more afraid of supervisors and 181 then criminals in the streets. I live in N/E div I know that too many criminal/gang members get away with anything they want because police officers are not aggressive and don't believe the courts, brass and don't give a dam. Soon the citz of LA will feel the same way! You don't make things better for the street cop. You just promote each other.

(Police Officer, Male, Hispanic, 42 years old, 20 years PO, 20 years LAPD, Chief when hired: Davis)

#251

Ofcrs feel like they are being told to go out there and do the job with one hand tied behind their back. You can't do aggressive police work (and generate the recap demanded by supervision) without generating 181s & use of force; management is going to have to tolerate lower recap, or tolerate uof [use of force] incidents as a necessary job occurance & not a "pattern of misconduct."

(Police Officer, Male, Caucasian, 38 years old, 8 years PO, 8 years LAPD, Chief when hired: Gates)

#252

How can you expect officers to feel confident about job when they are not backed up. One must wonder if one should back up a Capt or staff in the field because of tendency to neg scrutinize the ofc to point of dysfunction. It is like you don't back me up so why should I back up?

(Police Officer, Male, Caucasian, 47 years old, 25 years PO, 25 years LAPD, Chief when hired: Parker)

#253

The upper management (Captain & above) are dinosaurs. They are too quick to jump on the working bees for every little thing. I took a 5 day suspension and my partner who had 22 years on the job at the time took 10 days for the horrible crime of stopping to have a piece of pie without asking permission. The department stresses promotion entirely too much. It takes an attitude that if you are happy being a police officer then you are either lazy, stupid or crooked. The upper management is full of self serving hypocritical individuals who have one concern and that is how can they achieve the next level. We are grossly understaffed and under paid (no cash for overtime). We should be on a 4–10 plan or 3–12 plan [4–10 officers work 4 days per week, 10 hours; 3–12, three days per week, 12 hours]. That would eliminate a great deal of the stress. We should go to a civilian body for disciplinary decisions.

(Police Officer, Male, Hispanic, 37 years old, 10 years PO, 10 years LAPD, Chief when hired: Gates)

#254

Upper Management (Capt's & above) is the most poorly appointed positions on this dept & in most cases are a true embarrassment to our dept than those lower grade ofcrs whom they punish daily for misconduct they commit but is swept under the table by their peers.

(Police Officer, Male, Hispanic, 45 years old, 18 years PO, 18 years LAPA, Chief when hired: Davis)

#254

Command level contact with the working officer is sadly lacking. There appears to be too much interest in personal programs and feathering individual beds. The reality of what goes on at the street level is watered down and smoother over in too many cases. Command needs to hear what the street officer has to say and come down and experience police work today.

#255 (see #6)

#256 (see #57)

#257 (see #32)

#258

Fuck Management.

(Detective, Male, Caucasian, 47 years old, 26 years PO, 26 years LAPD, Chief when hired: Parker)

#259

In my opinion the Command Staff on this dept are more preoccupied with promoting & making themselves look good than considering the needs of the policeman working the street. These particular individuals (command staff) cannot make a decision for fearing how it will affect their career, thus they don't make any decisions. There is too much back biting & self service. When you have this attitude in the command staff you have a do nothing attitude among the police rank working the street because no one will back up the working policeman.

(Police Officer, Male, Hispanic, 44 years old, 22 years PO, 22 years LAPD, Chief when hired: Davis)

#260

Let's see some leadership from this department—with some guts.

(Male, Caucasian, 48 years old, 23 years PO, 23 years LAPD, Chief when hired: Reddin)

#261

The staff from capt & above are nothing but back stabbing, self serving thiefs. This deps need to get rid of more than ½ of these do nothing people. They think they are Gods & don't know what the streets are like and don't care. They care nothing about the citizens of LA & don't care. All they want is their own power & making themselves jobs where no one knows what they are doing from capt. up. Why do you need two capts of the Divisions. You will have answers which say nothing. (Officer information not available)

#262

It appears that the brass & upper management is out for their own glory & benefit. Do what is good for them at the expense of the troops and working class.

(Sergeant, Male, Caucasian, 57 years old, 32 years PO, 32 years LAPD, Chief when hired: Parker)

#263

In regards to morale, the reason that it is so low in the patrol ranks, which is supposed to be the "backbone of the Department," is the strong feelings that the upper management people are not concerned about the field officers and are only involved in taking Chief Gates seat. It is common knowledge that these higher ups are stabbing each other in the back and whose goals sway with each change in the community and media. Opinion, we are also overworked and severely under deployed. We need more officers in the street.

(Police Officer, Male, Caucasian, 32 years old, 11 years PO, 11 years LAPD, Chief when hired: Gates)

#264

I have seen through my contact with other officers the nearly complete lack of confidence in the loyalty of the department's middle to upper management. A great number of junior officers are looking for new jobs.

(Police Officer, Male, Caucasian, 34 years old, 5 years PO, 4 years LAPD, Chief when hired: Gates)

#265

Brass has no balls.

(Police Officer, Male, Caucasian, 31 years old, 10 years PO, 10 years LAPD, Chief when hired: Gates)

#266

I find the department leaning toward being a social agency rather than concentrating on crime prevention.

(Detective, Male, Caucasian, 53 years old, 28 years PO, 28 years LAPD, Chief when hired: Parker)

#267

This department needs to return to basics. Trendy programs with cute names won't replace good street cops. Relations with the community is an important part of police work as long as you have knowledgeable, aggressive "street wise" loyal officers. Affirmative action has divided this dept and no survey is going to mend the wounds. This dept places no emphasis on arrests/convictions/expertise in the patrol force. To say that a patrol ofcr is generally qualified in this period of time, is a joke!

(Detective, Male, Caucasian, 39 years old, 16 years PO, 16 years LAPD, Chief when hired: Davis)

#268

Community based policing is extremely important. However, it appears the dept is forgetting force is absolutely necessary at times & should not discourage the use of it. An ofcr is going to get seriously hurt or killed because of the doubts the admin has set up. If we reach out to the community & explain our actions & do role playing it's guaranteed to change attitudes about what is excessive force & what's necessary force. I would like nothing better than to be proud again to be a Los Angeles Police ofcr. What happened to our backbone?

(Police Officer, Female, Caucasian, 32 years old, 8 years PO, 8 years LAPD, Chief when hired: Gates)

#269

The LAPD is in Full Retreat from the criminal elements in our once beautiful city! Unless the LAPD reassumes its once aggressive, no nonsense & professional stance, we will continue our decline into the depths of apathy, foolishness, & social chaos.

(Police Officer, Male, Caucasian, 26 years old, 3 years PO, 3 years LAPD, Chief when hired: Gates)

#270

Community policing while in theory may sound good, will eventually offer no significant positive results in combating crime. As long as officers are used as scapegoats for societies' inability to deal with criminals, we will continue to see ineffective policing in our communities. Tying police officers hands and taking away proven tools in combating crime will only lead to more crime and apathy in the dept.

(Police Officer, Male, Caucasian, 33 years old, 8 years PO, 8 years LAPD, Chief when hired: Gates)

#271

Get the street back for the citizens of LA and put the fear back into the susps. Try and give the citizens a sense of security in knowing that we can protect them to some degree.

(Police Officer, Male, Caucasian, 44 years old, 22 years PO, 22 years LAPD, Chief when hired: Davis)

#272 (see #116)

#273

Eliminate the God Squad good old boys. Someone should realize that we are not selling bedsheets at a white sale at Nordstroms. Until you separate the vict & susp the service satisfaction issue will never fly. I didn't spend twenty years on the street to kiss the ass of some robber or burglar. I could care less if the child molester is satisfied with the service.

(Sergeant, Male, Caucasian, 45 years old, 20 years PO, 20 years LAPD, Chief when hired: Davis)

#274

The recruiting at the Acad. is structured so that recruits go out in the field ill-prepared for how susp. will treat them. Instructors are too easy on them on the P.T. field. If they can't handle stress in the academy then let them quit & good riddance to them. They can be trained to be polite but firm. This dept. seems like it doesn't want to hire anyone that may look too intimidating to the public. The brass on this dept. doesn't care if they humiliate us, especially at a demonstration. Show some balls! Handle all demonstrators the same. The queer nation doesn't deserve special treatment. My bureau commander is a good example. I'm running out of room.

(Police Officer, Male, Caucasian, 43 years old, 22 years PO, 22 years LAPD, Chief when hired: Davis)

#275

My opinion is that the high brass (Sgt's & above) forget what patrol is all about. So they want to burn people (ofcrs) for any little citizen complaint (181) so that they will promote faster. Now as a patrol officer, you go out to the streets & you won't get respect from suspects, gang members, etc.... They will come right up to you & say "Fuck You" ... Now what do we do? Nothing because we don't have a backbone like LASO-Sheriff Block!!! You want community based policing ... that's Bullshit, just ask New York PD and look at their crime rate. C-YA.

(Police Officer, Male, Hispanic, 22 years old, 2 years PO, 2 years LAPD, Chief when hired: Gates)

#276

The focus of attention has shifted and the main goal in the street has shifted. Change takes time. We've always had good ofcrs. When I came on 20 years ago, the emphasis was on running things with a strong hand and public opinion was secondary. Now community involvement is primary and the "battering ram" is un-acceptable. It'll work out for the best.

(Sergeant, Male, Hispanic, 45 years old, 21 years PO, 21 years LAPD, Chief when hired: Davis)

#277

Stop coming up with new ideas. The problem is that all the oxygen deprivated brass keep thinking of new things for us to try and new "buzz" words for us and the community. Let's get back to the basics. No bullshit.

(Sergeant, Male, Caucasian, 30 years old, 9 years PO, 9 years LAPD, Chief when hired: Gates)

#278

This is a start toward building a better dept. Hopefully mgmt will not crumble in the face of individual political goals, as we are seeing actually happen today. Let's not lose sight of our goal to have a crime free community, rather than a bend over backwards weak dept that gives in to the concept of leaving all persons smiling. We can't make everyone happy all the time, and I really don't think we should make criminals happy about LAPD.

(Police Officer, Male, Caucasian, 37 years old, 12 years PO, 8 years LAPD, Chief when hired: Gates)

#279

Community-based policing, though a great concept, will never work in a city as diverse and transient as Los Angeles. It looks like the bad guys have won and the decent citizens will suffer the consequences. The squeaky wheel got the grease while the bike as a whole fell apart!

(Police Officer, Male, Hispanic, 25 years old, 7 years PO, 4 years LAPD, Chief when hired Gates)

#280

Community based policing is a good idea. But we are a police dept. and need to remain in an "aggressive arrest mode." This is the priority of the LAPD I joined. Help out patrol. We love to work, we just need some help from the administrators when it comes to supporting us. Please don't sell out LAPD to the liberals.

(Police Officer, Male, Hispanic, 25 years old, 4 years PO, 4 years LAPD, Chief when hired: Gates)

#281

Community based policing is proven ineffective. Keep LAPD the way it was.

(Police Officer, Male, Filipino, 29 years old, 4 years PO, 4 years LAPD, Chief when hired: Gates)

#282

I do not think we should become a Department that is not enforcement orientated. We should be involved with the community we serve but we should not give up putting crooks in jail.

(Detective, Male, Caucasian, 43 years old, 20 years PO, 20 years LAPD, Chief when hired: Davis)

#283

We should give the public the service they need, not bullshit them with coffee & tea.

(Police Officer, Male, Caucasian, 37 years old, 10 years PO, 3 years LAPD, Chief when hired: Gates)

#284

More decisions need to be made by officers who are sincere about the welfare of patrol officers, and not by the officers downtown sitting around playing "Monday Morning Quarterback." The majority of people making the rules do not and have not worked in the streets in years. A lot of these changes that have been implemented are going to cause officers to get hurt second guessing themselves because they're thinking about what the pencil pushers will think later, much later. This department was not formed to be a dept of psychologists. We are people just like everyone else. We are not sponges to soak up the frustration of the community. We are here to stop, prevent and catch criminal activity. The public as a whole still support the police. The criminals and those people who have never been victims of crimes and/or have lived sheltered lives are the people so bent on change. Granted, some things should be changed. But making officers more sensitive to everyone who may be a little different than the rest just magnifies their difference. Training people (recruits) to be nice in a society where more & more criminals are arising is somewhat CRAZY!!

(Police Officer, Male, African American, 27 years old, 4 years PO, 4 years LAPD, Chief when hired: Gates)

#285

I feel that our Department has lost sight of its mission. With upper level administrators thinking more of their individual reputations & political aspirations, they seem to have the tendency to cower down to the liberal politicians and various ad hoc committees instead of backing the very working force that keeps them in their various administrative kingdoms. This Department is dying & it is not being destroyed from the outside.

(Police Officer, Male, Hispanic, 43 years old, 22 years LAPD, Chief when hired: Davis)

Index

Q

For Product Safety Concerns and Information please contact our EU
representative GPSR@taylorandfrancis.com
Taylor & Francis Verlag GmbH, Kaufingerstraße 24, 80331 München, Germany

www.ingramcontent.com/pod-product-compliance
Ingram Content Group UK Ltd.
Pitfield, Milton Keynes, MK11 3LW, UK
UKHW020015200926
475702UK00014B/1895
* 9 7 8 0 3 6 7 8 6 6 9 9 0 *